SPEED G-TELP LEVEL 2

스피드
지텔프
레벨2

G

시대에듀

정윤호

약력

現 Jk정앤감 어학원 대표
現 정윤호 영어 연구소 소장
前 국민대학교 영어 강의
前 분당 차의과대학교 간호 영어 강의
前 상명대학교 TOEIC 강의
前 EBS G-TELP 강의
前 노량진 남부고시학원 9급 · 7급 영어 강의
前 노량진 위비스공무원학원 공무원 영어 강의

저서

우선순위 지텔프 보카(Level 2)
EBS 지텔프 VOCA
EBS 정윤호의 G-TELP 전략독해 Level.2
EBS 지텔프 코리아 공식지정 실전 모의고사

이정미

약력

호주 Sydney University 간호학 졸업
호주 Sydney University 간호학 석사 졸업
서울대학교 석박사 종합 중퇴
現 강남미키어학원 아이엘츠 수석강사

편집진행 윤승일 · 장민영
표지디자인 현수빈
본문디자인 박지은 · 하한우

머리말
PREFACE

약 90분 동안 총 80문항의 정답을 4지선다 중에서 골라야 하는 지텔프(Level 2) 시험을 어떻게 준비를 하는 것이 가장 효율적일까? 수험생들이 지원하고자 하는 기관 및 기업체에서 요구하는 점수에 따라 지텔프를 학습하는 방법과 전략이 서로 각자 다르겠지만, 〈스피드 지텔프 레벨2〉는 바로 이러한 점을 '한 방'에 해결할 수 있도록 내용을 구성했다.

우선, 지텔프 시험을 개략적으로 정리하자면, '문법은 26문항/20분', '청취는 26문항/약 30분', '독해 및 어휘는 28문항/40분'으로 구성되어 있고, 각 파트는 100점으로 총 300점 만점이다. 시험 시간은 약 90분이지만, 2018년 5월 이후부터 파트별 시험 시간제한 규정이 폐지되었다는 점은 정말이지 지텔프를 준비하는 수험생들이 목표 점수를 획득하는 데 '꿀'이다! 현실적으로 말하자면, 문법 파트에서 80분을 모두 쓰고, 나머지 파트는 '한 줄'로 찍어도 된다는 뜻이다. 무엇보다 가장 중요한 점은 상대평가인 토익과는 다르게 '절대평가'로 된 공인영어시험이고 다른 공무원과목과는 다르게 파트별 과락이 없다는 것이다.

지텔프 문법은 6가지 문법 사항만 물어보고, 그중에서도 '출제되는 곳에서만 출제된다!' 이 책에서는 그 출제 원리와 자주 출제되는 문법 사항을 모두 망라했으니, 모든 수험생들은 문법 파트에서 만점을 얻을 수 있을 것이다!

청취는 다소 어려울 수 있지만 질문을 두 번씩 읽어주고 '필기(Note-Taking)'를 할 수 있기에 나름 전략이 생긴다.

독해 및 어휘 파트는 글의 논리가 꼬여 있거나 전문성을 띠는 글보다는, '인물, 시사, 백과사전, 비즈니스 편지'의 내용이 담긴 '꿀잼' 내용이 나와 지루함이 없을 것이고, 어휘를 묻는 문제는 명사, 형용사, 동사 위주의 동의어를 묻는 문제로 한정되어 평소 이에 대한 훈련을 하면 되겠다.

청취와 독해 및 어휘 파트의 문제의 정답은 스크립트 순서와 거의 비슷하게 정답과 해설이 있고, 이 두 가지 파트의 주된 스킬은 '바꿔 쓰기(Paraphrasing)'인데 이 책에서는 문제마다 이 부분을 해설했으니 고득점에 도움이 되길 바란다. 독해 및 어휘 파트에 나오는 중요 지문은 철저하게 '구문 분석(Syntax)'을 했다는 점이 타 교재와의 차별성이라 할 수 있다. 따라서 해석하는 방법에 자신이 없는 수험생들에게 이 책은 '필수품(Musthave)'이 될 것이다. 이 책으로 고득점을 최단기간에 달성하기를 바란다.

정윤호 · 이정미

G-TELP 시험 소개
INTRODUCTION

G-TELP 시험이란?
지텔프(G-TELP)는 General Tests of English Language Proficiency의 약자로 듣기(Listening), 말하기(Speaking), 쓰기(Writing), 읽기(Reading) 등 언어의 4대 영역을 종합 평가하는 영어 평가 교육 시스템입니다.

G-TELP 시험 구성

문법	청취	독해 및 어휘
26문항 20분	26문항 약 30분	28문항 40분

G-TELP 시험 특징
❶ 문법 / 청취 / 독해 및 어휘 3영역의 종합 영어 능력 평가
❷ G-TELP Level 2만 국가고시, 국가자격증 등에 인정

G-TELP 시험의 강점
❶ 토익보다 접근하기 쉽다!
 토익에 비해 정형화된 문법 영역, 적은 학습량, 빠른 성적 확인, 문항 수 대비 넉넉한 시험 시간으로 원하는 점수를 빠르게 획득할 수 있습니다.
❷ 과락이 없다!
 과목당 과락이 없어 문법, 청취, 독해의 평균 점수만 맞추면 됩니다.
❸ 빠르게 성적 확인이 가능하다!
 응시일로부터 일주일 이내에 성적 발표를 해서 단기간에 영어 공인 점수를 취득할 수 있습니다.

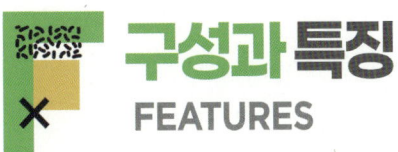

구성과 특징
FEATURES

| 문법 |

PART 1 현재진행형 핵심이론

이렇게 나와요

Macarthur High School's choir will be performing next. Right now, the choir members ________ plenty of water to keep their vocal cords from drying out.

(a) drink
(b) have drunk
(c) are drinking
(d) would drink

이렇게 풀어요

Linda was late for work this morning. She had to go back home to get the materials for meeting she'd left on the desk. She ________ the bus when she remembered about the documents.

(a) ~~would already get off~~
(b) ~~already got off~~
(c) was already getting off
(d) ~~had already got off~~

이렇게 나와요로 문제를 확인하고, 이렇게 풀어요로 풀이방법을 확인할 수 있습니다.

② 현재진행형(Present Continuous)

현재 말하는 시점에서 진행 중인 일시적 행위를 나타낼 때 사용한다.

현재진행형 ~하고 있다 or ~하고 있는 중이다
- 긍정문: am(are, is) + Ving
- 부정문: am(are, is) + not + Ving
- 의문문: am(are, is) + 주어 + Ving ~?

핵심만 공부할 수 있도록 필수 이론을 설명하고 있습니다.

이런 게 답이에요

*while + 주어 + 현재동사형 / *now / *right now / *nowadays / *currently / *still / *at this very moment / *at the moment / at the present time / at this time / today / these days / this week[year] ▶ 현재진행형

Tip right now는 '바로 지금, 지금 당장'이라는 의미로 현재, 현재진행, 즉시 일어날 미래시제와 주로 같이 사용한다.

이렇게 활용해요

① 현재 시점에서 지금 진행 중임을 강조하고 벌어지고 있는 일을 말할 때

I **am driving** now.
나는 지금 운전하고 있어.

22 시대에듀 | 지텔프 레벨2 대비

이런 게 답이에요와 이렇게 활용해요로 '핵심 이론'을 학습할 수 있습니다.

PART 3 If 생략 가정법 도치 문제풀이

TEST 1 – 22번

My grandfather Tony knocked over a glass of orange juice while I was cleaning in the living room. Had he not spilled the juice, I would have prepared dinner to serve before 6 pm.

(a) He had not spilled
(b) If he did not spilled
(c) Had he not spilled
(d) Were he not spilled

답 (c)

꼼꼼한 | 해설 |로 문제풀이의 순서를 확인하고 답을 찾아나갈 수 있습니다.

| 해설 |

가정법 과거완료(If 생략 가정법 도치)

정치: If + 주어 + had p.p. ~, 주어 + would have p.p.

도치: ②Had + 주어 + not p.p. ~, 주어 + ①would have p.p.

| 구문독해 |를 통해 긴 독해 지문도 막힘없이 해석할 수 있습니다.

| 구문독해 |

while(종속접속사) + 주어 + 동사: ~동안, during(전치사) + 명사

102 시대에듀 | 지텔프 레벨2 대비

구성과 특징
FEATURES

| 독해 & 청취 |

본인의 레벨에 따라 영어 지문과 한글 지문을 따로 활용할 수 있도록 해설을 분리해 두었습니다.

- QR코드를 활용하여 구문독해 파일과 청취파일을 확인할 수 있습니다.

- 문제의 정답이 되는 부분은 문제 번호를 표시해 두었고 정답의 핵심 내용은 형광펜으로 확인할 수 있습니다.

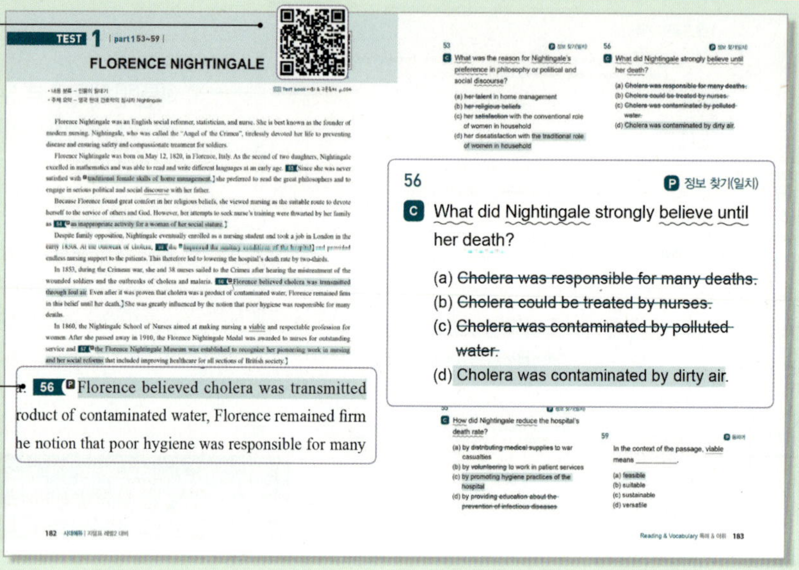

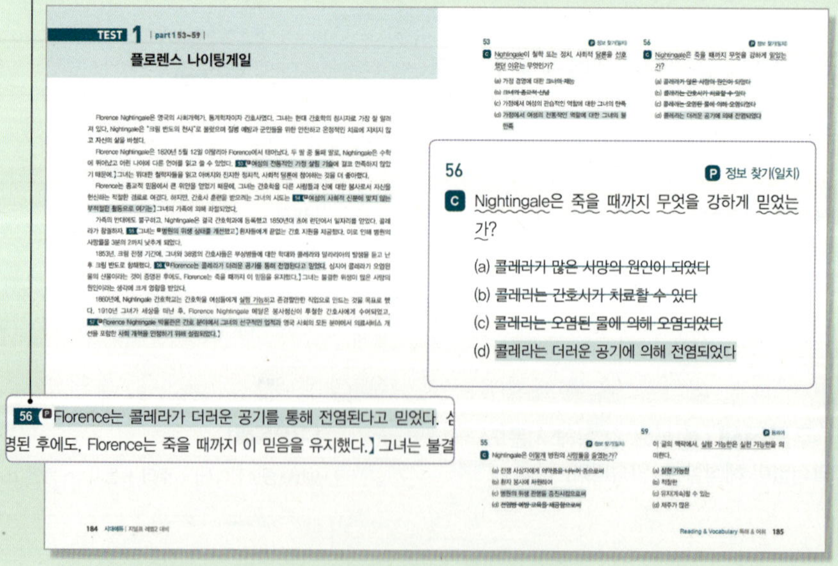

SPEED G-TELP LEVEL 2

합격의 공식 Formula of pass | 시대에듀 www.sdedu.co.kr

| 모의고사 |

실전과 동일한 유형의 모의고사로 실력을 확인할 수 있습니다.

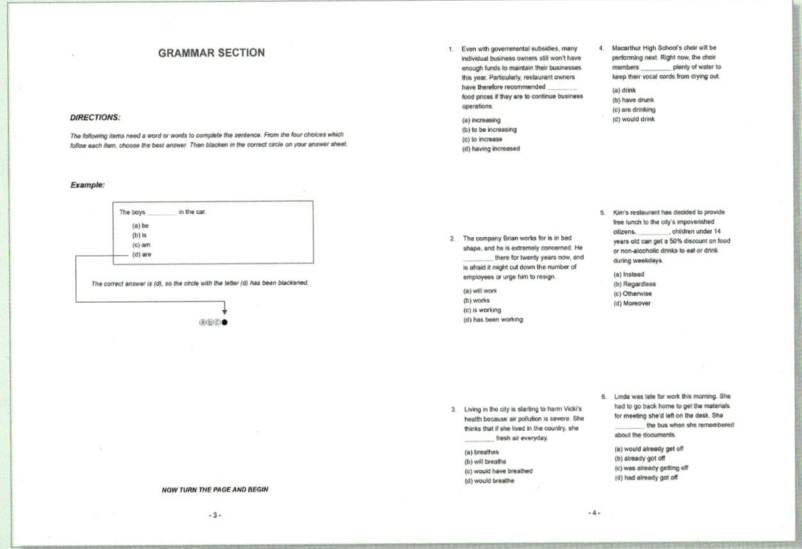

| 어휘 & 구문독해 |

❶ 어디서나 편리하게 학습할 수 있도록 구성하였습니다.

❷ 어휘와 구문독해로 청취와 독해의 문장을 완벽하게 이해하고 파악할 수 있습니다.

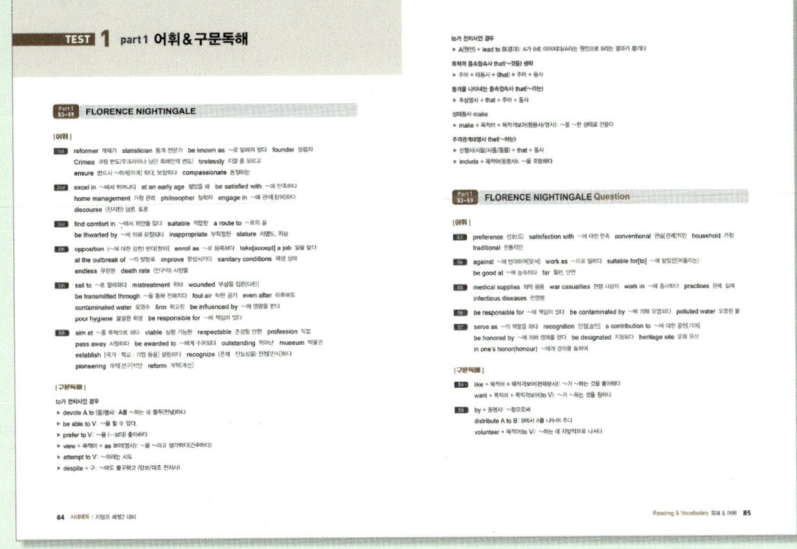

GRAMMAR 문 법

PART 1	동사의 시제	012
PART 2	조동사	050
PART 3	가정법	078
PART 4	to 부정사와 동명사	104
PART 5	연결사(어)	132
PART 6	관계대명사와 관계부사	152

READING & VOCABULARY 독해 & 어휘

PART 1	과거 역사 속의 사건이나 현시대의 이야기	182
PART 2	잡지나 신문의 기사	194
PART 3	백과사전	206
PART 4	비즈니스 편지	218

LISTENING 청 취

PART 1	개인적인 이야기	238
PART 2	일의 진행이나 과정에 대한 설명	250
PART 3	비공식적인 협상 등의 대화	262
PART 4	공식적인 담화	274

책속의 책

모의고사

TEST 1	001
TEST 2	025
TEST 3	049

어휘 & 구문독해

독해 & 어휘	082
청취	108

스피드 지텔프 레벨2

G-TELP 핵심이론 + 상세한 문제풀이 + 모의고사 3회분

GRAMMAR

G-TELP 문법

PART 1 동사의 시제
PART 2 조동사
PART 3 가정법
PART 4 to 부정사와 동명사
PART 5 연결사(어)
PART 6 관계대명사와 관계부사

G-TELP 핵심이론 | Grammar

자주 출제되는 정답의 힌트를 모두 모아두었다. 해설에서 표현하는 동그라미 번호(①)로 문제를 확인하고 형광펜으로 표시된 부분에 해당하는 답을 찾아보자. 아래에 해당하는 내용을 모두 학습한 뒤 문제를 풀면, 보다 빠르고 정확하게 정답을 찾을 수 있다!

1 동사의 시제(Tense)

종류	정답과 관련된 시간 부사
과거진행형	when + 주어 + 과거동사형 / while + 주어 + 과거진행형 / always / at that time / the other night
현재진행형	while + 주어 + 현재동사형 / now / right now / nowadays / currently / still / at this very moment / at the moment
미래진행형	when + 주어 + 현재동사형 / by the time + 주어 + 현재동사형 / if + 주어 + 현재동사형 / for + 기간 표현 / until + 미래 시점 / until + (주어 + be동사) + Ving
과거완료진행형	before[when] + 주어 + 과거동사형 / since + 주어 + 과거동사형 / until + 주어 + 과거동사형 / by the time + 주어 + 과거동사형[과거시점] / for + 기간 표현
현재완료진행형	for + 기간 표현 / for + 기간 표현 + now / after + 주어 + 현재완료 / lately / (ever) since + 주어 + 과거동사형 / since + 과거 시점 / for(over) the past + 기간 표현 / in(during) the last + 기간 표현 / over + 기간 표현
미래완료진행형	by(by the time) + 미래 시점 / for + 기간 표현 / by the time + 주어 + 현재동사형

2 조동사(Modal Verb & Auxiliary Verb)

(1) 조동사의 종류와 용법

종류	용법		의미
can	현재형	가능성/능력	~할 수 있다
could	과거형	추측	~할 수도 있다
may	현재형	약한 추측	~할지도 모르다
might	과거형	불확실한 약한 추측	~일(할)지도 모르다
must	현재/과거형	강한 의무/필요/당위성	~해야(만) 한다
should	과거형	당위성	~해야(만) 한다

have to	현재형	의무	~해야(만) 한다
will	현재형	예정/미래	~할 것이다
would	과거형	현재 사실의 반대/소망/미래/예정	~하곤 했었다

(2) 조동사 + have + p.p.

종류	해석
may(might) have p.p.	~이었을지도 모른다 (과거 사실에 대한 약한 추측)
must have p.p.	~이었음에 틀림이 없다 (과거 사실에 대한 강한 추측)
should(ought to) have p.p.	~했었어야 했는데(하지 못했다)

(3) should 생략

주절			종속절		
주어	동사		종속접속사	주어	동사
	요구	ask, request			
주어	제안	suggest	(that)	주어	(should) 동사원형
	주장	insist, urge			
	충고(조언)	advise, recommend			

주절			종속절		
주어	동사	이성적 판단 형용사	종속접속사	주어	동사
It	be	best(가장 잘하는) / essential(필수적인, 중요한) / imperative(반드시 해야 하는, 긴요한) / important(중요[중대·소중]한)	(that)	주어	(should) 동사원형

G-TELP 핵심이론 | Grammar

3 가정법(Subjunctive Mood)

(1) 가정법 과거(종속절과 주절의 위치가 서로 바뀔 수 있음)

종속절			주절	
		과거형동사		
		were ~,		
		were not ~,		
		were Ving ~,		would V ~.
If	주어	were p.p. ~,	주어	would not V ~.
		were to V ~,		would be Ving ~.
		were to be p.p. ~,		could V ~.
		could V ~,		
		could not V ~,		
		would V ~,		
Even if	주어	were p.p. ~,		would V ~.
		were Ving ~,		wouldn't V ~.

(2) 가정법 과거완료(종속절과 주절의 위치가 서로 바뀔 수 있음)

종속절			주절	
		had p.p. ~,		would have p.p. ~.
If	주어	had not p.p. ~,	주어	would not have p.p. ~.
		had been Ving ~,		could have p.p. ~.
		had been p.p. ~,		would have been p.p. ~.

(3) If 생략 가정법 도치 구문(종속절과 주절의 위치가 서로 바뀔 수 있음)

종속절			주절	
Had	주어	not p.p. ~,	주어	would have p.p. ~.

4 to 부정사와 동명사

(1) 5형식에서 목적격보어로 to 부정사를 취하는 동사[S V O O·C (5)]

allow(~에게 ~하는 것을 허락[허가]하다) / ask(~에게 ~하는 것을 묻다) / beg(~에게 ~해 달라고 부탁/간청하다) / believe(~을 ~라고 믿다) / bother(~가 ~하는 것을 괴롭히다) / force(~가 ~하는 것을 강요하다) / tell(~에게 ~하라고 말[충고/명령]하다) / urge(~에게 ~하도록 강제[설득/간청/권]하다)

(2) 3형식에서 목적어로 동명사를 취하는 동사[S V O (3)]

avoid(~을 피하다) / consider(~을 고려하다) / deny(~을 부정하다) / enjoy(~을 즐기다) / experience(~을 경험하다) / favor(~을 찬성하다) / finish(~을 끝내다) / involve(~을 포함[수반]하다) / mind(~을 꺼려하다) / miss(~을 이해하지 못하다) / prohibit(~을 금지하다) / reconsider(~을 재고하다) / require(~을 필요로 하다) / resist(~에 저항하다) / tolerate(~을 묵인하다/관대하게 다루다)

(3) to 부정사와 동명사의 의미 구별

① 3형식에서 목적어 자리에 to 부정사와 동명사가 둘 다 나오는 경우(의미 차이 없음): 예 start(~을 시작하다)
② 3형식에서 목적어 자리에 to 부정사와 동명사가 둘 다 나오는 경우(의미 차이 있음)

타동사	목적어 자리	
	to 부정사	동명사
try	~하려고 노력하다(애쓰다) : 주어의 의지 있음	~을 시험 삼아 해보다(시도하다) : 주어의 의지 없음
stop/quit	~하기 위해 멈추다/그만두다	~을 멈추다/그만두다

타동사	목적어 자리	
	to 부정사(미래)	동명사(과거)
remember	~할 것을 기억하다	~한 것을 기억하다
forget	~할 것을 잊어버리다	~을 잊어버리다
regret	~을 하게 되어 유감이다	~한 일을 후회하다

타동사	목적어 자리	의미	해석
need	to 부정사(to V)	능동	(~할) 필요가 있다, ~해야 하다
	동명사(Ving)	수동	[사람·물건이] (~되어야 할) 필요가 있다

G-TELP 핵심이론 | Grammar

5 연결사(어)

(1) 연결사(어) 종류

단순 전치사(기능별 분류)	양보/대조: despite(~에도 불구하고)
구 전치사	because of(~ 때문에) / instead of(~대신에) / rather than(~보다 오히려) / regardless of(~을 개의치 않고)

(2) 전치사의 중요 논리적 역할: 순접과 역접

순접	시간: for(~동안에) / since(~이래로) 원인/이유/동기: because of(~ 때문에)
역접	대체: instead of(~대신에) 양보/대조: despite(~에도 불구하고) / regardless of(~을 개의치 않고)

(3) 대등(등위)접속사(Coordinating Conjunction)

종류	해석	용법
and	그리고	'단어와 단어', '구와 구', '문장과 문장'을 이어줌(순접)
	~해라, 그러면 ~할 것이다	명령문 + and ~
	~가라, 와라, 해봐라	go, come, try + and (to) + 원형
so	그래서	원인 + so + 결과

(4) 종속접속사(Subordinator)

① 순접

인과관계	because(~ 때문에) / since(~ 때문에) / so (that)(그래서 ~하다)
결과	so 형용사(부사) that(너무 ~해서 그 결과 ~하다) / so 형용사 a(n) 명사 that(너무 ~해서 그 결과 ~하다)
목적	so that(~하기 위해서)
시간	as long as(~하는 한) / since(~한 이래로) / until(~할 때까지) / when(~할 때) / whenever(~할 때 마다)

② 역접

양보/대조	although(비록 ~일지라도) / even though(비록 ~일지라도) / however(아무리 ~한다 하더라도) / unless(~가 아니라면)

(5) 접속부사(Connective Adverb, Conjunct)

① 순접

도입	at the same time(동시에, 또한) / in the first place(먼저, 무엇보다도)
인과관계	thus(따라서) / in short(간단히 말해) / therefore(따라서) / so(그래서) / eventually(마침내)
강조	at length(상세히) / in fact(사실상) / indeed(사실상)
반복 & 동격	that is(즉, 다시 말해서)
비교	similarly(유사: 마찬가지로)
예시	for instance(예를 들면)
증거 & 확실성	additionally(부가적으로) / at the same time(동시에, 또한) / besides(게다가) / in fact(사실상) / in addition(to)(~외에도, 게다가) / moreover(게다가)
시간관련	afterward(s)(나중에)
시간의 순서	in the first place(우선)

② 역접

대조	although(~에도 불구하고) / but(그러나) / even though(비록 ~일지라도) / however(그러나) / nevertheless(~임에도 불구하고) / on the contrary(반대로, 반면에) / still(그러나) / while(반면에, ~동안에) / yet(그러나)
반박	instead(대신에, 그런게 아니라) / rather(그렇기는커녕, 반대로, 도리어)
양보 & 대조	even so(그렇기는 하지만) / instead(~ 대신에) / nevertheless(그럼에도 불구하고) / nonetheless(~에도 불구하고) / otherwise(그렇지 않다면) / still(그런데도, 그럼에도 불구하고)

(6) 전치사와 종속접속사: 해석은 같지만 구조가 다름

구분	해석	전치사	종속접속사
원인/이유	~때문에	because of	because, since
양보/대조	비록 ~일지라도	despite	even though, while

6 관계사(Relative)와 관계부사(Relative Adverb)

(1) 관계대명사(Relative Pronoun)

선행사 \ 격	주격	소유격	목적격
사람	who	whose	whom
사물/동물	which	whose / of which	which
사람 사물/동물	that	×	that
× (선행사 포함)	what	×	what

(2) 관계대명사 that만 사용하는 경우

선행사 앞에 있는 표현	선행사	쓰임
the + only/very/same	사람 / 사물 / 동물	주격 관계대명사: 주어가 없는 경우 목적격 관계대명사: 목적어가 없는 경우

(3) 관계부사(Relative Adverb)

용도	선행사	관계부사	전치사 + 관계대명사
시간	the time	when	in / at / on 등 + which
장소	the place	where	in / at / on 등 + which
이유	the reason	why	for which
방법	(the way)	how	in which
방법	\multicolumn{3}{ the way how는 같이 사용 못 함, the way, how, the way in which, the way that은 사용 가능 }

the way how는 같이 사용 못 함,
the way, how, the way in which, the way that은 사용 가능

합격의 공식
시대에듀

우리 인생의 가장 큰 영광은
결코 넘어지지 않는 데 있는 것이 아니라
넘어질 때마다 일어서는 데 있다

– 넬슨 만델라 –

PART 1
동사의 시제

과거진행형(Past Continuous)

현재진행형(Present Continuous)

미래진행형(Future Continuous)

과거완료진행형(Past Perfect Continuous)

현재완료진행형(Present Perfect Continuous)

미래완료진행형(Future Perfect Continuous)

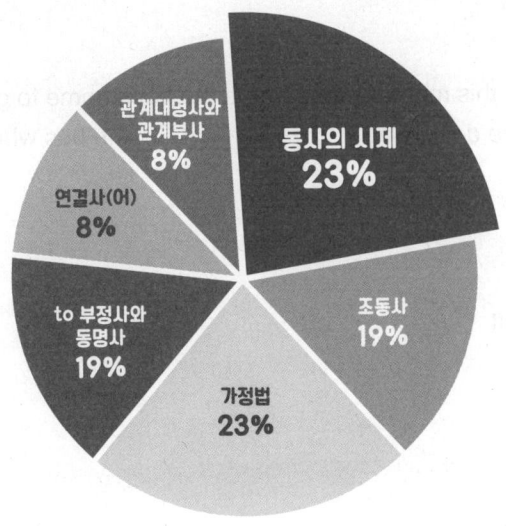

동사의 시제 출제원리

동사의 12시제 중, 6가지 시제만 출제된다.

〈진행형〉
1. 과거진행형: was/were Ving
2. 현재진행형: am/is/are Ving
3. 미래진행형: will be Ving

〈완료진행형〉
4. 과거완료진행형: had been Ving
5. 현재완료진행형: have been Ving
6. 미래완료진행형: will have been Ving

1. 시간을 나타내는 시점부사를 동사의 시제와 같이 묶어서 숙지한다.
2. 시간을 나타내는 연결사(어)를 동사의 시제와 같이 묶어서 숙지한다.
3. 오답이 되는 선택지는 출제되지 않는 6가지 시제이다.
   - 기본 3시제: 과거형(동사의 과거형, 조동사의 과거형 V) / 현재형[V/V(e)s] / 미래형(will V)
   - 완료형: 과거완료형(had p.p.) / 현재완료형(have/has p.p.) / 미래완료형(will have p.p.)

PART 1 과거진행형 핵심이론

📖 이렇게 나와요

Linda was late for work this morning. She had to go back home to get the materials for meeting she'd left on the desk. She _____ the bus when she remembered about the documents.

(a) would already get off
(b) already got off
(c) was already getting off
(d) had already got off

① 과거진행형 (Past Continuous)

과거 특정한 때에 하고 있었던 동작이나 **일시적 행위를 강조**하기 위해 사용한다.

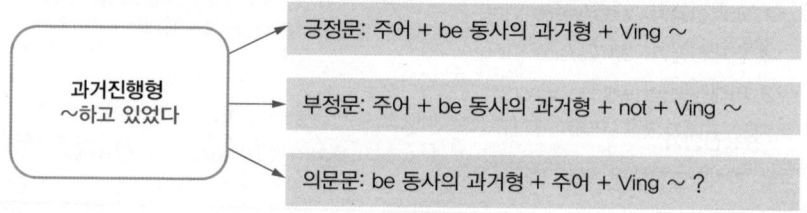

이런 게 답이에요

[*when + 주어 + 과거동사형 / *while + 주어 + 과거진행형 / *always / *at that time / *the other night / forever / constantly / continually / at + 시간 / in + 시간] ▶ 과거진행형

Linda was late for work this morning. She had to go back home to get the materials for meeting she'd left on the desk. She _____ the bus when she remembered about the documents.

(a) ~~would already get off~~
(b) ~~already got off~~
(c) was already getting off   be 동사의 과거형 + Ving
(d) ~~had already got off~~

이렇게 활용해요

① 과거 특정 시점에 진행 중이었던 일(행동·사건)

At 8 o'clock, he **was eating** dinner.
8시에, 그는 저녁 식사를 하던 중이었다.

② 과거에 있었던 짧고 임시적인 상황

They **were having** dinner when I got home.
내가 집에 도착했을 때, 그들은 저녁 식사를 하고 있었다.

③ 과거진행형과 단순 과거의 결합

She **was cooking** when the telephone rang.
전화벨이 울렸을 때, 그녀는 요리 중이었다.

④ 과거진행형과 과거진행형의 결합

She **was cooking** while I **was studying** yesterday.
어제 내가 공부를 하고 있는 동안에 그녀는 요리 중이었다.

PLUS 선택지에서 주로 혼동할 수 있는 경우

단순 과거형과 과거진행형의 차이점

단순 과거형	• 과거 특정 시점에 시작하여 종료된 행동이나 사건을 표현 • 연속해서 발생하는 행동이나 사건을 서술하기 위해 표현 • 과거 특정 시점을 표현하는 부사: yesterday, last week, two years ago 등 • 과거에 발생했던 반복적인 일이나 습관을 표현할 때 사용하는 부사: always, often, usually, never, when I was a child, when I was young, every weekend 등
과거진행형	• 과거 특정 시점에 진행 중이었던 행동이나 사건을 표현 • 행동이나 사건이 과거 특정 시점 전에 시작하였지만 종료되지 않은 상황 • 단순 과거와 결합하여 사용 가능 • 과거에 예상치 않게 매우 자주 또는 계획되지 않게 자주 발생한 상황을 표현 • 과거진행을 표현하는 부사: always, forever, constantly, continually, while 등

PART 1 과거진행형 문제풀이

TEST 1 – 6번

Linda was late for work this morning. She had to go back home to get the materials for meeting [1]she'd left on the desk. She was already getting off the bus when she remembered about the documents.

(a) would already get off
(b) already got off
(c) was already getting off
(d) had already got off

답 (c)

| 해설 |

주어 + [3]과거진행형(be 동사의 과거형 + Ving) + [1]when + 주어 + [2]과거동사형

(a) would V – 현재 사실의 반대/소망/미래/예정
(b) Ved – 과거 특정 시점에 시작하여 종료된 행동이나 사건을 표현
(c) was Ving – 과거 특정 시점에 진행 중이었던 행동이나 사건을 표현
(d) had p.p. – 단기간에 지속되고 일시적인 행위나 상황 혹은 행위가 완료됨을 강조할 경우

| 구문독해 |

[1]목적격 관계대명사 that(~하는) 생략
– 선행사 + (that) + 주어 + 타동사 + (목적어 없음)

| 해석 |

Linda는 오늘 아침에 직장에 지각했다. 그녀는 책상 위에 두고 온 회의 자료를 가지러 집으로 돌아가야만 했다. 그녀는 이미 버스에서 내리고 있었는데 그 서류들이 생각났다.

| 어휘 |

be late for 시간에 늦다
go back home 귀가하다
materials for meeting 회의 자료
get off the bus 버스에서 내리다(↔ get on the bus)
remember about ~에 대해 기억하다

PART 1
과거진행형 문제풀이

TEST 1 - 20번

Did you know ❶that Maggie has already returned home from her business trip? I saw her this afternoon while she was drinking coffee with her mom at the cafe.

(a) would drink
(b) drank
(c) was drinking
(d) had drunk

답 (c)

|해설|

주어 + ❷과거동사형 + ①while + 주어 + ③과거진행형(be 동사의 과거형 + Ving)

(a) would V – 현재 사실의 반대/소망/미래/예정
(b) Ved – 과거 특정 시점에 시작하여 종료된 행동이나 사건을 표현
(c) was Ving – 과거 특정 시점에 진행 중이었던 행동이나 사건을 표현
(d) had p.p. – 단기간에 지속되고 일시적인 행위나 상황 혹은 행위가 완료됨을 강조할 경우

|구문독해|

❶목적격 종속접속사 that
– 주어 + 동사 + that + 주어 + 동사 ~ (완전한 문장)
   생략 가능 (~하는 것을)

|해석|

Maggie가 이미 출장을 마치고 집으로 돌아왔다는 사실을 알고 있었나요? 오늘 오후에 그녀가 그녀의 엄마와 카페에서 커피를 마시고 있는 것을 봤어요.

|어휘|

return home 귀가하다, 귀향하다, 귀국하다
business trip 출장

TEST 2 – 8번

Jack has good memories of his high school music teacher, Ms. Hampton. Aside from giving interesting music theory lessons, she was always encouraging students ❶who were not confident in ❷playing musical instruments.

(a) always encourages
(b) had always encouraged
(c) was always encouraging
(d) would always have encouraged

답 (c)

| 해설 |

주어 + ①was + ③always + ②Ving

(a) V – 보통 일상적이고 반복적인 상황
(b) had p.p. – 단기간에 지속되고 일시적인 행위나 상황 혹은 행위가 완료됨을 강조할 경우
(c) was Ving – 과거 특정 시점에 진행 중이었던 행동이나 사건을 표현
(d) would have p.p. – 과거 사실에 대한 단순한 유감이나 후회

| 구문독해 |

❶주격관계대명사 who(~하는)
– 선행사(사람) + who + 동사
❷play + the(정관사) + 악기: (어떤 악기)를 연주하다

| 해석 |

Jack은 그의 고등학교 음악 선생님인 Hampton 선생님에 대해 좋은 기억을 가지고 있다. 흥미로운 음악 이론 수업을 하는 것 외에도, 그녀는 악기 연주에 자신감이 없는 학생들을 항상 격려하고 있었다.

| 어휘 |

Ms. [여성이 미혼(Miss)인지 기혼(Mrs.)인지 모를 때 성·성명에 붙여] ~씨, ~님
aside from ~ 외에는, ~을 제외하고
give(teach) a lesson ~을 가르치다
encourage 격려[고무]하다, 용기를 북돋우다
be confident in ~에 대해 자신이 있다
musical instrument 악기

PART 1
과거진행형 문제풀이

TEST 3 – 20번

While I was studying for an important exam the other night, I found my lovely dogs sleeping on my bed peacefully.

(a) studied
(b) was studying
(c) would study
(d) had studied

답 (b)

| 해설 |

①While + 주어 + ②과거진행형(be 동사의 과거형 + Ving) + 주어 + ③과거동사형

(a) Ved – 과거 특정 시점에 시작하여 종료된 행동이나 사건을 표현
(b) was Ving – 과거 특정 시점에 진행 중이었던 행동이나 사건을 표현
(c) would V – 현재 사실의 반대/소망/미래/예정
(d) had p.p. – 단기간에 지속되고 일시적인 행위나 상황 혹은 행위가 완료됨을 강조할 경우

| 구문독해 |

③find + 목적어 + 목적격보어(현재분사): ~가 ~하고 있는 것을 발견하다

| 해석 |

며칠 전 밤 중요한 시험을 위해 **공부하고 있는 동안**, 나는 내 사랑스러운 개들이 내 침대에서 평화롭게 자고 있는 것을 발견했다.

| 어휘 |

the other night 며칠 전 밤
study for ~을 위해 공부하다

TEST 3 - 23번

Jenny was late for school yesterday. She had to go back home to bring her history assignment. She ❶wanted to ask her old brother for a ride, but he was sleeping at that time.

(a) would sleep
(b) had slept
(c) slept
(d) was sleeping

답 (d)

| 해설 |

주어 + ❷과거진행형(be 동사의 과거형 + Ving) + ❶at that time

(a) would V – 현재 사실의 반대/소망/미래/예정
(b) had p.p. – 단기간에 지속되고 일시적인 행위나 상황 혹은 행위가 완료됨을 강조할 경우
(c) Ved – 과거 특정 시점에 시작하여 종료가 된 행동이나 사건을 표현
(d) was Ving – 과거 특정 시점에 진행 중이었던 행동이나 사건을 표현

| 구문독해 |

❶want + 목적어(to V): 목적어가 ~하기를 원하다

| 해석 |

Jenny는 어제 학교에 지각했다. 그녀는 역사 과제를 가져오기 위해 집으로 돌아가야 했다. 그녀는 그녀의 오빠에게 차를 태워달라고 부탁하고 싶었지만, 그는 그때 자고 있었다.

| 어휘 |

be late for ~시간에 늦다
go(come) back home 귀향하다
assignment 숙제, 과제
ask A for B A에게 B를 요청/부탁하다
at that time 그때(에)

Grammar 문법 **21**

PART 1 현재진행형 핵심이론

📖 이렇게 나와요

Macarthur High School's choir will be performing next. Right now, the choir members _____ plenty of water to keep their vocal cords from drying out.

(a) drink
(b) have drunk
(c) are drinking
(d) would drink

② 현재진행형(Present Continuous)

현재 말하는 시점에서 진행 중인 일시적 행위를 나타낼 때 사용한다.

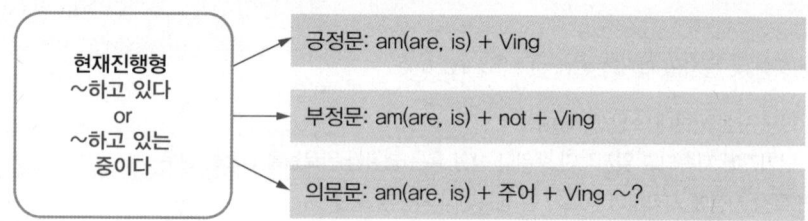

이런 게 답이에요

*while + 주어 + 현재동사형 / *now / *right now / *nowadays / *currently / *still / *at this very moment / *at the moment / at the present time / at this time / today / these days / this week[year] ▶ 현재진행형

Tip right now는 '바로 지금, 지금 당장'이라는 의미로 현재, 현재진행, 즉시 일어날 미래시제와 주로 같이 사용한다.

이렇게 활용해요

① 현재 시점에서 지금 진행 중임을 강조하고 벌어지고 있는 일을 말할 때

I **am driving** now.
나는 지금 운전하고 있어.

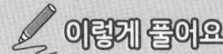

Macarthur High School's choir will be performing next. Right now, the choir members _____ plenty of water to keep their vocal cords from drying out.

현재 시점   주어

(a) ~~drink~~
(b) ~~have drunk~~
(c) are drinking be + Ving
(d) ~~would drink~~

② 현재 시점을 넓혀서 말할 때: 일정한 주기를 반복과 멈춤 그리고 시작이 반복될 때

Tip 오늘(today), 요즘(these days), 이번 주(this week), 올해(this year) 등의 표현과 주로 사용한다.

I **am reading** a book today.
나는 오늘 책을 읽었어. (오늘 하루 동안 책을 읽기도 하고 읽지 않기도 하는 행위를 반복했다는 의미)

③ 일정 기간 동안 진행되고 있던 행위 또는 점진적으로 변화되고 있는 것을 말할 때

More and more people **are becoming** a meaterarian.
점점 많은 사람들이 육식주의자가 되고 있어.

④ 예정되어 있는 미래를 말할 때

I **am meeting** my girlfriend tomorrow.
나는 내일 여자 친구를 만날 거야.

⑤ 너무 자주(too often) 일어나는 상황을 말하는 것으로 강조의 의미

Tip 주로 always, forever와 같이 사용한다.

He **is** always **getting up** late!
그는 항상 늦게 일어나!

Tip 단순 현재 시제: 보통 일상적이고 반복적인 상황

I **get up** at 7 a.m. every day.
나는 매일 아침 7시에 일어나.

PART 1 현재진행형 문제풀이

TEST 1 – 4번

Macarthur High School's choir will be performing next. Right now, the choir members are drinking plenty of water to ⓐkeep their vocal cords from drying out.

(a) drink
(b) have drunk
(c) are drinking
(d) would drink

답 (c)

| 해설 |

①Right now, 주어 + ②현재진행형(be + Ving)

(a) V – 보통 일상적이고 반복적인 상황
(b) have p.p. – 행위의 결과에 중점을 두는 표현으로 이미 완료되었다는 점에 초점
(c) be Ving – 현재 말하는 시점에서 진행 중인 일시적 행위
(d) would V – 현재 사실의 반대/소망/미래/예정

| 구문독해 |

ⓐkeep + 목적어 + from Ving: ~가 ~하는 것을 못하게 하다(keep + 목적어 + Ving: ~가 계속 ~하다)

| 해석 |

다음 공연에는 Macarthur 고등학교의 합창단이 공연할 것이다. 바로 지금, 합창단원들은 성대가 마르지 않도록 물을 많이 마시고 있는 중이다.

| 어휘 |

choir 합창단, 성가대
perform 공연/연기/연주하다
plenty of 많은
vocal cords 성대
dry out 메마르다, 건조하다

TEST 2 – 26번

James is unable to make it to the post office before it closes. Fortunately, his girlfriend works near the post office. He is now talking to her over the phone about letters and parcels ❶she ❷needs to pick up from the post office.

(a) now talks
(b) is now talking
(c) would now talk
(d) has now talked

답 (b)

| 해설 |

주어 + be ① now Ving

(a) V – 보통 일상적이고 반복적인 상황
(b) be Ving – 현재 말하는 시점에서 진행 중인 일시적 행위
(c) would V – 현재 사실의 반대/소망/미래/예정
(d) have/has p.p. – 행위의 결과에 중점을 두는 표현으로 이미 완료되었다는 점에 초점

| 구문독해 |

❶목적격 관계대명사 that(~하는) 생략
– 선행사 + (that) + 주어 + 타동사 + (목적어 없음)
❷need + 목적어(to V): ~하는 것이 필요하다

| 해석 |

James는 우체국이 문 닫기 전에 도착할 수 없다. 다행히도, 그의 여자친구는 우체국 근처에서 일한다. 그는 우체국에서 찾아와야 할 편지와 소포에 대해 전화로 그녀에게 **지금 이야기하고 있는 중이다**.

| 어휘 |

be unable to V ~할 능력이 없다
make it (어떤 곳에 간신히) 시간 맞춰 가다
talk to ~에게 말을 걸다
over the phone 전화 통화상으로
pick up (어디에서) ~을 찾다[찾아오다]

PART 1
현재진행형 문제풀이

TEST 3 - 5번

If someone rings Dr. Lee, kindly [1]ask the person to call her back later. Dr. Lee is conducting a very delicate surgical operation right now. She doesn't [2]want to be disturbed under any circumstances.

(a) conducts
(b) will conduct
(c) is conducting
(d) conducted

답 (c)

| 해설 |

주어 + [2]현재진행형(be Ving) + [1]right now

(a) V – 보통 일상적이고 반복적인 상황
(b) will V – 단순히 미래를 예측/추측
(c) be Ving – 현재 말하는 시점에서 진행 중인 일시적 행위
(d) Ved – 과거 특정 시점에 시작하여 종료된 행동이나 사건을 표현

| 구문독해 |

[1]ask + 목적어 + 목적격보어(to V): ~가 ~하도록 부탁하다
[2]want + 목적어(to V): ~하기를 원하다

| 해석 |

만약 누군가가 Lee 박사님에게 전화를 걸면, 그 사람에게 다시 전화 해달라고 부탁해라. Lee 박사님은 지금 매우 까다로운 수술을 하고 있다. 그녀는 어떤 상황에서도 방해받는 것을 원하지 않는다.

| 어휘 |

call back (전화를 해 왔던 사람이나 누구에게) 다시 전화를 하다
delicate 섬세한, 정밀한, 정교한, 까다로운
surgical operation 외과수술
under(in) any circumstances 어떠한 일이 있어도, 여하한 일이 있더라도

예제문제

Because Oliver needs a certificate to graduate from university, he decided to study hard to get a certificate during this vacation. Although it's his lunch break, he _____ in the library.

(a) now studies
(b) is now studying
(c) will now have studied
(d) has now studied

답 (b)

| 해설 |

현재진행(be Ving) 시제는 현재 시점에서 지금 진행 중인 행위를 강조할 때 또는 예정된 미래를 말하는 경우에 사용한다. Oliver는 졸업하기 위해 점심시간임에도 불구하고 도서관에서 지금(now) 열심히 공부하고 있다는 내용으로 현재 시점에서 행위의 진행을 강조하고 있으므로 현재진행시제인 (b) is now studying이 정답이다.

| 해석 |

Oliver는 대학교를 졸업하기 위해 자격증이 필요했기 때문에 이번 방학 때 열심히 공부해서 자격증을 따기로 결심했다. 비록 점심시간이지만, 그는 도서관에서 **지금 공부를 하는 중**이다.

| 어휘 |

certificate 자격증
graduate 졸업하다
lunch break (직장·학교의) 점심시간(= lunch hour)

PART 1 미래진행형 핵심이론

📖 이렇게 나와요

Lisa can't wait to finish work. Her husband is preparing dinner for her. She is sure their kitchen _____ of baked lamb, and pizza when she gets home later.

(a) smells
(b) is smelling
(c) has smelled
(d) will be smelling

③ 미래진행형 (Future Continuous)

한정된 미래 시점에서 진행되고 있을 상황을 묘사하는 시제로 미래의 어느 시점에 '~하고 있겠지'라는 의미이다.

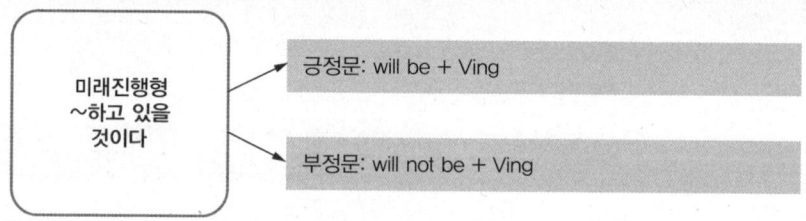

이런 게 답이에요

*when + 주어 + 현재동사형 / *by the time + 주어 + 현재동사형 / *if + 주어 + 현재동사형 / *for + 기간 표현 / *until + 미래 시점 / *until + (주어 + be 동사) + Ving / tomorrow[someday/next] + 시간 표현 / start + 미래 시점 ▶ 미래진행형

Lisa can't wait to finish work. Her husband is preparing dinner for her. She is sure their
주어
kitchen _____ of baked lamb, and pizza when she gets home later.
　　　　　　　　　　　　　　　　　　　　　　　　　　　　주어　현재동사형

(a) ~~smells~~
(b) ~~is smelling~~
(c) ~~has smelled~~
(d) will be smelling will be Ving

이렇게 활용해요

① 미래의 어느 기간 동안 이루어지는 동작의 연속

They **will be traveling** Europe next year.
그들은 내년에 유럽을 여행하고 있을 거야.

② 미래에 일어날 일들이 이미 이전의 결정이나 약속으로 고정이 된 경우

I **will be seeing** you.
너를 보게 될 거야.

③ 미래 어느 시점에 진행 중인 동작이나 상태

By this time next week, we'**ll be sunning** ourselves on a beach in Bali.
다음 주 이 시간이면 우리는 발리 해변에서 햇볕을 쬐고 있을 거야.

④ 늘 반복되는 일들에 대한 언급할 때

We'**ll be going** to my brother's house again for Christmas.
우리는 크리스마스 동안 다시 나의 형 집에 가 있을 거야.

⊕ PLUS 선택지에서 주로 혼동할 수 있는 경우

① 미래진행 시제와 미래를 나타내는 현재진행 시제의 차이점

공통점	미래에 하기로 되어 있었던 일들을 언급할 경우 We **will be leaving** / **are leaving** for London at 7:00 in the evening. 우리는 저녁 7시에 런던으로 떠나고 있겠지 / 떠날 거야.
차이점	현재진행형이 좀 더 예기치 못한 깜짝 놀랄 만한 일이 발생할 때 사용 Have you heard the news? Mr. Kevin **is leaving**! 너 그 소식 들었어? Kevin씨가 떠난대!

② 미래진행 시제와 미래 시제의 차이점
※ 미래진행 시제가 미래 시제보다 먼저 일어나는 일을 말한다.

미래진행 시제	We**'ll be making** dinner when you arrive. 네가 도착할 때 우리는 저녁을 만들고 있을 거야.
미래 시제	We**'ll make** dinner together when you arrive. 네가 도착할 때 우리는 저녁을 같이 만들 거야.

PART 1 미래진행형 문제풀이

TEST 1 – 21번

Lisa can't **①wait** to finish work. Her husband is preparing dinner for her. She **②is** sure their kitchen will be smelling of baked lamb, and pizza **③when** she gets home later.

(a) smells
(b) is smelling
(c) has smelled
(d) will be smelling

답 (d)

| 해설 |

주어 + ③미래진행형(will be Ving) + ①when + 주어 + ②현재동사형

(a) V – 보통 일상적이고 반복적인 상황
(b) be Ving – 현재 말하는 시점에서 진행 중인 일시적 행위
(c) have/has p.p. – 행위의 결과에 중점을 두는 표현으로 이미 완료되었다는 점에 초점
(d) will be Ving – 미래의 어느 시점에 진행 중인 동작이나 상태

| 구문독해 |

①wait to V: ~하기를 기다리다
②be sure + (that) + 주어 + 동사: ~을 확신하다(= be sure to V/be sure of Ving)
③미래대용
 – 시간/조건의 부사절에서는 현재(완료)가 미래(완료)를 대신한다.

| 해석 |

Lisa는 일을 끝내기를 기다릴 수 없다. 그녀의 남편은 지금 그녀를 위해 저녁 식사를 준비하고 있다. 그녀는 나중에 집에 들어가면 부엌에서 구운 양고기와 피자 **냄새가 날 것이라고** 확신한다.

| 어휘 |

prepare ~을 준비하다
smell of ~의 냄새가 나다
lamb (새끼 양의) 양고기
get home 귀가하다

PART 1
미래진행형 문제풀이

TEST 2 - 12번

①It is already nine o'clock in the morning, and I still have a lot of housework to do. ②I will be staying home until noon cleaning rooms and washing dishes.

(a) am staying
(b) have stayed
(c) stay
(d) will be staying

답 (d)

| 해설 |

주어 + ②미래진행형(will be Ving) + ①until + 미래 시점

(a) be Ving – 현재 말하는 시점에서 진행 중인 일시적 행위
(b) have p.p. – 행위의 결과에 중점을 두는 표현으로 이미 완료되었다는 점에 초점
(c) V – 보통 일상적이고 반복적인 상황
(d) will be Ving – 미래 어느 시점에 진행 중인 동작이나 상태

| 구문독해 |

①비인칭 주어 it
– 날씨/시각(간)/요일/날짜/거리/명암 등을 나타낼 때 주어 it을 비인칭 주어라고 하고, 이때 it은 "그것은"이라고 해석하지 않는다.
②분사구문
– 주어 + 동사 ~, 현재분사[Ving: 능동(~하면서)]

| 해석 |

벌써 아침 9시 정각인데, 나는 아직 해야 할 집안일이 많아. 나는 정오까지 방을 청소하고 설거지를 하면서 집에 머물러 있을 거야.

| 어휘 |

housework 가사, 집안일
stay home 집에 머물다
wash dishes 접시를 닦다

예제문제

Portman Corporation recently announced its recruitment announcement. The company said that starting next week, they _____ prospective candidates from all over the country for one month.

(a) would interview
(b) have been interviewing
(c) interview
(d) will be interviewing

답 (d)

| 해설 |

미래진행(will be Ving)은 미래의 어느 시점에 진행 중일 동작이나 상태를 말한다. 다음 주(next week)를 시작으로 한 달 동안 예비 후보들을 면접 볼 것이라는 미래의 시점에 진행 중인 경우이므로 미래진행 시제인 (d) will be interviewing이 정답이다.

| 해석 |

Portman 기업은 최근 회사 모집공고를 발표하였다. 회사는 다음 주부터, 한 달 동안 전국에서 온 예비 후보들을 <u>면접 볼 것이라고</u> 말했다.

| 어휘 |

announce 발표하다
recruitment 신규 모집
prospective 장래의
candidate 지원자
all over the country 나라 안 방방곡곡에

PART 1 과거완료진행형 핵심이론

📖 이렇게 나와요

I was supposed to go shopping with my sister yesterday, but my last client meeting went longer than expected. She was really angry because she _____ for an hour by the time I finally met her.

(a) waited
(b) would have waited
(c) was waiting
(d) had been waiting

4. 과거완료진행형(Past Perfect Continuous)

대과거에 시작한 일이 과거까지 이어져 와서 끝나는 과거완료(had p.p.)와 일이 끝나지 않고 계속해서 진행되는 진행형(be Ving)의 합성으로 대과거에 시작한 일이 끝나지 않고 과거 어느 시점에도 진행 중이고 이 시점을 넘어 계속 진행될 때 사용한다.

과거완료진행형 ~해오고 있었다
- 긍정문: had + been + Ving
- 부정문: had + not + been + Ving
- 의문문: Had + 주어 + been + Ving ~?

이런 게 답이에요

[*before[when] + 주어 + 과거동사형 / *since + 주어 + 과거동사형 / *until + 주어 + 과거동사형 / *by the time + 주어 + 과거동사형[과거시점] / *for + 기간 표현 / last night / how long / ever since + 주어 + 과거동사형] ▶ 과거완료진행형

I was supposed to go shopping with my sister yesterday, but my last client meeting went longer than expected. She was really angry because she _____ for an hour by the time I finally met her.

(a) ~~waited~~
(b) ~~would have waited~~
(c) ~~was waiting~~
(d) had been waiting   had been Ving

이렇게 활용해요

① 대과거에서 과거까지 진행: 모두 과거에서 시작해 과거에서 끝남

My brother had just turned TV off before I got home. He **had been watching** TV.
나의 형은 내가 집에 들어오기 전에 막 TV를 껐다. 그는 TV를 보고 있었다.

② 원인과 결과

He **had been working** all day, so he was very tired.
그는 하루 종일 일을 해왔기 때문에 그는 매우 피곤했다.

③ 대과거부터 경과된 지속시간: 의문문의 경우 how long~?, 긍정문의 경우 for, since 등과 같이 사용

How long **had** you **been studying** English before you moved to America?
당신은 미국으로 떠나기 전에 얼마나 영어를 공부해오셨나요?

Kevin **had been working** at that company for twenty years when he retired in 2002.
Kevin이 2002년에 은퇴를 했을 때, 그는 20년 동안 그 회사에서 일을 해오고 있었다.

PLUS 선택지에서 주로 혼동할 수 있는 경우

① 과거완료진행형과 과거완료형 비교

과거완료 진행형	장기간에 지속되고 영구적인 상황 혹은 어떤 일을 과거의 어느 시점까지 계속 해왔음을 강조할 경우 He **had been standing** on the street corner for 10 minutes when Julie arrived. Julie가 도착했을 때 그는 길 모퉁이에서 10분 정도 서 있어왔다.
과거완료형	단기간에 지속되고 일시적인 행위나 상황 혹은 행위가 완료됨을 강조할 경우 That statue **had stood** in the square for three hundred years before a heavy earthquake hit in 2000. 2000년에 대지진이 발생하기 전 그 조각상은 광장에서 300년 동안 서 있었다.

② 과거완료진행형과 과거진행형 비교

과거완료 진행형	과거의 어느 시점에서 어떤 일을 막 하고 있었다는 것을 강조 When I saw her, she **had been talking** to her friends. 내가 그녀를 보았을 때, 그녀는 친구들에게 말을 해오고 있었다.
과거진행형	과거의 어느 시점에서 어떤 일이 한창 진행 중이었던 일 When I saw her, she **was talking** to her friends. 내가 그녀를 보았을 때, 그녀는 친구들에게 한창 말을 하고 있었다. (그러나 곧 끝냈다)

③ 과거완료진행형과 현재완료진행형 비교

과거완료 진행형	과거를 기준으로 대과거부터 과거까지 행동이 지속됨을 강조 I **had been waiting** there for five hours when she arrived. 나는 거기서 5시간째 기다리고 있었는데, 그때 그녀가 도착했다.
현재완료 진행형	현재를 기준으로 과거부터 현재까지 행동이 지속됨을 강조 I **have been waiting** here for five hours. 나는 여기서 5시간 동안 기다리고 있다.

PART 1 과거완료진행형 문제풀이

TEST 1 - 14번

I was supposed to ⁰go shopping with my sister yesterday, but my last client meeting went longer ⁰than expected. She was really angry because she had been waiting for an hour by the time I finally met her.

(a) waited
(b) would have waited
(c) was waiting
(d) had been waiting

답 (d)

| 해설 |

주어 + ⁰과거완료진행형(had been Ving) + ⁰for + 기간 표현 + ⁰by the time + 주어 + ⁰과거동사형/과거 시점

(a) Ved – 과거 특정 시점에 시작하여 종료가 된 행동이나 사건을 표현
(b) would have p.p. – 과거 사실에 대한 단순한 유감이나 후회
(c) was/were Ving – 과거 특정 시점에 진행 중이었던 행동이나 사건을 표현
(d) had been Ving – 장기간에 지속되고 영구적인 상황 혹은 어떤 일을 과거의 어느 시점까지 계속 해왔음을 강조할 경우

| 구문독해 |

⁰go + Ving(동명사): ~하러 가다
⁰유사관계대명사 than
– 관계대명사는 아니지만 관계대명사처럼 사용되는 경우

| 해석 |

어제 언니와 쇼핑을 가기로 했는데, 마지막 고객 미팅이 예상보다 길어졌다. 내가 마침내 그녀를 만났을 때 그녀는 한 시간 동안 기다렸었기 때문에 그녀는 정말 화가 났다.

| 어휘 |

be supposed to V ~하기로 되어 있다, ~할 의무가 있다
wait for ~를 기다리다

PART 1
과거완료진행형 문제풀이

TEST 2 – 3번

Jack was ⁰one of the national top marathon runners. He had been winning five gold medals at the 1936 Olympic Games in Berlin until he had a car accident.

(a) would win
(b) was winning
(c) won
(d) had been winning

답 (d)

| 해설 |

주어 + ③과거완료진행형(had been Ving) + ①until + 주어 + ②과거동사형

(a) would V – 현재 사실의 반대/소망/미래/예정
(b) was/were Ving – 과거 특정 시점에 진행 중이었던 행동이나 사건을 표현
(c) Ved – 과거 특정 시점에 시작하여 종료된 행동이나 사건을 표현
(d) had been Ving – 장기간에 지속되고 영구적인 상황 혹은 어떤 일을 과거의 어느 시점까지 계속 해왔음을 강조할 경우

| 구문독해 |

⁰one of + 복수명사: ~중의 하나

| 해석 |

Jack은 전국 최고의 마라톤 선수들 중 한 명이었다. 그는 자동차 사고를 당하기 전까지 1936년 베를린 올림픽에서 5개의 금메달을 땄었다.

| 어휘 |

win a medal 메달(상패)을 획득하다
car accident 자동차 사고

TEST 3 – 11번

One week ago, Heather ❶decided to take a short trip. She had been studying nonstop for ten years before she was ❷appointed as a full professor of anatomy at Cambridge last month. She's now on her way to Bangkok in Thailand.

(a) studied
(b) studies
(c) had been studying
(d) was studying

답 (c)

| 해설 |

주어 + ③과거완료진행형(had been Ving) + ①for + 기간 표현 + before + 주어 + ②과거동사형

(a) Ved – 과거 특정 시점에 시작하여 종료된 행동이나 사건을 표현
(b) V – 보통 일상적이고 반복적인 상황
(c) had been Ving – 장기간에 지속되고 영구적인 상황 혹은 어떤 일을 과거의 어느 시점까지 계속 해왔음을 강조할 경우
(d) was/were Ving – 과거 특정 시점에 진행 중이었던 행동이나 사건을 표현

| 구문독해 |

❶decide + 목적어(to V): ~하기를 결정하다
❷appoint + 목적어 + 목적격보어(as + 명사): ~을 ~로 임명하다[수동태 시, be appointed + 주격보어(as + 명사)]

| 해석 |

일주일 전에, Heather는 짧은 여행을 가기로 결정했다. 그녀는 지난 달 케임브리지 대학 해부학 정교수로 임명되기 전까지 10년 동안 쉬지 않고 **공부해왔다**. 그녀는 지금 태국의 방콕으로 가는 중이다.

| 어휘 |

take a short trip 짧은 여행을 하다
nonstop 쉬지 않고
a full professor 정교수
anatomy 해부학
on one's way to ~으로 가는 길에

PART 1 현재완료진행형 핵심이론

📖 이렇게 나와요

The company Brian works for is in bad shape, and he is extremely concerned. He _____ there for twenty years now, and is afraid it might cut down the number of employees or urge him to resign.

(a) will work
(b) works
(c) is working
(d) has been working

⑤ 현재완료진행형(Present Perfect Continuous)

과거에 시작해서 꾸준하게 지금까지 진행되고 있는 동작 또는 상태가 지속되고 있는 경우에 사용한다.

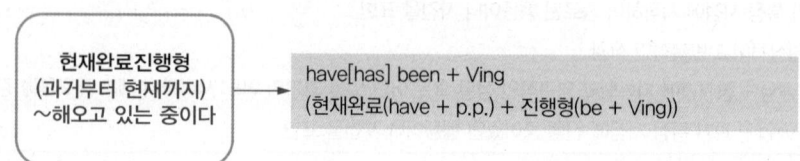

현재완료진행형
(과거부터 현재까지)
~해오고 있는 중이다

have[has] been + Ving
(현재완료(have + p.p.) + 진행형(be + Ving))

이런 게 답이에요

*for + 기간 표현 / *for + 기간 표현 + now / *after + 주어 + 현재완료 / *lately / *[ever] since + 주어 + 과거동사형 / *since + 과거 시점 / *for[over] the past + 기간 표현 / *in[during] the last + 기간 표현 / *over + 기간 표현 / recently / up to now / all day / already / just ▶ 현재완료진행형

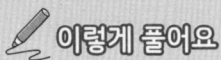

The company Brian works for is in bad shape, and he is extremely concerned. He (주어) _____ there for twenty years now, and is afraid it might cut down the (for + 기간 표현 + now) number of employees or urge him to resign.

(a) ~~will work~~
(b) ~~works~~
(c) ~~is working~~
(d) has been working have[has] been Ving

이렇게 활용해요

① 행위 자체에 중점을 두는 표현
- 어떤 행동이 계속 진행되어 왔다는 점에 초점
- 과거의 특정 시점에서 시작한 일이 현재까지 영향을 미치는 경우

> **Tip** 시간의 길이를 나타내는 for, since와 주로 같이 사용한다.

I have been doing my homework for about 3 hours.
나는 3시간 동안 숙제를 하고 있는 중이다.

> **Tip** 현재완료(Present Perfect): 행위의 결과에 중점을 두는 표현으로 이미 완료되었다는 점에 초점

I have done my homework.
나는 숙제를 했다. (숙제를 끝마친 행위의 결과에 중점)

② 시간의 길이가 없는 경우: 근래에 꽤 오랜 시간 동안 진행 중

I have been trying to stop smoking.
나는 금연하려고 노력 중이다.

③ 바로 얼마 전에 끝난 동작 표현: 지금은 진행되지 않고 과거에 시작해서 최근에 끝난 일을 표현하는 경우

You are sweating a lot.
Yeah, I **have been running**.
너 땀이 많이 나네.
응, 달리기를 했거든.

PART 1 현재완료진행형 문제풀이

TEST 1 – 2번

The company [1]Brian works for is in bad shape, and he is extremely concerned. He has been working there for twenty years now, and [2]is afraid it might cut down [3]the number of employees or [4]urge him to resign.

(a) will work
(b) works
(c) is working
(d) has been working

답 (d)

| 해설 |

주어 + [2]현재완료진행형(have[has] been Ving) + [1]for + 기간 표현 + now

(a) will V – 단순히 미래를 예측/추측
(b) V – 보통 일상적이고 반복적인 상황
(c) be Ving – 현재 말하는 시점에서 진행 중인 일시적 행위
(d) have[has] been Ving – 현재를 기준으로 과거부터 현재까지 행동이 지속됨을 강조

| 구문독해 |

[1]목적격 관계대명사 that(~하는) 생략
– 선행사 + (that) + 주어 + 동사 + 전치사 (목적어 없음)
[2]be afraid (that) + 주어 + 동사: ~을 두려워하다 (= be afraid of + Ving)
[3]the number of + 복수명사: ~수
[4]urge + 목적어 + 목적격보어(to V): ~가 ~하도록 재촉하다

| 해석 |

Brian이 일하는 회사는 불황이고, 그는 극도로 걱정하고 있다. 그는 지금 20년 동안 그곳에서 **일해왔으며**, 이로 인해 직원 수를 줄이거나 그에게 사직을 권고하지 않을까 우려하고 있다.

| 어휘 |

work for ~을 위해 일하다
be in bad shape 나쁘다, 불황이다
extremely 극도로, 극히
cut down (무엇의 크기·양·수를) 줄이다
resign 사직하다

TEST 2 – 13번

I really respect mothers who completely [1]devote [2]themselves to child-rearing. [3]One of those [4]I admire most is my mother, who has been working for 7 days a week to support my family [5]as well as other poor people.

(a) is working
(b) works
(c) has been working
(d) will work

답 (c)

| 해설 |

주어 + 동사 + ①선행사, who + ③현재완료진행형(have[has] been Ving) + ②for + 기간 표현

(a) be Ving – 현재 말하는 시점에서 진행 중인 일시적 행위
(b) V – 보통 일상적이고 반복적인 상황
(c) have[has] been Ving – 현재를 기준으로 과거부터 현재까지 행동이 지속됨을 강조
(d) will V – 단순히 미래를 예측/추측

| 구문독해 |

[1]devote + 목적어 + to (동)명사: ~을/를 ~하는 데 전념(몰두)하다
[2]재귀대명사의 재귀적 용법(생략 불가)
– 주어(주체)와 같으면 재귀대명사를 사용하고 다르면 대명사를 사용
[3]주어와 동사의 수의 일치
– one of + 복수명사 + 단수동사: ~중의 하나는 ~이다
[4]목적격 관계대명사 that(~하는) 생략
– 선행사 + (that) + 주어 + 타동사 + (목적어 없음)
[5]상관접속사
– not only A but also B = B as well as A: A뿐만 아니라 B도 (주어로 사용 시, 주어는 B)

| 해석 |

나는 육아에 완전히 전념하는 엄마들을 정말 존경한다. 내가 가장 존경하는 사람들 중 한 명은 나의 엄마인데, 그녀는 일주일 내내 다른 가난한 사람들뿐만 아니라 가족을 부양하기 위해 **일해오셨다**.

| 어휘 |

child-rearing 자녀 양육

PART 1
현재완료진행형 문제풀이

TEST 3 – 10번

Olivia is upset with her brother [1]for not washing dad's car with her. He has been playing computer games since this early morning without having breakfast and lunch.

(a) plays
(b) is playing
(c) has been playing
(d) played

답 (c)

| 해설 |

주어 + [2]현재완료진행형(have[has] been Ving) + [1]since + 과거 시점

(a) V – 보통 일상적이고 반복적인 상황
(b) be Ving – 현재 말하는 시점에서 진행 중인 일시적 행위
(c) have[has] been Ving – 현재를 기준으로 과거부터 현재까지 행동이 지속됨을 강조
(d) Ved – 과거 특정 시점에 시작하여 종료된 행동이나 사건을 표현

| 구문독해 |

[1]동명사 부정
– not/never + 동명사 / 전치사 + not/never + 동명사 (no는 형용사로 동명사를 수식할 수 없어서 사용 불가)

| 해석 |

Olivia는 자기와 함께 아버지의 차를 세차하지 않은 동생에게 화가 났다. 그는 오늘 아침 일찍부터 아침과 점심을 먹지 않고 컴퓨터 게임을 해오고 있다.

| 어휘 |

be[get] upset (with) ~에 역정이 나다
play game 놀이를 하다
have[eat] breakfast 아침을 먹다
have[eat] lunch 점심을 먹다

TEST 3 – 25번

[1]Adam Miller, one of the best neurologists, was actually a pianist [2]during his high school years. In fact, he hasn't been playing the piano over a year [3]due to his busy schedule.

(a) weren't playing
(b) isn't playing
(c) didn't play
(d) hasn't been playing

답 (d)

| 해설 |

주어 + [2]현재완료진행형(have[has] not been Ving) + [1]over + 기간 표현

(a) was/were Ving – 과거 특정 시점에 진행 중이었던 행동이나 사건을 표현
(b) be Ving – 현재 말하는 시점에서 진행 중인 일시적 행위
(c) Ved – 과거 특정 시점에 시작하여 종료된 행동이나 사건을 표현
(d) have[has] been Ving – 현재를 기준으로 과거부터 현재까지 행동이 지속됨을 강조

| 구문독해 |

[1]동격
– 명사(A), 명사(B): B라는 A(주어로 사용 시, A가 주어)
[2]during(전치사) + 명사: ~동안[while(종속접속사) + 주어 + 동사]
[3]due to(전치사) + 명사: ~ 때문에[because(종속접속사) + 주어 + 동사]

| 해석 |

최고의 신경과 의사 중 한 명인 Adam Miller는 고등학교 시절 실제로 피아노 연주가였다. 사실, 그는 바쁜 일정 때문에 1년 넘게 피아노를 연주해 오지 않고 있다.

| 어휘 |

neurologist 신경학자, 신경과 전문의

PART 1 미래완료진행형 핵심이론

📖 이렇게 나와요

Prince Laboratories has poured massive sums into a new drug for diabetes. However, the FDA is still examining the drug's safety. By October, the company _____ for FDA approval for two years before they can distribute the drug to people all over the world.

(a) will have been waiting
(b) has waited
(c) would have waited
(d) will wait

6 미래완료진행형 (Future Perfect Continuous)

미래 한 시점에서 계속 진행 중인 일의 기간(Duration)을 표현하기 위해 사용되거나 미래에 있을 일의 확신의 근거로써 사용한다.

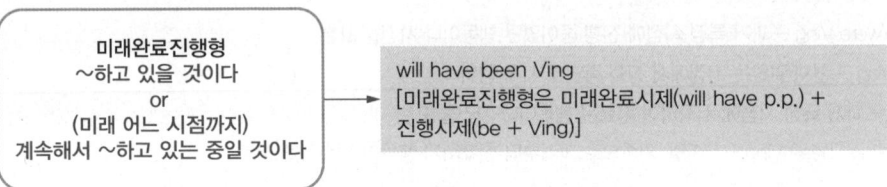

이런 게 답이에요

*by(by the time) + 미래 시점 / *for + 기간 표현 / *by the time + 주어 + 현재동사형 / since + 시간 ▶ 미래완료진행형

Prince Laboratories has poured massive sums into a new drug for diabetes. However, the FDA is still examining the drug's safety. By October, the company _____ for FDA approval for two years before they can distribute the drug to people all over the world.

by + 미래 시점
for + 기간 표현

(a) will have been waiting *will have been Ving*
(b) ~~has waited~~
(c) ~~would have waited~~
(d) ~~will wait~~

이렇게 활용해요

① 기간(Duration)을 강조: 미래의 특정 시점 이전에 시작되어 그때까지 진행되고 있는 일

By the time Kevin arrives, we **will have been waiting for** thirty minutes.
Kevin이 도착할 쯤, 우리는 30분 동안 기다리고 있을 것이다.

② 미래의 일에 대한 확신의 근거(Cause)

Kevin will be tired when he gets home because he **will have been working for** over ten hours.
Kevin이 집에 도착하고 나면 피곤할 것인데 왜냐하면 그는 10시간 넘게 일을 했을 것이기 때문이다.

③ 미래의 특정 시점까지 진행될 일

If you arrive at 12 o'clock, I'**ll have been standing** here for two hours.
네가 12시에 도착하면, 나는 두 시간째 여기 서 있는 게 될 거야.

④ 과거부터 계속 진행하던 동작이 미래의 어느 시점에 딱 완료될 때 사용: '~하는 게 될 것이다'라는 의미

Next month, I **will have been working** here for 10 years.
다음 달에 나는 여기에서 10년 동안 일하는 게 될 것이다.

PART 1 미래완료진행형 문제풀이

TEST 1 - 9번

Prince Laboratories has poured massive sums into a new drug for diabetes. However, the FDA is still examining the drug's safety. By October, the company will have been waiting for FDA approval for two years before they can [1]distribute the drug to people all over the world.

(a) will have been waiting
(b) has waited
(c) would have waited
(d) will wait

답 (a)

| 해설 |

[1]By + 미래 시점 + 주어 + [3]미래완료진행(will have been Ving) + [2]for + 기간 표현

(a) will have been Ving – 미래 한 시점에서 계속 진행 중인 일의 기간(duration)을 표현하기 위해 사용되거나 미래에 있을 일의 확신의 근거로써 사용
(b) have[has] p.p. – 행위의 결과에 중점을 두는 표현으로 이미 완료되었다는 점에 초점
(c) would have p.p. – 과거 사실에 대한 단순한 유감이나 후회
(d) will V – 단순히 미래를 예측/추측

| 구문독해 |

[1]전치사 to
- distribute A to B: A를 B에 나누어 주다

| 해석 |

Prince 연구소는 당뇨병을 위한 새로운 약에 막대한 금액을 쏟아 부었다. 하지만, FDA는 여전히 이 약의 안전성을 조사하고 있다. 전 세계 사람들에게 그 약을 나누어 줄 수 있기 전에 10월까지, 그 회사는 2년 동안 FDA의 승인을 기다리고 있을 것이다.

| 어휘 |

laboratory 연구실[소], 랩(lab)
massive 대규모의, 대량의
diabetes 당뇨병
examine 조사[검토]하다
approval (정식) 승인, 인가
pour A into B A를 B에 쏟아 넣다
sum 금액
FDA 미국 식품 의약국
wait for ~를 기다리다
all over the world 전 세계에

TEST 2 - 22번

Annabelle is in her last year as a nursing student and is ①looking forward to graduation. By the time she finishes this semester, she will have been studying nothing but ②how to improve patient care for more than four years.

(a) was studying
(b) will have been studying
(c) studied
(d) would have studied

답 (b)

| 해설 |

①By the time + 주어 + ②현재동사형 + 주어 + ④미래완료진행(will have been Ving) + ③for + 기간 표현

(a) was/were Ving – 과거 특정 시점에 진행 중이었던 행동이나 사건을 표현
(b) will have been Ving – 미래 한 시점에서 계속 진행 중인 일의 기간(duration)을 표현하기 위해 사용되거나 미래에 있을 일의 확신의 근거로써 사용
(c) Ved – 과거 특정 시점에 시작하여 종료된 행동이나 사건을 표현
(d) would have p.p. – 과거 사실에 대한 단순한 유감이나 후회

| 구문독해 |

①전치사 to
– look forward to + (동)명사: ~을 기대하다, 즐거운 마음으로 기다리다
②간접의문문
– 의문문이 문장 내에서 품사적 기능을 가지는데, 특히 명사절(주어/목적어/보어)로 주로 사용
– 의문사 to V = 의문사 + 주어 + should + V

| 해석 |

Annabelle은 간호학과 학생으로 마지막 해를 보내고 있고 졸업을 기대하고 있다. 그녀가 이번 학기를 마칠 때까지, 그녀는 4년 이상 동안 환자 치료를 어떻게 개선할 것인가를 공부만 하고 있을 것이다.

| 어휘 |

be in one's last year ~의 마지막 해에 있다
nothing but 오직, 그저[단지] ~일 뿐인(= only)
semester (특히 미국에서) 학기
patient care 환자 치료

PART 2
조동사

조동사

should 생략

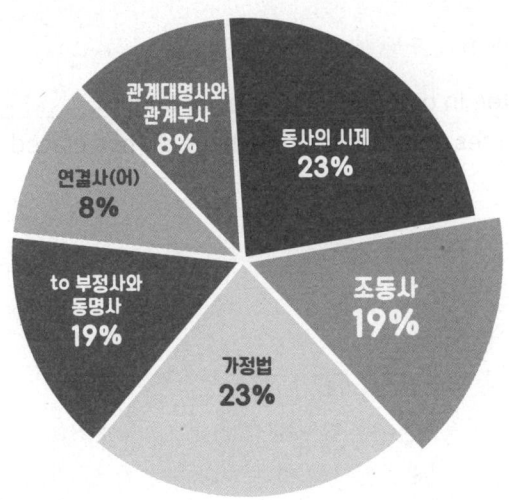

🔍 조동사의 출제원리

1. **조동사의 쓰임과 우리말 뜻을 알아야 한다.**
   - can/could: 가능
   - may/might: 추측
   - must/should/have to: 의무
   - will/would: 예정
   - 조동사 have Ved: 추측/후회(가정법에 주로 적용)

2. **should 생략**
   - 주절에 나오는 '요구/제안/주장/충고(제안) 관련 동사'와 '이성적 판단 형용사'를 숙지한다.
   - 종속절에 나오는 동사는 무조건 동사원형(V)을 사용한다.
   - 종속절을 이끄는 that은 목적격 종속접속사로 생략되기도 하니 주의해야 한다.

 Tip

1. 조동사의 종류는 출제 원리에서 언급한 이외의 것들이 많이 있지만 출제 원리에 제시한 조동사의 종류와 의미만 알고 있으면 된다.
2. 조동사의 뜻만 안다고 해서 문장이 해석이 되지 않는 경우 문제의 정답을 찾지 못할 수도 있기 때문에 평소 단어와 문법 및 구문 학습도 필요하다.
3. 'should 생략'은 관련 동사와 형용사를 숙지했을 경우에 누구나 정답을 빠르고 쉽게 찾을 수 있으니 본 서에 제시된 동사와 형용사를 반드시 숙지하자.

PART 2 조동사 핵심이론

📖 이렇게 나와요

The Sea level rises faster. In order to survive, polar bears _____ walk a long way to search for food. Sometimes, they forage in garbage dumps placed in the areas where the locals live.

(a) must
(b) can
(c) might
(d) should

① 조동사의 종류

동사에 어떤 특정한 의미를 더해 동사의 의미를 구체적으로 설명해주는 동사이다.

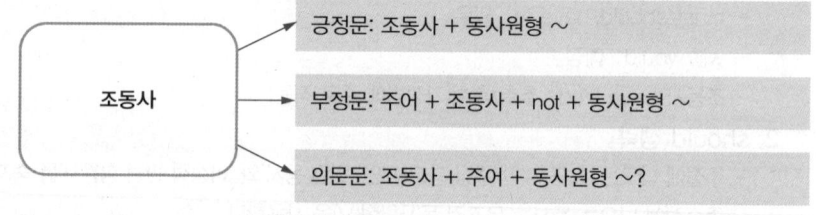

※ 위치: be동사나 일반 동사 앞

Tip '조동사 + 조동사' 불가

이런 게 답이에요

종류	시제	용법	의미
can	현재형	가능성/능력	~할 수 있다
could	과거형	추측	~할 수도 있다
may	현재형	약한 추측	~할지도 모르다
might	과거형	불확실한 약한 추측	~일(할)지도 모르다

The Sea level rises faster. In order to survive, polar bears _____ walk a long way to search for food. Sometimes, they forage in garbage dumps placed in the areas where the locals live.

(a) must ~해야만 한다.
(b) ~~can~~
(c) ~~might~~
(d) ~~should~~

must	현재/과거형	강한 의무/필요/당위성	~해야(만) 한다
should	과거형	당위성	~해야(만) 한다
will	현재형	예정/미래	~할 것이다
would	과거형	현재 사실의 반대/소망/미래/예정	~하곤 했었다

② can/could 용법

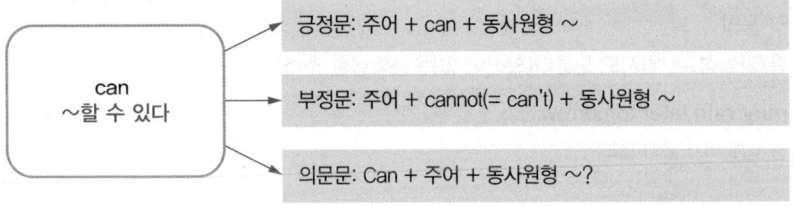

이렇게 활용해요

① can 용법: 가능성과 능력에 주로 사용
- 현재의 가능성(possibility): ~할 수 있다

　The sales **can go up** again.
　매출액은 다시 <u>올라갈 수 있다</u>.

- 현재의 능력(ability): ~할 수 있다

    I **can drive** a car.
    나는 차를 운전할 수 있다.

    Can you **speak** any foreign languages?
    외국어를 할 수 있습니까?

    The child **can't walk** yet.
    그 아이는 아직 걸을 수 없다.

② could의 용법: can의 과거형
- 과거의 능력(past ability): ~할 수 있었다

    When I was younger, I **could run** for 10 kilometers without stopping.
    내가 젊었을 때는 10킬로미터를 쉬지 않고 달릴 수 있었다.

- 과거의 가능성(possibility): ~할 수 있었다(can보다 좀 더 낮은 가능성)

    It **could be** dangerous.
    위험할 수도 있었다.

③ may/might 용법

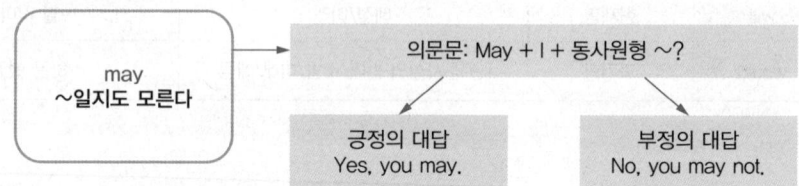

이렇게 활용해요

① may의 용법
- 추측/가능성: ~일지도 모른다(확신이 없는 불확실한 추측)

    It **may rain** later tomorrow.
    내일 늦게 비가 올지 몰라.

- 허락/허가: ~해도 좋다

    You **may have** lunch.
    점심을 먹어도 좋아.

- 제안: ~해드릴까요?(공손한 제안)

    May I **ask** you some questions?
    질문 몇 가지만 해도 되겠습니까?

- **소망/기원**: ~하시길!, 기원문으로 「May + 주어 + 동사원형~ !」 형태로 사용한다.

    May you **succeed**!
    당신이 성공하기를!

② might의 용법: 조동사 might는 조동사 may의 과거형으로 사용되는 경우도 있지만, 이 둘의 의미는 약간 다르다. 부정문은 might not으로 표현한다.

- **may의 과거형**: ~할지도 모르다

    He said that he **might come** tomorrow.
    그는 그가 내일 올지도 모른다고 말했다.

- **추측/가능성**: ~일지도 모르다

    It **might rain** today.
    오늘 비가 올 것 같아.

- **허락/허가(permission)**: ~해도 될까요?

    Might I **borrow** your pen?
    당신이 펜을 빌려도 되나요?

🔍 PLUS 선택지에서 주로 혼동할 수 있는 경우

may/might/can/could 공통점과 차이점

공통점	가능성(~일지도 모르다) (확신은 없음)	
차이점	may	• '~일지 모른다', '~해도 된다'(표현이 애매모호할 때) • 일반적으로 어떤 일이 일어날 가능성이 존재할 때 • 격식을 갖춘 문장에서는 더 선호
	might	• 일반적으로 어떤 일이 일어날 가능성이 존재할 때 • 가능성이 좀 더 낮을 때
	can	• '~할 수 있다', '~해도 된다'(표현이 확실할 때) • 좀 더 일반적인 상황에서 가능한 사건들에 대해 언급할 때 • 특별한 상황의 가능성에서는 잘 쓰이지 않음
	could	확신을 갖지 못한 것에 대한 의견을 개진할 때
가능성의 강도 차이	might < may < could < can	

④ must/should/have to 용법

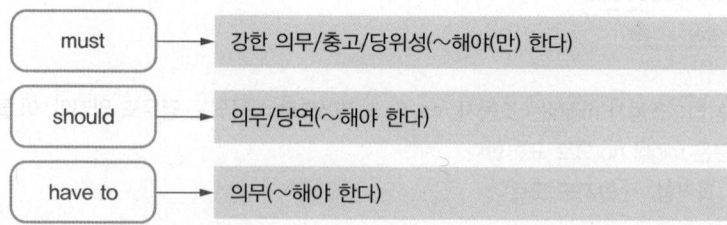

> **PLUS** 선택지에서 주로 혼동할 수 있는 경우

① must와 have to 공통점과 차이점

공통점		어떤 행동을 하는 것이 꼭 필요한 상황일 때
차이점	must	필요하다고 느끼는 사람은 바로 화자 자신 I **must see** my boss. 나는 나의 직장 상관을 보러 가야만 해. (주어 I가 직접 직장 상관을 찾아갈 필요가 있어 직접 가는 경우)
	have to	결정권은 화자가 아닌 다른 3자에게 있음, 격식이 없는 표현 I **have to see** my principal. 나는 교장선생님을 보러 가야만 해. (주어 I의 의지와는 상관없이 직장 상관이 불러서 어쩔 수 없이 가야 하는 경우)

② mustn't 와 don't/doesn't have to 차이점

mustn't	'절대 해서는 안 돼'라는 뜻 We must keep it a secret. We **mustn't tell** anyone. 우리는 그것에 비밀을 지켜야만 해. 절대로 누구에게도 말해서는 안 돼.
don't/doesn't have to	'~할 필요는 없다'라는 뜻으로, 즉 '~하지 않아도 돼'라는 의미이며 '상대방이 원하면 해도 돼'라는 뜻을 내포 You **don't have to tell** her, but you can if you want to. 너는 그녀에게 말할 필요는 없지만, 만약 네가 원한다면 말할 수 있어.

③ should/ought to/had better/have to/gotta/must 공통점과 차이점

공통점	~해야 한다
차이점	필요성의 강도 차이 should < ought to < had better < have to(have got to = gotta) < must 충고나 의견 및 조언 충고나 의견보다는 강함 강한 표현 아주 강함

⑤ will/would 용법

화자가 말하는 시점에서 결심한 일을 하려고 할 때 사용

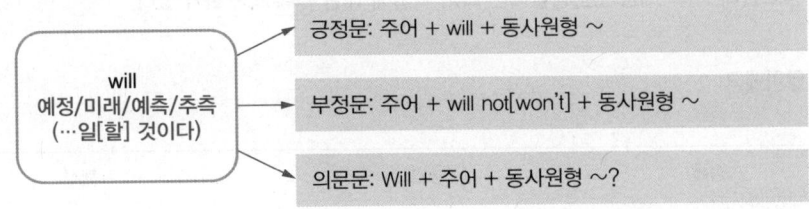

이렇게 활용해요

① will의 용법
- 단순 미래 예측: ~ 될 것이다(단순미래)

  Tip 미리 정해진 일은 아닌 경우

  It **will be** fine tomorrow.
  내일은 날씨가 좋을 것이다.

- 추측: (아마도) ~일 것이다

  Perhaps she **will be** free this afternoon.
  아마 그녀는 오늘 점심에는 한가할 것이다.

- be going to V(주어의 의지: ~할 예정이다, 가까운 미래: ~ 할 것이다)

  We **are going to have** a party.
  우리는 파티를 열 예정이다.

- 시간이나 조건의 부사절에서는 현재 시제로 미래 시제를 대신한다.

  If it snows tomorrow, **we will go skiing**.
  내일 눈이 오면, 우리는 스키 타러 갈 것이다.

② would의 용법: will의 과거형으로 will의 용법과 비슷하지만 would만의 특별한 의미를 갖기도 한다.
- will의 과거형

  I thought that he **would do** it at once.
  나는 그가 그 일을 즉시 하리라고 생각했다.

- 과거의 불규칙적인 습관: ~하곤 했다

  Jane **would sit** for hours doing nothing.
  Jane은 아무 것도 하지 않은 채 몇 시간 동안 앉아 있곤 했다.

6 조동사 + have + p.p.

'조동사 + have + p.p.'는 조동사를 이해하는 측면에서도 중요하지만, 가정법 특히 **가정법 과거완료를 이해하는 데 있어 중요**한데, 이에 해당하는 용법에는 과거 사실에 대한 **추측**과 **후회**가 있다.

이런 게 답이에요

종류	용법	해석
may[might] have p.p.	~이었을지도 모른다	과거 사실에 대한 약한 추측
must have p.p.	~이었음에 틀림이 없다	과거 사실에 대한 강한 추측
would have p.p.	~했을[이었을] 것이다	과거 사실에 대한 단순한 유감이나 후회
should[ought to] have p.p.	~했어야 했는데(하지 못했다)	과거 사실에 대한 후회

이렇게 활용해요

① may[might] have p.p.

He **may have got lost**.
그는 길을 잃었을지도 모른다.

② must have p.p.

It **must have rained** during the night.
밤새 비가 온 게 틀림없다.

③ would have p.p.

I **would have done** it differently.
나라면 다르게 그것을 했을 거야.

④ should[ought to] have p.p.

You **should have come** a little earlier.
네가 좀 더 일찍 왔어야 했다.

PART 2 조동사 문제풀이

TEST 1 – 13번

Sandra has just left home, and is on her way to the office. [1]Given [2]how close her office is to her house, [3]I'm sure she will be here before the meeting starts.

(a) should
(b) may
(c) will
(d) could

답 (c)

| 해설 |

(a) should(과거형) – 당위성: ~해야만 한다
(b) may(현재형) – 약한 추측: ~할지도 모르다
(c) will(현재형) – 예정/미래: ~할 것이다
(d) could(과거형) – 추측: ~할 수도 있다

| 구문독해 |

[1]given [전치사적 또는 접속사적]: ~이라고 가정하면, ~이 주어지면
[2]간접의문문
– how(의문부사) + 형용사/부사 + 주어 + 동사
[3]be sure + (that) 주어 + 동사: ~을 확신하다(= be sure to V/be sure of Ving)

| 해석 |

Sandra는 막 집을 떠나 사무실로 가는 길이다. 그녀의 사무실이 그녀의 집과 얼마나 가까운지 고려해본다면, 나는 그녀가 회의가 시작되기 전에 여기에 올 것이라고 확신한다.

| 어휘 |

on one's way to ~으로 가는 길[도중]에
be close ~에 근접해 있다
be here 왔다

PART 2
조동사 문제풀이

TEST1 - 25번

Stella took a medical leave of absence for two weeks. I wanted to visit her house to check on her. However, I ■was afraid Stella might ❷feel uncomfortable with my visit.

(a) can
(b) might
(c) will
(d) must

답 (b)

| 해설 |

(a) can(현재형) - 가능성/능력: ~할 수 있다
(b) might(과거형) - 불확실한 약한 추측: ~일[할]지도 모르다
(c) will(현재형) - 예정/미래: ~할 것이다
(d) must(현재/과거형) - 강한 의무/필요/당위성: ~해야(만) 한다

| 구문독해 |

■be afraid (that) + 주어 + 동사: ~을 두려워하다(= be afraid of + Ving)
❷feel + 주격보어(형용사): ~처럼 느끼다

| 해석 |

Stella는 2주 동안 병가를 냈다. 나는 그녀를 확인하기 위해 그녀의 집을 방문하고 싶었다. 하지만 Stella가 내 방문을 불편해**할지도 몰라** 걱정했다.

| 어휘 |

take a leave of absence 휴학하다
medical leave 병가
check on (이상이 없는지를) 확인하다[살펴보다]
uncomfortable with ~으로 불편한, ~으로 기분이 언짢은

TEST 2 – 6번

Our dog Felix is home now. He had been missing for three days before we found him near the park this morning. We are still wondering [1]what he might have eaten for three days.

(a) will
(b) might
(c) should
(d) can

답 (b)

| 해설 |

(a) will have p.p. – 미래 사실에 대한 추측: (미래에/나중에) ~할 것이다. ~일 것이다
(b) may[might] have p.p. – 과거 사실에 대한 약한 추측: ~이었을지도 모른다
(c) should[ought to] have p.p. – 과거 사실에 대한 후회: ~했었어야 했는데 (하지 못했다)
(d) can[would] have p.p. – 과거 사실에 대한 추측, 짐작 / 일어나지 않는 일: ~였을 수 있다 / ~할 수 있었는데 못했다

| 구문독해 |

[1]의문대명사 what: 무엇
– 타동사 + 목적어(what + 주어 + 동사)
〈간접의문문〉

| 해석 |

우리의 개 Felix는 지금 집에 있다. 그(Felix)가 사흘 동안 행방불명된 후 오늘 아침 우리가 공원 근처에서 그(Felix)를 발견했다. 우리는 아직도 그가 3일 동안 무엇을 **먹었는지** 궁금하다.

| 어휘 |

be home 집에 있다
wonder 궁금하다

PART 2
조동사 문제풀이

TEST 2 - 19번

[1]Greenfield, a new fiber optic cable system [2]designed to prevent power outages, has been developed. It can eliminate the possibility of electrical outages and even detect an outage before it happens.

(a) can
(b) may
(c) would
(d) must

답 (a)

| 해설 |

(a) can(현재형) - 가능성/능력: ~할 수 있다
(b) may(현재형) - 약한 추측: ~할지도 모르다
(c) would(과거형) - 현재 사실의 반대/소망/미래/예정: ~하곤 했었다
(d) must(현재/과거형) - 강한 의무/필요/당위성 : ~해야(만) 한다

| 구문독해 |

[1]동격
- 명사(A), 명사(B): B라는 A(주어로 사용 시, A가 주어)

[2]생략
- 선행사 + (주격관계대명사 + be동사) + 과거분사 p.p.(~되어진): 형용사(선행사를 수식함)

| 해석 |

정전 방지를 위해 설계된 새로운 광섬유 케이블 시스템인 Green field가 개발되어 왔다. 그것은 정전 가능성을 제거하고 정전이 발생하기 전에 감지까지 <u>할 수 있다</u>.

| 어휘 |

power outages 정전(power cut)
fiber optic cable system 광섬유 케이블 시스템
eliminate 없애다, 제거[삭제]하다
possibility 가능성
outage 정전, (수돗물의) 단수
detect 발견하다, 감지하다

TEST 3 – 6번

Children and teenagers can be physically and psychologically damaged by their smartphones and tablet computers. Thus, doctors strongly claim ❶that parents should limit their children's screen time.

(a) may
(b) would
(c) should
(d) will

답 (c)

| 해설 |

(a) may(현재형) – 약한 추측: ~할지도 모르다
(b) would(과거형) – 현재 사실의 반대/소망/미래/예정: ~하곤 했었다
(c) should(과거형) – 당위성: ~해야만 한다
(d) will(현재형) – 예정/미래: ~할 것이다

| 구문독해 |

❶목적격 종속접속사 that
– 주어 + 타동사 + 목적어[that + 주어 + 동사 ~ (완전한 문장)]
　　　　　　　　　　생략 가능(~하는 것을)

| 해석 |

어린이와 청소년들은 스마트폰과 태블릿 컴퓨터에 의해 신체적, 심리적 손상을 입을 수 있다. 따라서, 의사들은 부모가 자녀가 화면을 보는 시간을 제한**해야 한다**고 강력히 주장한다.

| 어휘 |

physically 신체[육체]적으로
psychologically 심리학적으로, 심리적으로
be damaged by ~에 의해 피해를 받다
screen time (휴대폰, PC, TV 등, 전자기기의) 화면/스크린을 응시하는 시간

PART 2
조동사 문제풀이

TEST 3 - 17번

George has been working as a car salesman for 15 years. Although he loves his job, ❶dealing with complaints from bad customers ❷stresses him out enormously. ❸If given the chance, he would get a stress management therapy.

(a) may
(b) should
(c) can
(d) would

답 (d)

| 해설 |

(a) may(현재형) - 약한 추측: ~할지도 모르다
(b) should(과거형) - 당위성: ~해야만 한다
(c) can(현재형) - 가능성/능력: ~할 수 있다
(d) would(과거형) - 현재 사실의 반대/소망/미래/예정: ~하곤 했었다, ~일 것이다

| 구문독해 |

❶주어와 동사의 수의 일치
- 동명사 주어 + 단수 동사

❷이어동사
- 타동사 + 대명사 + 부사(O), 타동사 + 부사 + 대명사(X), 타동사 + 명사 + 부사(O), 타동사 + 부사 + 명사(O)

❸생략(분사구문)
- 종속접속사(If) + (주어 + be동사) + 과거분사(given) ~, 주어 + 동사

| 해석 |

George는 15년 동안 자동차 판매원으로 일해오고 있다. 비록 그는 자신의 직업을 사랑하지만, 나쁜 고객들의 불평을 다루는 것은 그에게 매우 큰 스트레스를 준다. 만약 기회가 주어진다면, 그는 스트레스 관리 요법을 받을 것이다.

| 어휘 |

work as ~로 일하다
deal with ~을 다루다
complaint 불평, 불만
stress out 스트레스를 주다(가하다)
enormously 엄청나게, 대단히
get a stress management therapy 스트레스 관리 요법을 받다

TEST 3 - 19번

The Sea level rises faster. [1]In order to survive, polar bears must walk a long way to search for food. Sometimes, they forage in garbage dumps [2]placed in the areas [3]where the locals live.

(a) must
(b) can
(c) might
(d) should

답 (a)

| 해설 |

(a) must(현재/과거형) – 강한 의무/필요/당위성: ~해야(만) 한다
(b) can(현재형) – 가능성/능력: ~할 수 있다
(c) might(과거형) – 불확실한 약한 추측: ~일(할)지도 모르다
(d) should(과거형) – 당위성: ~해야만 한다

| 구문독해 |

[1]in order to V: ~하기 위해서
[2]명사 + (주격 관계대명사 + be동사) + 과거분사(앞 명사를 수식)
[3]선행사(장소) + where + 주어 + 동사

| 해석 |

해수면은 더 빨리 상승하고 있다. 살아남기 위해서, 북극곰은 먹이를 찾기 위해 먼 길을 걸어**야만 한다**. 때때로, 그들은 지역 주민들이 사는 곳에 있는 쓰레기 더미를 뒤지며 찾아다닌다.

| 어휘 |

sea level 해수면
polar bear 북극곰, 흰곰
walk a long way 먼 길을 걷다
search for ~를 찾다
forage 마구 뒤지며 찾다
garbage dump 쓰레기 처리장
placed 놓여진
local (특정 지역에 사는) 주민, 현지인

PART 2 should 생략 핵심이론

📖 이렇게 나와요

Many roads in the countryside are so narrow that accidents commonly happen. While farmers and residents have sent request letters for road construction, the government advises that the public _____ bikes, bicycles and small cars in the meantime.

(a) are using
(b) will use
(c) use
(d) uses

⑦ 결정/명령/요구/제안/주장/충고(제안) 동사와 should 생략

G-TELP 문법에서, 주절에 있는 동사가 결정/명령/요구/제안/주장/충고(조언)과 관련된 동사라면 종속절 안에 있는 동사는 <u>조동사 should를 사용해서 'should + 동사원형(영국식)'</u> 또는 <u>should를 생략(미국식)하고 '동사원형'</u>을 사용해야 한다.

이런 게 답이에요

주절			종속절		
	동사		종속접속사		동사
주어	요구	ask	(that)	주어	(should) 동사원형
		request			
	제안	suggest			
	주장	insist			
		urge			
	충고(조언)	advise			
		recommend			

Tip 당위성(마땅히 해야 한다)과 관련된 사항이라면 주절의 동사의 시제와는 상관없이 종속절 안에 있는 동사는 무조건 '(should) + 동사원형'으로, 일반적인 사실과 관련된 내용이라면 주절에 있는 동사와 종속절 안에 있는 동사와 시제를 일치시켜야 한다. 참고로 종속절을 이끌고 가는 **that**은 목적격 종속접속사로 생략할 수 있다.

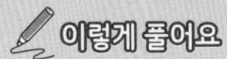

Many roads in the countryside are so narrow that accidents commonly happen. While farmers and residents have sent request letters for road construction, the government advises that the public _____ bikes, bicycles and small cars in the meantime.
촉고 동사

(a) ~~are using~~
(b) ~~will use~~
(c) use (should) V
(d) ~~uses~~

8 이성적/감성적 판단 형용사와 should 생략

종속접속사 that 앞에 '이성적 판단 형용사' 또는 '감성적 판단 형용사'가 있을 때 that절 안에 있는 동사는 'should + 동사원형(영국식)' 또는 should를 생략(미국식)하고 '동사원형'을 사용한다.

이런 게 답이에요

주절				종속절		
주어	동사	이성적 판단 형용사		종속접속사	주어	동사
It	be	*best	가장 잘하는	(that)	주어	(should) 동사원형
		compulsory	강제[의무/필수]적인			
		desirable	바람직한			
		*essential	필수적인, 중요한			
		*imperative	반드시 해야 하는, 긴요한			
		*important	중요[중대/소중]한			
		necessary	필요한			
		urgent	긴급[시급]한			

PLUS

1. G-TELP 문법에서, 현재로는 감성적 판단 형용사보다는 이성적 판단 형용사가 주로 출제된다.
2. 감성적 판단 형용사: curious(호기심이 강한, 이상한), fortunate(운이 좋은, 행운의), regrettable(유감스러운, 후회되는), strange(이상한), stupid(어리석은), surprising(놀라운) 등이 있다.

PART 2 should 생략 문제풀이

TEST 1 – 11번

Many roads in the countryside are ❶so narrow that accidents commonly happen. While farmers and residents have sent request letters for road construction, the government advises that the public use bikes, bicycles and small cars in the meantime.

(a) are using
(b) will use
(c) use
(d) uses

답 (c)

| 해설 |

주어 + ①advise + ②(that) + 주어 + ③(should) V

| 구문독해 |

❶so + 형용사/부사 that + 주어 + 동사: 너무 ~해서 그 결과 ~하다

| 해석 |

시골의 많은 도로는 너무 좁아서 사고가 흔하게 일어난다. 농민과 주민들이 도로 건설 요청서를 보낸 가운데, 정부는 사람들에게 그동안 오토바이, 자전거 그리고 소형차를 이용해야 한다고 조언하고 있다.

| 어휘 |

countryside 시골 지역
narrow 좁은
accident 사고, 재난
commonly 흔히, 보통
resident (특정 지역) 거주자[주민]
send A for B B를 위해 A를 보내다
request letter 요청[구]편지
road construction 도로 건설
in the meantime (두 가지 시점·사건들) 그동안[사이]에

TEST 1 - 15번

We expect a huge crowd at the Korean music concert tomorrow. ❶To get a good seat, it is imperative that you arrive at the venue at least four hours before the concert begins.

(a) will arrive
(b) have arrived
(c) arrive
(d) to arrive

답 (c)

| 해설 |

It is ①imperative ②(that) + 주어 + ③(should) V

| 구문독해 |

❶To 동사원형, 주어 + 동사: ~하기 위하여

| 해석 |

우리는 내일 있을 한국 음악 콘서트에 많은 인파를 기대하고 있다. 좋은 좌석을 확보하려면, 최소한 콘서트가 시작되기 4시간 전에 행사장에 반드시 도착해야만 합니다.

| 어휘 |

a huge crowd 엄청난 수의 군중
get a good seat[place] 좋은 좌석을 잡다
imperative 반드시 해야 하는, 긴요한
arrive at ~에 도착하다
venue (콘서트 · 스포츠 경기 · 회담 등의) 장소
at least 적어도[최소한]

PART 2
should 생략 문제풀이

TEST 1 - 23번

Cindy is reluctant to eat lunch and dinner because she ▫is afraid of putting on weight. Her doctor insists that she exercise more, so she can burn more calories or speed up her metabolism.

(a) will exercise
(b) is exercising
(c) exercises
(d) exercise

답 (d)

| 해설 |

주어 + ①insist + ②(that) + 주어 + ③(should) V

| 구문독해 |

▫be afraid of + Ving: ~을 두려워하다 = be afraid + (that) + 주어 + 동사

| 해석 |

Cindy는 살이 찌는 것을 두려워하기 때문에 점심과 저녁을 먹는 것을 꺼린다. 그녀의 주치의는 그녀가 더 많은 칼로리를 소모하거나 그녀의 신진대사를 증가시킬 수 있도록 운동을 더 많이 해야만 한다고 주장한다.

| 어휘 |

be reluctant to V ~을 주저하다, 망설이다
put on weight 체중이 늘다, 살찌다
burn calories 칼로리를 태우다
speed up metabolism 신진대사를 활성화하다

TEST 2 – 10번

¹It was so windy this afternoon. I called my mother to close the window in my room as soon as she gets home. I asked that she drive slowly and safely ²due to strong wind.

(a) drove
(b) drive
(c) drives
(d) was driving

답 (b)

| 해설 |

주어 + ①ask + ②(that) + 주어 + ③(should) V

| 구문독해 |

¹비인칭 주어 it
- 날씨/시각(간)/요일/날짜/거리/명암 등을 나타낼 때 주어 it을 비인칭 주어라고 하고, 이때 it은 "그것은"이라고 해석하지 않는다.
²전치사: 원인/이유
- due to + (동)명사(구): ~ 때문에

| 해석 |

오늘 오후에는 바람이 너무 많이 불었다. 나는 엄마에게 집에 오자마자 내 방의 창문을 닫으라고 전화했다. 나는 그녀에게 강풍으로 인해 천천히 안전하게 **운전해야만 한다**고 말했다.

| 어휘 |

windy 바람이 많이 부는
as soon as ~하자마자
get home 귀가하다

PART 2
should 생략 문제풀이

TEST 2 - 18번

Harris has to conduct his study all over again [1]because he found an error in calculating chemical formulas. The professor recommends that he use a new model of calculator.

(a) will use
(b) uses
(c) use
(d) is using

답 (c)

|해설|

주어 + [1]recommend + [2](that) + 주어 + [3](should) V

|구문독해|

[1]종속접속사: 원인/이유 – because + 주어 + 동사: ~ 때문에

|해석|

Harris는 화학 공식 계산에서 오류를 발견했기 때문에 그의 연구를 처음부터 다시 해야 한다. 교수님은 그에게 새로운 계산기 모델을 <u>사용해야만 한다</u>고 권한다.

|어휘|

conduct study 연구를 수행하다
all over again 처음부터 다시
find a(n) mistake[error] 오류를 발견하다
calculate 계산하다, 산출하다
a chemical formula 화학 공식
calculator 계산기

TEST 2 – 24번

My mom will open her second Italian restaurant on George Street this weekend. [1]To attract a crowd, I am requiring that all my friends and relatives [2]attend the opening party to act as regular customers.

(a) have attended
(b) are attending
(c) will attend
(d) attend

답 (d)

|해설|

주어 + [1]require + [2](that) + 주어 + [3](should) V

|구문독해|

[1]to 부정사의 부사적 용법
– 목적(~하기 위해서)

[2]자동사로 착각하기 쉬운 완전타동사
– attend 타동사(~에 참석하다): attend to (×)
– attend 자동사(시중들다, 전념하다): attend to (○)

|해석|

우리 엄마는 이번 주말에 George Street에 두 번째 이탈리아 식당을 열 것이다. 사람들을 끌어 모으기 위해, 나는 내 모든 친구들과 친척들이 단골 고객 역할을 하기 위해 개업식에 참석해야만 한다고 요구하고 있다.

|어휘|

attract a crowd 사람들을 끌다
relative 친척, 인척, 일가
opening party 개관식
act as ~으로서의 역할을 하다[맡다]
a regular customer 단골 손님

PART 2
should 생략 문제풀이

TEST 3 – 2번

The majority of animals in Antarctica are dying ①due to rising water temperatures. ②That is why environmentalists are urging that the public take urgent action on climate change in order to save the remaining animals.

(a) are taking
(b) take
(c) to take
(d) will take

답 (b)

| 해설 |

주어 + ①urge + ②(that) + 주어 + ③(should) V

| 구문독해 |

①due to(전치사) + 명사: ~ 때문에[because(종속접속사) + 주어 + 동사]
②That(원인) is why + 주어 + 동사(결과): 그것은(원인) ~ (결과)이다

| 해석 |

남극 대륙의 대부분의 동물들은 수온 상승으로 인해 죽어가고 있다. 그렇기 때문에 환경보호론자들은 남은 동물들을 구하기 위해 기후 변화에 대해 사람들이 긴급 조치를 취해야만 한다고 촉구하고 있다.

| 어휘 |

the majority of 대부분의, 다수의
Antarctica 남극 대륙(the Antarctic Continent)
die 죽다(die – died – died – dying)
rise 오르다(rise – rose – risen – rising)
water temperature 수온
take action on ~에 대해 조치를 취하다
climate change 기후 변화
(in order) to V ~하기 위해서

TEST 3 – 12번

Thousands of factory workers are staging a protest over the permanent termination of employment. ❶They have been standing in front of factories since yesterday, insisting that the company rethink workforce planning.

(a) rethink
(b) would rethink
(c) rethinks
(d) is rethinking

답 (a)

| 해설 |
주어 + ①insist + ②(that) + 주어 + ③(should) V

| 구문독해 |
❶주어 + 현재완료진행(have been Ving) + since + 과거 시점: ~한 이래로 ~해오고 있다

| 해석 |
수천 명의 공장 근로자들이 영구적인 고용 해지를 놓고 시위를 벌이고 있다. 그들은 어제부터 회사가 노동 인력 계획을 **재고해야만 한**다고 주장하며 공장 앞에 서 있어 왔다.

| 어휘 |
thousands of 수천의, 무수한, 많은
stage a protest 시위/항의 집회를 벌이다
permanent 영구[영속]적인
termination of employment 고용기간 종료
in front of ~의 앞쪽에[앞에]
rethink 다시 생각하다[재고하다]
workforce planning 노동 인력 계획

PART 2
should 생략 문제풀이

TEST 3 – 24번

①Working in a group is not easy ②because people have different qualifications, knowledge, ideas, and work experience. ③In order to avoid conflicts or arguments, it is <u>essential</u> that you <u>improve</u> communication and interpersonal skills.

(a) are improving
(b) will improve
(c) improved
(d) improve

답 (d)

| 해설 |

It is ①<u>essential</u> ②(that) + 주어 + ③(should) V

| 구문독해 |

①주어와 동사의 수의 일치
- 동명사 주어(Ving) + 단수 동사
②because(종속접속사) + 주어 + 동사: ~ 때문에
③(in order) to V: ~하기 위해서

| 해석 |

사람들이 서로 다른 자격, 지식, 아이디어, 그리고 업무 경험을 가지고 있기 때문에 단체로 일하는 것은 쉽지 않다. 갈등이나 말다툼을 피하기 위해서는 의사소통과 대인관계 능력을 <u>향상시켜야만 하는</u> 것이 필수적이다.

| 어휘 |

qualification 자격[자질/능력]
argument 말다툼
interpersonal skill 대인 관계 기술

예제문제

Pearl is relieved that her son is safe. She was worried that he didn't come back home till late at night. She now requires that he _____ his phone regularly whenever he goes out of the house.

(a) will check
(b) checks
(c) check
(d) is checking

답 (c)

| 해설 |

주절 안에 있는 동사 require는 '요구하다'라는 뜻으로 요구와 관련된 동사로 that 이하 종속절 안에 있는 동사는 should check 또는 check이어야 한다. 따라서 조동사 should가 생략된 (c) check이 정답이다.

| 해석 |

Pearl은 그녀의 아들이 안전하다는 것에 안도했다. 그녀는 그가 밤늦게까지 집에 돌아오지 않아 걱정했었다. 그녀는 이제 그가 집 밖에 있을 때마다 전화를 규칙적으로 **확인해야만 한다**고 요구한다.

| 어휘 |

relieve 안도하게 하다
entire 전체의
regularly 규칙적으로
out of ~ 바깥에

PART 3
가정법

가정법

가정법 과거완료

If 생략 가정법 도치

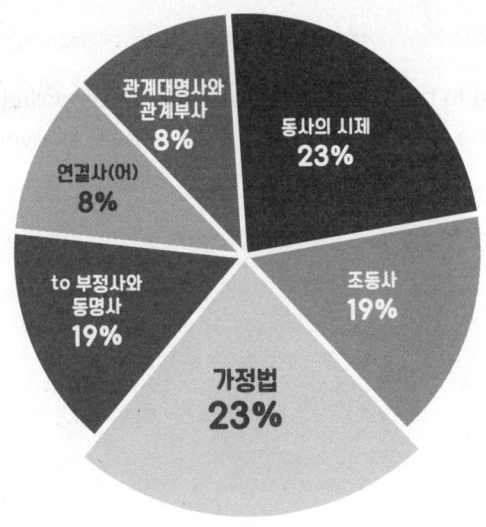

가정법의 출제원리

가정법에서 출제자가 묻고자 하는 것은 주절과 종속절 안에 있는 동사의 시제이니 가정법과 관련된 공식을 본 서를 통해 숙지하자.

1. 가정법 현재
2. 가정법 과거
3. 가정법 과거완료
4. If 생략 가정법 도치

1. 지텔프에서는 가정법 현재보다는 주로 가정법 과거와 과거완료가 주로 출제된다.
2. If 생략 시 주어와 동사가 서로 자리가 바뀌는 것을 판단할 수 있기 위해서는 절의 개념을 알아야 한다.
   - 주절: 주어 + 동사
   - 종속절: 종속접속사 + 주어 + 동사 (종속접속사의 종류 중, 가정법에서는 If가 쓰인다.)
   - 종속절의 위치: 종속절 + 주절 / 주절 + 종속절 / 주어 + 종속절 + 동사

PART 3 가정법 핵심이론

📖 이렇게 나와요

Living in the city is starting to harm Vicki's health because air pollution is severe. She thinks that if she lived in the country, she _____ fresh air everyday.

(a) breathes
(b) will breathe
(c) would have breathed
(d) would breathe

가정법이란 실제 사실을 말하는 직설법(indicative mood)과 상반되는 것으로, <u>실제로 일어나지 않았거나, 일어날 것 같지 않은 일을 가정 또는 소망하여 표현하는 것</u>을 말한다.

① 가정법 현재(Subjunctive Present)

막연한 상상이나 일반적인 가정을 말할 때 사용한다.

이런 게 답이에요

종속절 (만약 ~한다면)			주절 (~할 것이다)	
If	주어	현재형 동사 동사원형	주어	will V shall V can V may V

> **Tip** 1. If로 시작하는 조건절, 즉 종속절(부사절) 안에 있는 동사는 '시간과 조건의 부사절에서는 현재 시제가 미래 시제를 대신한다'라는 규칙하에 미래형으로 사용할 수 없다. 단, 종속절이 부사절이 아니라 명사절(주어, 목적어, 보어)로 사용되는 경우에는 미래형으로 사용할 수 있다.
> 2. 종속절과 주절의 위치는 종속절이 부사절이기 때문에 서로 바뀔 수 있다.

Living in the city is starting to harm Vicki's health because air pollution is severe. She thinks that if she lived in the country, she _____ fresh air everyday.
　　　　　　　　　　　　　　　　　　　　　　　　　　주어

(a) ~~breathes~~
(b) ~~will breathe~~
(c) ~~would have breathed~~
(d) would breathe would V

이렇게 활용해요

① 부사절

I shall be glad **if I meet you tomorrow**. (○)
나는 내일 너를 만난다면 기쁠 것이다.

② 명사절

I don't know **if he will come here tomorrow**. (○)
나는 그가 내일 여기에 올지 안 올지를 모르겠다.

② 가정법 과거(Subjunctive Past)

현재 사실과 반대되는, 즉 다른 일이나 실현 가능성이 희박한 일을 나타낼 때 사용한다.

이런 게 답이에요

종속절			주절	
If	주어	과거형동사	주어	would V ~. would not V ~. would be Ving ~. could V ~.
		were ~,		
		were not ~,		
		were Ving ~,		
		were p.p. ~,		
		were to V ~,		
		were to be p.p. ~,		
		could V ~,		
		could not V ~,		
		would V ~,		
Even if		were p.p. ~,		would V ~ .
		were Ving ~,		wouldn't V ~.

Tip 종속절과 주절의 위치는 종속절이 부사절이기 때문에 서로 바뀔 수 있다.

PART 3 가정법 문제풀이

TEST 1 – 3번

[1]Living in the city is [2]starting to harm Vicki's health [3]because air pollution is severe. She thinks [4]that if she lived in the country, she would breathe fresh air everyday.

(a) breathes
(b) will breathe
(c) would have breathed
(d) would breathe

답 (d)

| 해설 |

가정법 과거: [1]If + 주어 + [2]과거형 동사, 주어 + [3]would V

| 구문독해 |

[1]주어와 동사의 수의 일치 – 동명사 주어(Ving) + 단수 동사
[2]start + 목적어(to V/Ving): ~하기를 시작하다
[3]종속접속사: 원인/이유
– because + 주어 + 동사: ~ 때문에
[4]목적격 종속접속사 that
– 주어 + 타동사 + 목적어[that + 주어 + 동사 ~ (완전한 문장)]
　　　　　　　　　생략 가능(~하는 것을)

| 해석 |

공기 오염이 심하기 때문에 도시에 사는 것은 Vicki의 건강을 해치기 시작하고 있다. 그녀는 만약 시골에 산다면, 매일 맑은 공기로 **숨을 쉴 것이라**고 생각한다.

| 어휘 |

harm the health 건강을 해치다
air pollution 공기[대기] 오염
severe 극심한, 심각한
breathe 호흡하다, 숨을 쉬다
fresh air 맑은 공기

PART 3
가정법 문제풀이

TEST 1 – 16번

Sales of printed newspapers are decreasing in many countries ❶because newspapers are increasingly replaced by online news sources. If Internet technologies did not develop today, printed newspapers would ❷remain prevalent.

(a) would have remained
(b) remain
(c) have remained
(d) would remain

답 (d)

| 해설 |

가정법 과거: ①If + 주어 + ②과거형 동사, 주어 + ③would V

| 구문독해 |

종속접속사: 원인/이유
❶because + 주어 + 동사: ~ 때문에
❷remain + 주격보어(형용사): 계속[여전히] ~이다

| 해석 |

신문은 점점 더 온라인 뉴스 매체에 의해 대체되기 때문에 많은 나라에서 인쇄된 신문의 판매가 감소하고 있다. 오늘날 인터넷 기술이 발달하지 않았다면, 인쇄된 신문은 여전히 널리 퍼져 있을 것이다.

| 어휘 |

printed newspapers 인쇄된 신문
decrease 줄다, 감소하다
increasingly 점점 더, 갈수록 더
be replaced by ~에 의해 대체되다
online news source 온라인 뉴스 매체
develop 발달하다
prevalent 널리 퍼진

TEST 1 - 26번

Anthony's expenses for ongoing roof repairs have just reached $1000. He is on a tight budget nowadays, and if he could make the repairs ①himself, he would be able to use that $1000 to donate for families ②living in poverty.

(a) would be able
(b) would have been able
(c) was able
(d) has been able

답 (a)

| 해설 |

가정법 과거: ①If + 주어 + ②could V, 주어 + ③would V

| 구문독해 |

①재귀대명사의 강조적 용법(생략 가능)
- 주어(주체)와 같으면 재귀대명사를 사용하고, 다르면 대명사를 사용

②생략
- 선행사 + (주격관계대명사 + be동사) + 현재분사 Ving(~하고 있는): 형용사, 선행사를 수식함

| 해석 |

Anthony가 계속 진행 중인 지붕 수리에 드는 비용은 이제 막 1000달러에 달했다. 그는 요즘 예산이 빠듯해서, 만약 그가 직접 수리를 할 수 있다면, 그 1000달러를 가난한 생활을 하고 있는 가정을 위해 기부하는 데 쓸 수 있을 것이다.

| 어휘 |

expense (어떤 일에 드는) 돈, 비용
ongoing 계속 진행 중인
roof repair 지붕 수리
reach (비용 등이) 총 ~가 되다
be on a tight budget 돈에 쪼들리다
make a repair 수리하다
be able to V ~할 수 있다
donate for ~을 위해 기부하다
live in poverty 가난한 생활을 하다

PART 3
가정법 문제풀이

TEST 2 - 11번

Julia is often late for work [1]because she has to take her daughter to school every morning. If she could [2]allow her daughter to walk to school by herself, she wouldn't get complaints from her work colleagues.

(a) isn't getting
(b) doesn't get
(c) wouldn't get
(d) hadn't got

답 (c)

| 해설 |

가정법 과거: [1]If + 주어 + [2]could V, 주어 + [3]would V

| 구문독해 |

[1]because(종속접속사) + 주어 + 동사: ~ 때문에(due to(전치사) + 명사)
[2]allow + 목적어 + 목적격보어(to V): ~가 ~하는 것을 허락하다

| 해석 |

Julia는 매일 아침 딸을 학교에 데려다 줘야 하기 때문에 종종 직장에 늦는다. 만약 Julia가 딸이 혼자서 학교에 걸어가는 것을 허락할 수 있다면, 그녀(Julia)는 직장 동료들로부터 불평을 듣지 않을 텐데.

| 어휘 |

be late for 시간에 늦다
take A to B A를 B에 데리고 가다
walk to school 도보로 통학하다
by oneself 혼자, 다른 사람 없이
complaint 불평, 불만
colleague 동료

TEST 2 – 25번

I'm so happy ①that I joined the dancing team ②our school formed early this semester. I usually ③prefer dancing alone or with close friends. However, if it weren't for the dancing team, I would be ④having trouble developing my dancing skills on my own.

(a) was having
(b) would be having
(c) am having
(d) will be having

답 (b)

| 해설 |

가정법 과거: ①If it weren't for ~, 주어 + ②would V

| 구문독해 |

①목적격 종속접속사 that
- 주어 + 타동사 + 목적어[that + 주어 + 동사 ~ (완전한 문장)]
  생략 가능(~하는 것을)

②목적격 관계대명사 that(~하는) 생략
- 선행사 + (that) + 주어 + 타동사 + (목적어 없음)

③prefer + 목적어(Ving): 오히려 ~을 좋아하다

④have trouble[a hard time, difficulty] (in) (동)명사: ~하는 데 어려움이 있다

| 해석 |

이번 학기 초에 우리 학교에서 결성한 댄스팀에 합류하게 되어 너무 기쁘다. 나는 보통 혼자 또는 가까운 친구들과 함께 춤추는 것을 더 좋아한다. 하지만, 만약 댄스팀이 아니었다면, 나는 나 스스로 내 춤 실력을 기르는 데 어려움을 <u>겪을 것이다</u>.

| 어휘 |

this semester 이번 학기
alone 혼자, 다른 사람 없이
close friends 막역한 친구
on one's own 혼자서, 단독으로

PART 3
가정법 문제풀이

TEST 3 – 4번

Karis Kulas is a famous hip-hop composer who has worked with many high-profile celebrities. My friend Jack, [1]who is always a fan of her, would greatly appreciate it if he were to be given the opportunity to collaborate with her in writing a new piece of music.

(a) had greatly appreciated
(b) is greatly appreciating
(c) will greatly appreciate
(d) would greatly appreciate

답 (d)

| 해설 |

가정법 과거: 주어 + ③would V ~ ①if + 주어 + ②were to V

| 구문독해 |

[1]주격관계대명사 who(~하는)
- 선행사(사람) + who + 동사

| 해석 |

Karis Kulas는 세간의 이목을 끄는 많은 유명 연예인들과 함께 작업해 왔던 유명한 힙합 작곡가이다. 항상 그녀의 팬인 내 친구 Jack이 그녀와 함께 새로운 음악을 작곡할 수 있는 기회를 얻는다면 매우 고마워할 것이다.

| 어휘 |

composer 작곡가
work with ~와 함께 일하다
high-profile 세간의 이목을 끄는
celebrity (유명) 연예인, 유명인
appreciate 고마워하다, 환영하다
collaborate with ~와 협동하다
a piece of music 하나의 음악 작품

TEST 3 – 14번

Kids sometimes say something **①**unexpected. Today, my six-year-old daughter said **②**that if she were a bird, she would fly in the sky **③**because she can be a good friend with all kinds of birds.

(a) will be flying
(b) would fly
(c) had flied
(d) flied

답 (b)

| 해설 |

가정법 과거: **①**If + 주어 + **②**were ~, 주어 + **③**would V

| 구문독해 |

①생략
 – 선행사 + (주격관계대명사 + be동사) + 과거분사 p.p.(~되어진): 형용사, 선행사를 수식함
②목적격 종속접속사 that
 – 주어 + 타동사 + 목적어[that + 주어 + 동사 ~ (완전한 문장)]
   생략 가능(~하는 것을)
③because(종속접속사) + 주어 + 동사: ~ 때문에(due to(전치사) + 명사)

| 해석 |

아이들은 가끔 예상치 못한 것을 말한다. 오늘, 여섯 살 난 내 딸은 자신이 새라면 모든 종류의 새들과 좋은 친구가 될 수 있기 때문에 하늘을 날 텐데라고 말했다.

| 어휘 |

fly in the sky(air) 하늘을 날다
be a good friend with ~와 좋은 친구가 되다

PART 3 가정법 과거완료 핵심이론

📖 이렇게 나와요

Luke wishes that he had better self-control around computer games. If he had not played games all day yesterday, he _____ his math exam.

(a) could be passing
(b) was passing
(c) passed
(d) could have passed

③ 가정법 과거완료 (Subjunctive Past Perfect)

이미 끝나버린 과거의 사실과 반대되는 상황을 가정하는 것을 말하거나 과거의 일에 대해 아쉽고 후회에 대한 의미에 사용한다.

이런 게 답이에요

종속절			주절	
If	주어	had p.p. ~,	주어	would have p.p. ~.
		had not p.p. ~,		could not have p.p. ~.
		had been Ving ~,		should have p.p. ~.
		had been p.p. ~,		might have been p.p. ~.

Tip 종속절과 주절의 위치는 종속절이 부사절이기 때문에 서로 바뀔 수 있다.

Luke wishes that he had better self-control around computer games. If he had not played games all day yesterday, he _____ his math exam.
주어   주어   had not p.p.

(a) ~~could be passing~~
(b) ~~was passing~~
(c) ~~passed~~
(d) could have passed 가정법 과거완료

이렇게 활용해요

① would have p.p.: ~이었을 것이다(주어의 의지가 있는 문장)

→ **If** he **had known** her phone number, he **would have called** her.
만약 그가 그녀의 전화번호를 알았더라면, 그는 그녀에게 전화했을 텐데.

② could have p.p.: ~할 수도 있었다(과거 사실에 대한 아쉬움이나 가능성)

→ **If** he **had known** her phone number, he **could have called** her.
만약 그가 그녀의 전화번호를 알았더라면, 그는 그녀에게 전화할 수 있었을 텐데.

③ should have p.p.: ~했었어야 했는데(하지 못했다)(과거 사실에 대한 후회)

→ **If** he **had known** her phone number, he **should have called** her.
만약 그가 그녀의 전화번호를 알았더라면, 그는 그녀에게 전화했어야 했는데(결국 하지 못했다).

④ might have p.p.: ~이었을지도 모른다(과거 사실에 대한 약한 추측)

→ **If** he **had known** her phone number, he **might have called** her.
만약 그가 그녀의 전화번호를 알았더라면, 그는 그녀에게 전화했을지도 모를 텐데.

PART 3 가정법 과거완료 문제풀이

TEST 1 - 7번

Luke wishes ①that he had better self-control around computer games. If he had not played games all day yesterday, he could have passed his math exam.

(a) could be passing
(b) was passing
(c) passed
(d) could have passed

답 (d)

| 해설 |

가정법 과거완료: ①If + 주어 + ②had not p.p. ~, 주어 + ③could have p.p.

| 구문독해 |

①목적격 종속접속사 that
- 주어 + 타동사 + 목적어[that + 주어 + 동사 ~ (완전한 문장)]
                 생략 가능(~하는 것을)

| 해석 |

Luke는 그가 컴퓨터 게임에 대해 더 잘 자제하기를 바란다. 만약 그가 어제 하루 종일 게임을 하지 않았다면, 그는 그의 수학 시험에 **합격할 수 있었을 텐데**.

| 어휘 |

all day 하루 종일
pass an exam 시험에 통과하다

TEST 1 – 18번

Jack is ①regretting buying a new laptop too soon ②because the laptop is now on sale. If he had waited a little bit longer, he would have saved a fair amount of money on the purchase.

(a) saved
(b) would have saved
(c) was saving
(d) would save

답 (b)

| 해설 |

가정법 과거완료: ①If + 주어 + ②had p.p. ~, 주어 + ③would have p.p.

| 구문독해 |

①regret + 목적어(to V: 미래, Ving: 과거): ~할 것을 잊다/~했던 것을 잊다
②because(종속접속사) + 주어 + 동사: ~ 때문에(due to(전치사) + 명사)

| 해석 |

Jack은 노트북이 지금 세일 중이기 때문에 너무 빨리 새 노트북을 산 것을 후회하고 있다. 그가 조금만 더 기다렸더라면, 그는 그 구매에 상당한 돈을 절약했을 텐데.

| 어휘 |

too soon 너무 일찍
be on sale (상품이) 할인판매 중이다
a little bit 조금

PART 3
가정법 과거완료 문제풀이

TEST 2 – 2번

Tina didn't tell her father about her plans [1]to go to the library after lunch. If she had told him about her plans this morning, he would not have booked a table at Gordon's restaurant for dinner.

(a) has not booked
(b) would not have booked
(c) did not book
(d) was not booking

답 (b)

| 해설 |

가정법 과거완료: [1]If + 주어 + [2]had p.p. ~, 주어 + [3]would not have p.p.

| 구문독해 |

[1]to 부정사의 형용사적 용법
- 명사 + to V: ~할 명사

| 해석 |

Tina는 점심 식사 후에 도서관에 갈 계획에 대해 아버지에게 말하지 않았다. 만약 그녀가 오늘 아침 그녀의 계획을 그에게 말했었다면, 그는 저녁 식사로 Gordon의 레스토랑에 좌석을 예약하지 않았을 텐데.

| 어휘 |

go to ~에 가다
book 예약하다

TEST 2 - 17번

Amy vomited more than three times and complained about nausea this early morning, so we took her to the hospital. ❶If we hadn't done so, we wouldn't have known that she has severe gastritis ❷which is inflammation of the lining of the stomach.

(a) were not knowing
(b) didn't know
(c) have not known
(d) wouldn't have known

답 (d)

| 해설 |

가정법 과거완료: ①If + 주어 + ②had not p.p. ~, 주어 + ③would not have p.p.

| 구문독해 |

❶대동사
– 동사의 반복을 피하기 위하여 대신 쓰는 동사로, be동사는 be동사로, 조동사는 조동사로, 일반동사는 do/does/did로 사용한다.
❷주격관계대명사 which(~하는) – 선행사(사물/동물) + which + 동사

| 해석 |

Amy는 오늘 아침 일찍 세 번 이상 구토를 했고 메스꺼움을 호소해서 우리는 그녀를 병원에 데려갔다. 만약 우리가 그렇게 하지 않았었다면, 우리는 그녀가 위 내벽에 염증이 심한 위염에 걸렸다는 것을 **몰랐었을 것이다**.

| 어휘 |

vomit 토하다
complain about ~에 대해 불평하다
nausea 메스꺼움
take A to B A를 B로 데려가다
gastritis 위염
inflammation (신체 부위의) 염증
the lining of the stomach 위벽

PART 3
가정법 과거완료 문제풀이

TEST 2 – 20번

I had no idea ❶passengers ❷were advised to arrive well ahead of listed departure time at least two hours, so I missed the flight to New York. If I had known about the announcement, I would have left home earlier.

(a) would know
(b) knew
(c) had known
(d) was knowing

답 (c)

| 해설 |

가정법 과거완료: ❶If + 주어 + ❸had p.p. ~, 주어 + ❷would have p.p.

| 구문독해 |

❶동격의 종속접속사 that(~라는) 생략
- 추상명사 + (that) + 주어 + 동사

❷advise + 목적어 + 목적격보어(to V): ~가 ~하도록 권고/충고하다(수동태 시, be advised to V)

| 해석 |

승객들이 적어도 두 시간 전에 게재된 출발 시간을 훨씬 앞당겨 도착하라는 권고를 받은 줄 몰라서 뉴욕행 비행기를 놓쳤다. 만약 내가 그 발표를 알았더라면, 나는 더 일찍 집을 떠났었을 텐데.

| 어휘 |

ahead of ~보다 빨리
list 리스트[목록/명단/일람표]에 언급하다[포함시키다](list – listed – listed – listing)
departure time 출발시각
at least 적어도
a flight to ~로의 비행(편)
know about ~에 대하여 알고[듣고] 있다
announcement 발표(내용), 소식

TEST 3 – 9번

Mina wasn't able to get a ticket for Maroon 5's London concert ❶because the tickets were already sold out. If she had known ❷that a lot of people would go to the concert tonight, she would have bought a ticket online instead of lining up for a ticket.

(a) was buying
(b) bought
(c) would buy
(d) would have bought

답 (d)

| 해설 |

가정법 과거완료: ①If + 주어 + ②had p.p. ~, 주어 + ③would have p.p.

| 구문독해 |

❶because(종속접속사) + 주어 + 동사: ~ 때문에[due to(전치사) + 명사]
❷목적격 종속접속사 that
– 주어 + 타동사 + 목적어[that + 주어 + 동사 ~ (완전한 문장)]
　　　　　　　　　생략 가능(~하는 것을)

| 해석 |

Mina는 Maroon 5의 런던 콘서트 표가 이미 매진되었기 때문에 표를 구할 수 없었다. 만약 그녀가 오늘 밤에 많은 사람들이 그 콘서트에 갈 것을 알았다면, 그녀는 표를 사기 위해 줄을 서는 대신 온라인으로 표를 구매했었을 텐데.

| 어휘 |

be able to V　~할 수 있다
get(buy) a ticket　표를 사다
be sold out　매진[품절]되다
go to　~로 가다
instead of　~대신에
line up for　~를 위해 줄지어 세우다

PART 3
가정법 과거완료 문제풀이

TEST 3 – 13번

[1]Due to sexual discrimination, Stacey quitted her job. Today, she constantly [2]reminds [3]herself [4]that if she had endured that poor working conditions, she would have suffered from various mental disorders.

(a) was suffering
(b) would suffer
(c) would have suffered
(d) suffered

답 (c)

| 해설 |

가정법 과거완료: [1]If + 주어 + [2]had p.p. ~, 주어 + [3]would have p.p.

| 구문독해 |

[1]due to(전치사) + 명사: ~ 때문에(because(종속접속사) + 주어 + 동사)
[2]remind + 간접목적어 + 직접목적어(that + 주어 + 동사): ~에게 ~을 상기시키다
[3]재귀대명사의 재귀적 용법(생략 불가)
 – 주어(주체)와 같으면 재귀대명사를 사용하고 다르면 대명사를 사용
[4]목적격 종속접속사 that
 – 주어 + 타동사 + 목적어[that + 주어 + 동사 ~ (완전한 문장)]
   생략 가능(~하는 것을)

| 해석 |

Stacey는 성 차별 때문에 그녀의 직장을 그만두었다. 오늘, 그녀는 자신이 그 열악한 근무 환경을 견뎌냈었다면, 다양한 정신장애로 **고통을 받았을 것이라고** 스스로에게 끊임없이 상기시킨다.

| 어휘 |

sexual discrimination 성 차별
quit one's job 사직하다
constantly 끊임없이
endure 견디다, 참다
poor working conditions 열악한 근무 조건[환경]
suffer from ~로 고통 받다
mental disorder[disease, illness] 정신장애

TEST 3 − 26번

Devastated after breaking up with his girlfriend, William ①wasn't sure ②whether he should ③go and see a therapist until his sister ④convinced him to go. If he had ⑤waited for all his pain to go away, his life would have been miserable.

(a) is waiting
(b) had waited
(c) waited
(d) would wait

답 (b)

| 해설 |

가정법 과거완료: ①If + 주어 + ③had p.p. ~, 주어 + ②would have p.p.

| 구문독해 |

①be sure + whether + 주어 + 동사: ~인지를 확신하다
②간접의문문 whether(~인지 아닌지) 용법
- 의문사 대용어로 사용된 whether는 간접의문문으로 사용될 수 있는데, that(~것을)은 사용할 수 없다.
③go and V = go to V = go V(~하러 가다) ⓔ go and see a doctor = go to see a doctor = go see a doctor = (진찰받으러 병원에 가봐라)
④convince + 목적어 + 목적격보어(to V): ~가 ~하도록 설득하다
⑤wait + for + 목적어 + to V: ~가 ~하기를 기다리다

| 해석 |

여자 친구와 헤어진 후 충격을 받은, William은 여동생이 가자고 설득하기 전까지 치료사를 찾아가야 할지 확신이 서지 않았다. 만약 그가 모든 고통이 사라지기를 **기다렸더라면**, 그의 삶은 비참했었을 텐데.

| 어휘 |

devastated 엄청난 충격을 받은
break up with ~와 결별하다
therapist 치료 전문가, 치료사
go away 없어지다
miserable 비참한

PART 3 If 생략 가정법 도치 핵심이론

📖 이렇게 나와요

My grandfather Tony knocked over a glass of orange juice while I was cleaning in the living room. _____ the juice, I would have prepared dinner to serve before 6 pm.

(a) He had not spilled
(b) If he did not spilled
(c) Had he not spilled
(d) Were he not spilled

4 If 생략 가정법 도치

종속절에 사용된 가정법 구조에서 종속접속사 If를 생략하면 종속절에 사용된 주어와 동사의 어순이 서로 바뀌게 되는데 이를 'If 생략 가정법 도치'라고 한다.

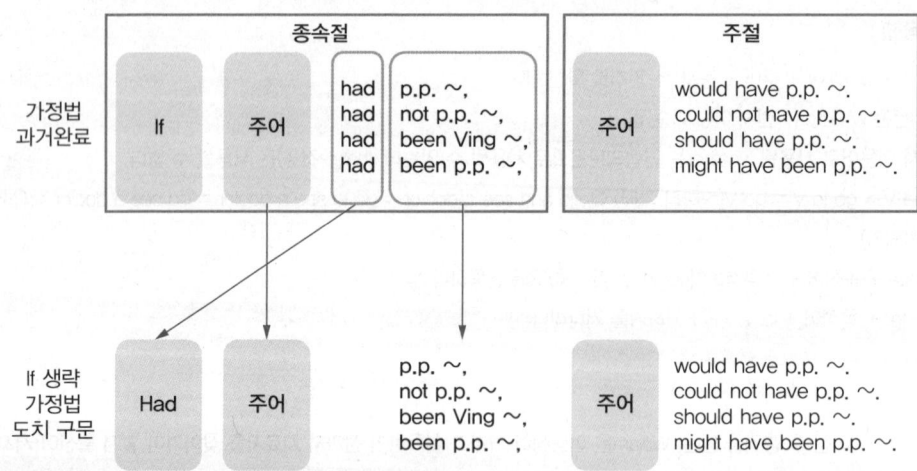

Tip 종속절과 주절의 위치는 종속절이 부사절이기 때문에 서로 바뀔 수 있다.

My grandfather Tony knocked over a glass of orange juice while I was cleaning in the living room. _____ the juice, I would have prepared dinner to serve before 6 pm.

주어   would have p.p.

(a) ~~He had not spilled~~
(b) ~~If he did not spilled~~
(c) Had he not spilled If 생략 가정법 도치
(d) ~~Were he not spilled~~

이런 게 답이에요

종속절			주절	
Had	주어	not p.p. ~,	주어	would have p.p. ~.

이렇게 활용해요

① If I had been you, I would have gone shopping.

→ **Had I been you**, I would have gone shopping.
만약 내가 너라면, 나는 쇼핑하러 갔었을 텐데.

② If I were a bird, I could fly to you.

→ **Were I a bird**, I could fly to you.
만약 내가 새라면, 나는 너에게 날아갈 수 있었을 텐데.

PART 3 If 생략 가정법 도치 문제풀이

TEST 1 - 22번

My grandfather Tony knocked over a glass of orange juice [1]while I was cleaning in the living room. Had he not spilled the juice, I would have prepared dinner to serve before 6 pm.

(a) He had not spilled
(b) If he did not spilled
(c) Had he not spilled
(d) Were he not spilled

답 (c)

| 해설 |

가정법 과거완료(If 생략 가정법 도치)
정치: If + 주어 + had p.p. ~, 주어 + would have p.p.
도치: [2]Had + 주어 + not p.p. ~, 주어 + [1]would have p.p.

| 구문독해 |

[1]while(종속접속사) + 주어 + 동사: ~동안, during(전치사) + 명사

| 해석 |

내 할아버지 Tony는 내가 거실에서 청소하는 동안 오렌지 주스 한 잔을 엎었다. 그가 주스를 엎지르지 않았다면, 나는 저녁 6시 전에 접대할 저녁을 준비했었을 텐데.

| 어휘 |

knock over 쓰러트리다, 엎지르다.
spill 흘리다, 엎지르다(spill - spilled - spilled - spilling)
serve 시중들다, 접대하다

TEST 2 – 9번

When I was growing up, I wished ①that I was speaking fluent French. My dream still holds true today. Could I travel to France, I would make ②as many friends as possible.

(a) I could travel
(b) Could I travel
(c) If I had traveled
(d) If I travels

답 (b)

|해설|

가정법 과거(If 생략 가정법 도치)
정치: If + 주어 + could V, 주어 + would V
도치: ②Could + 주어 + V, 주어 + ①would V

|구문독해|

①목적격 종속접속사 that
– 주어 + 타동사 + 목적어[that + 주어 + 동사 ~ (완전한 문장)]
                    생략 가능(~하는 것을)
②as 형용사/부사 as possible: 가능한 한 ~한/하게, 될 수 있으면 ~한/하게

|해석|

내가 자랄 때, 나는 프랑스어를 유창하게 했으면 하고 바랐다. 내 꿈은 오늘날에도 여전히 유효하다. **내가** 프랑스로 **여행을 갈 수 있다면**, 나는 가능한 한 많은 친구를 사귈 텐데.

|어휘|

grow up   성장[장성]하다
fluent   (언어, 특히 외국어 실력이) 유창한[능숙한]
hold true   진실이다, (규칙・말 따위가) 유효하다
travel to   ~로 여행하다[이동하다]
make a friend   친구가 되다
as much[many] as possible   되도록 많이

PART 4
to 부정사와 동명사

to 부정사

동명사

to 부정사와 동명사

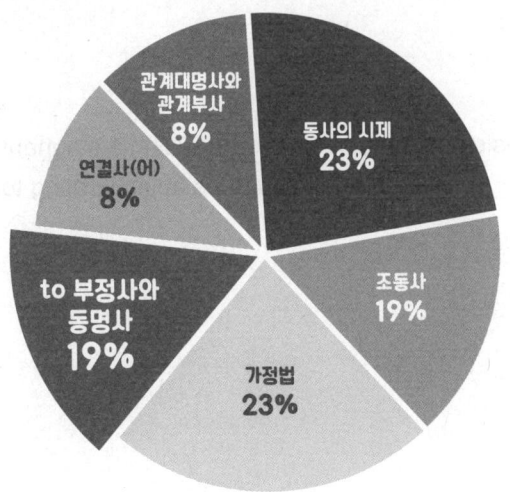

📖 to 부정사와 동명사의 출제 원리

1. to 부정사
- 명사 / 형용사 / 부사적 용법[주로 부사적 용법(목적: ~하기 위해서)이 출제된다.]
- 단순시제(to V)만 정답
- 3형식 구조에서 목적어 자리에 to 부정사를 취하는 완전타동사의 종류
- 5형식 구조에서 목적격보어 자리에 to 부정사를 취하는 불완전타동사의 종류
- to 부정사의 관용적 표현들

2. 동명사
- 단순시제(Ving)만 정답
- 3형식 구조에서 목적어 자리에 동명사를 취하는 완전타동사의 종류
- 동명사의 관용적 표현들

3. to 부정사와 동명사의 차이점
- 주어 자리는 주로 동명사 사용
- 3형식(주어 + 완전타동사 + 목적어) 구조에서 목적어 자리에 to 부정사와 동명사를 모두 취하는 완전타동사의 종류를 숙지하고 이에 대한 해석의 차이를 구별할 수 있어야 한다.

 Tip

1. to 부정사: to 부정사의 완료시제(to have p.p.) / 수동형(to be p.p.) / 완료수동형(to have been p.p.)은 무조건 오답
2. 동명사: 동명사의 완료시제(having p.p.) / 수동형(being p.p.) / 완료수동형(having been p.p.)은 무조건 오답
3. to 부정사와 동명사의 차이점: 주어 자리면 무조건 동명사의 단순시제가 정답(Ving)

PART 4 to 부정사 핵심이론

📖 이렇게 나와요

In many countries, consistent unemployment is causing a stagnant economy, forcing people _____ cities or their countries by emigrating to places where they can find a job.

(a) having left
(b) leaving
(c) to leave
(d) to have left

1 to 부정사

부정사에는 '원형부정사'(bare infinitive)와 **'to 부정사'**(to-infinitive)가 있다. 전자는 어형변화가 없는, 즉 to가 없는 동사원형이라고도 하고, 후자는 **동사원형 앞에 to가 있는 것**을 말한다.

이런 게 답이에요

1. to 부정사의 품사적 성질
2. to 부정사의 동사적 성질
3. to 부정사를 목적어로 취하는 동사
4. 자동사 + to V
5. to 부정사를 목적격보어로 취하는 동사
6. to 부정사의 관용적 표현

🔍 PLUS 선지에서 오답을 고르는 방법

1. to 부정사에서 완료 시제(to have p.p.)는 무조건 오답
2. to 부정사의 수동(to be p.p.)은 무조건 오답

In many countries, consistent unemployment is causing a stagnant economy, forcing people _____ cities or their countries by emigrating to places where they can find a job.

목적어   to 부정사를 목적격보어로 취하는 동사

(a) ~~having left~~
(b) ~~leaving~~
(c) to leave to V
(d) ~~to have left~~

---

to 부정사는 품사적 성질(명사/형용사/부사적 성질)과 동사적 성질을 동시에 가진다. 전자는 문장에서 주어, 목적어, 보어 역할을 하는 **명사적 용법**, 명사를 수식하는 **형용사적 용법**, 동사를 수식하는 **부사적 용법**으로 나뉜다. 동사가 문장의 형식에 따라 뒤에 목적어, 보어, 수식어 등의 어구들이 나올 수 있는 것처럼, to 부정사 역시 동사처럼 뒤에 동사가 가질 수 있는 어구들이 나올 수 있다. 동사는 아니지만 동사처럼 사용되기 때문에, 즉 동사적 성질을 가지기 때문에 시제, 태, 부정 등을 나타낼 수도 있다.

② to 부정사의 부사적 용법

G-TELP에서는 **'목적'**(~하기 위해서, ~하려고) 용법이 주로 출제된다.

Tip '목적'에 쓰이는 다른 표현들: so as to V / in order to V

이렇게 활용해요

She got up early **to catch the first train**.
그녀는 첫 기차를 타기 위해서 일찍 일어났다.

③ to 부정사의 동사적 성질

이런 게 답이에요

① to 부정사의 시제

종류	형태	의미
단순시제	to V	주절의 시제와 같거나 주절보다 미래를 의미
완료시제	to have p.p.	주절의 시제보다 한 시제 과거이거나, 주절의 시제가 과거인 경우 과거에 실제 일어나지 않은 일

Tip G-TELP에서는 완료 시제(to have p.p.)는 무조건 오답이다.

② to 부정사의 태

종류	형태	의미
to 부정사의 능동	to V	행위의 주체와의 관계가 능동일 때
to 부정사의 수동	to be p.p.	행위의 주체와의 관계가 수동일 때
to 부정사의 완료 수동	to have been p.p.	행위의 주체와의 관계가 수동이고, 본동사 시제보다 한 시제 앞설 때

Tip G-TELP에서는 to 부정사의 수동(to be p.p.)과 to 부정사의 완료 수동(to have been p.p.)은 무조건 오답이다.

이렇게 활용해요

① to 부정사의 시제

- It seems that he is ill.
  그는 아픈 것처럼 보인다.
  = He seems **to be** ill.

- It seems that she was a nurse.
  = She seems **to have been** a nurse.
  그녀는 간호사였던 것 같다. (지금은 간호사가 아님)

② to 부정사의 태

- I expect that you will visit me soon.
  = I expect you **to visit** me soon.
  저를 방문해 주시길 바랍니다.

- I expect that you will be visited me.
  나는 당신이 곧 방문을 받을 것이라고 예상한다.
  = I expect you **to be visited** me.

④ to 부정사를 목적어로 취하는 동사

3형식에서 목적어 자리에 사용되는 to 부정사이다.

이런 게 답이에요

[
choose(~을 택하다) / claim(~을 (사실이라고) 주장하다) / decide(~을 결심[결정]하다) / expect(~을 기대[예기/예상]하다) / hope(~을 바라다, 희망하다) / learn(~을 배우다, 익히다, 습득하다) / manage(용케[잘] ~을 해내다) / *promise(~을 약속[계약]하다) / refuse(~하는 것을 거부하다) / seek(~하려고 노력[시도]하다) / want(~하고 싶다) / wish(~을 희망하다, 바라다)
]

이렇게 활용해요

① He began **to think so**.
그는 그렇게 생각하기 시작했다.

② We decided **to accept her offer**.
우리는 그녀의 제안을 받아들이기로 결정했다.

⑤ 자동사 + to V

자동사 뒤에 to 부정사를 사용해 마치 타동사처럼 사용되며, G-TELP에서는 동사 tend가 주로 출제된다.

이런 게 답이에요

[
tend(~하는 경향이 있다)
]

이렇게 활용해요

Women **tend to be more sensitive** than men.
여성이 남성보다 더 예민한 성격을 가지는 경향이 있다.

⑥ to 부정사를 목적격보어로 취하는 동사

5형식에서 목적격보어 자리에 사용되는 to V이다.

이런 게 답이에요

> advise(~에게 ~하는 것을 충고[조언]하다) / *allow(~에게 ~하는 것을 허락[허가]하다) / *ask(~에게 ~하는 것을 묻다) / *believe(~을 ~라고 믿다) / encourage(~에게 ~하도록 격려하다) / expect(~가 ~하는 것을 기대하다) / *force(~가 ~하는 것을 강요하다) / instruct(~에게 ~하라고 지시[명령]하다) / order(~에게 ~하도록 지시[명령]하다) / require(~에게 ~하도록 요구[명령]하다) / *tell(~에게 ~하라고 말[충고/명령]하다) / *urge(~에게 ~하도록 강제[설득/간청/권]하다) / want(~가 ~하기를 원하다)

Tip G-TELP에서는 능동태와 수동태 둘 다 출제된다. 전자의 구조는 '불완전타동사 + 목적어 + 목적격보어(to V)'이고, 후자는 '주어(능동태의 목적어) + be + 불완전타동사의 과거분사형 + 주격보어(to V)'이다.

이렇게 활용해요

Her father **does not allow** his daughter **to come home late**.
그녀의 아빠는 그녀의 딸이 늦게 집에 오는 것을 허락하지 않는다.

⑦ to 부정사의 관용적 표현

이런 게 답이에요

> be able to V(~할 수 있다) / be unwilling to V(~하기를 꺼리다) / have no choice but to V(~하지 않을 수밖에 없다) / too ~ to V(너무 ~해서 ~할 수 없다)

Tip too는 부사로 '너무나, 유감이지만 (너무) ~한'의 의미로 too 다음에 to 부정사를 뒤에 사용하면 '~하기에 너무 ~하다' 또는 '너무 ~해서 ~할 수 없다'로 해석된다(too + 형용사/부사 + to 부정사 = so + 형용사 + that + 주어 + cannot: '~하기에 너무 ~하다', '너무 ~해서 ~할 수 없다').

이렇게 활용해요

He is **too** busy **to have** a long holiday.
= He is **so** busy **that** he **cannot have** a long holiday.
그는 너무 바빠서 긴 휴가를 가질 수 없다.

PART 4 to 부정사 문제풀이

TEST 1 – 8번

In many countries, the high unemployment rate is causing a stagnant economy, **①**forcing people **to leave** cities or their countries **②**by emigrating to places **③**where they can find a job.

(a) having left
(b) leaving
(c) to leave
(d) to have left

답 (c)

| 해설 |

①force + 목적어 + **②**목적격보어(to V): ~가 …하도록 강요하다

(a) 현재분사/동명사 – having p.p.(완료시제): 본동사 시제와 다름
(b) 현재분사/동명사 – Ving(단순시제): 본동사 시제와 동일, 동사 force는 뒤에 현재분사/동명사를 목적격보어로 취할 수 없음
(c) to 부정사 – to V(단순시제): 본동사 시제와 동일, force는 목적격보어 자리에 to V를 가짐
(d) to 부정사 – to have p.p.(완료시제): 본동사 시제와 다름

| 구문독해 |

①분사구문
– 주어 + 동사 ~, 현재분사(Ving): 능동(~하면서)
②by + 동명사(Ving): ~함으로써
③관계부사 where: ~하는 (장소)
– 선행사(장소) + where + 주어 + 동사

| 해석 |

많은 나라에서, 높은 실업률은 사람들이 일자리를 구할 수 있는 곳으로 이주함으로써 도시나 그들의 나라를 **떠나도록** 강요하면서, 침체된 경제를 야기시키고 있다.

| 어휘 |

unemployment rate 실업률
cause ~을 야기하다[초래하다](cause – caused – caused – causing)
stagnant (물·공기가) 고여 있는, 침체된
emigrate to ~로 이주하다
find[get] a job 직장을 얻다

PART 4
to 부정사 문제풀이

TEST 1 – 17번

The police ①wanted to ensure ②that their primary suspect was definitively the one ③who smuggled drugs. Therefore, several witnesses were asked to identify the man in police custody.

(a) having identified
(b) identifying
(c) to identify
(d) to have identified

답 (c)

| 해설 |

ask + 목적어 + 목적격보어(to V): ~가 ~하도록 부탁하다[수동태 시, 주어 + ①be asked + ②to V(주격보어)]

(a) 현재분사/동명사 – having p.p.(완료시제): 본동사 시제와 다름
(b) 현재분사/동명사 – Ving(단순시제): 본동사 시제와 동일, 동사 ask가 수동태 시 현재분사/동명사 사용 불가
(c) to 부정사 – to V(단순시제): 본동사 시제와 동일, 동사 ask는 목적격보어 자리에 to V를 가짐
(d) to 부정사 – to have p.p.(완료시제): 본동사 시제와 다름

| 구문독해 |

①want + 목적어(to V)
②목적격 종속접속사 that
– 주어 + 타동사 + 목적어[that + 주어 + 동사 ~ (완전한 문장)]
　　　　　　　　생략 가능(~하는 것을)
③주격 관계대명사 who(~하는)
– 선행사(사람) + who + 동사

| 해석 |

경찰은 그들의 주요 용의자가 분명히 마약을 밀반입한 사람이라는 것을 확실히 확인하기를 원했다. 따라서, 몇몇 목격자들은 경찰에 구금되어 있는 그 남자의 **신원을 밝혀달라는** 요청을 받았다.

| 어휘 |

primary 주된, 주요한
definitively 결정적으로, 명확하게
witness 목격자
police custody 경찰서 구류
suspect 혐의자, 용의자
smuggle 밀수입[밀수출]하다, 밀수하다
identify (신원 등을) 확인하다[알아보다]

TEST 2 – 21번

The profits ❶earned by milk companies ❷should have been reviewd when higher taxes were imposed on their products. However, these companies have increased the prices of their milk products to make up for their losses.

(a) making up
(b) to make up
(c) to have made up
(d) having made up

답 (b)

| 해설 |

(a) 현재분사/동명사 – 현재분사는 '~하는', 동명사는 '~것'이라는 의미를 가지는데, 의미상 '~하기 위해서'라고 해석해야 하기 때문에 오답
(b) to 부정사 – to V(단순시제): 본동사 시제와 동일, to 부정사의 부사적 용법 중 '목적'으로 '~하기 위해서'라고 해석함
(c) to 부정사 – to have p.p.(완료시제): 본동사 시제와 다름
(d) 현재분사/동명사 – having p.p.(완료시제): 본동사 시제와 다름

| 구문독해 |

❶생략
– 선행사 + (주격 관계대명사 + be동사) + 과거분사[p.p.(~되어진): 형용사], 선행사를 수식함
❷should have p.p.: ~했어야 했는데(결국 못했다)(과거 사실에 대한 후회)

| 해석 |

우유 회사들이 그들의 제품에 더 높은 세금이 부과됐을 때 벌어들인 이익을 재검토했어야 했다. 하지만, 이 회사들은 그들의 손실을 **보충하기 위해** 우유 제품의 가격을 인상했다.

| 어휘 |

review 다시 조사하다, 재검토하다
tax 세금
impose A on B A를 B에 부과하다 (수동태 시, A be imposed on B)
make up for (손실 따위를) 보상하다, 보전하다

PART 4
to 부정사 문제풀이

TEST 3 – 3번

The Seoul City Council has set up a new public bike-sharing system [1]which makes use of an online application. [2]Called Ddareungi, the app allows bikers to pay for renting a bicycle by using their smartphones.

(a) to be paid
(b) having paid
(c) to be paying
(d) to pay

답 (d)

| 해설 |

[1]allow + 목적어 + [2]목적격보어(to V): ~가 ~하도록 허락하다

(a) to 부정사 – to be p.p.(단순수동): 본동사 시제와 동일, 목적어인 bikers와 수동관계
(b) 현재분사/동명사 – having p.p.(완료시제): 본동사 시제와 다름
(c) to 부정사 – to be Ving(단순시제): 본동사 시제와 동일, 목적어인 bikers와 능동관계, to be Ving은 앞으로 그러한 동작이 진행 될 것을 의미
(d) to 부정사 – to V(단순시제): 본동사 시제와 동일, 동사 allow는 목적격보어 자리에 to V를 가짐

| 구문독해 |

[1]주격 관계대명사 which(~하는)
– 선행사(사물/동물) + which + 동사
[2]분사구문
– 과거분사 p.p.: 수동(~되어진), 주어 + 동사

| 해석 |

서울시 의회는 온라인 응용 프로그램을 이용하는 새로운 공공 자전거 공유 체계를 마련했다. 따릉이라고 불리는 이 앱은 자전거를 타는 사람들이 스마트폰을 사용하여 자전거를 빌리는 데 비용을 **지불할** 수 있게 해준다.

| 어휘 |

set up 건립하다, 설립[수립]하다
bike-sharing system 자전거 공유 체계
make use of ~을 이용하다
pay for 대금을 지불하다
rent a bicycle 자전거를 대여하다

TEST 3 – 15번

The teachers are ⓐhaving a difficult time choosing the best essay of this year's writing competition. Many of the essays are equally outstanding. Nevertheless, they promised to report the winner at 11 a.m.

(a) will report
(b) reporting
(c) to report
(d) to have reported

답 (c)

| 해설 |

①promise + ②목적어(to V): ~을 약속/계약하다

(a) will V – 단순히 미래를 예측/추측, 문장에서 동사 promise가 있기 때문에 동사를 또 사용할 수 없음
(b) 동명사 – Ving(단순시제): 본동사 시제와 동일, 동사 promise는 뒤에 동명사를 목적어로 취할 수 없음
(c) to 부정사 – to V(단순시제): 본동사 시제와 동일
(d) to 부정사 – to have p.p.(완료시제): 본동사 시제와 다름

| 구문독해 |

ⓐhave trouble, have a hard(difficult) time, have difficulty (in) (동)명사: ~하는 데 어려움이 있다

| 해석 |

교사들은 올해 글짓기 대회에서 최고의 에세이를 고르는 데 어려움을 겪고 있다. 많은 에세이가 똑같이 뛰어나다. 그럼에도 불구하고, 그들은 오전 11시에 우승자를 **발표하기로** 약속했다.

| 어휘 |

competition 경쟁, 대회
outstanding 뛰어난, 걸출한

PART 4 동명사 핵심이론

📖 이렇게 나와요

Even with governmental subsidies, many individual business owners still won't have enough funds to maintain their businesses this year. Particularly, restaurant owners have therefore recommended _____ food prices if they are to continue business operations.

(a) increasing
(b) to be increasing
(c) to increase
(d) having increased

⑧ 동명사의 동사적 성질

이런 게 답이에요

1. 동명사를 목적어로 취하는 동사
2. 동명사의 시제: 단순/완료 시제
3. 동명사의 태: 능동/수동
4. 동명사의 관용적 표현
5. to 부정사와 동명사의 의미 구별

🔍 PLUS 선지에서 오답을 고르는 방법

1. 동명사에서 완료 시제(having p.p.)는 무조건 오답
2. 동명사의 수동(being p.p.)은 무조건 오답

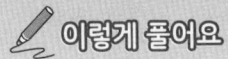

Even with governmental subsidies, many individual business owners still won't have enough funds to maintain their businesses this year. Particularly, restaurant owners have therefore recommended _____ food prices if they are to continue business operations.

동명사를 목적어로 취하는 동사

(a) increasing Ving
(b) ~~to be increasing~~
(c) ~~to increase~~
(d) ~~having increased~~

이렇게 활용해요

① 동명사의 시제

종류	형태	의미
단순시제	Ving	주절의 시제와 같거나 주절보다 미래를 의미
완료시제	having p.p.	주절의 시제보다 한 시제 과거이거나, 주절의 시제가 과거인 경우 과거에 실제 일어나지 않은 일

Tip G-TELP에서는 동명사의 완료시제(having p.p.)는 무조건 오답이다.

• 단순시제

I am proud of **being** rich.
→ I am proud that I am rich.
나는 부자가 된 것을 자랑스러워한다.

• 완료시제

I am proud of **having been** rich.
→ I am proud that I was rich.
나는 부자가 되었던 것을 자랑스러워한다.

② 동명사의 태

종류	형태	의미
동명사의 능동	Ving	행위의 주체와의 관계가 능동일 때
동명사의 수동	being p.p.	행위의 주체와의 관계가 수동일 때
동명사의 완료 수동	having been p.p.	행위의 주체와의 관계가 수동이고, 본동사 시제보다 한 시제 앞설 때

Tip G-TELP에서는 동명사의 수동(being p.p.)과 동명사의 완료 수동(having been p.p.)은 무조건 오답이다.

- 동명사의 능동

    He likes **treating** his teacher kindly.
    그는 그의 선생님을 친절하게 대우하는 것을 좋아한다.

- 동명사의 수동

    He doesn't like **being treated** like a child.
    그는 어린 아이처럼 대접받는 것을 좋아하지 않는다.

- 동명사의 완료 수동

    She complained of **having been insulted**.
    그녀는 모욕 당했던 것에 대해 불평했다.

⑨ 동명사를 목적어로 취하는 동사

이런 게 답이에요

[advocate(~을 옹호[지지]하다) / anticipate(~을 기대하다) / appreciate(~을 고맙게 여기다[감사하다]) / *avoid(~을 피하다) / ban(~을 금지하다) / conduct(~을 수행하다) / *consider(~을 고려하다) / contemplate(~을 생각하다) / delay(~을 늦추다) / *deny(~을 부정하다) / *enjoy(~을 즐기다) / *experience(~을 경험하다) / *favor(~을 찬성하다) / *finish(~을 끝내다) / imagine(~하는 것을 상상하다) / include(~을 포함시키다) / *involve(~을 포함[수반]하다) / *mind(~을 꺼려하다) / overcome(~을 극복하다) / postpone(~을 연기하다) / practice(~을 연습[훈련]하다) / *prohibit(~을 금지하다) / recall(~을 상기하다) / recommend(~을 추천하다) / *reconsider(~을 재고하다) / report(~을 보고하다[전하다]) / *require(~을 필요로 하다) / *resist(~에 저항하다) / suggest(~을 제안하다) / take up(~을 계속하다) / *tolerate(~을 묵인하다[관대하게 다루다])]

⑩ 동명사의 관용적 표현

이런 게 답이에요

[be used to Ving(~하는 데 익숙하다) / *go Ving(~하러 가다) / keep (on) Ving(계속 ~하다) / keep (목적어) from Ving(~을 ~하는 것으로부터 막다) / upon Ving(~하자마자)]

PART 4 동명사 문제풀이

TEST 1 – 1번

Even with governmental subsidies, many individual business owners still won't have ①enough funds to maintain their businesses this year. Particularly, restaurant owners have therefore recommended increasing food prices if they are ②to continue business operations.

(a) increasing
(b) to be increasing
(c) to increase
(d) having increased

답 (a)

| 해설 |

①recommend + ②목적어(Ving)

(a) 동명사 – Ving(단순시제): 본동사 시제와 동일, 동사 recommend는 목적어 자리에 동명사 사용
(b) to 부정사 – to be Ving(단순시제): 본동사 시제와 동일, 동사 recommend는 목적어 자리에 to V 사용 불가, to be Ving은 앞으로 그러한 동작이 진행될 것을 의미
(c) to 부정사 – to V(단순시제): 본동사 시제와 동일, 동사 recommend는 목적어 자리에 to V 사용 불가
(d) 동명사 – having p.p.(완료시제): 본동사 시제와 다름

| 구문독해 |

①enough 쓰임
– enough + 명사 (O) / 명사 + enough (O) / 형용사/부사 + enough (O) / enough + 형용사/부사 (X)
②to 부정사의 형용사적 용법: be to 용법
– be 동사 + V: 예정(~할 예정이다) / 의무(~해야만 한다) / 가능(~할 수 있다) / 의도(~할 의도이다) / 운명(~할 운명이다)

| 해석 |

정부 보조금에도 불구하고, 많은 개인 사업주들은 올해 사업을 유지할 충분한 재원을 가지고 있지 못할 것이다. 특히, 식당 주인들은 영업을 계속하려면 음식값을 올려야 한다고 권고했다.

| 어휘 |

subsidy (국가의) 보조금, 장려금
won't ~않을 것이다(will not의 축약형)
maintain 유지하다[지키다]
particularly 특히
business operations 경영 활동, 사업 운영

PART 4
동명사 문제풀이

TEST 1 – 10번

Eric is [1]disappointed that he cannot go to the cinema with his friends on the weekend. He is considering meeting them after the movie, but is worried [2]that he will not be able to finish work.

(a) to be meeting
(b) having met
(c) meeting
(d) to meet

답 (c)

| 해설 |

[1]consider + [2]목적어(Ving)

(a) to 부정사 – to be Ving(단순시제): 본동사 시제와 동일, 동사 consider는 목적어 자리에 to V 사용 불가, to be Ving은 앞으로 그러한 동작이 진행될 것을 의미
(b) 동명사 – having p.p.(완료시제): 본동사 시제와 다름
(c) 동명사 – Ving(단순시제): 본동사 시제와 동일, 동사 consider는 목적어 자리에 동명사 사용
(d) to 부정사 – to V(단순시제): 본동사 시제와 동일, 동사 consider는 목적어 자리에 to V 사용 불가

| 구문독해 |

[1]감정과 관련된 타동사
– appoint, excite, satisfy 등
– 주어(사람) + 동사 + 주격보어(과거분사 p.p.): 감정과 관련된 타동사가 보어 자리에 사용될 때 주어가 사람이면 과거분사를 사용한다.

[2]목적격 종속접속사 that
– 주어 + 타동사 + 목적어[that + 주어 + 동사 ~ (완전한 문장)]
　　　　　　　　　생략 가능(~하는 것을)

| 해석 |

Eric은 주말에 친구들과 영화관에 갈 수 없어서 실망했다. 영화가 끝난 뒤 그들을 만날지를 고민하고 있지만, 일을 끝내지 못할까 봐 걱정하고 있다.

| 어휘 |

go to ~에 가다
be able to V ~할 수 있다
finish work 근무를 마치다

TEST 1 – 12번

Melissa was very nervous when she first [1]started swimming in the sea. She only had experienced swimming in the swimming pool.

(a) to be swimming
(b) swimming
(c) to swim
(d) having swum

답 (b)

| 해설 |

[1]experience + [2]목적어(Ving)

(a) to 부정사 – to be Ving(단순시제): 본동사 시제와 동일, 동사 experience는 목적어 자리에 to V 사용 불가, to be Ving은 앞으로 그러한 동작이 진행될 것을 의미
(b) 동명사 – Ving(단순시제): 본동사 시제와 동일, 동사 experience는 목적어 자리에 동명사 사용
(c) to 부정사 – to V(단순시제): 본동사 시제와 동일, 동사 experience는 목적어 자리에 to V 사용 불가
(d) 동명사 – having p.p.(완료시제): 본동사 시제와 다름

| 구문독해 |

[1]start + 목적어(to V/Ving): ~를 시작하다

| 해석 |

Melissa는 바다에서 수영을 처음 시작했을 때 매우 긴장했다. 그녀는 단지 수영장에서 **수영하는 것**을 경험했을 뿐이다.

| 어휘 |

nervous 불안해[초조해/두려워]하는

PART 4
동명사 문제풀이

TEST 2 – 1번

It's been a year now ❶since Kim lost her job. Nonetheless, she has intentionally avoided finding a new job ❷because she doesn't ❸want to work.

(a) to find
(b) will find
(c) finding
(d) having found

답 (c)

| 해설 |

①avoid + ②목적어(Ving)

(a) to 부정사 – to V(단순시제): 본동사 시제와 동일, 동사 avoid는 목적어 자리에 to V 사용 불가
(b) will V – 단순미래: 단순히 미래를 예측/추측, 한 문장 안에 2개의 동사 사용 불가
(c) 동명사 – Ving(단순시제): 본동사 시제와 동일, 동사 avoid는 목적어 자리에 동명사 사용
(d) 동명사 – having p.p.(완료시제): 본동사 시제와 다름

| 구문독해 |

❶주어 + 현재완료(have p.p.) + since + 주어 + 과거동사: ~한 이래로 ~해오고 있다
❷because(종속접속사) + 주어 + 동사: ~ 때문에(due to(전치사) + 명사)
❸want + 목적어(to V)

| 해석 |

Kim 씨가 실직한 지 1년이 됐다. 그럼에도 불구하고, 그녀는 일하기 싫어서 일부러 새 직장을 구하는 것을 피했다.

| 어휘 |

intentionally 의도적으로, 고의로
find[get] a job 직장을 잡다

TEST 2 – 14번

Christine and Annabelle have been friends **①**since they were in kindergarten. Even after they got married, **②**they have been enjoying spending time for their favorite hobbies together.

(a) having spent
(b) to spend
(c) will spend
(d) spending

답 (d)

| 해설 |

①enjoy + ②목적어(Ving)

(a) 동명사 – having p.p.(완료시제): 본동사 시제와 다름
(b) to 부정사 – to V(단순시제): 본동사 시제와 동일, 동사 enjoy는 목적어 자리에 to V 사용 불가
(c) will V – 단순미래: 단순히 미래를 예측/추측, 한 문장 안에 2개의 동사 사용 불가
(d) 동명사 – Ving(단순시제): 본동사 시제와 동일, 동사 enjoy는 목적어 자리에 동명사 사용

| 구문독해 |

①주어 + 현재완료(have p.p.) + since + 주어 + 과거동사: ~한 이래로 ~해오고 있다
②주어 + 현재완료진행형(have[has] been + Ving) + for + 기간 표현

| 해석 |

Christine과 Annabelle은 유치원에 다닐 때부터 친구였다. 그들은 결혼한 후에도 그들이 가장 좋아하는 취미를 위해 함께 시간을 <u>보내는 것</u>을 즐기고 있다.

| 어휘 |

kindergarten 유치원
even after 이후에도, 심지어 ~한 후에도
get married 결혼하다
favorite 매우 좋아하는

PART 4
동명사 문제풀이

TEST 3 – 18번

On his way home, Jeff, by chance, saw **①**Brandy, an old friend **②**who has been working as an accountant in England. He couldn't resist inviting her to dinner.

(a) having invited
(b) to invite
(c) inviting
(d) to be inviting

답 (c)

| 해설 |

①resist + ②목적어(Ving)

(a) 동명사 – having p.p.(완료시제): 본동사 시제와 다름
(b) to 부정사 – to V(단순시제): 본동사 시제와 동일, 동사 resist는 목적어 자리에 to V 사용 불가
(c) 동명사 – Ving(단순시제): 본동사 시제와 동일, 동사 resist는 목적어 자리에 동명사 사용
(d) to 부정사 – to be Ving(단순시제): 본동사 시제와 동일, 동사 resist는 목적어 자리에 to V 사용 불가, to be Ving은 앞으로 그러한 동작이 진행될 것을 의미

| 구문독해 |

①동격
– 명사(A), 명사(B): B라는 A(주어로 사용 시, A가 주어)
②주격 관계대명사 who(~하는)
– 선행사(사람) + who + 동사

| 해석 |

집에 오는 길에, Jeff는 영국에서 회계사로 일해오고 있는 옛 친구 Brandy를 우연히 보게 되었다. 그는 그녀를 저녁 식사에 초대하지 않을 수 없었다.

| 어휘 |

on one's way home[back] 돌아가는 길에
by chance 우연히, 뜻밖에
accountant 회계사

TEST 3 - 22번

Every summer, Clare tries ❶one of the water activities ❷she has on her wish list. She has already done snorkeling, sea walking, and jet skiing. Next summer, she will go windsurfing with her sisters and parents.

(a) to be windsurfing
(b) windsurfing
(c) to windsurf
(d) having windsurfed

답 (b)

| 해설 |

①go + ②동명사(Ving)

(a) to 부정사 – to be Ving(단순시제): 본동사 시제와 동일, to be Ving은 앞으로 그러한 동작이 진행될 것을 의미
(b) 동명사 – Ving(단순시제): 본동사 시제와 동일, 동사 go는 바로 뒤에 동명사 사용 가능
(c) to 부정사 – to V(단순시제): 본동사 시제와 동일, go to V는 '~하기 위해 가다'
(d) 동명사 – having p.p.(완료시제): 본동사 시제와 다름

Tip go + Ving: '~하러 가다'(어떤 행위와 동작을 나타내어 평상시에 하던 일이나 습관처럼 하던 일의 반복성을 의미)
go + to V: '~하기 위해서 가다'

| 구문독해 |

❶one of + 복수명사: ~중의 하나
❷목적격 관계대명사 that(~하는) 생략
 – 선행사 + (that) + 주어 + 타동사 + (목적어 없음)

| 해석 |

매년 여름, Clare는 그녀의 소원 목록에 있는 수상 스포츠 중 하나를 시도한다. 그녀는 이미 스노클링, 바다 걷기, 제트 스키를 했다. 내년 여름, 그녀는 여동생들과 부모님과 함께 **윈드서핑을 하러** 갈 것이다.

| 어휘 |

water activities 수상 스포츠
wish list 소원 목록

PART 4 to 부정사와 동명사 핵심이론

📖 이렇게 나와요

Mr. Lee is advising his sister to exercise at least three times a week instead of eating one meal a day. He warns that she may regret _____ her health, since regular exercise is the most effective way to prevent weight gain.

(a) harming
(b) to harm
(c) being harmed
(d) to be harming

⑪ to 부정사와 동명사의 차이점

이런 게 답이에요

> 1. to 부정사와 동명사의 차이점: 주어 자리에는 동명사를 주로 사용
> 2. 3형식에서 목적어 자리에 to 부정사와 동명사가 둘 다 나오는 경우(의미 차이 없음)
> 3. 3형식에서 목적어 자리에 to 부정사와 동명사가 둘 다 나오는 경우(의미 차이 있음)

이렇게 활용해요

구분		to 부정사	동명사
차이점	시간	앞으로 일어날 미래의 일	이미 일어난 과거의 일
		*미래 지향적	*과거/현재
	주어 자리	주로 사용하지 않음	*주로 사용

Tip G-TELP에서는 주로 주어 자리에 동명사를 더 선호하는데, to 부정사가 주어로 사용될 경우에는 가주어 It을 사용해 진주어 자리에 to 부정사를 사용한다. 선지(보기)에 to 부정사와 동명사가 동시에 나오는 경우에는 동명사를 선택하자.

Mr. Lee is advising his sister to exercise at least three times a week instead of eating one meal a day. He warns that she may regret _____ her health, since regular exercise is the most effective way to prevent weight gain.
과거

(a) harming Ving
(b) ~~to harm~~
(c) ~~being harmed~~
(d) ~~to be harming~~

⑫ 3형식에서 목적어 자리에 to 부정사와 동명사가 둘 다 나오는 경우(의미 차이 없음)

이런 게 답이에요

> begin(~을 시작하다) / cease(~을 중단하다) / continue(~을 계속하다) / deserve(~할 가치[자격/권리]가 있다) / dislike(~을 싫어하다) / fail(~하지 못하다) / hate(~을 싫어하다) / like(~을 좋아하다) / love(~을 사랑하다) / prefer(~쪽을 좋아하다) / require(~을 요구하다) / *start(~을 시작하다)

Tip G-TELP에서는 start 동사가 주로 출제된다.

⑬ 3형식에서 목적어 자리에 to 부정사와 동명사가 둘 다 나오는 경우(의미 차이 있음)

이렇게 활용해요

타동사	목적어 자리	
	to 부정사	동명사
stop/quit	~ 하기 위해 멈추다/그만두다	~을 멈추다/그만두다

타동사	목적어 자리	
	to 부정사(미래)	동명사(과거)
remember	~할 것을 기억하다	~한 것을 기억하다
forget	~할 것을 잊어버리다	~을 잊어버리다
regret	~을 하게 되어 유감이다	~한 일을 후회하다

Tip G-TELP에서는 주로 remember/forget/regret/need 동사가 주로 출제된다.

	목적어 자리	의미	해석
need	to V	능동	(~할) 필요가 있다, ~해야 한다
	동명사(Ving)	수동	[사람·물건이] (~되어야 할) 필요가 있다

* 수동의 의미를 지닌 동명사
 '주어(사물) + need + 동명사(= to be p.p.)'

PART 4 to 부정사와 동명사 문제풀이

TEST 2 – 16번

Mr. Lee is ❶advising his sister to exercise at least three times ❷a week instead of eating one meal a day. He warns ❸that she may regret harming her health, ❹since regular exercise is the most effective way to prevent weight gain.

(a) harming
(b) to harm
(c) being harmed
(d) to be harming

답 (a)

| 해설 |

①regret + ②목적어(Ving): 과거(~한 일을 후회하다)

Tip regret + 목적어(to V): 미래(~을 하게 되어 유감이다)

(a) 동명사 – Ving(단순시제): 본동사 시제와 동일
(b) to 부정사 – to V(단순시제): 본동사 시제와 동일
(c) 동명사 – being p.p.(단순수동): 본동사 시제와 동일, 주어와 수동관계
(d) to 부정사 – to be Ving(단순시제): 본동사 시제와 동일, to be Ving은 앞으로 그러한 동작이 진행될 것을 의미

| 구문독해 |

❶advise + 목적어 + 목적격보어(to V): ~가 ~하도록 권고/충고하다
❷a(n) [단위를 나타내는 낱말에 붙여]: ~당, ~마다(= per)
❸목적격 종속접속사 that
– 주어 + 타동사 + 목적어[that + 주어 + 동사 ~ (완전한 문장)]
　　　　　　　　　　생략 가능(~하는 것을)
❹종속접속사 since
– 이유(~이므로, ~이니까) / 시간(~이래(쭉), ~한 때부터 내내)

| 해석 |

Lee 선생님은 그의 여동생에게 하루에 한 끼를 먹는 거 대신에 적어도 일주일에 세 번 운동을 하라고 충고하고 있다. 그는 규칙적인 운동이 체중 증가를 예방하는 가장 효과적인 방법이기 때문에 건강을 <u>해치는 것을</u> 후회할지도 모른다고 경고한다.

| 어휘 |

at least 적어도[최소한]
harm 해치다, 상하게 하다
effective 효과적인

instead of ~대신에
regular exercise 규칙적인 운동
weight gain 체중 증가

PART 4
to 부정사와 동명사 문제풀이

TEST 2 - 23번

Beth ¹asked me to go with her to the ²newly opened hair salon on Milson Street. She will be going on a date with Greg on Christmas Eve, and needs to get a haircut for the date.

(a) to have got
(b) to be getting
(c) getting
(d) to get

답 (d)

| 해설 |

①need + ②목적어(to V): 능동(~할 필요가 있다, ~해야 한다)

Tip need + 목적어(Ving): 수동(~되어야 할 필요가 있다)

(a) to 부정사 - to have p.p.(완료시제): 본동사 시제와 다름
(b) to 부정사 - to be Ving(단순시제): 본동사 시제와 동일, to be Ving은 앞으로 그러한 동작이 진행될 것을 의미
(c) 동명사 - Ving(단순시제): 본동사 시제와 동일
(d) to 부정사 - to V(단순시제): 본동사 시제와 동일

| 구문독해 |

¹ask + 목적어 + 목적격보어(to V): ~가 ~하도록 부탁하다
²어순 주의
- 부사는 형용사(과거분사/현재분사)를 수식할 수 있고, 분사는 명사를 수식한다.
- 부사 + 과거분사(p.p. 형용사) + 명사

| 해석 |

Beth는 나에게 Milson street에 새로 문을 연 미용실에 같이 가자고 했다. 그녀는 크리스마스 이브에 Greg과 데이트를 할 예정이고, 데이트를 위해 머리 손질을 **해야** 한다.

| 어휘 |

go with ~와 함께 가다
hair salon 미용실, 이발소
go on a date with ~와 데이트하다
get a haircut 이발하다

TEST 3 - 8번

A new hybrid car was lately recalled from the market. Selling the car was banned ❶due to a faulty engine control system. So, affected customers ❷were offered full refunds.

(a) Selling
(b) Having sold
(c) To sell
(d) To have sold

답 (a)

| 해설 |

②동명사(Ving) 주어 + ①단수 동사

(a) 동명사 – Ving(단순시제): 본동사 시제와 동일, 주어 자리는 주로 동명사 사용
(b) 동명사 – having p.p.(완료시제): 본동사 시제와 다름
(c) to 부정사 – to V(단순시제): 본동사 시제와 동일, G-TELP에서는 주어 자리에 to 부정사보다 동명사를 더 선호
(d) to 부정사 – to have p.p.(완료시제): 본동사 시제와 다름

| 구문독해 |

❶due to(전치사) + 명사: ~ 때문에[because(종속접속사) + 주어 + 동사]
❷offer + 간접목적어(A) + 직접목적어(B): ~에게 ~을 제공하다[수동태 시, 주어(A) + be offered + 목적어(B)]

| 해석 |

신형 하이브리드 자동차는 최근에 시장에서 회수되었다. 엔진 제어 시스템의 결함으로 인해 그 차를 **판매하는 것은** 금지되었다. 그래서 충격받은 고객들은 전액 환불을 받았다.

| 어휘 |

hybrid car 하이브리드[휘발유·전기 병용] 승용차
recall (물건을) 회수하다
faulty 흠[결함]이 있는, 불완전한
affect (강한 정서적) 충격을 주다(affect – affected – affected – affecting)
full refund 전액 환불
lately 최근에, 얼마 전에
ban 금(지)하다
engine control system 엔진 조정 장치

PART 5
연결사(어)

전치사(Preposition)

접속사(Conjunction)

접속부사(Connective Adverb, Conjunct)

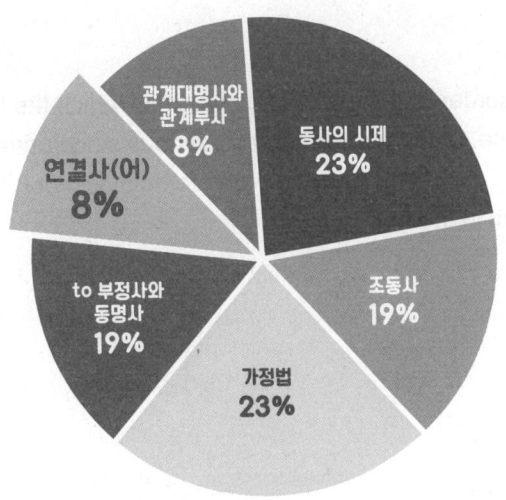

연결사(어)의 출제 원리

1. 전치사
- 양보/대조 관련 전치사
- 구 전치사
- 순접과 역접에 사용되는 전치사

2. 접속사
- 대등접속사: and/or 용법
- 종속접속사: 순접과 역접에 사용되는 종속접속사

3. 접속부사
- 순접과 역접에 사용되는 접속부사

4. 전치사 vs. 종속접속사
- 해석은 같지만 구조가 다른 전치사와 종속접속사 종류 숙지

 Tip

1. 전치사는 뒤에 명사나 명사 상당어구(동명사 / 대명사 / 관계대명사 what절 / 간접의문문 등)가 나온다.
2. 접속사 중 종속접속사는 종속절을 이끈다(주절은 '주어 + 동사', 종속절은 '종속접속사 + 주어 + 동사').
3. 접속부사는 문장과 문장을 주로 이어준다(주어 + 동사 ~. 접속부사, 주어 + 동사 ~).

PART 5 전치사 핵심이론

이렇게 나와요

Hypothyroidism is a disorder of the endocrine system in which the thyroid gland does not produce thyroid hormone. Many people find this serious since untreated cases of hypothyroidism _____ pregnancy can lead to delays in body growth and intellectual development in the baby.

(a) while
(b) during
(c) because of
(d) despite

1 전치사(Preposition)

이런 게 답이에요

1. 단순/구 전치사 숙지
2. 전치사를 기능별로 숙지: 순접/역접

이렇게 활용해요

① 전치사의 종류

단순 전치사 (기능별 분류)	양보/대조: *despite
구 전치사	*because of(~ 때문에) / *instead of(~ 대신에) / *rather than(~보다 오히려) / *regardless of(~을 개의치 않고)

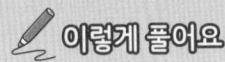

Hypothyroidism is a disorder of the endocrine system in which the thyroid gland does not produce thyroid hormone. Many people find this serious since untreated cases of hypothyroidism _____ pregnancy can lead to delays in body growth and intellectual development in the baby.

(명사)

(a) ~~while~~
(b) during   ~동안에: 시간
(c) ~~because of~~
(d) ~~despite~~

② 전치사의 중요 논리적 역할

순접	시간	*during(~ 동안에) / *for(~ 동안에) / *since(~ 이래로)
	원인/이유/동기	*because of(~ 때문에)
역접	대체	*instead of(~ 대신에)
	양보/대조	*despite(~에도 불구하고) / *regardless of(~을 개의치 않고)

PART 5 전치사 문제풀이

TEST 3 – 16번

Hypothyroidism is a disorder of the endocrine system in which the thyroid gland does not produce thyroid hormone. Many people [1]find this serious since untreated cases of hypothyroidism during pregnancy [2]can lead to delays in body growth and intellectual development in the baby.

(a) while
(b) during
(c) because of
(d) despite

답 (b)

| 해설 |

during + 명사
〈시간〉: ~동안에
(a) 종속접속사 while – 주어 + 동사 + while + 주어 + 동사(~ 동안에: 시간)
(b) 전치사 during – during + 명사(~ 동안에: 시간)
(c) 전치사 because of – because of + 명사(~ 때문에: 원인)
(d) 전치사 despite – despite + 명사(~에도 불구하고: 양보/대조)

| 구문독해 |

[1] find + 목적어 + 목적격보어[(to be) 형용사]: ~이 ~하다는 것을 알다
[2] 주어(A: 원인) + lead to + 목적어(B: 결과): A라는 원인 때문에 B라는 결과가 발생하다, A는 B로 이어지다

| 해석 |

갑상선 기능 저하증은 갑상선이 갑상선 호르몬을 생성하지 않는 내분비계통의 질환이다. 많은 사람들은 임신 **동안에** 갑상선 기능 저하증이 치료되지 않은 경우들이 아기의 신체 성장 지연과 지적 발달 지연으로 이어질 수 있기 때문에 이것을 심각하게 생각한다.

| 어휘 |

hypothyroidism 갑상선 기능 저하증
endocrine system 내분비계
thyroid hormone 갑상샘 호르몬
pregnancy 임신
intellectual development 지력의 발달
disorder (신체 기능의) 장애[이상]
thyroid gland 갑상샘
untreated 치료를 받지 않은
delay 지연, 연기

예제문제

Mason participated in the Olympics for the first time as a marathoner. He usually prepared for the Olympics with constant training and practice. He could win a bronze medal _____ he practiced hard.

(a) despite
(b) because
(c) although
(d) instead of

답 (b)

| 해설 |

'그는 연습을 열심히 했기 때문에 동메달을 딸 수 있었다.'가 해석상 가장 올바른 내용이므로, 원인/이유/동기를 나타내는 (b) because가 정답이다.

| 해석 |

Mason은 이번 올림픽에 마라톤 선수로 처음 참가했다. 그는 평소에 꾸준한 훈련과 연습을 하며 올림픽 준비를 했다. 연습을 열심히 했기 **때문에** 그는 동메달을 딸 수 있었다.

| 어휘 |

participate 참가[참여]하다
prepare 준비하다[시키다]

PART 5 접속사 핵심이론

📖 이렇게 나와요

I'm so glad that my mom has promised to go shopping with me this weekend. I really hope she doesn't change her mind _____ she hardly buys anything for herself. My mom is always working for us nowadays.

(a) so
(b) although
(c) but
(d) because

② 접속사(Conjunction)

접속사에는 **대등접속사, 상관접속사, 종속접속사, 접속부사**가 있다.

이런 게 답이에요

1. 대등접속사: and, so
2. 종속접속사를 기능별로 숙지: 순접/역접
3. 접속부사를 기능별로 숙지: 순접/역접

③ 대등(등위)접속사(Coordinating Conjunction)

단어와 단어를, 구와 구를, 절과 절을 대등하게 연결해 주는 기능을 가진다.

이렇게 활용해요

대등(등위)접속사의 종류

종류	해석	용법
for	왜냐하면	For + 주어 + 동사 ~, 주어 + 동사 (×)
		주어 + 동사 ~, for + 주어 + 동사 (○)

I'm so glad that my mom has promised to go shopping with me this weekend. I really hope she doesn't change her mind _____ she hardly buys anything for herself.
〈결과〉   주어 동사
My mom is always working for us nowadays.

(a) ~~so~~
(b) ~~although~~
(c) ~~but~~
(d) because 원인

*and	그리고	'단어와 단어', '구와 구', '문장과 문장'을 이어줌(순접)
	~해라, 그러면 ~할 것이다	명령문 + and ~
	~가라, 와라, 해봐라	go, come, try + and + (to) + 원형
nor	역시 아니다	–
but	그러나	'단어와 단어', '구와 구', '문장과 문장'을 이어줌(역접)
or	또는(선택의 의미)	'단어와 단어', '구와 구', '문장과 문장'을 이어줌(순접)
	~해라, 그렇지 않으면 ~할 것이다	명령문 + or ~
yet	아직	–
*so	그래서	원인 so 결과

Tip 'fanboys(for, and, nor, but, or, yet, so)'가 있는데 그중 G-TELP에서는 and와 so가 주로 출제된다.

PLUS

1. 대등(등위)접속사는 문장 맨 앞에 사용할 수 없다.
2. 대등(등위)접속사는 'A 대등(등위)접속사 B' 형식으로 A와 B가 같은 형태로 사용되는 병렬구조로 사용된다.
3. G-TELP에서는 주로 and와 so가 주로 출제된다.
4. 대등(등위)접속사는 'fanboys(for, and, nor, but, or, yet, so)'로 암기하면 좀 더 쉽게 숙지할 수 있다.

4 종속접속사(Subordinator)

종속접속사가 이끄는 절을 **종속절(종속접속사 + 주어 + 동사)**이라 하고 종속접속사가 없는 절을 **주절(주어 + 동사)** 이라 한다. 종속절의 종류는 명사절, 형용사절, 부사절이 있는데, G-TELP에서는 부사절이 주로 시험에 출제된다.

이렇게 활용해요

① 명사절을 이끄는 종속접속사: 주어/목적어/보어/동격 자리에 사용

	종류
종속접속사	that(~하는 것)
의문사	who(누가) / when(언제 ~하는지) / where(어디서 ~하는지) / what(무엇 ~하는지) / why(왜 ~하는지) / how(어떻게 ~하는지)
의문사 대용어	whether(~인지 아닌지) / if(~인지 아닌지)
관계대명사	what(~하는 것)
복합관계대명사	whoever(~하는 사람이면 누구나) / whichever(~하는 것은 어느 것이나) / whatever(~하는 것은 무엇이나)

- if는 부사절(만약 ~하면)과 명사절(~인지 아닌지)로 사용되는데, 후자일 경우 타동사의 목적어 자리에는 사용 가능하지만 주어자리, 전치사 뒤, 보어자리, 동격자리에는 사용할 수 없다.
- 관계대명사 what과 복합관계대명사 whoever/whichever/whatever는 앞에 선행사(주로 명사)가 없어야 하는 점이 공통점이라 동격절로 사용할 수 없다.

② 형용사절을 이끄는 종속접속사: 관계사 앞에 있는 명사(선행사)를 수식

관계사	종류
관계대명사	who / whose / whom / which / that(~하는)
관계부사	when(~하는/~할 때(시간)) / where(~하는(장소)) / why(~하는(이유)) / how(~하는(방법))

- 관계대명사 what은 명사절로 문장에서 주어/목적어/보어 자리에 사용가능하지만, 선행사(명사)를 포함하고 있어 명사(선행사)를 수식할 수 없다.

③ 부사절을 이끄는 종속접속사: 주로 동사 수식

순접 관계	인과관계		*because(~ 때문에) / *so (that)(그래서 ~하다) / now (that)(~이기 때문에) / *since(~ 때문에)
	결과		*so 형용사(부사) that(너무 ~해서 그 결과 ~하다) / *so 형용사 a(n) 명사 that(너무 ~해서 그 결과 ~하다)
	목적		*so that(~하기 위해서)
	시간		*as long as(~하는 한) / ever since(~ 이후로 줄곧[계속]) / *since(~한 이래로) / *until(~할 때까지) / *when(~할 때) / *whenever(~할 때마다) / while(~하는 동안)
	조건/가정	순접	if(만약 ~라면)
		역접	unless(만약 ~하지 않는다면)
	제한		as(so) long as(~하는 동안은 (시간)) / as(so) far as[~에 관한(지역적 범위)]
역접 관계	양보/대조		*although(비록 ~일지라도) / *even though(비록 ~일지라도) / *however(아무리 ~한다 하더라도) / *unless(~가 아니라면)

Tip 부사절을 이끄는 종속접속사는 앞서 살펴본 전치사처럼 순접과 역접으로 나누어 학습하자.

PART 5 접속사 문제풀이

TEST 2 - 5번

I'm ①so glad that my mom has ②promised to ③go shopping with me this weekend. I really hope ④she doesn't change her mind because she hardly buys anything for herself. My mom is always working for us nowadays.

(a) so
(b) although
(c) but
(d) because

답 (d)

| 해설 |

주어 + 동사 + because + 주어 + 동사
  〈결과〉   〈원인〉: ~하기 때문에

(a) 대등접속사 so - 순접(인과관계): 원인 + so(그래서) + 결과
(b) 종속접속사 although - 역접(양보/대조): A + although(비록 ~일지라도) + B
(c) 대등접속사 but - 역접(반대): A + but(그러나) + B
(d) 종속접속사 because - 순접(인과관계): 결과 + because(~하기 때문에) + 원인

| 구문독해 |

①so + 형용사/부사 that + 주어 + 동사: 너무 ~해서 그 결과 ~하다
②promise + 목적어(to V): ~하기로 결정하다
③go + Ving(동명사): ~하러 가다
④목적격 종속접속사 that
- 주어 + 타동사 + 목적어[that + 주어 + 동사 ~ (완전한 문장)]
                    생략 가능(~하는 것을)

| 해석 |

엄마가 이번 주말에 나와 같이 쇼핑 가기로 약속해서 너무 기쁘다. 나는 그녀(엄마)가 스스로 물건을 사는 일이 거의 없기 **때문에** 마음을 바꾸지 않았으면 좋겠다. 우리 엄마는 요즘 항상 우리를 위해 일하신다.

| 어휘 |

change one's mind 의견[생각, 결심]을 바꾸다, 고쳐 생각하다
hardly 거의 ~아니다[없다]
for oneself 스스로, 혼자 힘으로
work for ~을 위해 일하다
nowadays 요즘에는

TEST 2 – 7번

Jackson is leaving on a trip to Taiwan this Wednesday. Even though he is taking a long vacation, he is bringing a small suitcase. Perhaps he ❶plans to buy a big suitcase ❷once he arrives there.

(a) Despite
(b) Even though
(c) Unless
(d) As long as

답 (b)

| 해설 |

Even though + 주어 + 동사 ~, 주어 + 동사
〈양보/대조〉: 비록 ~일지라도

(a) 전치사 despite – 역접(양보/대조): Despite(비록 ~일지라도) A, B
(b) 종속접속사 even though – 역접(양보/대조): even though(비록 ~일지라도) A, B
(c) 종속접속사 unless – 역접(조건): Unless(만약 ~하지 않는다면) A, B
(d) 종속접속사 as long as – 순접(시간): As long as(~하는 한) A, B

| 구문독해 |

❶plan + 목적어(to V): ~할 작정이다
❷종속접속사 once
– 조건(일단 ~하면), 시간(~하자마자, 언제 ~하더라도)

| 해석 |

Jackson은 이번 수요일에 대만으로 여행을 떠날 것이다. 그는 긴 휴가를 얻었지만, 작은 여행 가방을 가지고 왔다. 아마도 그는 그곳에 도착하면 큰 여행 가방을 구입할 작정이다.

| 어휘 |

leave on a trip 여행을 가다[출발하다]
take a vacation(holiday) 휴가를 얻다
suitcase 여행 가방

PART 5 접속부사 핵심이론

이렇게 나와요

Kim's restaurant has decided to provide free lunch to the city's impoverished citizens. _____, children under 14 years old can get a 50% discount on food or non-alcoholic drinks to eat or drink during weekdays.

(a) Instead
(b) Regardless
(c) Otherwise
(d) Moreover

⑤ 접속부사(Connective Adverb, Conjunct)

두 개의 문장이나 문장의 일부를 연결시켜 주는 부사 역할을 한다.

Tip 접속부사 역시 앞서 살펴본 전치사와 종속접속사처럼 순접과 역접으로 나누어 학습하자.

이렇게 활용해요

① 순접

도입	*at the same time(동시에, 또한) / *in the first place(먼저, 무엇보다도)
결과	*thus(따라서, 그러므로) / hence(그래서) / *in short(간단히 말해) / *therefore(따라서) / *so(그래서)
결론	finally(마침내, 결국)
인과관계	*eventually(마침내) / *therefore(그러므로) / *thus(그러므로)
요약 & 종합	altogether(전체적으로 보아, 요컨대)
강조	*at length(상세히) / *in fact(사실상) / *indeed(사실상)
반복 & 동격	in other words(다시 말해서, 달리 말하자면) / *that is(즉, 다시 말해서)
비교	*similarly(유사: 마찬가지로)
예시	for example(예를 들어) / *for instance(예를 들면)
증거 & 확실성	*indeed(실로, 사실상) / naturally(당연히, 물론)
부가 & 첨가	*additionally(부가적으로) / *at the same time(동시에, 또한) / *besides(게다가) / *in fact(사실상) / *in addition (to)(~ 외에도, 게다가) / *moreover(게다가)

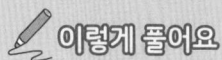

Kim's restaurant has decided to provide free lunch to the city's impoverished citizens. _____, children under 14 years old can get a 50% discount on food or non-alcoholic drinks to eat or drink during weekdays.

(a) ~~Instead~~
(b) ~~Regardless~~
(c) ~~Otherwise~~
(d) Moreover 부가 & 첨가

시간 관련	*afterward(s)(나중에) / in the meantime(한편) / meanwhile(한편)
시간의 순서	*in the first place(우선)

② 역접

대조	*although(~에도 불구하고) / *but(그러나) / *even though(비록 ~일지라도) / *however(그러나) / *nevertheless(~임에도 불구하고) / *on the contrary(반대로, 반면에) / *still(그러나) / *while(반면에, ~ 동안에) / *yet(그러나)
반박	*instead(대신에, 그런게 아니라) / *rather(그렇기는커녕, 반대로, 도리어)
양보 & 대조	*even so(그렇기는 하지만) / instead(~ 대신에) / *nevertheless(그럼에도 불구하고) / *nonetheless(~에도 불구하고) / *otherwise(그렇지 않다면) / *still(그럼에도 불구하고)
역접	however(하지만, 그러나) / otherwise(그렇지 않으면) / unfortunately(불행하게도)

6 전치사 vs. 종속접속사

서로 해석은 같지만 구조가 다른 경우이다.

이런 게 답이에요

구분	해석	전치사	종속접속사
시간	~ 동안에	during	while
원인/이유	~ 때문에	*because of	*because *since
양보/대조	비록 ~일지라도	*despite	although *even though *while

PLUS

1. 전치사 구조: 전치사 + 명사/명사 상당어구[동명사, 대명사, 관계대명사, what절, 의문사절(간접의문문)]
2. 종속접속사 구조: 종속접속사 + 주어 + 동사

PART 5 접속부사 문제풀이

TEST 1 – 5번

Kim's restaurant has ❶decided to ❷provide free lunch to the city's impoverished citizens. Moreover, children under 14 years old can get a 50% discount on food or non-alcoholic drinks to eat or drink ❸during weekdays.

(a) Instead
(b) Regardless
(c) Otherwise
(d) Moreover

답 (d)

| 해설 |

주어 + 동사 ~. Moreover, 주어 + 동사 ~.
　　순접: 〈부가 & 첨가〉 게다가

(a) 접속부사 instead – 역접(반박): Instead(대신에), S + V
(b) 접속부사 regardless – 역접(양보 & 대조): Regardless(그럼에도 불구하고), S + V
(c) 접속부사 otherwise – 역접(양보 & 대조): Otherwise(그럼에도 불구하고), S + V
(d) 접속부사 moreover – 순접(부가 & 첨가): Moreover(게다가), S + V

| 구문독해 |

❶decide + 목적어(to V): ~하기를 결정하다
❷provide + 목적어(사람/동물) + with 목적어(사물): ~에게 ~을 제공하다[= provide + 목적어(사물) + to/for 목적어(사람/동물)]
❸during(전치사) + 명사: ~동안[while(종속접속사) + 주어 + 동사]

| 해석 |

Kim 씨의 식당은 그 도시의 가난한 시민들에게 무료 점심을 제공하기로 결정했다. 게다가, 14세 미만의 어린이들은 주중에 먹거나 마실 수 있는 음식이나 무알코올 음료를 50% 할인을 받을 수 있다.

| 어휘 |

impoverished 빈곤한
get a discount 할인을 받다
non-alcoholic 알코올을 포함하지 않은

PART 5
접속부사 문제풀이

TEST 1 – 19번

Rehabilitating old buildings to their original appearance can **①**help attract **②**investment as well as tourists if the structures are historically significant. For instance, a historic but abandoned industrial building **③**can be turned into small business space.

(a) Moreover
(b) For instance
(c) In fact
(d) Thus

답 (b)

| 해설 |

주어 + 동사 ~. For instance, 주어 + 동사 ~.

순접: 〈예시〉 예를 들어

(a) 접속부사 moreover – 순접(부가 & 첨가): Moreover(게다가), S + V
(b) 접속부사 for instance – 순접(예시): For instance(예를 들어), S + V
(c) 접속부사 in fact – 순접(강조): In fact(사실상), S + V
(d) 접속부사 thus – 순접(결과): Thus(그러므로), S + V

| 구문독해 |

①help + 목적어[(to) V]: ~하는 것을 돕다
②B as well as A: A뿐만 아니라 B도(= not only A but also B, 주어로 사용 시, 주어는 B)
③turn A into B: A를 B로 바꾸다(수동태 시, A be turned into B)

| 해석 |

오래된 건물들을 원래의 모습대로 복원하면 그 구조물이 역사적으로 중요한 경우 관광객뿐만 아니라 투자 유치에도 도움이 될 수 있다. **예를 들어**, 역사적이지만 버려진 산업 건물은 작은 사업 공간으로 바뀔 수 있다.

| 어휘 |

rehabilitate A to B A를 B로 복구시키다
attract investment 투자를 유치하다
historically 역사상(으로)
abandoned 버려진, 유기된
business space 업무(사업) 공간
original appearance 본래의 모습
structure 구조물, 건축물
significant 중요한
industrial 산업[공업]의

TEST 3 – 1번

Parents have **¹**warned us **²**not to eat fast food. They say **³**that fast food has high calories, sugar, salt, and cholesterol and is harmful to health. Nevertheless, we still eat fast food **⁴**because its taste is irresistible.

(a) Otherwise
(b) Eventually
(c) Nevertheless
(d) In fact

답 (c)

| 해설 |

주어 + 동사 ~. Nevertheless, 주어 + 동사 ~.
　　　　　역접: 〈양보 & 대조〉 그럼에도 불구하고

(a) 접속부사 otherwise – 역접(양보 & 대조): Otherwise(그럼에도 불구하고), S + V
(b) 접속부사 eventually – 순접(결과): Eventually(그 결과적으로), S + V
(c) 접속부사 nevertheless – 역접(양보 & 대조): Nevertheless(그럼에도 불구하고), S + V
(d) 접속부사 in fact – 순접(강조): In fact(사실상), S + V

| 구문독해 |

¹warn + 목적어 + 목적격보어(to V): ~에게 ~하라고 통고(경고)하다
²to 부정사의 부정
– not/never + to V
³목적격 종속접속사 that
– 주어 + 타동사 + 목적어[that + 주어 + 동사 ~ (완전한 문장)]
　　　　　　　　　　생략 가능(~하는 것을)
⁴because(종속접속사) + 주어 + 동사: ~ 때문에(due to(전치사) + 명사)

| 해석 |

부모들은 우리에게 패스트푸드를 먹지 말라고 경고했다. 그들은 패스트푸드는 높은 칼로리, 설탕, 소금, 그리고 콜레스테롤이 있고 건강에 해롭다고 말한다. 그럼에도 불구하고, 우리는 여전히 패스트푸드의 맛을 거부할 수 없기 때문에 패스트푸드를 먹는다.

| 어휘 |

be harmful to　~에 해롭다
irresistible　억누를[저항할] 수 없는

PART 5
접속부사 문제풀이

TEST 3 - 21번

If you really **①**want to be a doctor, you **②**need to put more effort into your study. Otherwise, you won't get into a medical school and will regret **③**what you have done.

(a) Instead
(b) Therefore
(c) Additionally
(d) Otherwise

답 (d)

|해설|

주어 + 동사 ~. Otherwise, 주어 + 동사 ~.
  역접: 〈양보 & 대조〉 그렇지 않으면

(a) 접속부사 instead – 역접(반박): Instead(대신에), S + V
(b) 접속부사 therefore – 순접(결과): Therefore(그러므로), S + V
(c) 접속부사 additionally – 순접(부가 & 첨가): Additionally(부가적으로), S + V
(d) 접속부사 otherwise – 역접(양보 & 대조): Otherwise(그럼에도 불구하고), S + V

|구문독해|

①want + 목적어(to be 명사): ~가 되기를 원하다
②need + 목적어(to V): ~할 필요가 있다(능동)
③선행사를 포함한 관계대명사 what: ~하는 것
– (선행사 없음) + what + 주어 + 타동사 + (목적어 없음)

|해석|

만약 여러분이 정말 의사가 되고 싶다면, 여러분은 공부에 더 많은 노력을 기울일 필요가 있다. **그렇지 않으면**, 여러분은 의대에 들어가지 못하고 여러분이 해온 일을 후회하게 될 거다.

|어휘|

put effort(labor, work) into 힘을 들이다
won't ~않을 것이다(will not의 축약형)
get into ~에 들어가다
medical(med) school 의과 대학
regret 후회하다

예제문제

I used to think that reading was difficult, and I even gave up reading a book that I read many times. _____, when I stopped harboring this negative perception, reading actually became easier.

(a) However
(b) In fact
(c) Therefore
(d) Moreover

답 (a)

| 해설 |

However는 접속부사로 '그러나, 그렇지만'이라는 뜻을 가지고, 앞 문장에서 한 말과 뒤 문장의 논리적 상관관계가 서로 반대되는 내용을 말할 때 사용한다. 앞 문장에서 'I(나)'는 독서가 어렵다고 생각했고 몇 번 포기하기도 했다고 말한다. 뒤 문장에서는 독서가 어렵다는 내용의 앞 문장과 반대되는 내용으로 독서가 재밌어졌다고 말하고 있으므로 (a) However가 정답이다.

| 해석 |

나는 한때 독서가 어렵다고 생각했고, 심지어 여러 번 읽던 책을 포기했다. <u>그러나</u>, 내가 이런 부정적인 인식을 품는 것을 그만두었을 때, 독서는 사실 더 쉬워졌다.

| 어휘 |

give up 포기하다
harbor (계획·생각 등을) 품다
negative perception 부정적 지각(인식)

PART 6
관계대명사와 관계부사

관계대명사(Relative Pronoun)

관계부사(Relative Adverb)

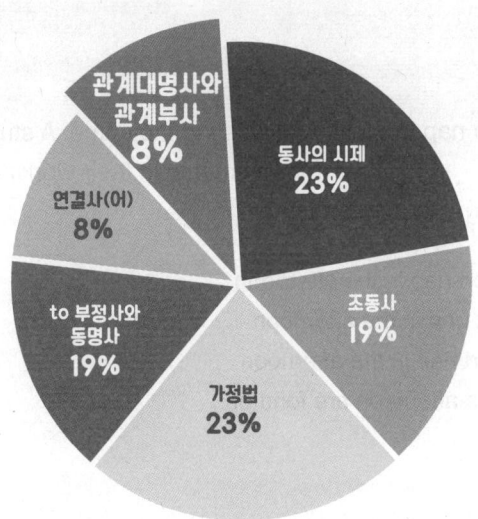

 관계대명사와 관계부사의 출제 원리

1. 관계대명사
- 선행사가 사람, 동물 또는 사물, 사람 + 사물, 없는 경우를 구분해서 숙지하자.
- 관계대명사 뒤에 주어 / 목적어 / 소유격 중 무엇이 없는지를 찾자.
- 관계대명사의 계속적 용법과 제한적 용법을 구별하자.
- 관계대명사 that만 사용하는 경우를 숙지하자.

2. 관계부사
- 관계부사의 종류와 용법은 선행사와 관계부사의 관계를 통해 숙지하자.

> **Tip**
>
> 〈관계대명사〉
> 1. '선행사(명사) + what'은 절대 불가하다.
> 2. '선행사, that'은 절대 불가하다.
> 3. '선행사(사람) + which'는 절대 불가하다.
> 4. '선행사(사물) + who'는 절대 불가하다(예외: 선행사를 의인화할 때 가능).
> 5. 'who / which / that / what + 완전한 문장'은 절대 불가하다.
> 6. 'the only / very / same + 선행사 + who / which / what'은 절대 불가하다.
>
> 〈관계부사〉
> 1. 'when / where / why / how + 불완전한 문장'은 절대 불가하다.
> 2. 'the way how'는 절대 불가하다.

PART 6 관계대명사 핵심이론

📖 이렇게 나와요

Not all people who take a nap are lazy and wasting their time. A study shows that people _____ have improvements in their working memory and a 37% less chance of contracting a fatal heart condition.

(a) which are fond of a short nap in the afternoon
(b) who are fond of a short nap in the afternoon
(c) when are fond of a short nap in the afternoon
(d) whom a short nap in the afternoon are fond of

1 관계대명사(Relative Pronoun)

'접속사 + 대명사' 역할을 한다.

이런 게 답이에요

관계대명사의 종류: 격과 선행사에 따라 결정

선행사 \ 격	주격	소유격	목적격
사람	who	whose	whom
사물/동물	which	whose of which	which
사람 사물/동물	that	×	that
× (선행사 포함)	what	×	what

> **Tip** 관계대명사 what을 제외한 관계대명사는 앞에 선행사를 수식하는 형용사절로 '~하는'이라고 해석하고, what은 명사절로 '~하는 것'으로 해석한다.

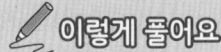

Not all people who take a nap are lazy and wasting their time. A study shows that people <u>선행사</u> _____ <u>have improvements</u> in their working memory and a 37% 본동사

less chance of contracting a fatal heart condition.

(a) ~~which are fond of a short nap in the afternoon~~
(b) who are fond of a short nap in the afternoon   who + (주어없음) + 동사
(c) ~~when are fond of a short nap in the afternoon~~
(d) ~~whom a short nap in the afternoon are fond of~~

이렇게 활용해요

① 선행사

'선행사'란 관계대명사절(접속사 + 대명사)의 수식을 받는 '명사'를 말한다.

(A) I have a friend. + (B) He lives in London.

→ (C) I have a friend **and he** lives in London.

→ (D) I have a friend **who** lives in London.

(A)와 (B)를 합친 (C)에서 대등접속사 and와 대명사 he를 동시에 수행하는 관계대명사 who를 사용해서 (D)처럼 바꿀 수 있다. 여기에서 <u>a friend</u>를 <u>선행사</u>라고 한다.

② 격

'격'이란 관계대명사가 관계대명사절에서 무슨 역할을 하는지에 따라 '격'이 결정된다.

(D) I have a friend **who** lives in London.

who가 이끄는 절에서 동사 lives에 대한 **주어가 없기 때문에 who를 주격 관계대명사**라고 부르고, who lives in London을 주격 관계명사절이라고 말한다.

> **Tip** '격 = 선행사'

Grammar 문법 **155**

③ 관계대명사의 해석 용법
  • 제한적 용법
    형태: 관계대명사 앞에 콤마(,)가 없는 경우
    해석: 관계대명사절이 앞에 있는 선행사(명사)를 수식하는 형용사절로 '~하는'이라고 해석
  • 계속적 용법
    형태: 관계대명사 앞에 콤마(,)가 있는 경우
    해석: '대등접속사[and(그리고), but(그러나), for(~ 때문에), though(비록 ~일지라도)] + 대명사(선행사)'로 바꿔 해석

    Tip 계속적 용법으로는 관계대명사 that과 what은 사용할 수 없다.

② 선행사가 사람일 경우

이렇게 활용해요

① 주격 관계대명사 who의 용법
  • 선행사(사람) + who + 주어 + 동사
    　　　　　　　주격 관계대명사절(that 사용 가능)
  • 선행사(사람: 주어) + (who + 주어 + 동사) + 동사
    　　　　　　　주격 관계대명사절: 삽입(that 사용 가능)
  선행사가 사람이고 who 뒤 문장에서 주어가 없을 때 who를 주격 관계대명사라고 부른다.

  Tip 주격 관계대명사 who절 안에 있는 동사는 선행사와 수의 일치를 시켜야 한다.

  (a) Kevin is a teacher **who** [teach / **teaches**] us English.
    Kevin은 우리에게 영어를 가르치는 선생님이다.

  위 (a) 문장에서 어법상 올바른 것은 선행사가 a teacher로 단수형이기 때문에 단수 동사인 teaches이다.

② 소유격 관계대명사 whose의 용법
  선행사(사람) + whose + 소유격 + 명사 + 동사
  　　　　　　　소유격 관계대명사절
  선행사가 사람이고 whose 뒤 문장에서 소유격이 없을 때 whose를 소유격 관계대명사라고 부른다.

  Tip whose 대신에 관계대명사 that은 소유격이 없기 때문에 사용할 수 없다.

  (b) Kevin is an English teacher and his pronunciation is good.
  → Kevin is an English teacher [**whose** / who] pronunciation is good.
    Kevin은 발음이 좋은 영어 선생님이다.

  위 (b) 문장에서 어법상 올바른 것은 선행사가 사람 an English teacher이고, 뒤에 명사 pronunciation으로 시작하기 때문에 whose가 올바르다. who는 주격 관계대명사로 선행사가 사람인 것은 올바르지만 주어 없이 바로 동사가 나와야 하기 때문에 올바르지 않다.

③ 목적격 관계대명사 whom의 용법

- 선행사(사람) + whom + 주어 + 타동사 + 목적어
  목적격 관계대명사절(whom 생략 가능, that 사용/생략 가능)

- 선행사(사람) + whom + 주어 + 자/타동사 ~ 전치사 + 목적어
  목적격 관계대명사절(whom 생략 가능, that 사용/생략 가능)

= 선행사(사람) + 전치사 + whom + 주어 + 자/타동사
  (whom 생략 불가, *that 사용 불가)

Tip 영어에서 반드시 뒤에 목적어를 가져야 하는 경우는 타동사와 전치사이다.

선행사가 사람이고 whom 뒤 문장에서 목적어가 없을 때 whom을 목적격 관계대명사라고 부른다.

(c) Kevin is an English teacher **and** she met **him** in the classroom yesterday.
→ Kevin is an English teacher [**whom** / **whose**] she met in the classroom yesterday.
 Kevin은 그녀가 교실에서 어제 만났던 영어 선생님이다.

위 (c) 문장에서 어법상 올바른 것은 선행사가 사람 an English teacher이고, 뒤에 타동사 met의 목적어가 없기 때문에 목적격 관계대명사 whom이 올바르다. 소유격 관계대명사 whose는 '선행사 + whose + 명사 + 동사~' 구조로 whose 다음에 있는 동사 뒤에 완전한 문장이 나와야 하기 때문에 올바르지 않다.

(d) This is the student **and** Kevin played baseball **with** him.
→ This is the student [**whom** / **who**] Kevin played baseball **with**.
→ This is the student [**with whom** / **with that**] Kevin played baseball.
 이 사람이 Kevin이 야구를 같이 했던 그 학생이다.

위 (d) 문장 중 두 번째 문장에서 어법상 올바른 것은 선행사가 사람 the student이고, 뒤에 전치사 with의 목적어가 없기 때문에 목적격 관계대명사 whom 또는 that이 올바르다. who는 주격 관계대명사로 선행사가 사람인 것은 올바르지만 뒤에 주어 없이 바로 동사가 나와야 하기 때문에 올바르지 않다. 세 번째 문장에서 어법상 올바른 것은 with whom으로 관계대명사 that은 바로 앞에 전치사를 사용할 수 없다.

Tip '전치사 + 관계대명사'에서 that은 사용 불가

③ 선행사가 사물/동물일 경우

이렇게 활용해요

① 주격 관계대명사 which의 용법

- 선행사(사물/동물) + which + 주어 + 동사
  주격 관계대명사절(that 사용 가능)

- 선행사(사물/동물: 주어) + (which + 주어 + 동사) + 동사
  주격 관계대명사절: 삽입(that 사용 가능)

선행사가 사물이나 동물이고 which 뒤 문장에서 주어가 없을 때 which를 주격 관계대명사라고 부른다.

Tip 주격 관계대명사 which절 안에 있는 동사는 선행사와 수의 일치를 시켜야 한다.

(e) I have a dog and it is so cute.
→ I have a dog **which** [**is** / **are**] so cute.
 나는 매우 귀여운 강아지 한 마리를 가지고 있다.

위 (e) 문장에서 어법상 올바른 것은 선행사가 a dog로 단수형이기 때문에 단수 동사인 is이다.

② 소유격 관계대명사 whose의 용법

• 선행사(사물/동물) + <u>whose + 소유격 + 명사</u> ~
　　　　　　　　　　소유격 관계대명사절

선행사가 사물이나 동물이고 whose 뒤 문장에서 소유격이 없을 때 whose를 소유격 관계대명사라고 부른다.

Tip whose 대신에 관계대명사 that은 사용할 수 없다.

(f) I have a book. + Its cover is blue.
→ I have a book **and its** cover is blue.
→ I have a book [**whose** / that] cover is blue.
나는 표지가 파란색인 책을 가지고 있다.

위 (f) 문장에서 어법상 올바른 것은 선행사가 사물 a book이고, 뒤에 명사 cover로 시작하기 때문에 whose가 올바르다. that은 소유격 관계대명사로 사용할 수 없기에 올바르지 않다.

③ 목적격 관계대명사 which의 용법

• 선행사(사물/동물) + <u>which + 주어 + 타동사 + 목적어</u>
　　　　　　　　　　목적격 관계대명사절(which 생략 가능, that 사용/생략 가능)

• 선행사(사물/동물) + <u>which + 주어 + 자/타동사 ~ 전치사 + 목적어</u>
　　　　　　　　　　목적격 관계대명사절 (which 생략가능, that 사용/생략 가능)

= 선행사(사물/동물) + <u>전치사 + which + 주어 + 자/타동사</u>
　　　　　　　　　　목적격 관계대명사절 (which 생략 불가, *that 사용 불가)

Tip 영어에서 반드시 뒤에 목적어를 가져야 하는 경우는 타동사와 전치사이다.

선행사가 사물이나 동물이고 which 뒤 문장에서 목적어가 없을 때 which를 목적격 관계대명사라고 부른다.

(g) This is the dog. + I saw it yesterday.
→ This is the dog [**which** / whom] I saw yesterday.
이것은 내가 어제 보았던 강아지이다.

위 (g) 문장에서 어법상 올바른 것은 선행사가 동물 the dog이고, 뒤에 타동사 saw의 목적어가 없기 때문에 목적격 관계대명사 which가 올바르다. whom는 목적격 관계대명사로 선행사가 사람일 때 사용하기 때문에 어법상 올바르지 않다.

(h) This is the house. + I live in it.
→ This is the house [**which** / who] I live **in**.
→ This is the house [**in which** / in that] I live.
이곳은 내가 살고 있는 집이다.

위 (h) 문장 중 두 번째 문장에서 어법상 올바른 것은 선행사가 사물 the house이고, 뒤에 전치사 in의 목적어가 없기 때문에 목적격 관계대명사 which가 올바르다. 주격관계대명사 who는 '선행사(사람) + who + 동사~' 구조로 사용되기에 올바르지 않다. 세 번째 문장에서 어법상 올바른 것은 in which로 관계대명사 *that은 바로 앞에 전치사를 사용할 수 없다.

④ 선행사가 사람/사물/동물일 경우

이렇게 활용해요

① 주격 관계대명사 that의 용법

- 선행사(사람/사물/동물) + that + 주어 + 동사
  <u>주격 관계대명사절</u>
- 선행사(사람/사물/동물: 주어) + (that + 주어 + 동사) + 동사
  <u>주격 관계대명사절(삽입)</u>

주격 관계대명사 that은 선행사를 사람, 사물, 동물일 경우에 사용하기 때문에 선행사가 사람인 주격 관계대명사 who와 선행사가 사물이나 동물인 which 대신에 사용할 수 있다.

(b) Kevin is a teacher **who(= that)** teaches us English.
Kevin은 우리에게 영어를 가르치는 선생님이다.

(e) I have a dog **which(= that)** is are so cute.
나는 매우 귀여운 강아지 한 마리를 가지고 있다.

* 선행사 a dog가 의인화(Personification)된 경우 which와 that 대신 who를 사용할 수 있다.

② 목적격 관계대명사 that의 용법

- 선행사(사람/사물/동물) + that + 주어 + 타동사 + 목적어
  <u>목적격 관계대명사절</u>
- 선행사(사람/사물/동물) + that + 주어 + 자/타동사 ~ 전치사 + 목적어
  <u>목적격 관계대명사절</u>
- 선행사(사람/사물/동물) + 전치사 + that + 주어 + 자/타동사 (×)

> **Tip** that은 바로 앞에 전치사를 사용할 수 없다.

목적격 관계대명사 that 역시 목적격 관계대명사로 사용된 whom과 which처럼 사용될 수 있다.

⑤ 선행사가 없는 경우

이렇게 활용해요

① 관계대명사 what의 용법

관계대명사 what은 '**선행사를 포함한 관계대명사**'로 이때 what은 '**the thing(s) which/that, all that**'과 동일한 표현으로 '~하는 것(들)'로 해석하고, 형용사절이 아니라 **명사절**로 사용되어 문장에서 **주어, 목적어, 보어 역할**을 한다.

> **Tip** 관계대명사 who, which, that으로 바꿔 사용할 수 없다.

(i) **What** Kevin said is true.
Kevin이 말한 것은 사실이다. (주어)

(j) Kevin doesn't believe **what** she said.
Kevin은 그녀가 말한 것을 믿지 않는다. (목적어)

(k) Kevin is not **what** he was.
Kevin은 예전의 그가 아니다. (보어)

> **Tip** what Kevin said는 주어, what she said는 목적어, what he was는 보어의 역할을 한다.

② 주격 관계대명사 what의 용법
- 선행사 + what + 주어 + 동사
  _{주격 관계대명사절}
- 선행사 + what + 주어 + 동사 (×)
  _{주격 관계대명사절}

선행사를 포함했으니 선행사가 없고 what 뒤 문장에서 주어가 없을 때 what을 주격 관계대명사라고 부른다.

Tip 모든 구와 절은 단수 취급하기 때문에 구와 절이 주어로 사용된 경우에는 단수 동사를 사용해야 한다.

(l) **What** is important for success [**is** / are] hard work.
성공을 위해 중요한 것은 노력이다.

위 (l) 문장에서 관계대명사 what절이 주어로 사용되었기 때문에 동사는 단수형 is가 어법상 올바르다.

③ 목적격 관계대명사 what의 용법
- 선행사 + what + 주어 + 타동사 + 목적어
  _{목적격 관계대명사절}
- 선행사 + what + 주어 + 자/타동사 ~ 전치사 + 목적어
  _{목적격 관계대명사절}
- 선행사 + 전치사 + what + 주어 + 타동사 + 목적어
  _{목적격 관계대명사절}
- 선행사 + what + 주어 + 타동사 + 목적어 (×)
  _{목적격 관계대명사절}

선행사를 포함했으니 선행사가 없고 what 뒤 문장에서 목적어가 없을 때 what을 목적격 관계대명사라고 부른다.

(m) He couldn't believe **what** he saw.
그는 그가 본 것을 믿을 수가 없었다.

(n) **What** I'm most interested in is your personal reactions.
내가 가장 관심을 갖는 것은 네 개인적인 반응이다.

(o) She is interested in **what** he wants.
그녀는 그가 원한 것에 관심이 있다.

6 관계대명사 that의 특별 용법

이렇게 활용해요

① 관계대명사 that만 사용하는 경우

주격 관계대명사 who/which와 목적격 관계대명사 whom/which는 관계대명사 that으로 서로 바꿔 사용 가능하지만, 관계대명사 that만 사용해야 할 경우가 있다.

선행사 앞에 있는 표현	선행사	쓰임
*the + only / very / same	사람 사물 동물	주격 관계대명사: 주어가 없는 경우 목적격 관계대명사: 목적어가 없는 경우

② 관계대명사 that을 사용할 수 없는 경우

• 소유격 관계대명사: 선행사 + that + 소유격 + 명사 + 동사 (×)
　　　　　　　　　　　　　　　소유격 관계대명사절

관계대명사 that은 주격이나 목적격일 경우에 관계대명사 who(whom)와 which 대신에 사용할 수 있지만 소유격이 없기 때문에 관계대명사 who와 which의 소유격인 whose 대신에 사용할 수 없다.

(b) Kevin is an English teacher **whose(≠ that)** pronunciation is good.
Kevin은 발음이 좋은 영어 선생님이다.

(f) I have a book **whose(≠ that)** cover is blue.
나는 표지가 파란색인 책을 가지고 있다.

• 계속적 용법: 선행사, that + 주어 + 동사 (×)
　　　　　　　　　　　　목적격 관계대명사절
　　　　　　　선행사, that + 주어 + 타동사 + 목적어 (×)
　　　　　　　　　　　　　목적격 관계대명사절

관계대명사 who와 which는 계속적 용법으로 사용될 수 있지만 선행사 바로 다음에 콤마(,)를 사용한 관계대명사 that은 사용할 수 없다.

(p) I have a friend, **who(≠ that)** lives in London.
나는 친구 한 명이 있는데 그는 런던에서 산다.

• 전치사의 목적어: 선행사 + 전치사 + that + 주어 + 자/타동사 (×)
　　　　　　　　　　　　　　　　목적격 관계대명사절

더불어 전치사의 목적어로 관계대명사 who와 which의 목적격인 whom과 which 대신에 관계대명사 that은 사용할 수 없다.

(d) This is the student **with whom(≠ with that)** Kevin played baseball.
이 사람이 Kevin이 야구를 같이 했던 그 학생이다.

(h) This is the house **in which(≠ in that)** I live.
이곳은 내가 살고 있는 집이다.

> **Tip** 관계대명사 that이 계속적 용법으로 사용될 수 없고 전치사의 목적어로 사용될 수 없는 이유는 지시대명사라는 오해를 불러일으킬 수 있기 때문이다.

PART 6 관계대명사 문제풀이

TEST 1 - 24번

Jimmy's math teacher is very strict about punctuality. In fact, she said ❶that missing the school bus, which she never allows as an excuse for tardiness, is the last explanation ❷she ❸wants to hear when one student is late for school.

(a) what she never allows as an excuse
(b) that she never allows as an excuse
(c) whom she never allows as an excuse
(d) which she never allows as an excuse

답 (d)

| 해설 |

선행사 + 콤마(,) + [which + 주어 + 동사 + (목적어 없음)] + 동사
주어(사물) 〈계속적 용법〉   〈목적격 관계대명사〉: 불완전한 문장   본동사

(a) 목적격 관계대명사 what - (선행사 없음) + what + 주어 + 동사 (불완전한 문장: 목적어 없음)
(b) 목적격 관계대명사 that - 선행사(사람/사물/동물) that + 주어 + 동사 (불완전한 문장: 목적어 없음) 〈that은 계속적 용법 사용 불가〉
(c) 목적격 관계대명사 whom - 선행사(사람) + whom 주어 + 동사 (불완전한 문장: 목적어 없음)
(d) 목적격 관계대명사 which - 선행사(사물/동물) + 주어 + 동사 (불완전한 문장: 목적어 없음)

| 구문독해 |

❶목적격 종속접속사 that
- 주어 + 타동사 + 목적어[that + 주어 + 동사 ~ (완전한 문장)]
             생략 가능(~하는 것을)
❷목적격 관계대명사 that(~하는) 생략
- 선행사 + (that) + 주어 + 타동사 + (목적어 없음)
❸want + 목적어(to V): ~하는 것을 원하다

| 해석 |

Jimmy의 수학 선생님은 시간 엄수에 대해 매우 엄격하다. 실제로, 그녀는 지각의 핑계로 절대 허용하지 않는 것으로, 스쿨버스를 놓치는 것은 한 학생이 지각했을 때 듣고 싶은 마지막 설명(변명)이라고 했다.

| 어휘 |

punctuality 시간 엄수, 정확함
allow (무엇을 하도록) 허락하다, 용납하다
tardiness 느림, 지각
be late for[at] school 학교(의 수업)에 늦다

strict about ~에 엄격한
an excuse for ~에 대한 구실[변명]
explanation 설명, 변명

TEST 2 – 4번

Graham bought a bracelet ❶for his wife to wear for their 5th wedding anniversary. The bracelet, which ❷is made of platinum with 1000 sparkling diamonds, ❸caused Graham to pay a fair amount of money. The bracelet is designed by a famous designer.

(a) what is made of platinum with 1000 sparkling diamonds
(b) how it is made of platinum with 1000 sparkling diamonds
(c) which is made of platinum with 1000 sparkling diamonds
(d) that is made of platinum with 1000 sparkling diamonds

답 (c)

| 해설 |

선행사   + 콤마(,) +   [which + (주어 없음) + 동사]   +   동사
주어(사물)   〈계속적 용법〉   〈주격 관계대명사〉: 불완전한 문장   본동사

(a) 주격 관계대명사 what – what + 동사 (불완전한 문장: 주어 없음)

> **Tip** 선행사 포함[what = the thing(s) which(that)]

(b) 관계부사 how – how + 주어 + 동사 (완전한 문장)
(c) 주격 관계대명사 which – 선행사(사물/동물) which + 동사 (불완전한 문장: 주어 없음)
(d) 주격 관계대명사 that – 선행사(사람/사물/동물) that + 동사 (불완전한 문장: 주어 없음)

| 구문독해 |

❶to 부정사의 의미상 주어: 문장의 주어와 to 부정사의 주체가 다를 경우 to 부정사 앞에 'for + 목적격'을 사용함
– 주어 ~ + to V(to 부정사의 주체가 주어와 같을 경우)
– 주어 ~ for + 목적격 + to V (to 부정사의 주체가 주어와 다를 경우)

❷~로 만들어지다: be made of + 물리적 변화 / be made from + 화학적 변화 / be made with + 재료 / be made into + 제품(원료)
❸cause + 목적어 + 목적격보어(to V): ~가 ~하도록 야기시키다

| 해석 |

Graham은 결혼 5주년을 맞아 아내가 착용할 팔찌를 샀다. 1000개의 반짝이는 다이아몬드가 박힌 백금으로 만들어진 이 팔찌는 Graham이 상당한 액수의 돈을 지불하게 만들었다. 그 팔찌는 유명한 디자이너에 의해 디자인되었다.

| 어휘 |

bracelet 팔찌
platinum 백금
wedding anniversary 결혼기념일
sparkling 반짝거리는

PART 6
관계대명사 문제풀이

TEST 3 - 7번

¹Not all people who take a nap are lazy and wasting their time. A study shows ²that people ³who are fond of a short nap in the afternoon have improvements in their working memory and a 37% less chance of contracting a fatal heart condition.

(a) which are fond of a short nap in the afternoon
(b) who are fond of a short nap in the afternoon
(c) when are fond of a short nap in the afternoon
(d) whom a short nap in the afternoon are fond of

답 (b)

| 해설 |

선행사   +   [who + (주어 없음) + 동사 ~]   +   동사
주어(사람)   〈주격 관계대명사〉: 불완전한 문장   본동사

(a) 주격 관계대명사 which – 선행사(사물/동물) + which + 동사 (불완전한 문장: 주어 없음)
(b) 주격 관계대명사 who – 선행사(사람) + who + 동사 (불완전한 문장: 주어 없음)
(c) 관계부사/종속접속사 when – 관계부사: 선행사(시간) + when + (완전한 문장) / 종속접속사: 주어 + 동사 ~ when + (완전한 문장)
(d) 목적격 관계대명사 whom – 선행사(사람) + whom + 주어 + 동사 + 전치사 (불완전한 문장: 목적어 없음)

| 구문독해 |

¹부분부정: 부정어(not/never) + 전체를 나타내는 표현 (~하는 것은 아니다)
– 전체를 나타내는 표현: all(모두), always(항상), every(모든) necessarily(필연적으로), entirely(전적으로), altogether(완전히), exactly(정확히), totally(전체적으로), absolutely(절대적으로), completely(완전히), wholly(완전히)

²목적격 종속접속사 that
– 주어 + 타동사 + 목적어[that + 주어 + 동사 ~ (완전한 문장)]
           생략 가능(~하는 것을)

³주격 관계대명사 who(~하는)
– 선행사(사람) + who + 동사

| 해석 |

낮잠을 자는 모든 사람들이 게으르고 시간을 낭비하는 것은 아니다. **오후에 짧은 낮잠을 좋아하는** 사람들은 작업 기억력이 향상되고 치명적인 심장 질환에 걸릴 확률이 37% 낮다는 연구 결과가 나왔다.

| 어휘 |

take[have] a nap[siesta] 낮잠을 자다
be fond of ~을 좋아하다
contract (병에) 걸리다
a heart condition 심장 질환

waste (돈·시간·재능 등을) 낭비하다, 허비하다
improvement 향상, 개량
fatal 치명적인

예제문제

Abbey played well in the second game of the season. Her batting average, _____ remarkably since last season, is the reason why her team beat the heavily favored home team, Big Mountain.

(a) that was improved
(b) who has improved
(c) which has improved
(d) what has improved

답 (c)

| 해설 |

Her batting average를 선행사로 하고 주어 역할을 하는 주격 관계대명사 which가 필요하다. '현재 완료 + since + 과거'형식에 맞는 'has improved'동사가 필요하다. what은 선행사를 포함한 관계대명사로 선행사가 없어야 하기에 정답이 될 수 없다. 따라서 (c) which가 정답이다.

| 해석 |

Abbey는 시즌 2번째 게임에서 잘했다. 작년 시즌부터 현저하게 **향상되어 왔던** 그녀의 타율은, 그녀의 팀이 Big Mountain이라는 크게 선호되는 홈팀을 이길 수 있었던 이유이다.

| 어휘 |

batting average 타율
remarkably 현저하게
heavily 크게

PART 6 관계부사 핵심이론

📖 이렇게 나와요

Seoul National University Hospital is the oldest public hospital in South Korea. Since 1946, _____, the hospital has hired professional doctors and nurses to ensure proper treatment.

(a) when it was established
(b) how it was established
(c) where it was established
(d) that it was established

⑦ 관계부사(Relative Adverb)

'접속사 + 부사' 역할을 한다.

이런 게 답이에요

용도	선행사	관계부사	전치사 + 관계대명사
시간	the time	when	in / at / on 등 + which
장소	the place	where	in / at / on 등 + which
이유	the reason	why	for which
방법	(the way)	how	in which

※ 관계부사의 종류와 용법: 선행사에 따라 결정

💡 PLUS

1. 관계부사는 선행사를 수식하는 형용사절로 '~하는'이라고 해석한다.
2. 관계부사는 관계대명사와는 다르게 '격'이 없기 때문에 완전한 문장이 수반된다.
3. '전치사 + 관계대명사 = 관계부사'는 관계대명사절은 불완전하지만, 전치사가 관계대명사 앞에 붙으면 완전한 문장으로 사용된다.
4. the way how는 같이 사용 불가, the way, how, the way in which, the way that은 사용 가능하다.
5. 관계부사는 관계대명사처럼 제한적 용법 또는 계속적 용법으로 사용될 수 있지만, 관계부사 why와 how는 계속적 용법이 없다.

Seoul National University Hospital is the oldest public hospital in South Korea. <u>Since 1946</u>, _____, the hospital has hired professional doctors and nurses to ensure proper treatment.
<u>시간</u>

(a) when it was established 관계부사 + 주어 + 동사
(b) ~~how it was established~~
(c) ~~where it was established~~
(d) ~~that it was established~~

이렇게 활용해요

① 관계부사 where

선행사(장소) + <u>where + 주어 + 동사</u>
관계부사절(완전한 절)

This is the place **where(= at which)** I used to sleep.
여기는 내가 예전에 잠을 자던 장소이다.

Tip • 관계부사 where 대신에 that을 사용할 수 있지만 where가 더 일반적이다.
• 관계부사 where의 선행사는 '상황(Situation)'인 경우도 있다.

② 관계부사 when

선행사(시간) + <u>when + 주어 + 동사</u>
관계부사절(완전한 절)

It was the first day of June **when(= on which)** she arrived home.
그녀가 집에 도착한 것은 6월의 첫 번째 날이었다.

③ 관계부사 why

선행사(이유) + <u>why + 주어 + 동사</u>
관계부사절(완전한 절)

The reason **why(= for which)** he did it is complicated.
그가 그 짓을 한 이유는 복잡하다.

④ 관계부사 how

선행사(방법) + how + 주어 + 동사
　　　　　　　관계부사절(완전한 절)

This is **how** I solved the problem.
이것은 내가 그 문제를 해결한 방법이다.

= This is **the way** I solved the problem. (O)
= This is **the way in which** I solve the problem. (O)
= This is **the way that** I solve the problem. (O)
= This is **the way how** I solved the problem. (X)

Tip 관계부사 how와 선행사 the way는 서로 같이 사용할 수 없다.

PART 6 관계부사 문제풀이

TEST 2 – 15번

Seoul National University Hospital is the oldest public hospital in South Korea. [1]Since 1946, when it was established, the hospital has hired professional doctors and nurses to ensure proper treatment.

(a) when it was established
(b) how it was established
(c) where it was establisehd
(d) that it was established

답 (a)

| 해설 |

선행사 + 콤마(,) + [when + 주어 + 동사(수동태)]
시간   〈계속적 용법〉   〈관계부사〉: 완전한 문장

(a) 관계부사 when – 선행사(시간) + when + 주어 + 동사 (완전한 문장)
(b) 관계부사 how – how + 주어 + 동사 (완전한 문장)
(c) 관계부사 where – 선행사(장소) + where + 주어 + 동사 (완전한 문장)
(d) 종속접속사 that – that + 주어 + 동사 (완전한 문장): 명사절(주어/목적어/보어), 부사절(동사 수식)로 사용

| 구문독해 |

[1]Since + 과거 시점, 주어 + 현재완료(have p.p.): ~한 이래로 ~해오고 있다

| 해석 |

서울대병원은 한국에서 가장 오래된 공립병원이다. **설립 당시인** 1946년부터, 그 병원은 적절한 치료를 받도록 하기 위해서 전문 의사와 간호사를 고용해왔다.

| 어휘 |

public hospital 공공(공립)병원
establish 설립하다
hire 고용하다
professional 전문적인
ensure (insure) 반드시 ~하게[이게] 하다, 보장하다
proper treatment 적절한 치료

READING & VOCABULARY

G-TELP 독해 & 어휘

PART 1 과거 역사 속의 사건이나 현시대의 이야기
PART 2 잡지나 신문의 기사
PART 3 백과사전
PART 4 비즈니스 편지

G-TELP 핵심이론 | Reading & Vocabulary

독해 & 어휘에서 자주 출제되는 힌트표현을 모았다. 답을 찾는 전략과 오답을 피하는 전략을 학습하여 독해 만점에 한걸음 더 다가갈 수 있다. 지텔프에서 가장 어려운 부분으로 꼽히는 독해에서도 만점을 받을 수 있도록 학습해보자!

1 문제 구성

Reading 문항 수: 독해 & 어휘 28문항 (약 40분)

(1) Part 별 문제 구성

구분	문제	문항 번호	문항 수
Part 1	Biographical / Historical Article	53~57	5
	Vocabulary	58~59	2
Part 2	Web / Magazine Article	60~64	5
	Vocabulary	65~66	2
Part 3	Encyclopedia Article	67~71	5
	Vocabulary	72~73	2
Part 4	Business Letter	74~78	5
	Vocabulary	79~80	2

(2) 독해 문제 유형

유형	중요 단어
일치 & 불일치	not / true / false
추론	could be
Vocabulary	명사 / 동사 / 형용사

(3) 독해 내용

구분	소재 및 주제	내용 및 서술 방법
Part 1	Biographical / Historical Article 일대기	특정 인물과 관련된 사실적 이야기: 연대기순

Part 2	Web / Magazine Article 흥미 유발, 사실 전달	최근의 사회적이고 기술적인 묘사에 초점을 맞춘 잡지나 신문기사로 주로 실험/연구와 관련된 글
Part 3	Encyclopedia Article 정보 제공	지역 이름, 사물, 운동 등 다양한 소재의 생성 배경과 과거와 현재를 조명: 연대기순
Part 4	Business Letter 도움 요청	어떤 것을 설명하거나 설득하는 서신으로 주로 문제점과 해결책 제시

2 G-TELP 독해 단락 순서와 글의 구조의 공통점

(1) Part 1 공통점

단락 순서	글의 구조		공통점(인물의 소개와 성공 일대기)
1	주제문	서론	주인공 소개, 과거와 현재의 직업 및 업적 소개
2	연대기순	본론1	출생, 가족관계, 주로 유년 시절
3		본론2	사건의 전환으로 문제, 갈등, 성격, 성과 제시와 극복한 과정 설명
4		본론3	사건의 절정과 문제에 대한 해결점 제시
5	주제문(재진술)	결론	주인공 사망, 주제문 재진술, 새로운 미래 방향 제시

(2) Part 2 공통점

단락 순서	글의 구조		공통점(실험/연구에 대한 결과로 문제점에 대한 해결책 제시)
1	주제문	서론	주제문 제시, 실험/연구 방향, 실험 대상자, 연구 기관 제시, 문제점과 해결책 제시
2	실험 과정	본론1	연구 책임자, 시험 대상, 실험 조건, 연구자, 전문가 제시
3		본론2	유사 실험, 비교와 대조로 통한 문제점과 해결책 제시
4		본론3	전문가, 이론(정의), 해결책의 장점 제시
5	실험 결과 (주제문 재진술)	결론	실험의 결과를 촉구, 장려, 충고, 권장으로 제시

(3) Part 3 공통점

단락 순서	글의 구조	공통점(소재 소개 및 정보 제공)
1	서론	소재 이름, 위치, 현 상황, 과정, 설명 제시
2	본론1	유래, 생성 과정 제시
3	본론2	성장 배경과 원인, 일정 제시
4	본론3	장점과 단점 제시
5	(본론4)	현재 그리고 미래 방향 제시

(4) Part 4 공통점

단락 순서	공통점(편지 형식의 글로 문제점 및 해결책 제시)
1	보낸 날짜, 받는 사람 및 주소(편지 내용 제시)
2	인사말
3	문제점과 이에 대한 예시, 원인과 결과, 편지의 목적
4	문제점의 원인과 이에 대한 결과, 해결책, 계약의 세부 사항 제시
5	해결의 구체적 진술, 해결책 도움 요청, 팀에 대한 소개
6	해결의 구체적 진술, 해결책 도움 요청, 계약 조건 확인 후 답장
7	보내는 사람

3 G-TELP 독해 전략: Part별 공략 방법

(1) Part 1 (Biographical / Historical Article) 정답 표현

최상급	most
접속부사	nevertheless, however, thus
연도	in + 연도
특정단어	found, founder, famous, favorite
전환	change, shift
부사	also, later

(2) Part 2 (Web / Magazine Article) 정답 표현

실험/연구	study, experiment, researcher, professor, survey, observe
결과	show, conduct, response, reveal, result, find, urge, encourage, advise, suggest, discover, finding, lead to, claim, state, help, hope
비교급	more, longer, higher, stronger, easier
조건	when, if
배수 표현	twice as much ~ as
퍼센트	%
접속부사	on the other hand, in contrast, but, also, quite the opposite, not, unlike, moreover, in contrast to
유사 표현	similar
증가	increase
감소	decline
강조	in order to 동사원형
균형	balance, mutual, tie, alike, adjustable
최상급	most, biggest
인용	according to, " "
전환	exchange, new
형용사	easy
부사	easily

(3) Part 3(Encyclopedia Article) 정답 표현

접속부사	but, however, still, because
최상급	best, most, largest
전환	new
증가	grow, peak, increase
비교급	more than
감소	decline, close, shut down
시간 강조	today
첨가	as well, also
유사	similar
인용	according to
결과	eventually
인정	realize
형용사	important
순서	first

(4) Part 4(Business Letter) 정답 표현

문제점	problem, hard, difficult, difficulty, serious, problem, low, below, challenge, struggle
접속부사	but, futhermore, no, because, also, verse
확신	assured
전환	repaint
시간 강조	now
시도	in an attempt to
해결책	address, propose, suggest, appreciate, prompt response, need, surely, more importantly, critically, help, support, this letter, as agreed, assure, please, thank you
최상급	most
형용사	important
비교급	further

G-TELP 핵심이론 | Reading & Vocabulary

4 G-TELP 독해 TIP

(1) 독해 기출 정답의 Signal Word

최상급	most			nevertheless
	best			however
	the -est			in contrast
형용사	famous		대조	in contrast to
	favorite			but
	new	접속부사		quite the opposite
시간부사	later			unlike
전환동사	shift		비교	similar
	change		인과관계	thus
	exchange			also
강조	new		첨가	on the other hand
	in order to 동사원형			moreover

(2) 독해 문제 유형 및 해결책

유형	중요 단어	해결책
일치 & 불일치	not/true/false	사실성을 묻는 문제 본문과의 일치성을 묻는 문제 Paraphrasing 표현 찾기
추론	could be	전체 지문을 이해해야 함(주제 이해) 많은 시간 소요 제목에 정답의 근거 있음 다른 문제와의 상관관계 이해
Vocabulary	명사/동사/형용사	수준은 그리 높지 않음 동의어 학습 모르는 단어 유추하는 습관 선지에 나오는 단어를 밑줄 친 부분에 대입

(3) 어휘 학습의 문제점과 해결책

① 어휘 학습의 문제점

분류	설명
의미의 다양성	한 단어의 의미는 1 : 多
품사의 다양성	한 단어의 품사는 1 : 多
구조의 다양성	한 단어의 구조는 1 : 多
숙어의 다양성	하나의 숙어의 의미는 1 : 多
유의어의 다양성	비슷한 의미를 지닌 단어의 뉘앙스 구별

② 어휘 학습의 해결책

분류	설명
동의어/반의어	같고 다른 의미를 지닌 단어 정리
어휘 유추	사전 찾기 전 모르는 단어를 문맥에서 유추
빈칸에 어휘 대입	선지에 있는 단어를 빈칸에 대입
빈칸 앞뒤 단어 보기	빈칸에 있는 어휘 앞뒤 단어를 보고 적절성 판단
주어, 동사, 빈칸 단어 보기	빈칸이 속해 있는 단어의 주어와 동사와의 상관관계 판단
Paraphrasing	빈칸 단어 전후 문장을 보고 유추
전문적인 용어, 명사	암기하지 말자

G-TELP 핵심이론 | Reading & Vocabulary

(4) 오답을 피하는 전략

논리	특징
Could be true but not enough information	가장 오답률이 높은 문제로 어휘력이 필요함
True for the passage but not for the specific lines in question	전체적인 지문에 대한 정답은 되지만 질문 자체에 대한 답변은 되지 않는 오답
Factually true but not stated in the passage	지문에서 언급되지 않았다면 정답이 될 수가 없음
Half-right, Half-wrong	고득점에 필수! 선지 4개 중 2개까지 걸러냈다면 나머지 2개에서 정답을 골라야 정답
Too broad	주제보다 넓은 것은 오답
Too extreme	너무 negative하거나 strong한 것은 오답
Off-topic	주제에 완전히 벗어난 것은 오답

(5) G-TELP Reading & Vocabulary 절대 전략 Point

Point	설명
선 문제(Question), 후 지문(Paragraph)	문제 보고, 지문 보고를 반복 훈련하자
문제에서 신호어(Signal Word)를 찾자	의문사, 비교급, 최상급, 주어, 명사, 동사, 부사, 접속사 등
문제 순서와 단락의 순서는 거의 동일	각각의 문항에서 키워드 파악
신호어를 찾아서 단락에서 그 신호어와 재진술(Paraphrasing) 되는 것을 찾자	문항에서 사용된 키워드는 지문에서 paraphrasing 되거나 동일 단어로 사용
Clue Sentence에 사용된 단어가 선택지에 Paraphrasing 되어 제시	해당 지문에 대한 제목을 통해 지문 유형 파악
Note-Taking으로 간단하게 핵심 정리	Clue를 찾자
절대적인 단어가 있다면 정답에서 배제	only, never, all 등
Chunk와 Chunking(Clustering) 활용	덩어리로 묶어서 이해하자
Skimming(=Previewing)	시간 절약, 개요 파악
첫 번째 문장	'큰 그림'을 파악하는 데 중요, 그 다음 전개될 내용 예측에 중요
모든 지문을 다 본다는 생각을 버려라	모든 단락에는 중요한 문장이나 핵심 단어가 있으므로 주제문이나 키워드를 파악하는 훈련이 중요

소거법을 알자	정답의 근거는 늘 존재
정답과 오답 사이	정답의 근거에 혼동이 없는 문제 vs 혼동이 있는 문제
선택지 중 2개가 혼동되는 것	각각의 선택지를 간단화하여 비교 분석하면 보다 쉽게 정답과 오답 구분 가능
시간 관리	시험시간은 40분으로 각 세트당 10분 정도 배분 (지문 독해에 35분, 문제당 40초)
직독 직해 연습을 꾸준히, 반복적으로 하자	시간을 줄이자
평소 다양한 소재의 글을 읽는 것이 필요	배경지식을 쌓자
속도보다는 정확도에 초점	시간부족은 정확도가 떨어지기 때문
어휘 정리를 평상시에 하자	단어장을 만들자
독해 시 모르는 어휘는 문맥으로 파악하고, 때로는 과감히 넘기자	단어를 다 알 수는 없다
시험장에서 독해 문제 푸는 순서	Part 4 → Part 2 → Part 1 → Part 3 순이 효율적

FLORENCE NIGHTINGALE

- 내용 분류 – 인물의 일대기
- 주제 요약 – 영국 현대 간호학의 창시자 Nightingale

Florence Nightingale was an English social reformer, statistician, and nurse. She is best known as the founder of modern nursing. Nightingale, who was called the "Angel of the Crimea", tirelessly devoted her life to preventing disease and ensuring safety and compassionate treatment for soldiers.

Florence Nightingale was born on May 12, 1820, in Florence, Italy. As the second of two daughters, Nightingale excelled in mathematics and was able to read and write different languages at an early age. 53 (Since she was never satisfied with traditional female skills of home management,) she preferred to read the great philosophers and to engage in serious political and social discourse with her father.

Because Florence found great comfort in her religious beliefs, she viewed nursing as the suitable route to devote herself to the service of others and God. However, her attempts to seek nurse's training were thwarted by her family as 54 (an inappropriate activity for a woman of her social stature.)

Despite family opposition, Nightingale eventually enrolled as a nursing student and took a job in London in the early 1850s. At the outbreak of cholera, 55 (she improved the sanitary conditions of the hospital) and provided endless nursing support to the patients. This therefore led to lowering the hospital's death rate by two-thirds.

In 1853, during the Crimean war, she and 38 nurses sailed to the Crimea after hearing the mistreatment of the wounded soldiers and the outbreaks of cholera and malaria. 56 (Florence believed cholera was transmitted through foul air. Even after it was proven that cholera was a product of contaminated water, Florence remained firm in this belief until her death.) She was greatly influenced by the notion that poor hygiene was responsible for many deaths.

In 1860, the Nightingale School of Nurses aimed at making nursing a viable and respectable profession for women. After she passed away in 1910, the Florence Nightingale Medal was awarded to nurses for outstanding service and 57 (the Florence Nightingale Museum was established to recognize her pioneering work in nursing and her social reforms that included improving healthcare for all sections of British society.)

53 What was the reason for Nightingale's preference in philosophy or political and social discourse?

(a) her talent in home management
(b) her religious beliefs
(c) her satisfaction with the conventional role of women in household
(d) her dissatisfaction with the traditional role of women in household

54 Why was Nightingale's family against Nightingale becoming a nurse?

(a) Males did not like women working as a nurse.
(b) Working as a nurse wasn't suitable for her social position.
(c) She was far good at mathematics and languages.
(d) Her family wanted her to be a politician.

55 How did Nightingale reduce the hospital's death rate?

(a) by distributing medical supplies to war casualties
(b) by volunteering to work in patient services
(c) by promoting hygiene practices of the hospital
(d) by providing education about the prevention of infectious diseases

56 What did Nightingale strongly believe until her death?

(a) Cholera was responsible for many deaths.
(b) Cholera could be treated by nurses.
(c) Cholera was contaminated by polluted water.
(d) Cholera was contaminated by dirty air.

57 Which serves as a recognition of Nightingale's contributions to nursing and social reforms?

(a) She was honored by nursing students.
(b) Her school was designated as a heritage site.
(c) Her museum was established in England.
(d) British society named all nursing medals in her honour.

58 In the context of the passage, discourse means _____.

(a) conflict
(b) discussion
(c) lesson
(d) matter

59 In the context of the passage, viable means _____.

(a) feasible
(b) suitable
(c) sustainable
(d) versatile

TEST 1 | part 1 53~59 |

플로렌스 나이팅게일

  Florence Nightingale은 영국의 사회개혁가, 통계학자이자 간호사였다. 그녀는 현대 간호학의 창시자로 가장 잘 알려져 있다. Nightingale은 "크림 반도의 천사"로 불렸으며 질병 예방과 군인들을 위한 안전하고 온정적인 치료에 지치지 않고 자신의 삶을 바쳤다.

  Florence Nightingale은 1820년 5월 12일 이탈리아 Florence에서 태어났다. 두 딸 중 둘째 딸로, Nightingale은 수학에 뛰어났고 어린 나이에 다른 언어를 읽고 쓸 수 있었다. **53** 「**P**여성의 전통적인 가정 살림 기술에 결코 만족하지 않았기 때문에,」 그녀는 위대한 철학자들을 읽고 아버지와 진지한 정치적, 사회적 담론에 참여하는 것을 더 좋아했다.

  Florence는 종교적 믿음에서 큰 위안을 얻었기 때문에, 그녀는 간호학을 다른 사람들과 신에 대한 봉사로서 자신을 헌신하는 적절한 경로로 여겼다. 하지만, 간호사 훈련을 받으려는 그녀의 시도는 **54** 「**P**여성의 사회적 신분에 맞지 않는 부적절한 활동으로 여기는」 그녀의 가족에 의해 좌절되었다.

  가족의 반대에도 불구하고, Nightingale은 결국 간호학과에 등록했고 1850년대 초에 런던에서 일자리를 얻었다. 콜레라가 창궐하자, **55** 그녀는 「**P**병원의 위생 상태를 개선했고」 환자들에게 끝없는 간호 지원을 제공했다. 이로 인해 병원의 사망률을 3분의 2까지 낮추게 되었다.

  1853년, 크림 전쟁 기간에, 그녀와 38명의 간호사들은 부상병들에 대한 학대와 콜레라와 말라리아의 발생을 듣고 난 후 크림 반도로 항해했다. **56** 「**P**Florence는 콜레라가 더러운 공기를 통해 전염된다고 믿었다. 심지어 콜레라가 오염된 물의 산물이라는 것이 증명된 후에도, Florence는 죽을 때까지 이 믿음을 유지했다.」 그녀는 불결한 위생이 많은 사망의 원인이라는 생각에 크게 영향을 받았다.

  1860년에, Nightingale 간호학교는 간호학을 여성들에게 실행 가능하고 존경할만한 직업으로 만드는 것을 목표로 했다. 1910년 그녀가 세상을 떠난 후, Florence Nightingale 메달은 봉사정신이 투철한 간호사에게 수여되었고, **57** 「**P**Florence Nightingale 박물관은 간호 분야에서 그녀의 선구적인 업적과 영국 사회의 모든 분야에서 의료서비스 개선을 포함한 사회 개혁을 인정하기 위해 설립되었다.」

53
정보 찾기(일치)

C Nightingale이 철학 또는 정치, 사회적 담론을 선호했던 이유는 무엇인가?

(a) 가정 경영에 대한 그녀의 재능
(b) 그녀의 종교적 신념
(c) 가정에서 여성의 관습적인 역할에 대한 그녀의 만족
(d) 가정에서 여성의 전통적인 역할에 대한 그녀의 불만족

54
추론

C Nightingale의 가족이 Nightingale이 간호사가 되는 것에 반대했던 이유는 무엇인가?

(a) 남성들은 여성들이 간호사로 일하는 것을 좋아하지 않았다
(b) 간호사로 일하는 것은 그녀의 사회적 지위에 적합하지 않았다
(c) 그녀는 수학과 언어에 매우 뛰어났다
(d) 그녀의 가족은 그녀가 정치인이 되기를 원했다

55
정보 찾기(일치)

C Nightingale은 어떻게 병원의 사망률을 줄였는가?

(a) 전쟁 사상자에게 의약품을 나누어 줌으로써
(b) 환자 봉사에 지원하여
(c) 병원의 위생 관행을 증진시킴으로써
(d) 전염병 예방 교육을 제공함으로써

56
정보 찾기(일치)

C Nightingale은 죽을 때까지 무엇을 강하게 믿었는가?

(a) 콜레라가 많은 사망의 원인이 되었다
(b) 콜레라는 간호사가 치료할 수 있다
(c) 콜레라는 오염된 물에 의해 오염되었다
(d) 콜레라는 더러운 공기에 의해 전염되었다

57
추론

C Nightingale이 간호와 사회 개혁에 기여한 공로를 인정하는 것은 무엇인가?

(a) 그녀는 간호학과 학생들로부터 존경받았다
(b) 그녀의 학교는 유산으로 지정되었다
(c) 그녀의 박물관이 영국에 세워졌다
(d) 영국 사회는 그녀를 기리기 위해 모든 간호 훈장을 명명했다

58
동의어

이 글의 맥락에서 담론은 토론을 의미한다.

(a) 갈등
(b) 토론
(c) 교훈
(d) 문제

59
동의어

이 글의 맥락에서, 실행 가능한은 실현 가능한을 의미한다.

(a) 실현 가능한
(b) 적절한
(c) 유지(계속)할 수 있는
(d) 재주가 많은

KRISTI YAMAGUCHI

- 내용 분류 – 인물의 일대기
- 주제 요약 – 미국의 피겨 스케이팅 선수 Kristi Yamaguchi

Kristi Yamaguchi is an American former figure skater. Yamaguchi, a two-time world champion, the 1992 Olympic champion, and the 1992 U.S. champion, is one of the most decorated figure skaters in U.S. history.

Yamaguchi was born on July 12, 1971, in Hayward, California, to Jim, a dentist, and Carole Yamaguchi, a medical secretary. She has two siblings, Brett and Lori. Because she was born with clubfoot, she put casts on legs for much of the first year of her life and then wore corrective shoes connected by a brace for the next year.

At the age of 6, **53** Yamaguchi started skating as physical therapy for her clubfoot. Although her older sister, Lori, quickly dropped out of skating lessons, Yamaguchi's love of ice skating kept growing. In addition to helping strengthen her feet, skating also provided an outlet for Yamaguchi's shyness.

54 In order to accommodate herself to the training schedule, Yamaguchi was privately homeschooled for the first two years of high school. She started competing in junior high, and in 1986 she won the junior pairs title at the U.S. championships with her partner, Rudy Galindo. Two years later, they took home the same honor at the World Junior Championships and won the senior pairs title at the U.S. championships in 1989 and 1990.

After graduating from high school, she moved to Alberta, Canada, to train full-time with her coach, Christy Ness and **55** to focus on her singles figure skating. Yamaguchi developed her artistry and triple-triple combinations in hopes of becoming a more well-rounded skater.

56-c Yamaguchi won the 1991 World Championships. **56-b** In the 1992 Winter Olympics in Albertville, France, she won a gold medal in the ladies' singles figure skating. After her Olympic win, **56-d** Yamaguchi toured for many years with *Stars on Ice*. Yamaguchi was inducted into the U.S. Figure Skating Hall of Fame in 1998 and the World Figure Skating Hall of Fame in 1999.

57 In 1996, she established the Always Dream Foundation, a nonprofit organization that provides funding for underprivileged, disabled and at-risk children. Her foundation has been trying to make a positive difference in children's lives through education. Yamaguchi is also an author. In 2011, she published an award-winning children's book and received the Gelett Burgess Children's Book Award. In 2018, she was honored by the U.S. Olympic Committee with the Jesse Owens Olympic Spirit Award.

53 정보 찾기(일치)

What made Kristi Yamaguchi begin skating as a child?

(a) her outgoing personality
(b) watching her brother skate
(c) her parents' insistence
(d) her rotated feet

54 추론

Why most likely did Yamaguchi study from home for a couple of years of high school?

(a) because her parents could no longer pay for her training
(b) because she needed to adapt to her training schedule
(c) because she could not find a training coach
(d) because she did not cope with school stress well

55 정보 찾기(일치)

What did Yamaguchi do in Canada?

(a) She was trained for her singles figure skating.
(b) She competed at the Olympics.
(c) She was trained with Rudy Galindo.
(d) She succeeded in triple-triple combinations for the first time.

56 정보 찾기(불일치)

Which did not happen to Yamaguchi from the early 1990s onwards?

(a) She won the junior pairs title at the U.S. championships.
(b) She won first place in an Olympic event.
(c) She became a world champion.
(d) She joined *Stars on Ice*.

57 추론

What was the reason that the Always Dream Foundation was founded?

(a) to help poor kids to learn figure skating
(b) to prevent kids from crimes
(c) to help kids with financial and physical difficulties
(d) to help kids find their parents

58 동의어

In the context of the passage, well-rounded means _____.

(a) famous
(b) inspirational
(c) healthy
(d) versatile

59 동의어

In the context of the passage, underprivileged means _____.

(a) needy
(b) advantaged
(c) wealthy
(d) illiterate

TEST 2 | part 1 53~59 |

크리스티 야마구치

Kristi Yamaguchi는 미국의 전 피겨 스케이팅 선수이다. Yamaguchi는 세계 챔피언 2회 우승자로 1992년 올림픽 챔피언, 그리고 1992년 미국 챔피언이었으며, 미국 역사상 가장 많은 훈장을 받은 피겨 스케이팅 선수 중 한 명이다.

1971년 7월 12일, 캘리포니아 헤이워드에서 치과의사 Jim과 의료 담당 비서인 Carole Yamaguchi 사이에서 태어났다. 그녀는 Brett과 Lori와 자매이다. 그녀는 내반족을 가지고 태어났기 때문에, 그녀의 생애 첫해의 대부분 동안 다리에 깁스를 했고, 다음 해에는 브레이스(부목)로 연결된 교정용 신발을 신었다.

6살 때, 53 〖Yamaguchi는 ■내반족에 대한 물리치료로 스케이트를 타기 시작했다.〗 언니 Lori는 빠르게 스케이팅 강습을 그만두었지만, Yamaguchi의 빙상 스케이팅에 대한 사랑은 계속 커져만 갔다. 스케이팅은 그녀의 발을 튼튼하게 해주는 것 외에도, Yamaguchi의 수줍음을 발산하는 수단으로 제공하기도 했다.

54 〖■훈련 일정에 적응하기 위해,〗 Yamaguchi는 고등학교 첫 2년 동안 개인 홈스쿨링을 받았다. 그녀는 주니어 하이 부분에서 경쟁하기 시작했고, 1986년 그녀의 파트너인 Rudy Galindo와 함께 미국 선수권에서 주니어 페어 타이틀(2인조 선수권)을 획득했다. 2년 후, 그들은 세계 주니어 선수권 대회에서 같은 영예를 안았고 1989년과 1990년 미국 선수권 대회에서 시니어 페어 타이틀을 획득했다.

고등학교를 졸업한 후, 그녀는 코치 Cristy Ness와 함께 풀타임 훈련을 하고 55 〖■싱글 피겨 스케이팅에 집중하기 위해〗 캐나다 앨버타로 이사했다. Yamaguchi는 좀 더 다재다능한 스케이터가 되기를 바라면서 그녀의 예술성과 트리플-트리플 콤비네이션(연속 3회전의 조합)을 개발했다.

56-c 〖Yamaguchi는 ■1991년 세계 선수권 대회에서 우승했다.〗 56-b 〖■1992년 프랑스 알베르빌 동계 올림픽 여자 싱글 스케이팅에서 그녀는 금메달을 획득했다.〗 올림픽 우승 후, 56-d 〖■Yamaguchi는 *Stars on Ice*와 함께 여러 해 동안 순회공연을 했다.〗 Yamaguchi는 1998년 미국 피겨 명예의 전당과 1999년 세계 피겨 명예의 전당에 추대되었다.

57 〖1996년, 그녀는 ■혜택을 받지 못한, 장애를 가진 그리고 위험에 처한 어린이들을 위한 기금을 제공하는 비영리 단체인 Always Dream Foundation을 설립했다.〗 그녀의 재단은 교육을 통해 아이들의 삶에 긍정적인 변화를 만들기 위해 노력해 왔다. Yamaguchi는 작가이기도 하다. 2011년, 그녀는 상을 받은 어린이 책을 출판했고 게렛 버지스 아동문학상을 받았다. 2018년, 그녀는 미국 올림픽 위원회로부터 제시 오웬스 올림픽 스피릿 어워드를 수여받았다.

53 🅟 정보 찾기(일치)

ⓒ Kristi Yamaguchi가 어렸을 때 스케이트를 시작하게 된 계기는 무엇인가?

(a) 그녀의 외향적인 성격
(b) 그녀의 남동생이 스케이트 타는 것을 보면서
(c) 그녀의 부모님의 고집
(d) 그녀의 휜 발

54 🅟 추론

ⓒ Yamaguchi가 고등학교 2년 동안 집에서 공부했던 이유로 가능성이 가장 높은 것은 무엇인가?

(a) 그녀의 부모는 더 이상 그녀의 훈련비용을 지불 할 수 없었기 때문에
(b) 훈련 일정에 적응해야 했기 때문에
(c) 훈련 코치를 찾을 수 없었기 때문에
(d) 학교 스트레스에 잘 대처하지 못했기 때문에

55 🅟 정보 찾기(일치)

ⓒ Yamaguchi는 캐나다에서 무엇을 했나?

(a) 그녀는 싱글 피겨 스케이팅 훈련을 받았다
(b) 그녀는 올림픽에 참가했다
(c) 그녀는 루타 갈린도와 함께 훈련을 받았다
(d) 그녀는 처음으로 트리플-트리플 콤비네이션에 성공 했다

56 🅟 정보 찾기(불일치)

ⓒ 1990년대 초반부터 Yamaguchi에게 일어나지 않았 던 것은 무엇인가?

(a) 그녀는 미국 선수권 대회에서 주니어 페어 타이틀을 우승했다
(b) 그녀는 올림픽 종목에서 1등을 했다
(c) 그녀는 세계 챔피언이 되었다
(d) 그녀는 *Stars on Ice*에 합류했다

57 🅟 추론

ⓒ Always Dream Foundation이 설립된 이유는 무엇 인가?

(a) 가난한 아이들이 피겨스케이팅을 배울 수 있도록 돕 기 위해
(b) 범죄로부터 아이들을 보호하기 위해
(c) 경제적, 신체적 어려움을 겪고 있는 아이들을 돕기 위해
(d) 아이들이 자신의 부모를 찾도록 돕기 위해

58 🅟 동의어

이 글의 맥락에서, 다재다능한은 다재다능한을 의미 한다.

(a) 유명한
(b) 영감을 주는
(c) 건강한
(d) 다재다능한

59 🅟 동의어

이 글의 맥락에서, 혜택을 못 받는은 궁핍한을 의미 한다.

(a) 궁핍한
(b) 유리한
(c) 부유한
(d) 글을 (읽거나 쓸 줄) 모르는

TEST 3 | part 1 53~59 |

STEVE JOBS

- 내용 분류 – 인물의 일대기
- 주제 요약 – 기업가 Steve Jobs

Steve Jobs was an American inventor, designer and entrepreneur who was the co-founder, chief executive and chairman of Apple Computer. 53 [Jobs is also widely recognized as a pioneer of the personal computer revolution of the 1970s and 1980s.]

Steve Jobs was born on February 24, 1955, in San Francisco, California. As an infant, Jobs was adopted by Clara and Paul Jobs. As a boy, Paul showed his son how to take apart and reconstruct electronics, a hobby that instilled confidence, tenacity and mechanical prowess in young Jobs. While Jobs was always smart and innovative thinker, 54 [he was directionless and dropped out of college after six months and spent the next 18months dropping in on creative classes at the school. Jobs later recounted how one course in calligraphy developed his love of typography.]

In 1976, when Jobs was just 21, he and Steve Wozniak started Apple Computer in the Jobs' family garage and 55 [are credited with revolutionizing the computer industry with Apple by democratizing the technology and making machines smaller, cheaper, intuitive and accessible to everyday consumers.] In 1980, Apple Computer became a publicly-traded company, with a market value of $1.2 billion.

Despite positive sales and performance superior to IBM's PC, 56 [several products from Apple suffered significant design flaws and resulted in recalls and consumer disappointment. This pushed Jobs into a marginalized position and therefore he left Apple in 1985.] Jobs purchased Pixar Animation Studios in 1986. The studio went on to produce wildly popular movies and these films have collectively netted $4 billion. The studio merged with Walt Disney in 2006, making Jobs Disney's largest shareholder.

In 1997, Jobs returned to his post as Apple's CEO. With a new management team, altered stock options and a self-imposed annual salary of $1 a year, Jobs put Apple back on track. 57 [Jobs' ingenious products, effective branding campaigns and stylish designs caught the attention of consumers once again.] Jobs died in 2011 after battling pancreatic cancer. He was 56 years old.

53 What is Steve Jobs known for?

(a) being the second chairman of Apple Computer
(b) being the sole founder of Apple Computer
(c) being the first popular Apple Computer personality
(d) being the leader of the personal computer revolution

54 When most likely did Jobs find out about his interest in typography?

(a) upon establishing Apple Computer
(b) before he left college
(c) after dropping out of college
(d) while he was in high school

55 How did Jobs and Wozniak revolutionize the computer industry?

(a) They decreased prices of all products they were selling.
(b) They led the widespread use of computers.
(c) They competed with IBM.
(d) They made Apple as the most famous company in the world.

56 Why most likely did Jobs leave Apple?

(a) Because he was Disney's largest shareholder.
(b) Because he bought Pixar Animation Studios.
(c) Because Walt Disney was merged with Pixar Animation Studio.
(d) Because he was responsible for product recalls and customer dissatisfaction caused by faulty design.

57 How did Jobs catch consumers' eyes again?

(a) by encouraging them to buy Apple's stock
(b) by producing creative and stylish products
(c) by inspiring them to design Apple's computer
(d) by persuading them to join in a new management team

58 In the context of the passage, tenacity means _____.

(a) ambition
(b) persistence
(c) courage
(d) patience

59 In the context of the passage, democratizing means _____.

(a) distributing
(b) specifying
(c) developing
(d) popularizing

TEST 3 | part 1 53~59 |

스티브 잡스

Steve Jobs는 미국의 발명가, 디자이너 및 기업가로, Apple Computer의 공동 창립자이자 CEO 및 회장을 역임했다. 53 [Jobs는 또한 1970년대와 1980년대 개인용 컴퓨터 혁명의 선구자로 널리 알려져 있다.]

Steve Jobs는 1955년 2월 24일 캘리포니아주 샌프란시스코에서 태어났다. 유아 시절, Jobs는 Clara와 Paul Jobs에게 입양되었다. 소년 시절, Paul은 아들에게 전자제품을 분해하고 재구성하는 방법을 보여주었는데, 이는 어린 Jobs에게 자신감, 끈기, 기계적 능력을 심어주는 취미였다. Jobs는 늘 똑똑하고 혁신적인 사상가였지만, 54 [방향성이 없어 6개월 만에 대학을 중퇴했고, 이후 18개월 동안 학교에서 창의적인 수업을 들으며 시간을 보냈다. Jobs는 나중에 서예의 한 과정이 어떻게 타이포그래피에 대한 그의 사랑으로 발전되었는지 설명했다.]

Jobs가 겨우 21살이던 1976년, 그와 Steve Wozniak은 Jobs의 가족 차고에서 Apple Computer를 시작했으며, 55 [기술을 대중화시키고 기계를 더 작고 저렴하며 직관적이며 일상적인 소비자가 이용할 수 있도록 만들어 Apple과 함께 컴퓨터 산업에 혁명을 일으킨 공로로 인정받았다.] 1980년에 Apple Computer는 시장 가치가 12억 달러인 상장기업이 되었다.

IBM의 PC보다 우월한 판매실적과 성능에도 불구하고, 56 [애플의 몇몇 제품들은 중요한 디자인 결함으로 어려움을 겪었으며 그 결과 제품 회수와 소비자 실망으로 이어졌다. 이것은 Jobs를 낭떠러지로 몰아넣었고 그래서 그는 1985년에 애플을 떠났다.] Jobs는 1986년에 픽사 애니메이션 스튜디오를 인수했다. 이 스튜디오는 계속해서 엄청나게 인기 있는 영화들을 제작했고 이 영화들은 총 40억 달러의 순익을 올렸다. 이 스튜디오는 2006년 월트 디즈니와 합병하여 Jobs를 디즈니의 최대 주주로 만들었다.

1997년 Jobs는 애플의 최고 경영자로 복귀했다. 새로운 경영진과 변경된 스톡 옵션 및 자발적인 1달러 연봉으로, Jobs는 애플을 정상 궤도에 올려놓았다. 57 [Jobs의 기발한 제품, 효과적인 브랜딩 캠페인과 스타일리시한 디자인이 소비자들의 눈길을 다시 한번 사로잡았다.] Jobs는 췌장암 투병 후 2011년 사망했다. 그는 56세였다.

53 　　　　　　　　　　　　　　　　　ⓟ 정보 찾기(일치)
ⓒ Steve Jobs는 무엇으로 유명한가?

(a) Apple Computer의 두 번째 회장이 된 것
(b) Apple Computer의 유일한 설립자가 된 것
(c) 최초의 인기 있는 Apple Computer 유명인이 된 것
(d) 개인용 컴퓨터 혁명의 리더가 된 것

54 　　　　　　　　　　　　　　　　　ⓟ 정보 찾기(일치)
ⓒ Jobs는 언제 타이포그래피에 대한 그의 관심을 알게 되었는가?

(a) Apple Computer의 설립 시
(b) 그가 대학을 떠나기 전에
(c) 대학을 중퇴한 후
(d) 그가 고등학교에 다닐 때

55 　　　　　　　　　　　　　　　　　ⓟ 정보 찾기(일치)
ⓒ Jobs와 Wozniak은 어떻게 컴퓨터 산업에 혁명을 일으켰는가?

(a) 그들이 판매하는 모든 제품의 가격을 내렸다
(b) 그들은 컴퓨터의 광범위한 사용을 주도했다
(c) 그들은 IBM과 경쟁했다
(d) 그들은 애플을 전세계에서 가장 유명한 회사로 만들었다

56 　　　　　　　　　　　　　　　　　ⓟ 추론
ⓒ Jobs가 왜 애플을 떠난 이유는 무엇인가?

(a) 그는 디즈니와 최대 주주였기 때문이다
(b) 그가 픽사 애니메이션 스튜디오를 샀기 때문이다
(c) 월트 디즈니가 픽사 애니메이션 스튜디오와 합병되었기 때문이다
(d) 그에게는 디자인 결함으로 인한 제품 리콜과 고객 불만족에 대한 책임이 있기 때문이다

57 　　　　　　　　　　　　　　　　　ⓟ 정보 찾기(일치)
ⓒ Jobs는 어떻게 다시 소비자들의 눈길을 끌었는가?

(a) 애플 주식을 사도록 장려함으로써
(b) 창의적이고 세련된 제품을 생산함으로써
(c) 그들이 애플 컴퓨터를 설계하도록 고무함으로써
(d) 그들이 새로운 경영진에 합류하도록 설득함으로써

58 　　　　　　　　　　　　　　　　　ⓟ 동의어
이 글의 맥락에서, 끈기는 끈기를 의미한다.

(a) 야망
(b) 끈기
(c) 용기
(d) 인내심

59 　　　　　　　　　　　　　　　　　ⓟ 동의어
이 글의 맥락에서, 대중화시키는은 대중화시키는을 의미한다.

(a) 분배하는
(b) 명시하는
(c) 개발시키는
(d) 대중화 시키는

TEST 1 | part 2 60~66 |
LACK OF SLEEP CAUSES ALZHEIMER'S DISEASE

- 내용 분류 – 기사문
- 주제 요약 – 수면 부족인 사람들은 알츠하이머병에 걸릴 가능성이 더 높다

Several studies have found an association between sleep problems and a higher risk of accumulating beta-amyloid in the brain. 60 (The studies showed that people who do not sleep enough are more likely to suffer from Alzheimer's disease, one of the most pervasive and debilitating forms of dementia.)

Based on a research conducted by Dr. Nora D. Volkow and Dr. Gene-Jack Wang of NIH's National Institute on Alcohol Abuse and Alcoholism, 61 (after a loss of sleep, levels of beta-amyloid were 5% more than after adequate sleep.) 62 (During a good night's sleep, the brain has time to flush out the beta-amyloid known as a protein being a catalyst in Alzheimer's, whereas beta-amyloid builds up and forms plaque on the brain tissue when sleep gets interrupted at night.)

Studies published in Nature Neuroscience discovered that adults over age 65 with beta-amyloid plaques in their brain have reduced the deep sleep, even though these people do not yet show signs of Alzheimer's, like memory loss and cognitive decline.

The recent research by Dr. Kristine Yaffe, professor of psychiatry, neurology and epidemiology at the University of California, also revealed that those who reported spending less time in bed actually sleeping were more likely to develop dementia five to ten years earlier than those who got the deep sleep. However, the good news is that beta-amyloid starts to build up in healthy adults before the onset of symptoms of Alzheimer's. So, 63 (it might be possible to delay the onset of more severe symptoms of dementia, if it could be detected early through screening.)

According to Dr. Michael Twery, director of the National Heart, Lung, and Blood Institute Center on Sleep Disorders Research, 64 (for the brain to fully rest and reset,) adults generally require 7-8 hours of quality sleep, infants need 16 hours, young children need 10 hours, and teenagers should aim for 9 hours. Moreover, there is strong evidence that regular aerobic exercise helps to improve sleep quality.

60 　　　　　　　　　　　정보 찾기(일치)

What is the result of people experiencing sleep deprivation?

(a) They become dependent on alcohol.
(b) They are invulnerable to Alzheimer's disease.
(c) They have a low deposition of beta-amyloid protein plaque in the brain.
(d) They are likely afflicted with an illness associated with Alzheimer's disease.

61 　　　　　　　　　　　정보 찾기(일치)

What could happen to the brain if people are lacking in night sleep?

(a) Poor night sleep clears beta-amyloid out of the brain.
(b) The level of beta-amyloid is elevated on the brain.
(c) No plaque on the brain tissue is shown in the brain.
(d) The level of beta-amyloid is lowered on the brain

62 　　　　　　　　　　　추론

Based on the passage, which of the following statement about beta-amyloid in the brain is true?

(a) Elderly people with beta-amyloid plaques frequently experience the deep sleep.
(b) Elderly people with beta-amyloid plaques always indicate the decreased deep sleep along with signs of Alzheimer's.
(c) Adequate sleep at night prevents the formation of beta-amyloid in the brain.
(d) Adequate sleep at night promotes the formation of beta-amyloid in the brain.

63 　　　　　　　　　　　추론

According to Dr. Kristine Yaffe, how can screening be used?

(a) as a means to promptly relieve symptoms of Alzheimer's
(b) as the best way to get the deep sleep
(c) as a means to quickly discover beta-amyloid in adults
(d) as a means to measure the severity of symptoms in adults

64 　　　　　　　　　　　추론

Why are recommended hours of sleep different depending on age?

(a) because the brain needs time to remove plaques on brain tissues
(b) because the brain needs time to arrange the function of each body organ
(c) because the brain needs time to relax and return to its original and functioning condition
(d) because each body organ burns a different amount of calories

65 　　　　　　　　　　　동의어

In the context of the passage, interrupted means _____.

(a) disturbed　　(b) obstructed
(c) shortend　　(d) postponed

66 　　　　　　　　　　　동의어

In the context of the passage, onset means _____.

(a) treatment　　(b) end
(c) beginning　　(d) peak

TEST 1 | part 2 60~66 |

수면 부족은 알츠하이머병을 유발한다

여러 연구에서 수면 문제와 뇌에 베타 아밀로이드가 축적될 높은 위험 사이의 연관성을 발견했다. 60 연구에 따르면 〔잠을 충분히 자지 못하는 사람들은 가장 널리 퍼지고 쇠약하게 만드는 치매 형태 중 하나인 알츠하이머병에 걸릴 가능성이 더 높다는 것을 보여주었다.〕

NIH's National Institute on Alcohol Abuse and Alcoholism(NIH의 국립 알코올 남용 및 알코올 중독 연구소)의 Nora D. Volkow 박사와 Gene-Jack Wang 박사가 수행한 연구에 따르면, 61 〔수면 부족 후 베타 아밀로이드 수치는 적절한 수면 후보다 5% 더 높았다.〕 62 〔숙면을 취하는 동안, 뇌는 알츠하이머병의 촉매 역할을 하는 단백질로 알려진 베타-아밀로이드를 씻어 낼 시간이 있는 반면, 밤에 수면이 방해받으면 베타-아밀로이드는 뇌 조직에 축적되어 플라크를 형성한다.〕

Nature Neuroscience(네이처 뉴로사이언스)에 발표된 연구에 따르면 뇌 속에 베타 아밀로이드 플라크가 있는 65세 이상의 성인들이 아직 기억력 상실과 인지력 저하 같은 알츠하이머 증세를 보이지 않더라도 숙면이 줄었다는 것을 발견했다.

캘리포니아 대학의 정신의학, 신경학 및 역학 교수인 Kristine Yaffe 박사의 최근 연구는 또한 실제 수면시간에 침대에서 보내는 시간이 더 적다고 보고한 사람들은 숙면을 취한 사람들보다 5년에서 10년 더 일찍 치매에 걸릴 가능성이 높다는 것을 밝혀냈다. 하지만, 좋은 소식은 베타 아밀로이드가 알츠하이머 증상이 시작되기 전에 건강한 성인들에게서 축적되기 시작한다는 것이다. 따라서, 63 〔검사를 통해 조기에 발견될 수 있다면 치매의 더 심각한 증상의 시작을 늦출 수 있을 것이다.〕

National Heart, Lung, and Blood Institute on Sleep Disorders Research Center(국립 심장, 폐, 혈액 연구소 수면 장애 연구 센터)의 책임자인 Michael Twery 박사에 따르면, 64 〔뇌가 완전히 쉬고 재설정하기 위해〕 일반적으로 성인은 7~8시간의 양질의 수면을 필요로 하고, 유아들은 16시간이 필요하고, 어린 아이들은 10시간이 필요하고, 청소년들은 9시간을 목표로 해야 한다. 게다가 규칙적인 유산소 운동이 수면의 질을 향상시키는 데 도움이 된다는 강력한 증거가 있다.

60   ⓟ 정보 찾기(일치)

ⓒ 수면 부족을 경험한 사람들의 결과는 무엇인가?

(a) 그들은 알코올에 의존하게 된다
(b) 그들은 알츠하이머병에 취약하지 않다
(c) 그들은 뇌에 베타 아밀로이드 단백질 플라크의 수치가 낮다
(d) 그들은 알츠하이머 병 관련 질병으로 고통받을 가능성이 높다

61   ⓟ 정보 찾기(일치)

ⓒ 만약 사람들이 야간 수면이 부족하면 뇌에 무슨 일이 생기는가?

(a) 잠을 잘 못 자면 베타 아밀로이드가 뇌에서 사라진다
(b) 뇌에 베타 아밀로이드 수치가 상승한다
(c) 뇌 조직에는 플라크가 없다
(d) 뇌에서 베타 아밀로이드의 수치가 낮아진다

62   ⓟ 추론

ⓒ 이 글에 따르면, 다음 중 뇌의 베타 아밀로이드에 관한 설명 중 어떤 것이 사실인가?

(a) 베타 아밀로이드 플라크가 있는 노인들은 자주 숙면을 경험한다
(b) 베타 아밀로이드 플라크가 있는 노인들은 항상 알츠하이머의 징후와 함께 숙면의 감소를 나타낸다
(c) 충분한 야간 수면은 뇌에서 베타 아밀로이드의 형성을 막는다
(d) 충분한 수면은 뇌에서 베타 아밀로이드의 형성을 촉진한다

63   ⓟ 추론

ⓒ Kristine Yaffe 박사에 따르면, 검사는 어떻게 사용할 수 있는가?

(a) 알츠하이머 증상을 즉시 완화하기 위한 수단으로써
(b) 숙면을 취하는 최선의 방법으로
(c) 성인들에게 베타 아밀로이드를 조기 발견하기 위한 수단으로써
(d) 성인의 증상의 심각성을 측정하기 위한 수단으로써

64   ⓟ 추론

ⓒ 나이에 따라 권장 수면 시간이 다른 이유는 무엇인가?

(a) 왜냐하면 뇌는 뇌조직의 플라크들을 제거할 시간이 필요하기 때문이다
(b) 왜냐하면 뇌는 각 신체 기관의 기능을 정리할 시간이 필요하기 때문이다
(c) 왜냐하면 뇌는 긴장을 풀고 본래의 기능적인 상태로 돌아갈 시간이 필요하기 때문이다
(d) 왜냐하면 각 신체 기관은 다른 양의 칼로리를 소모하기 때문이다

65   ⓟ 동의어

이 글의 맥락에서, 방해받는다는 방해받다를 의미한다.

(a) 방해받다   (b) 차단되다
(c) 짧아지다   (d) 연기되다

66   ⓟ 동의어

이 글의 맥락에서, 시작은 시작을 의미한다.

(a) 치료   (b) 끝
(c) 시작   (d) 절정

TEST 2 | part 2 60~66 |
STUDIES FIND THAT COW'S MILK MAY PREVENT MUSCLE LOSS

- 내용 분류: 기사
- 주제 요약: 근육 손실을 예방하는 우유

Recent studies have found that cow's milk is good for building muscle. The findings show that milk prevents the loss of muscle mass and is effective in increasing muscle strength.

In a study published in the American Journal of Clinical Nutrition, researchers from McMaster University found that 60 the daily consumption of cow's milk after workout including resistance exercise promotes greater muscle growth than soy or sport drinks.

To conduct the study, for 12 weeks, 56 young male participants were asked to drink either cow's milk, a soy protein drink or a carbohydrate drink after completing weight lifting workouts. 61 The results showed that the group drinking the cow's milk came out on top in terms of muscle gain with an estimated 40 percent more muscle mass than the soy protein drinkers. In addition, milk drinkers gained 63 percent more muscle mass than the carbohydrate drinkers.

An earlier study demonstrated the effects of cow's milk consumption on young athletic women. Researchers from Texas University found that only women in the cow's milk consumption group experienced greater muscle gains. After a workout, regular consumption of cow's milk is likely to support the build-up of muscle mass. This is because cow's milk contains two types of proteins named casein and whey. Most importantly, 62 casein protein provides a high amount of leucine which is responsible for muscle growth by reducing protein breakdown.

The studies shed light on the type of milk people drink in recent years. Stuart Phillips, associate professor of kinesiology from the American College of Sports Medicine believes 63 drinking whole fat milk after lifting weights promotes muscle growth 2.8 times more than drinking skim milk does.

However, the studies in established literature were mainly based on consuming cow's milk-based protein after workouts. Thus, the study was only able to conclude the effectiveness of cow's milk for increasing muscle mass. 64 The researchers hope to do future studies about how other proteins like eggs or lean meats affect muscle growth after workouts.

60 　　　　　　　　　　　　　　정보 찾기(일치)

What did researchers find out?

(a) that cow's milk helps build more muscle
(b) that people who prefer to drink cow's milk are healthy
(c) that cow's milk helps weight loss
(d) that cow's milk is better than soy and sports drinks

61 　　　　　　　　　　　　　　추론

How could the cow's milk drinking group be described?

(a) They gain weight easier than the soy and carbohydrate drinking groups.
(b) They have 63 percent more muscle growth than the soy protein drinkers.
(c) They drink a large amount of milk after weight lifting workouts.
(d) They have greater muscle mass than the soy and carbohydrate drinking groups.

62 　　　　　　　　　　　　　　추론

Why does drinking cow's milk enhance muscle mass?

(a) because cow's milk has the only one protein that cannot be found in other kinds of drinks
(b) because cow's milk accelerates protein breakdown
(c) because cow's milk has casein protein that gives high concentrations of leucine
(d) because cow's milk hinders the production of proteins in the muscle

63 　　　　　　　　　　　　　　정보 찾기(일치)

What do the recent studies tell cow's milk drinkers?

(a) Whole fat milk is more effective than skim milk if drinkers want to build muscle mass.
(b) Skim milk is more effective than whole milk if drinkers want to build muscle mass.
(c) Drinkers need to do lifting weights if they want to build muscle mass.
(d) Drinking both whole fat milk and skim milk before lifting weights is highly recommended.

64 　　　　　　　　　　　　　　정보 찾기(일치)

What does the article suggest that the researchers should do in the future?

(a) The researchers should measure the period muscle growth after workouts.
(b) The researchers should investigate the influences of other kinds of proteins on muscle growth after workouts.
(c) The researchers should compare advantages and disadvantages of each protein drink.
(d) The researchers should prove that the ingestion of eggs or lean meats is better than drinking cow's milk in terms of health.

65 　　　　　　　　　　　　　　동의어

In the context of the passage, consumption means _____.

(a) waste   (b) expenditure
(c) intake   (d) utilization

66 　　　　　　　　　　　　　　동의어

In the context of the passage, demonstrated means _____.

(a) concealed   (b) determined
(c) measured   (d) proved

연구에 따르면 우유는 근육 손실을 예방한다

최근 연구에 따르면 우유는 근육을 만드는 데 좋다. 연구 결과에 따르면 우유는 근육량 손실을 방지하고 근력을 높이는 데 효과적이다.

American Journal of Clinical Nutrition(미국 임상 영양 저널)에 발표된 연구에서, McMaster University의 연구원들은 60 【근력증강운동을 포함한 운동 후 우유를 매일 섭취하면 콩이나 스포츠 음료보다 근육 성장이 더 커진다는】 사실을 발견했다.

이 연구를 수행하기 위해, 12주 동안 56명의 젊은 남성 참가자들은 역도 운동을 마친 후 우유, 콩 단백질 음료 또는 탄수화물 음료를 마시도록 요청받았다. 61 【그 결과 우유를 마신 그룹이 콩 단백질 음료를 마신 사람들보다 약 40% 더 많은 근육량으로 근육 증가 측면에서 1위를 차지했다. 게다가, 우유를 마신 사람은 탄수화물 음료를 마시는 사람보다 63% 더 많은 근육량을 얻었다.】

이전 연구에서 우유 소비가 젊은 운동 여성에게 미치는 영향을 입증했다. 텍사스 대학교의 연구원들은 우유 소비 집단의 여성만이 더 큰 근육 증가를 경험한 것을 발견했다. 운동 후, 우유를 규칙적으로 섭취하면 근육량의 증가에 도움이 될 것으로 예상된다. 이는 우유에 카세인과 유장이라는 두 종류의 단백질이 들어 있기 때문이다. 가장 중요한 것은, 62 【카세인 단백질이 단백질 분해를 줄임으로써 근육 성장을 담당하는 다량의 류신을 제공한다는 것이다.】

이 연구는 최근 몇 년 동안 사람들이 마시는 우유의 종류를 밝혀냈다. 미국 스포츠 의학 대학의 운동 생리학 부교수인 Stuart Phillips는 역도를 한 후 63 【전유(지방을 빼지 않은)를 마시는 것이 탈지유를 마시는 것보다 근육 성장을 2.8배 더 촉진한다】고 믿고 있다.

그러나 기존 문헌의 연구는 주로 운동 후 우유 기반 단백질을 섭취하는 것을 기초로 하고 있다. 따라서, 이 연구는 근육량 증가에 우유가 미치는 영향을 판단하는 데만 그쳤다. 64 【연구원들은 계란이나 살코기와 같은 다른 단백질이 운동 후 근육 성장에 어떻게 영향을 미치는지에 대하여 향후 연구를 수행하기를 희망한다.】

60 정보 찾기(일치)

연구원들은 무엇을 알아냈는가?

(a) 우유가 더 많은 근육을 만드는 데 도움이 된다
(b) 우유를 마시는 것을 선호하는 사람들이 건강하다
(c) 우유가 체중 감량에 도움이 된다
(d) 우유가 콩과 스포츠 음료보다 낫다

61 추론

우유를 마시는 집단을 어떻게 묘사할 수 있는가?

(a) 그들은 콩과 탄수화물을 마시는 집단보다 더 쉽게 체중이 늘어난다
(b) 그들은 콩 단백질 음료를 마시는 사람들보다 63% 더 많은 근육 성장을 가진다
(c) 그들은 역도 운동 후에 우유를 많이 마신다
(d) 그들은 콩과 탄수화물 음료를 마시는 집단보다 더 많은 근육량을 가진다

62 추론

왜 우유를 마시는 것이 근육량을 증가시키는가?

(a) 우유는 다른 종류의 음료에서 찾을 수 없는 유일한 단백질을 가지고 있기 때문에
(b) 우유는 단백질 분해를 촉진하기 때문에
(c) 우유는 높은 농도의 류신을 제공하는 카세인 단백질을 함유하고 있기 때문에
(d) 우유는 근육 내 단백질 생성을 방해하기 때문에

63 정보 찾기(일치)

최근의 연구는 우유를 마시는 사람들에게 무엇을 말해주는가?

(a) 근육량을 증가시키고 싶다면 전유가 탈지유보다 더 효과적이다
(b) 근육량을 증가시키기를 원한다면 탈지유는 전유보다 더 효과적이다
(c) 근육량을 증가시키려면 역도를 해야 한다
(d) 역기를 들기 전에 전유와 탈지유를 둘 다 마시는 것이 매우 권장된다

64 정보 찾기(일치)

이 기사는 연구원들이 미래에 무엇을 해야 한다고 제안하는가?

(a) 연구원들은 운동 후 근육 성장 기간을 측정하여야 한다
(b) 연구원들은 운동 후 근육 성장에 미치는 다른 단백질의 영향을 조사하여야 한다
(c) 연구원들은 각 단백질 음료의 장단점을 비교해야 한다
(d) 연구원들은 건강 측면에서 계란이나 살코기를 섭취하는 것이 우유를 마시는 것보다 낫다는 것을 증명해야 한다

65 동의어

이 글의 맥락에서, 소비는 섭취를 의미한다.

(a) 낭비   (b) 지출
(c) 섭취   (d) 활용

66 동의어

이 글의 맥락에서, 입증했다는 증명했다를 의미한다.

(a) 숨겼다   (b) 결정했다
(c) 측정했다   (d) 증명했다

TEST 3 | part 2 60~66 |
STUDY SHOWS AUTISTIC CHILDREN TEND TO BE OBESE

- 내용 분류: 기사
- 주제 요약: 아동의 비만과 자폐증의 연관성

Recent studies have found a link between obesity and autism among children. The studies showed that 60 the risk of obesity is highest among the children with autism and childhood obesity further raises the risk of several disorders like diabetes, heart disease, sleep apnoea, menstrual irregularities and orthopaedic problems.

Based on a study conducted by Chanaka N. Kahathuduwa, clinical assistant professor in the department of psychiatry at Texas Tech University Health Sciences Center, children with autism have a 41.1% greater risk for development of obesity than typically developing children. Also, the prevalence of obesity among children and adolescents between ages 2 and 19 years in the United States is 16.3% and the prevalence of those that are overweight is 31.9%.

In the study performed by Carol Curtin, co-director of the Healthy Weight Research Network at the University of Massachusetts, 61 children with autism have unusual eating habits and prefer energy dense foods including high fat foods. It is possible that these eating patterns may contribute to the development of obesity. Particularly, 63 children with severe autism are more than three times as likely to be obese as those with mild autism because they tend to be less active and have more restricted diets than other autistic children.

Meanwhile, a survey by Tanja Kral, associate professor of nursing at the University of Pennsylvania in Philadelphia found that it is still unclear why children with autism are more likely to be obese than their peers. The study carried out by researchers from Duke University Medical Center and Virginia Commonwealth University revealed that 62 women who were overweight before they became pregnant have about a one-third increased risk of having a child with autism, compared with normal-weight women.

64 However, many studies are unable to prove there is a direct link between autism and women who were overweight or obese before falling pregnant. This is because the findings are based on observational studies that varied widely in their studied populations and it is possible that genetics, health, lifestyle and other family environmental factors could have played a role in the likelihood of having a child with autism.

60 정보 찾기(일치)

What is the result of children with autism?

(a) They have a greater risk of suffering from a number of disorders.
(b) They have a greater risk of being overweight or obese.
(c) They are highly affected by many disorders.
(d) They have a lesser risk of being overweight or obese.

61 정보 찾기(일치)

According to Carol Curtin, which of the following statement about autistic children's eating patterns is true?

(a) Their eating habits are similar to typically developing children.
(b) They avoid eating foods that have the high amount of energy or calories per gram of food.
(c) They enjoy eating foods that have the low amount of energy or calories per gram of food.
(d) They favor foods that have the high amount of energy or calories per gram of food.

62 추론

What could happen to children born to mothers who were severly obese before pregnancy?

(a) They could be more likely to be underweight than their friends.
(b) They might be more vulnerable to autism.
(c) They could be within the healthy weight range.
(d) They could be fatter than their friends.

63 추론

Why are children with high level autism more likely to be obese than those with low level of autism?

(a) because they do not stay active as much as those with low level of autism
(b) because they spend more time eating than those with low level of autism
(c) because they do not have a diet that limits or increases specific foods
(d) because they take medications that increase hunger

64 정보 찾기(일치)

What do many researchers find it hard to demonstrate?

(a) how exactly pregnant women in different ages are associated with autism
(b) how normal-weight women and obese women are different while they are pregnant
(c) how exactly women who were obese before having a baby are associated with autism
(d) how exactly women who were obese after pregnancy are having autistic children

65 동의어

In the context of the passage, typically means _____.

(a) mainly   (b) normally
(c) regularly   (d) frequently

66 동의어

In the context of the passage, likelihood means _____.

(a) consequence   (b) perception
(c) probability   (d) severity

TEST 3 | part 2 60~66 |

연구에 따르면 자폐 아동은 비만 경향이 있다

　최근 연구에 따르면 아동의 비만과 자폐증 사이의 연관성이 발견되었다. 연구에 따르면 60 (비만의 위험은 자폐 아동에서 가장 높으며, 소아 비만은 당뇨병, 심장병, 수면 무호흡증, 생리불순 및 정형외과적 문제 같은 여러 장애의 위험을 더욱 높인다고 나타났다.)

　텍사스 공대 보건과학센터 정신의학과 Charaka N. Kahathuduwa와 임상조교수가 실시한 연구에 따르면, 자폐 아동은 비만의 발병 위험이 정상적인 발달 아동보다 41.1% 더 높다. 또한, 미국의 2세에서 19세 사이의 아동과 청소년의 비만율은 16.3%이고 과체중인 비만율은 31.9%이다.

　매사추세츠 대학교의 Healthy Weight Research network 공동 책임자인 Carol Curtin이 수행한 연구에서, 61 (자폐 아동은 특이한 식습관을 가지고 있으며 고지방 식품을 포함한 에너지 밀도가 높은 음식을 선호한다.) 이런 식습관이 비만의 발달에 원인이 될 수도 있다. 특히, 63 (중증 자폐 아동은 다른 자폐 아동보다 활동성이 떨어지고 식습관이 더 제한돼 있어 경증 자폐 아동보다 비만일 확률이 3배 이상 높다.)

　한편, 필라델피아 펜실베이니아대 간호학과 Tanja Kral 부교수의 조사결과 자폐 아동이 또래 아동보다 비만 가능성이 더 높은 이유는 아직 불분명한 것으로 나타났다. 듀크 대학교 의료 센터와 버지니아 연방 대학교의 연구원이 실시한 연구에 따르면 62 (임신 전에 과체중이었던 여성들이 정상 체중의 여성들에 비해 자폐아를 출산할 위험이 약 3분의 1 증가했다.)

　64 (하지만, 많은 연구들은 자폐증과 임신하기 전에 과체중이거나 비만이었던 여성 사이에 직접적인 연관이 있다는 것을 증명하지 못하고 있다.) 이는 연구결과가 연구 집단에서 광범위하게 변화한 관찰연구를 바탕으로 한 연구결과로, 자폐 아동 출산 가능성에 유전학, 건강, 생활습관 및 다른 가정 환경적 요인이 작용했을 가능성이 있다.

60 정보 찾기(일치)

자폐 아동의 결과는 무엇인가?

(a) 그들은 많은 장애로 고통받을 위험이 더 크다
(b) 그들은 과체중이나 비만이 될 위험이 더 크다
(c) 그들은 많은 장애의 영향을 많이 받는다
(d) 그들은 과체중이나 비만이 될 위험이 더욱 적다

61 정보 찾기(일치)

Carol Curtin에 따르면, 자폐 아동들의 식습관에 대한 다음 진술 중 사실은 무엇인가?

(a) 그들의 식습관은 정상적으로 발달하는 아동과 유사하다
(b) 그들은 음식 1g당 에너지 또는 칼로리가 높은 식품의 섭취를 피한다
(c) 그들은 음식 1g당 에너지 또는 칼로리가 적은 식품 섭취를 즐긴다
(d) 그들은 음식 1g당 에너지 또는 칼로리가 높은 식품을 선호한다

62 추론

임신 전에 심하게 비만인 엄마들 사이에서 태어난 아동에게 무슨 일이 일어날 수 있는가?

(a) 그들은 친구보다 저체중일 가능성이 더 높다
(b) 그들은 자폐증에 더 취약할 수 있다
(c) 그들은 건강한 체중 범위 내에 있을 수 있다
(d) 그들은 친구들보다 더 뚱뚱할 수 있다

63 추론

중증 자폐 아동이 경증 자폐 아동보다 더 비만이 될 가능성이 높은가?

(a) 그들은 경증 자폐 아동만큼 활동적이지 않기 때문에
(b) 그들은 경증 자폐 아동보다 식사에 더 많은 시간을 보내기 때문에
(c) 그들은 특정 음식을 제한하거나 증가시키는 식단이 없기 때문에
(d) 그들은 배고픔을 증가시키는 약을 복용하기 때문에

64 정보 찾기(일치)

많은 연구자들이 증명하기가 어렵다고 생각하는 것은 무엇인가?

(a) 연령대가 다른 임산부가 자폐증과 정확히 연관되는 정도
(b) 정상 체중 여성과 비만 여성이 임신하는 동안 어떻게 다른가
(c) 아이를 갖기 전에 비만이었던 여성들이 자폐증과 정확히 얼마나 관련이 있는가
(d) 임신 후 비만이었던 여성이 자폐 아동을 정확히 어떻게 낳고 있는지

65 동의어

이 글의 맥락에서, 일반적으로는 정상적으로를 의미한다.

(a) 주로
(b) 정상적으로
(c) 정기적으로
(d) 자주

66 동의어

이 글의 맥락에서, 가능성은 가망성을 의미한다.

(a) 결과
(b) 인식
(c) 가망성
(d) 심각성

GREAT DANE

  The Great Dane is a breed of German origin. The Great Dane descends from hunting dogs known from the Middle Ages and 67 is recognized as the largest dog breed in terms of height.

  Great Danes are huge. 68-b Males can reach 87cm tall and weigh anywhere from about 50 to 54kg, while females may be 81cm tall and weigh from about 45 to 50kg. 68-a Their massive head is narrow and flat on top. The ears drop forward. The neck is long and strong. 68-c The body is long and muscular, and the front legs are straight.

  The Great Dane is a giant breed. The breed is thought to have been around for more than 400 years. 69 They were bred by German nobility to protect country estates and hunt wild boar. In the 18th century, Great Danes were prestigious guardians of estates and carriages. In 1880, the Germans banned the name "Great Dane" and called the breed "Deutsche Dogge", which means German mastiff, however, the breed continues to be called Great Dane in English speaking countries.

  70 Great Danes have a fast metabolism. This results in more energy and food consumption than in small breeds. Because of their size, their average lifespan is 6 to 8 years. A health condition known as bloat, which involves gas buildup and possible twisting of the stomach, is the number-one killer of Danes. Since these dogs do grow at a rapid pace, it takes a while for the bones and joints of Great Danes to become stable, so puppies are not allowed to jump and run until they are at least 18 months old.

  Great Danes are considered gentle giants. They are moderately playful, affectionate and good with children. However, 71 they must be obedience trained to assure they are manageable when fully grown because some individuals in the breed can be aggressive with dogs they do not know, although Great Danes generally get along with other animals.

  These dogs are primarily family pets and have become popular today among city dwellers who keep them to help guard against robbers.

67 　　　　　　　　　　　P 정보 찾기(일치)

C Which statement best characterizes the Great Dane?

(a) It is the first hunting dog in the Middle Ages.
(b) It lives in Germany.
(c) It is the world's tallest dog.
(d) It is the world's heaviest dog.

68 　　　　　　　　　　　P 정보 찾기(불일치)

C Which of the following descriptions about the Great Dane is false?

(a) that the top of its head is flat
(b) that a male dog is about 6cm taller than a female dog
(c) that its body is made up of firm muscles
(d) that it can walk upright on his hind legs

69 　　　　　　　　　　　P 추론

C Why were Great Danes raised by Germans holding the highest social status in the 18th century?

(a) because Great Danes were able to keep properties safe from danger
(b) because raising Great Danes could cost a lot of money
(c) because Great Danes ate wild boars
(d) because Germans did not want Great Danes to be called German mastiff

70 　　　　　　　　　　　P 정보 찾기(일치)

C What is the major reason for the Great Dane's high intake of food compared to small dogs?

(a) its ability to store food in the stomach for a long time
(b) its ability to convert food into energy at a very fast rate
(c) its body condition called bloat
(d) its short lifespan

71 　　　　　　　　　　　P 정보 찾기(일치)

C How most likely do Great Danes become compliant?

(a) by playing with other animals
(b) by a small amount of food
(c) through obedience instruction
(d) through animal hunting

72 　　　　　　　　　　　P 동의어

In the context of the passage, moderately means _____.

(a) gradually
(b) hugely
(c) massively
(d) reasonably

73 　　　　　　　　　　　P 동의어

In the context of the passage, aggressive means _____.

(a) hostile
(b) friendly
(c) obsessive
(d) addictive

TEST 1 | part 3 67~73 |

그레이트 데인

그레이트 데인은 독일 태생의 한 품종이다. 그레이트 데인은 중세 시대에 알려진 사냥개에서 유래했으며 67 (P 키 측면에서 가장 큰 개 품종으로 인정받고 있다.)

그레이트 데인은 거대하다. 68-b (P수컷은 키가 87cm에 이르며 몸무게는 약 50~54kg 정도이며, 반면에 P암컷은 키가 81cm,) 몸무게는 약 45~50kg 정도이다. 68-a (P그들의 거대한 머리는 좁고 정수리는 평평하다.) 귀는 앞으로 떨어진다. 목이 길고 튼튼하다. 68-c (P몸은 길고 근육질이며 앞다리는 곧다.)

그레이트 데인은 거대한 품종이다. 이 품종은 400년 이상 된 것으로 여겨진다. 69 (그들은 P시골 토지를 보호하고 야생 멧돼지를 사냥하기 위해 독일 귀족들에 의해 길러졌다.) 18세기에, 그레이트 데인은 토지와 마차를 지키는 명망있는 감시견이었다. 1880년에, 독일인들은 "Great Dane"이라는 이름을 금지하고, 그 품종을 독일어 마스티프를 뜻하는 "Deutsche Dogge"라고 불렀지만, 영어권 국가에서는 그레이트 데인이라고 계속 불린다.

70 (그레이트 데인은 P신진대사가 빠르다.) 그 결과 작은 품종보다 더 많은 에너지와 음식 소비로 이어진다. 그들의 크기 때문에, 그들의 평균 수명은 6년에서 8년이다. 가스 축적과 복부의 뒤틀림 가능성을 수반하는 팽창으로 알려진 건강 상태는 데인의 가장 큰 사망 원인이다. 이러한 개들은 빠른 속도로 자라기 때문에, 그레이트 데인의 뼈와 관절이 안정되기까지 시간이 걸리는 동안, 강아지들은 적어도 생후 18개월이 될 때까지는 점프하거나 뛰는 것이 허용되지 않는다.

그레이트 데인은 온화한 거인으로 여겨진다. 그들은 적당히 장난기 많고, 애정이 많으며, 아이들과 잘 지낸다. 하지만, 그레이트 데인이 일반적으로 다른 동물들과 잘 지내기는 하지만, 어떤 개들은 모르는 개들에게 공격적일 수 있기 때문에, 71 (그들은 완전히 자랐을 때 그들이 순종할 수 있다는 것을 확실히 하기 위해 P복종 훈련을 받아야 한다.)

이러한 개들은 주로 애완견으로 오늘날 도시 거주자들 사이에서 강도를 막기 위해 인기가 있다.

67 정보 찾기(일치)

어떤 진술이 그레이트 데인을 가장 잘 묘사하는가?

(a) 이 개는 중세 최초의 사냥개이다
(b) 이 개는 독일에 산다
(c) 이 개는 세계에서 가장 키가 큰 개이다
(d) 이 개는 세계에서 가장 무거운 개이다

68 정보 찾기(불일치)

그레이트 데인에 대한 다음 설명 중 잘못된 것은 무엇인가?

(a) 정수리가 평평하다는 것을
(b) 수컷이 암컷보다 약 6cm 더 크다는 것을
(c) 그것의 몸은 단단한 근육으로 이루어져 있다는 것을
(d) 그것의 뒷다리로 똑바로 걸을 수 있다는 것을

69 추론

그레이트 데인이 18세기에 가장 높은 사회적 지위를 가진 독일인에 의해 길러진 이유는 무엇인가?

(a) 왜냐하면 그레이트 데인이 위험으로부터 자산을 안전하게 지킬 수 있었기 때문이다
(b) 크레이트 데인을 키우는 데는 많은 돈이 들 수 있거 때문이다
(c) 왜냐하면 그레이트 데인이 멧돼지를 먹었거 때문이다
(d) 왜냐하면 독일인들은 그레이트 데인이 독일 마스티프라고 불리는 것을 원하지 않았거 때문이다

70 정보 찾기(일치)

그레이트 데인이 작은 개에 비해 음식을 많이 섭취하는 주된 이유는 무엇인가?

(a) 위장에 오랫동안 음식을 저장할 수 있는 능력
(b) 음식을 매우 빠른 속도로 에너지로 바꾸는 능력
(c) 팽창이라고 불리는 신체 상태
(d) 크것와 짧은 수명

71 정보 찾기(일치)

그레이트 데인은 어떻게 더 잘 순응할 수 있는가?

(a) 다른 동물들과 놀면서
(b) 적은 사료량으로
(c) 복종의 가르침을 받아
(d) 동물을 사냥하여

72 동의어

이 글의 맥락에서, 적당한은 알맞게를 의미한다.

(a) 차츰
(b) 거대하게
(c) 육중하게
(d) 알맞게

73 동의어

이 글의 맥락에서, 공격적은 적대적을 의미한다.

(a) 적대적인
(b) 우호적인
(c) 강박 관념의
(d) 중독성의

TEST 2 | part 3 67~73 |
RAFFLESIA ARNOLDII

- 내용 분류 – 지식 백과
- 주제 요약 – 꽃식물의 한 종인 라플레시아 아놀디

The Rafflesia Arnoldii is a species of flowering plant, **67** which produces the largest individual flower in the world. It is found in the rainforests of Sumatra and Borneo, Indonesia.

Rafflesia Arnoldii is a parasitic plant which has no visible leaves, roots, or stems. Similar to fungi, it grows as a mass of thread-like strands of tissue completely embedded within and in intimate contact with surrounding host cells from which nutrients and water are obtained. It can only be seen outside the host plant when it is ready to reproduce. The only part of **68** Rafflesia that is identifiable as distinctly plant-like are the flowers. Rafflesia Arnoldii has been found to infect hosts growing in alkaline, neutral and acidic soils.

69 The flower of Rafflesia Arnoldii grows to a diameter of around one meter and weighs up to 11 kilograms. These flowers emerge from very large cabbage-like or dark brown buds typically about 30 centimeters wide.

The buds take many months to develop and the flower lasts for just a few days. When Rafflesia is ready to reproduce, a tiny bud forms outside the root or stem of its host and develops over a period of a year. The cabbage-like head that develops eventually opens to reveal the flower.

Thriving in rainforests, **70** Rafflesia Arnoldii is in danger of extinction due to habitat loss as well as poaching. Its buds are harvested and sold for medicinal properties. The plant cannot grow in captivity and, as most occurrences of Rafflesia contain only male or female flowers, pollination is rare.

The flower of Rafflesia Arnoldii has a foul smell that attracts flies and beetles. **71** A fly must land first on a male flower, avoid being eaten, and then transport the pollen to a female flower. If pollination occurs, the flower produces a smooth-skinned fruit, which is actually a berry about 13 centimeters in diameter. Fortunately, squirrels and birds enjoy this fruit, and are therefore able to help with seed dispersal.

These days, Rafflesia Arnoldii have been found from 490 to 1024 meters in altitude and ecotourism is known as a main threat to the species since the number of flower buds at locations where many tourists visit, has decreased.

67 정보 찾기(일치)

Which statement best characterizes the Rafflesia Arnoldii?

(a) It grows in areas with ~~dry summers and snowy winters~~.
(b) It is the world's biggest ~~flowering plant~~.
(c) It provides the biggest flower in the world.
(d) It is the world's ~~tallest~~ flowering plant.

68 정보 찾기(일치)

Which of the following descriptions about the Rafflesia Arnoldii is true?

(a) It gets nutrients and water from ~~fungi~~.
(b) Its flowers are only distinguishable.
(c) It ~~is infected~~ by host plants.
(d) It has ~~roots or stems but no leaves~~.

69 추론

What is most likely the reason why Rafflesia Arnoldii has the largest flower on earth?

(a) The flower of Rafflesia Arnoldii has a long diameter and heavy.
(b) The flower of Rafflesia Arnoldii is from ~~the largest bud~~.
(c) The flower of Rafflesia Arnoldii ~~lasts for months~~ to produce fruits.
(d) The flower of Rafflesia Arnoldii is grown ~~by humans~~.

70 추론

Why most likely are Rafflesia Arnoldii endangered?

(a) because Rafflesia Arnoldii ~~can be grown by humans~~
(b) because ~~climate change leads to forest degradation~~
(c) because people sell ~~flowers~~ of Rafflesia Arnoldii for therapeutic purposes
(d) because people illegally remove Rafflesia Arnoldii from their natural habitats

71 정보 찾기(일치)

What roles do flies play before pollination successfully takes place?

(a) Flies transfer pollen from the male flower to the female flower.
(b) ~~Flies~~ make a disgusting smell to protect flowers from birds.
(c) ~~Flies~~ produce more pollen
(d) Flies land on a female flower ~~prior~~ to a male flower.

72 동의어

In the context of the passage, emerge means _____.

(a) vanish   (b) appear
(c) express   (d) arrive

73 동의어

In the context of the passage, foul means _____.

(a) ordinary   (b) unusual
(c) pleasant   (d) stinking

TEST 2 | part 3 67~73 |

라플레시아 아놀디

라플레시아 아놀디는 꽃식물의 한 종인데, 67 이것은 세상에서 가장 큰 독특한 꽃을 피운다. 그것은 인도네시아 수마트라와 보르네오의 열대 우림에서 발견된다.

라플레시아 아놀디는 잎, 뿌리 또는 줄기가 보이지 않는 기생 식물이다. 균류와 유사하게, 그것은 영양분과 물이 얻어지는 주변 숙주 세포 내에 완전히 박혀 있고 밀접하게 접촉하는 실과 같은 조직 가닥 덩어리로 자란다. 번식할 준비가 되었을 때만 숙주 식물 외부에서 볼 수 있다. 68 라플레시아에서 식물과 뚜렷하게 구별되는 유일한 부분은 꽃이다. 라플레시아 아놀디는 알칼리성, 중성 및 산성 토양에서 자라는 숙주를 감염시키는 것으로 밝혀졌다.

69 라플레시아 아놀디의 꽃은 지름이 약 1미터로 자라고 무게가 11킬로그램까지 나간다. 이 꽃들은 일반적으로 약 30센티미터 넓이의 매우 큰 양배추 모양이나 짙은 갈색 꽃봉오리에서 나온다.

꽃봉오리는 자라는 데 수개월이 걸리고 꽃은 단지 며칠 동안 지속된다. 라플레시아가 번식할 준비가 되었을 때, 작은 싹은 숙주의 뿌리나 줄기 바깥에서 형성되고 1년에 걸쳐 자란다. 발육하는 양배추 모양의 머리가 성장하여 결국 열리고 꽃이 드러난다.

열대 우림에서 번성하고 있는, 70 라플레시아 아놀디는 밀렵뿐만 아니라 서식지 손실로 인해 멸종 위기에 처해 있다. 그것의 싹은 수확되어 약재로 팔린다. 이 식물은 사육 상태에서는 자랄 수 없으며, 대부분의 라플레시아에는 수술 또는 암술만을 포함하고 있기 때문에 수분작용이 드물다.

라플레시아 아놀디의 꽃은 파리와 딱정벌레를 유인하는 역겨운 냄새가 난다. 71 파리는 먼저 수술에 착지하고, 먹히는 것을 피한 다음 그 꽃가루를 암술로 옮겨야 한다. 만약 수분작용이 일어난다면, 이 꽃은 껍질이 매끄러운 과일을 생산하는데, 이것은 실제로 직경 13센티미터의 열매이다. 다행히도, 다람쥐와 새들은 이 과일을 즐기며, 따라서 종자 분산을 도울 수 있다.

요즘, 라플레시아 아놀디는 고도 490~1024미터에서 발견되었으며, 많은 관광객이 방문하는 장소의 꽃봉오리 수가 감소함에 따라 생태 관광이 종의 주요 위협으로 알려져 있다.

67 정보 찾기(일치)

어떤 진술이 라플레시아 아놀디를 가장 잘 묘사하는가?

(a) 그것은 건조한 여름과 눈이 내리는 겨울 지역에서 자란다
(b) 그것은 세계에서 가장 큰 꽃식물이다
(c) 그것은 세계에서 가장 큰 꽃을 제공한다
(d) 그것은 세계에서 가장 커다란 꽃식물이다

68 정보 찾기(일치)

라플레시아 아놀디에 대한 다음 설명 중 어느 것이 사실인가?

(a) 그것은 균류로부터 영양분과 수분을 얻는다
(b) 그것의 꽃들은 구별할 수 있을 뿐이다
(c) 그것은 숙주 식물에 감염된다
(d) 그것은 뿌리나 줄기는 있지만 잎은 없다

69 추론

라플레시아 아놀디가 지구상에서 가장 큰 꽃을 가지고 있는 이유는 무엇인가?

(a) 라플레시아 아놀디의 꽃은 지름이 길고 무겁다
(b) 라플레시아 아놀디의 꽃은 가장 큰 꽃봉오리에서 왔다
(c) 라플레시아 아놀디의 꽃은 과일을 생산하기 위해 몇 달 동안 지속된다
(d) 라플레시아 아놀디의 꽃은 인간에 의해 재배된다

70 추론

왜 라플레시아 아놀디는 멸종 위기에 처했는가?

(a) 라플레시아 아놀디가 인간에 의해 자랄 수 있기 때문에
(b) 기후 변화가 산림 파괴를 초래하기 때문에
(c) 사람들이 라플레시아 아놀디의 꽃을 치료 목적으로 판매하기 때문에
(d) 사람들이 자연 서식지에서 라플레시아 아놀디를 불법적으로 제거하기 때문에

71 정보 찾기(일치)

수분작용이 성공적으로 이루어지기 전에 파리들은 어떤 역할을 하는가?

(a) 파리들은 수술에서 암술로 꽃가루를 옮긴다
(b) 파리들은 새로부터 꽃을 보호하기 위해 역겨운 냄새를 풍긴다
(c) 파리들은 더 많은 꽃가루를 생산한다
(d) 파리들은 수술보다 먼저 암술에 착륙한다

72 동의어

이 글의 맥락에서, 나온다는 나타나다를 의미한다.

(a) 사라지다   (b) 나타나다
(c) 표현하다   (d) 도착하다

73 동의어

이 글의 맥락에서, 역겨운은 악취가 나는을 의미한다.

(a) 평범한   (b) 특이한
(c) 즐거운   (d) 악취가 나는

TEST 3 | part 3 67~73 |
STONEFISH

- 내용 분류 – 지식 백과
- 주제 요약 – 해양 물고기 중의 한 종류인 스톤피쉬

The stonefish is a marine fish that is found in shallow water of the tropical Indo-Pacific. Stonefish are sluggish bottom-dwelling fish that live among rocks or coral and in mudflats and estuaries. 67 They are known as the most venomous fish in the sea.

Stonefish's dorsal areas is lined with 13 spines which are sharp and stiff and can even pierce boot soles. 68 Through its dorsal fin spines, the stonefish can inject a venom that is capable of killing an adult person in less than an hour. In nature, the stonefish does not use its venom to capture prey, but instead to avoid predation. The venom, which consists of a mixture of toxin proteins, is extremely painful and quite effective at turning away even the strongest potential predators.

The stonefish has evolved many adaptations to help them succeed in the reef bottom. They have large heads and mouths, and small eyes. 69 Their bumpy skins covered with wartlike lumps and fleshy flaps can help them hide and remain camouflaged in between rocks and corals. They reach up to 30~40 centimeters long.

They eat mostly other reef fish and some bottom dwelling invertebrates like shrimp. They capture prey by sitting motionless on the reef floor and waiting for potential prey to swim by. They have been recorded striking their pray in 0.015 seconds. 70 Their powerful jaws and large mouths create so much pressure that they are easily able to suck down their unsuspecting prey and swallow it whole.

There is no evidence to suggest that human activity threatens the stonefish. Although individuals are sometimes caught for the private aquarium trade, 71 stonefish are rarely eaten by people and there is not a targeted fishery for this species. Therefore, they are unlikely to become endangered anytime soon.

67.

What are stonefish famous for?

(a) being the most abundant fish on earth
(b) being one of the extinct fish on earth
(c) being the world's ugliest fish
(d) being the most poisonous fish on earth

68.

How are stonefish able to kill humans quickly?

(a) by sucking the blood of humans in the water
(b) by infecting the venomous wound
(c) by releasing a toxin from dorsal fin spines
(d) by laying toxic eggs from dorsal fin spines

69.

What is the benefit of the stonefish having rocky skins?

(a) getting less exhausted by the activity
(b) not being exposed to another type of prey and predator
(c) swimming easily between rocks and corals
(d) sustaining the high pressure in the deep ocean

70.

What is most likely the reason why stonefish have strong jaws and big mouths?

(a) to produce venoms quickly
(b) to protect themselves from predators quickly
(c) to eat prey quickly
(d) to hide from potential predators quickly

71.

Why are stonefish unlikely to become an endangered species?

(a) They have long average lifespans.
(b) They are not affected by seawater contamination.
(c) They still have a large population.
(d) They are not fished for food.

72.

In the context of the passage, camouflaged means _____.

(a) disguised
(b) engulfed
(c) exposed
(d) protruded

73.

In the context of the passage, unsuspecting means _____.

(a) inedible
(b) targeted
(c) unsuspicious
(d) unrecognizable

TEST 3 | part 3 67~73 |

스톤피쉬(독전갈 물고기)

 스톤피쉬는 열대 인도 태평양의 얕은 물에서 발견되는 해양 물고기이다. 스톤피쉬는 바위나 산호 사이와 갯벌과 강어귀에 서식하는 느린 바닥에 사는 어류이다. 67 「그것들은 바다에서 가장 독이 많은 물고기로 알려져 있다.」

 스톤피쉬의 등쪽 부분에는 날카롭고 뻣뻣한 13개의 가시가 줄지어 있고 부츠 밑창까지 뚫을 수 있다. 68 「그것의 등 지느러미 가시를 통해, 스톤피쉬는 한 시간 이내에 성인을 죽일 수 있는 독을 주입할 수 있다.」 자연에서, 스톤피쉬는 먹이를 잡기 위해 독을 사용하지 않는 대신에 포식을 피하기 위해 사용한다. 독소 단백질의 혼합물로 구성된 독은 매우 고통스럽고 가장 강력한 잠재적 포식자들까지도 쫓아내는 데 상당히 효과적이다.

 스톤피쉬는 암초 바닥에서 그들이 성공적으로 생존하기 위해 많은 적응을 하며 진화해왔다. 그들은 큰 머리와 입, 그리고 작은 눈을 가지고 있다. 69 「그것들의 울퉁불퉁한 껍질은 사마귀 모양의 혹과 두껍고 부드러운 날개로 덮여서 바위나 산호 사이에 숨어서 위장하는 데 도움을 줄 수 있다.」 그것들은 길이가 30~40센티미터에 이른다.

 그것들은 대부분 다른 암초 물고기와 새우와 같은 일부 바다에 거주하는 무척추동물을 먹는다. 그것들은 암초 바닥에 꼼짝 않고 앉아 잠재적인 먹이가 헤엄쳐 지나가는 것을 기다리면서 먹이를 잡는다. 그것들은 0.015초 만에 먹이를 공격하는 것으로 기록되었다. 70 「그것들의 강력한 턱과 큰 입은 너무 많은 압력을 만들어내기 때문에 그들은 의심하지 않는 먹이를 쉽게 빨아들이고 그것을 통째로 삼킬 수 있다.」

 인간의 활동이 스톤피쉬를 위협한다는 증거는 없다. 비록 개인들의 수족관 거래를 위해 종종 잡히기도 하지만, 71 「스톤피쉬는 사람들에 의해 거의 먹히지 않으며 이러한 종의 표적 어업은 없다.」 따라서, 그것들은 곧 멸종 위기에 처할 것 같지는 않다.

67 ⓟ 정보 찾기(일치)

ⓒ 스톤피쉬는 무엇으로 유명한가?

(a) 지구상에서 가장 풍부한 물고기
(b) 지구상에서 멸종된 어류 중 하나
(c) 세상에서 가장 못생긴 물고기
(d) 지구상에서 가장 독성이 강한 물고기

68 ⓟ 정보 찾기(일치)

ⓒ 어떻게 스톤피쉬가 인간을 빨리 죽일 수 있는가?

(a) 물속에서 인간의 피를 빨아들임으로써
(b) 독이 있는 상처를 감염시킴으로써
(c) 등 지느러미 가시에서 독소를 방출함으로써
(d) 등 지느러미 가시에서 독성 있는 알을 낳음으로써

69 ⓟ 정보 찾기(일치)

ⓒ 바위 같은 껍질을 가진 스톤피쉬의 이점은 무엇인가?

(a) 활동에 덜 지치는 것
(b) 다른 유형의 먹이와 포식자에 노출되지 않는 것
(c) 암석과 산호 사이에서 쉽게 헤엄치는 것
(d) 심해에서 고압을 유지하는 것

70 ⓟ 추론

ⓒ 스톤피쉬가 강한 턱과 큰 입을 가진 이유는 무엇인가?

(a) 빠르게 독을 생산하기 위해
(b) 포식자로부터 스스로를 빠르게 보호하기 위해
(c) 먹이를 빨리 먹기 위해
(d) 잠재적 포식자로부터 신속하게 숨기 위해

71 ⓟ 추론

ⓒ 왜 스톤피쉬가 멸종 위기에 처한 종이 될 것 같지 않은가?

(a) 평균 수명이 길다
(b) 해수 오염에 영향을 받지 않는다
(c) 여전히 많은 개체수를 가지고 있다
(d) 음식을 위해 어획되지 않는다

72 ⓟ 동의어

이 글의 맥락에서, 위장한은 위장한을 의미한다.

(a) 위장한
(b) 삼켜버린
(c) 노출된
(d) 돌출된

73 ⓟ 동의어

이 글의 맥락에서, 의심하지 않는은 의심의 여지가 없는을 의미한다.

(a) 먹을 수 없는
(b) 표적화 된
(c) 의심의 여지가 없는
(d) 인식할 수 없는

TEST 1 | part 4 74~80 |

FAULTY REFRIGERATOR

- 내용 분류: 비즈니스 편지
- 주제 요약: 냉장고 불량 해결 요구

Robert Kensington
Manager
Alpha Electrical Store

Dear Mr. Robert Kensington:

I bought a Loyald fridge that cost $2500 from your shop on 11th August 2020, bill No. LTN/22/17. Only after 3 days, **74** the fridge has started giving me the trouble.

The freezer compartment was not cooling properly. It took a lot of time to freeze the food items kept inside and the frozen foods kept inside the freezer got spooled. I called your customer service and informed them of the problem. Julia Kylim whom I spoke with, **75** told me that your company would send a replacement for the faulty product. She also assured me that it would arrive within a week.

No replacement arrived, although I waited for two weeks. I have made several phone calls to your shop stating the trouble. This time, I was told that the replacement would be delayed again because **76** the manufacturer needed another week to deliver a new fridge. Had I not called, I would have been kept waiting longer and putting up with inconveniences.

I am urging you to resolve this concern promptly. Since the fridge is under the warranty period, I demand a refund immediately. In case you fail to address this issue within the next 5 days, you can be assured of hearing from my lawyer soon because **77** I will file a formal complaint with the Better Business Bureau.

78 I have enclosed in this letter a copy of the order receipt and a photograph of the defective product. You can e-mail your response to me at goldstar@email.com or call me at 555-666-0000.

Annabelle Lee

74 주제 찾기

Why is Annabelle Lee writing a letter to Robert Kensington?

(a) to order a new product
(b) to make changes of the delivery date and address
(c) to ask for more information concerning a product
(d) to complain about a defective product

75 정보 찾기(일치)

What did Julia Kylim tell Lee that the company would do about her concern?

(a) offer a full refund
(b) report the concern to the manufacturer
(c) exchange the item with a new one
(d) repair the item back to its original condition

76 추론

Why most likely was Alpha Electrical Store unable to deliver the new fridge straight away?

(a) The manufacturer needed more time to deliver a new fridge.
(b) There were many customers waiting for their products to arrive.
(c) The manufacturer could not make fridges in large quantities.
(d) The deliveryman was off sick for a week.

77 정보 찾기(일치)

How will Lee respond if she doesn't receive a refund for her purchase quickly?

(a) by purchasing the same fridge from another store
(b) by reporting to the police
(c) by lodging a compensation claim against the store
(d) by filing a complaint with the Consumer Ombudsman Center

78 추론

Why most likely is Lee sending a photo of the defective product with her letter?

(a) She wants to compare the new product with the defective product.
(b) She wants to use it as proof of her complaint.
(c) She intends to threaten the store.
(d) She wants to upload the photo to social media.

79 동의어

In the context of the passage, urging means _____.

(a) begging
(b) demanding
(c) convincing
(d) offering

80 동의어

In the context of the passage, address means _____.

(a) tackle
(b) delay
(c) write
(d) mail

TEST 1 | part 4 74~80 |

불량 냉장고

Robert Kensington
매니저
알파 전기 매장

Mr. Kensington 님께:

저는 2020년 8월 11일에 당신의 가게에서 청구서 번호 LTN/22/17인 Loyald 냉장고를 $2500에 샀습니다. 딱 3일 후에, 74 냉장고가 문제를 일으키기 시작했습니다.

냉동실이 제대로 냉각되지 않고 있었습니다. 안에 보관되어 있던 음식물을 냉동하는 데 많은 시간이 걸렸고 냉동실에 보관되어 있던 냉동식품이 해동되었습니다. 저는 고객 서비스에 전화하여 문제를 알려주었습니다. 저와 통화했던 Julia Kylim이, 75 귀사에서 결함이 있는 제품에 대한 대체품을 보내준다고 했습니다. 그녀는 또한 저에게 그것이 일주일 안에 도착할 것이라고 장담했습니다.

2주 동안 기다렸지만, 대체품이 도착하지 않았습니다. 저는 당신의 가게에 여러 차례 전화를 걸어 그 문제를 언급했습니다. 이번에는, 76 제조사에서 새 냉장고를 배달하는 데 일주일이 더 걸리기 때문에 교체가 또 늦어진다고 들었습니다. 만약 제가 전화를 하지 않았다면, 저는 불편함을 참으며 계속 기다리고 있었을 것입니다.

저는 당신이 이 문제를 신속히 해결하기를 촉구합니다. 냉장고는 보증 기간 이내이므로 즉시 환불을 요청합니다. 앞으로 5일 이내에 이 문제를 해결하지 못할 경우, 77 제가 Better Business Bureau(소비자 고발 센터)에 정식으로 고소할 것이기 때문에 곧 제 변호사의 의견을 들을 수 있습니다.

78 이 편지에 주문 영수증 사본과 결함이 있는 제품의 사진을 동봉합니다. 답장을 goldstar@email.com으로 이메일을 보내주시거나 555-666-0000으로 전화 주세요.

Annabelle Lee

74 주제 찾기

Annabelle Lee가 Robert Kensington에게 편지를 쓰는 이유는 무엇인가?

(a) 신제품을 주문하기 위해서
(b) 배달 날짜와 주소를 변경하기 위해서
(c) 제품에 관한 더 많은 정보를 요청하기 위해서
(d) 불량품에 대해 불평하기 위해서

75 정보 찾기(일치)

Julia Kylim은 Lee에게 회사가 그녀의 불평에 대해 어떻게 할 것이라고 말했는가?

(a) 전액 환불하다
(b) 제조사에 불만 사항을 보고하다
(c) 그 물건을 새것으로 교환하다
(d) 그 물건을 원래의 상태로 되돌리다

76 추론

Alpha Electrical Store가 새 냉장고를 바로 배달하지 못한 이유는 무엇인가?

(a) 제조사에서 새 냉장고를 배달할 시간이 더 필요했다
(b) 많은 고객들이 그들의 제품이 도착하기를 기다리고 있었다
(c) 그 제조업자는 많은 양의 냉장고를 만들 수 없었다
(d) 배달원은 일주일 동안 아파서 결근했다

77 정보 찾기(일치)

구매에 대한 환불을 빨리 받지 못하면 Lee는 어떻게 대응할까?

(a) 다른 가게에서 같은 냉장고를 사서
(b) 경찰에 신고하여
(c) 그 상점에 대한 배상 청구를 함으로써
(d) 소비자 고발 센터에 고소함으로써

78 추론

Lee는 왜 그녀의 편지와 함께 불량품의 사진을 보내는가?

(a) 그녀는 신제품과 불량 제품을 비교하기를 원한다
(b) 그녀는 그것을 자신의 불평의 증거로 사용하기를 원한다
(c) 그녀는 그 가게를 위협할 작정이다
(d) 그녀는 그 사진을 소셜 미디어에 올리고 싶어 한다

79 동의어

이 글의 맥락에서, 촉구하는은 요구하는을 의미한다.

(a) 구걸하고 있는
(b) 요구하고 있는
(c) 설득력 있는
(d) 제공하고 있는

80 동의어

이 글의 맥락에서, 해결하다는 다루다를 의미한다.

(a) (문제를) 다루다
(b) 지연시키다
(c) 쓰다
(d) 메일을 보내다

TEST 2 | part 4 74~80 |
RESIGNATION LETTER

- 내용 분류: 비즈니스 편지
- 주제 요약: Keith Jung의 사직서

May 5, 2021
Cathy Tick
Manager
Forbitt Corporation

Dear Mr. Tick:

74 Please let this letter serve as my resignation as shift supervisor due to unsatisfactory work conditions. In accordance with our company policy, my last day of employment will be June 4, 2021.

On repeated occasions, I have been asked to work back-to-back shifts on weekends and holidays. Initially, I understood the need to help out with the increase in production. **75** But I was also promised that more employees would be hired to relieve the stress on current staff members.

76 To this point, many months later, there has been no added staff to take the pressure off the employees putting in upwards of 90 hours per week. I have been afraid that I can work in unsafe conditions I do not want to be responsible for heavy workload and long working hours.

To the HR department, I have raised concerns on several occasions and have even submitted these concerns in writing. Nonetheless, **77** I was merely told to wait for the resolution of the matter. The extra strain has now started to affect my health and I am forced to conclude that my needs are no longer part of the company's interests. Therefore, I must take immediate action and resign.

It would be a great kindness to ensure that my leaving documents and dues are processed on time. **78** I will train anyone you deem appropriate to replace me. And I wish the company all the best in your future endeavors.

Sincerely,
Keith Jung

74. Why did Keith Jung write Cathy Tick a letter?

(a) to request a promotion
(b) to negotiate his salary
(c) to complain his poor work conditions
(d) to tell her that he is quitting his job

75. Regarding working on weekends and holidays, which of the following was the company's assurance?

(a) regular performance incentives
(b) recruiting extra staff
(c) a reduction in production
(d) an all-expense-paid vacation

76. Based on the letter, which of the following statement about Keith Jung is true?

(a) He has worked less than 90 hours every week.
(b) His responsibility was to take care of current staff members.
(c) He has overworked for months.
(d) He has worked with new and old staff members.

77. How did the HR department respond to his complaints?

(a) by requesting an appointment to meet with Cathy Tick
(b) by solving them as soon as possible
(c) by offering monthly bonuses
(d) by telling him to wait without a specified time

78. What most likely will Keith Jung do for the company before the termination of his employment?

(a) He will be interviewing a number of candidates.
(b) He will train his replacement.
(c) He will look for a suitable replacement.
(d) He will claim his insurance benefits.

79. In the context of the passage, resolution means _____.

(a) continuation
(b) solution
(c) agreement
(d) intention

80. In the context of the passage, deem means _____.

(a) demand
(b) identify
(c) count
(d) consider

TEST 2 | part 4 74~80 |

사직서

2021년 5월 5일
Cathy Tick
매니저
포빗 코퍼레이션

친애하는 Tick 씨에게:

74 〔이 편지가 불만족스러운 근무조건으로 인해 교대 감독관직에서 사직한 것으로 보이길 바랍니다.〕 우리 회사 방침에 따라, 저의 마지막 근무일은 2021년 6월 4일이 될 것입니다.

반복적으로, 저는 주말과 휴일에 교대 근무를 하도록 요청받았습니다. 처음에는 생산 증가를 도울 필요가 있다는 것을 이해했습니다. **75** 〔그러나 저는 또한 현직 직원들의 스트레스를 완화하기 위해 더 많은 직원들이 고용될 것이라는 약속을 받았습니다.〕

76 〔수개월이 지난 지금 이 시점까지, 주당 90시간 이상을 투입하는 직원들의 부담을 덜어줄 추가 인력이 없었습니다. 과중한 업무량과 장시간 근로에 대한 책임을 지고 싶지 않기 때문에 불안전한 환경에서 일할까 봐 두려웠습니다.〕

인사부에, 저는 여러 차례 우려를 제기했고 이런 우려 사항을 서면으로 제출하기도 했습니다. 그럼에도 불구하고, **77** 〔저는 단지 그 문제의 해결을 기다리라는 말을 들었습니다.〕 그 추가적인 부담이 이제 제 건강에 영향을 미치기 시작했고 저는 회사가 더 이상 제 요구에 흥미가 없다는 결론을 내릴 수밖에 없습니다. 그러므로 저는 즉시 조치를 취하고 사임하려 합니다.

제 퇴사 서류와 퇴직금이 제시간에 처리하도록 하는 일은 큰 호의가 될 것입니다. **78** 〔당신이 저를 대신하기에 적당하다고 생각하는 누구라도 훈련시키겠습니다.〕 그리고 저는 회사가 앞으로의 노력에 최선을 다하기를 바랍니다.

진심으로,
Keith Jung

74 주제 찾기
왜 Keith Jung은 Cathy Tick씨에게 편지를 썼는가?

(a) 승진을 요청하기 위해서
(b) 그의 급여 협상을 위해서
(c) 그의 열악한 근무 조건을 불평하기 위해서
(d) 그녀에게 그가 직장을 그만둔다는 것을 말하기 위해서

75 정보 찾기(일치)
주말과 공휴일 근무와 관련하여, 회사가 약속한 것은 다음 중 어느 것인가?

(a) 정기적인 성과 장려금
(b) 추가 직원 모집
(c) 생산량 감소
(d) 전액 유급 휴가

76 추론
이 편지에 의하면, Keith Jung에 대한 다음 진술 중 어느 것이 사실인가?

(a) 그는 매주 90시간 이하로 일했다
(b) 그의 책임은 현직 직원을 돌보는 것이었다
(c) 그는 몇 달 동안 과로했다
(d) 그는 신규 및 기존 직원과 함께 일했다

77 정보 찾기(일치)
인사부는 그의 불평에 어떻게 대응했는가?

(a) Cathy Tick을 만나기 위해 약속을 요구함으로써
(b) 가능한 한 그것들을 빨리 해결함으로써
(c) 월별 보너스를 제공함으로써
(d) 그에게 지정한 시간 없이 기다리라고 말함으로써

78 추론
Keith Jung은 고용이 종료되기 전에 회사를 위해 무엇을 할 가능성이 가장 높은가?

(a) 그는 많은 지원자들을 인터뷰할 것이다
(b) 그는 후임자를 훈련시킬 것이다
(c) 그는 적절한 대체물을 찾을 것이다
(d) 그는 보험이익을 청구할 것이다

79 동의어
이 글의 맥락에서, 해결은 해결책을 의미한다.

(a) 계속
(b) 해결책
(c) 합의
(d) 의도

80 동의어
이 글의 맥락에서, 생각하다는 고려하다를 의미한다.

(a) 요구하다
(b) 식별하다
(c) 수를 세다
(d) 고려하다

TEST 3 | part 4 74~80 |

ENCOURAGED TO OPEN AN ACCOUNT

- 내용 분류: 비즈니스 편지
- 주제 요약: 은행의 새 지점 개설에 따른 계좌 개설 권유

October 11, 2020
Mr. John Nile
111 Cloudy Heights
Canterbury, NY 10000

Dear Mr. Nile:

74 It gives us pleasure to inform you that our bank has decided to open a branch this coming November 1, 2020. The new branch is located near the Transport Center in Canterbury.

75 You will realize that to open a branch at a place where business opportunities are still in the infancy requires great courage and conviction of duties. Fortunately, our bank is never found wanting where such courage is required. It is so because it has faith in its tradition of public goods and in its clients. We are, therefore opening the new branch even against all odds.

76 You have been our old patron. We invite you to open your account with us at the new branch and make full use of other banking facilities to be provided there. **77** We have decided to give 25% more interest on deposits in the new branch to the first 300 deposits for one year. Also, you will get all the customer facilities along with the foreign exchange facilities. From now, you will be able to receive any kind of foreign remittance within 48 hours and also can maintain accounts in foreign currency. It is our earnest desire that you make use of our offer and give us an opportunity to serve the public in greater good.

78 Should you have any inquires, don't hesitate to contact us at 300-40001 or at auzbank@uk.com. Thank you for your continued support of our bank.

Respectfully,
Brian Jo
Manager
AUZ Bank

74 주제 찾기

Why did Brian Jo write John Nile a letter?

(a) to notify John Nile that his bank account is closed
(b) to inform John Nile that AUZ Bank is closing
(c) to inform that John Nile has been registered for a service
(d) to inform John Nile that AUZ Bank opens a new branch

75 추론

What is the reason why opening the new branch is very unlikely to succeed?

(a) Business chances in the region of the new branch are just starting to develop.
(b) There are more young customers than old customers.
(c) Running a business in the region of the new branch is very difficult.
(d) The new branch is not ready to provide excellent customer service.

76 정보 찾기(일치)

Why was John Nile chosen to benefit from the new branch?

(a) because he is one of bank's founder members
(b) because he has been a regular customer of the bank
(c) because he has been a rich business man
(d) because he never borrows money from the bank

77 추론

What will most likely happen if Nile opens his account at the new branch?

(a) He will be able to transfer money to overseas within 48 hours.
(b) He will have extra interests on foreign accounts.
(c) He will have an instant account in foreign currency.
(d) He will have higher interests on his deposits within a given period of time.

78 정보 찾기(일치)

What should Nile do if he has inquires about the new branch?

(a) visit other branches
(b) meet Brian Jo
(c) ring up the bank
(d) send email to Brian Jo

79 동의어

In the context of the passage, conviction means _____.

(a) persuasion
(b) belief
(c) judgement
(d) uncertainty

80 동의어

In the context of the passage, earnest means _____.

(a) sincere
(b) intense
(c) willing
(d) keen

계좌 개설 권유

2020년 10월 11일
Mr. John Nile
111 클라우디 헤이츠
캔터베리, 뉴욕 주 10000

친애하는 Nile 씨:

74 [저희 은행이 오는 2020년 11월 1일에 ▣지점을 개설하기로 결정했다는 것을 알려드리게 되어 기쁩니다.] 새 지점은 캔터베리의 교통 센터 근처에 위치해 있습니다.

75 [▣사업 초기 단계인 곳에 지점을 개설하려면 큰 용기와 의무에 대한 확신이 필요하다는 것을 깨닫게 될 것입니다.] 다행히, 저희 은행은 그런 용기가 필요한 곳에서 결코 부족한 점을 발견하지 못했습니다. 그것은 그것이 공공재의 전통과 고객들에 대한 믿음을 가지고 있기 때문입니다. 그러므로 우리는 모든 역경에도 불구하고 새로운 지점을 열고 있습니다.

76 [▣당신은 저희의 오랜 후원자였습니다.] 저희는 당신이 새로운 지점에서 당사에 계좌를 개설하고 그곳에 제공될 다른 은행 시설을 충분히 이용하기를 바랍니다. 77 [저희는 ▣1년 동안 처음 300개의 예금에 대해 신규 지점 예금에서 25%의 이자를 더 주기로 결정했습니다.] 또한, 당신은 외환 시설과 함께 모든 고객 시설을 이용할 수 있습니다. 앞으로 48시간 이내에 모든 종류의 해외 송금을 받을 수 있으며 외화 계좌도 유지할 수 있습니다. 당신이 저희의 제안을 이용하여 더 큰 선의를 위해 대중에게 봉사할 기회를 주는 것이 바로 저희의 진심 어린 바람입니다.

78 [문의 사항이 있으시면 주저하지 마시고 ▣300-40001 또는 auzbank@uk.com으로 연락 주십시오.] 저희 은행을 계속 지원해 주셔서 감사합니다.

경의를 표하며
Brian Jo
매니저
AUZ 은행

74 **주제 찾기**

ⓒ 왜 Brian Jo는 John Nile에게 편지를 썼는가?

(a) John Nile에게 자신의 은행 계좌가 폐쇄되었음을 알리기 위해
(b) John Nile에게 AUZ 은행이 문을 닫는다는 것을 알리기 위해
(c) John Nile이 서비스에 등록되었음을 알리기 위해
(d) John Nile에게 AUZ 은행이 새로운 지점을 개설한다는 것을 알리기 위해

75 **추론**

ⓒ 신규 지점을 개설하는 것이 성공할 것 같지 않은 이유는 무엇인가?

(a) 새로운 지점의 지역에서 비즈니스 기회가 이제 막 개발되기 시작하고 있다
(b) 나이든 고객보다 젊은 고객이 더 많다
(c) 신설 지점 지역에서 사업을 운영하는 것은 매우 어렵다
(d) 신규 지점이 우수한 고객 서비스를 제공할 준비가 되어 있지 않다

76 **정보 찾기(일치)**

ⓒ 왜 John Nile은 새로운 지사로부터 이익을 얻기 위해 선택되었는가?

(a) 그가 은행 설립자 중 한 명이기 때문에
(b) 그가 은행의 단골 고객이었기 때문에
(c) 그가 부유한 사업가였기 때문에
(d) 그가 은행으로부터 돈을 빌린 적이 없기 때문에

77 **추론**

ⓒ Nile씨가 새 지점에서 계좌를 개설하면 어떤 일이 일어날 것 같은가?

(a) 그는 48시간 이내에 해외로 돈을 송금할 수 있을 것이다
(b) 그는 외국 계좌에 대한 추가 이익을 가질 것이다
(c) 그는 외화로 즉석 계좌를 가질 것이다
(d) 그는 일정 기간 내에 자신의 예금에 대해 더 높은 이자를 가질 것이다

78 **정보 찾기(일치)**

ⓒ 만약 Nile씨가 새 지사에 대한 문의가 있다면 어떻게 해야 할까?

(a) 다른 지점을 방문한다
(b) Brian Jo를 만난다
(c) 은행에 전화를 건다
(d) Brian Jo에게 이메일을 보낸다

79 **동의어**

이 글의 맥락에서, 확신은 믿음을 의미한다.

(a) 설득
(b) 믿음
(c) 판단
(d) 불확실성

80 **동의어**

이 글의 맥락에서, 진심 어린은 진지한을 의미한다.

(a) 진지한
(b) 강렬한
(c) 기꺼이 ~하는
(d) 예리한

LISTENING

G-TElP 청취

PART 1 개인적인 이야기
PART 2 일의 진행이나 과정에 대한 설명
PART 3 비공식적인 협상 등의 대화
PART 4 공식적인 담화

G-TELP 핵심이론 | Listening

청취에 자주 출제되는 힌트표현을 모았다. 답과 연결되는 표현을 학습하고 암기하면, 반드시 정답이 들릴 것이다. 많은 학생들이 어려워하는 청취에서도 고득점을 얻을 수 있다!

1 문제 구성

Listening 문항 수: 청취 26문항 (약 30분)

(1) Part별 문항 수

구분	문제	문항 번호	문항 수
Part 1	a conversation between two people	27~33	7
Part 2	a man/woman talking about a product/talking at an event	34~39	6
Part 3	a conversation between two people	40~45	6(7)
Part 4	an explanation of a process	46~52	7(6)

(2) Part별 듣기 문제 구성 요소

구분	Daily Conversation	Lecture & Speech	Informal Talk	Formal Talk
Part 1	○		○	
	두 명의 화자가 실생활에서 경험한 다양한 주제를 전달 및 교환하는 형식			
Part 2		○		○
	한 명의 화자(전문가)가 하나의 주제에 대한 정보를 제공하거나 세부요소 및 과정을 설명 또는 제안하는 형식			
Part 3	○		○	
	두 명의 화자가 특정 문제에 대하여 서로 정보를 교환하는 형식 (의견 제시 요청이나 이유 및 충고 요청)			
Part 4			○	○
	한 화자가 특정 주제에 대해서 청중에게 논리적으로 설명하는 형식			

(3) Listening 특징

① 듣기 순서: General Direction – Listening Script 듣기 – Question 듣기
  *General Direction: Direction(각 파트별 안내문) + Question(파트별 문제)
② 시험지에 질문(Question) 없이 선지 4개만 나와 있음

장점	1. Script를 읽기 전, 문제(Question)를 먼저 읽어주기 때문에 문제별로 Note-Taking 할 시간이 있다. → 6하 원칙, 의문사, 동사 위주로 문제지에 본인만의 방법으로 표시 2. 문제가 문장 흐름대로 배정되어 있다. → 일부러 꼬거나 난해하게 출제하지 않아 듣기 자체에만 집중한다면 기대한 만큼의 점수 획득 가능 3. 질문이 본론 내용을 듣기 전, 후 2번 제시된다. → 다시 질문을 들으면서, 정답 확인 가능 4. 시험의 전체 문항 수와 시간이 적다. (26문항, 30분) → 피로도↓, 집중도↑
단점	1. 다른 공인 영어 시험보다 Script 지문의 길이가 길다. 2. 다른 공인 영어 시험보다 한 지문에 딸려있는 문제 수가 많다. 3. 문제 푸는 요령을 익힐 적응기간이 필요하다. → 연습을 많이 해야 한다.

2 G-TELP 듣기 전략: Part별 공략 방법

(1) Part 1 공략 방법

① Informal Talk(Conversation) → interesting story
  • 자신의 경험담을 주변 사람들과 나누기
  • 화자는 2명 등장

② 내용
  • 실생활에서 쉽게 접할 수 있는 두 사람간 대화
  • 자신이 겪은 경험을 상대방에게 전달하는 내용
  • 상대방에게 도움을 요청하는 글

③ 듣기 TIP
  • Paraphrasing
  • 비교급 / 최상급 / 부정어 / 명령문 / 조동사 / now / 연결사(어)(but, also) / I want 등이 답과 관련됨

G-TELP 핵심이론 | Listening

(2) Part 2 공략 방법

① Formal Talk(Speech) → Advertisement
  • 상업성이 짙은 글로 형식적인 말로 소비자에게 광고하는 글
  • 화자는 1명 등장

② 내용
  • 화자의 자사 제품에 대한 광고가 목적
  • 자신의 기술, 제품, 서비스에 대한 세부사항을 전달하고 이용을 설득하는 내용

③ 듣기 TIP
  • Paraphrasing
  • today / different / 비교급 / 최상급 / 부정어 / 명령문 / 조동사(can, have to, must, should) / now / 연결사(어)(but, also) / I want 등이 답과 관련됨

(3) Part 3 공략 방법

① Informal Talk(Conversation) → Information exchange(Difference in position)
  • 특정 문제에 대하여 반대적인 입장을 가지고 대화함
  • 화자는 2명 등장

② 내용
  • 공통된 주제에 대한 입장을 얘기하고 정보와 감정을 교류하는 것이 목적
  • 두 가지 선택 중에서 장단점을 들어 한 가지를 선택하는 내용
  • 독해와 같은 논리가 약간 필요한데, 특히 '비교와 대조'가 주를 이룸

③ 듣기 TIP
  • Paraphrasing
  • only / very / really / today / different / 비교급 / 최상급 / 부정어 / 명령문 / 조동사(can, have to, must, should) / now / 연결사(어)(but, also, although, because of) / I want 등이 답과 관련됨

(4) Part 4 공략 방법

① Formal Talk(Speech) → explanation of a process
- 특정 주제에 대하여 청중에게 논리적으로 설명함
- 주로 사업, 교육, 광고 등 다양한 소재를 다룸
- 화자는 1명 등장

② 내용
- 사업이나 홍보 등의 주제를 전달하는 것이 목적
- 연설자의 아이디어를 단계별 순서별로 설명하고 당부하는 내용

③ 듣기 TIP
- Paraphrasing
- only / very / really / today / different / first / important / 비교급 / 최상급 / 부정어 / 명령문 / 조동사(can, have to, must, should) / now / 연결사(어)(but, also, although, because of) / I want 등

2 G-TELP 듣기 TIP

(1) 시간관리

① 잘못된 접근법: 질문을 적는데 급급해서, 흐름을 따라가지 못하는 경우 → 질문을 그대로 받아 적느라 다음 것을 듣지 못하거나, 이전 질문에 집착하게 됨
② Note-Taking: 들으면서 단어 형식으로 본인 방식대로 메모할 것
③ 영어, 한국어 상관없이 자기가 이해하기 쉽게 메모할 것(꼼꼼 X, 이해 O)
④ 의문사를 약자로 적어놓기(누가, 언제, 어디에서, 무엇을, 어떻게, 왜)
⑤ 무엇을 묻는지 빠르게 표시
⑥ 꼼꼼하게 읽는 것보다, 중요 정보에 본인의 방식대로 표시를 하며 스캔
⑦ Direction을 읽어주는 시간 활용
⑧ 주제를 미리 이야기 해주니 놓치지 말 것
⑨ 보기를 먼저 빠르게 읽자

G-TELP 핵심이론 | Listening

(2) Relax, I CAN LISTEN IT!

① 문제는 2번씩 들려주니 긴장하지 말고 차분한 태도를 가질 것
② 처음 문제를 들을 때, 질문이 인쇄되어 있지 않으므로 최대한 키워드를 잡아내자
③ 다시 문제를 들을 때, 문제 후 10초의 시간이 주어짐
④ 보기를 한 글자라도 더 읽어라
⑤ 포기하지 말고 끝까지 청취하자
⑥ 답을 정할 때는 기억하는 지문 내용과 메모를 종합해, 차분하게 선택하자
⑦ 평소 긴 지문 청취에 익숙해져라
⑧ 평소 1.2~1.5 배속 듣기 훈련을 하자
⑨ 한 번 만에 이해할 수 있도록 듣기 훈련을 하자

(3) 보기와 정답 Paraphrasing

① 보기를 읽으며, 문제를 유추
② 보기 선지를 분석해서 동그라미를 쳐라!
③ Script의 단어와 보기의 단어가 같은 경우가 많으니 참고하자
④ 문제를 들려준 후 4초 동안 각 문항의 보기에서 키워드 최대한 표시
⑤ 본문을 들을 때, 미리 파악한 키워드 또는 관련 내용이 나오면 빠르게 메모
⑥ 보기에는 명사 위주로 표시
⑦ 동사는 동의어가 많지만, 명사는 동의어가 많지 않아 들릴 가능성이 높음
⑧ 고득점을 위해서는 지문 표현 정리해서, 복습하기

(4) 문제 유형 숙지

① 왜 틀렸는지 오답 정리

② 문제 출제 순서 익히기

③ 반복되는 문제 유형 익히기: 첫 번째와 마지막 문제

④ 첫 번째 질문: 주제, 목적

⑤ 마지막 질문: 이어서 무슨 행동을 할 것인가? 대화에 기반하여~ ?

(5) 평상시에 영어를 많이 듣자

① EBS

② Arirang TV

③ TBS eFM(외국어 전용 라디오 방송)

④ American Drama

⑤ 기타

TEST 1 | part 1 27~33 |

문제풀이

- 내용 분류 – 일상 대화
- 주제 요약 – Donna의 바타네스 여행기

A: Donna, you're back! How was your trip to Batanes? I've heard that it's really amazing.

B: That's right. The island has its breathtaking views of the nature. Sam! 27 (You know how much I enjoy travelling to isolated islands, right?) Well, Batanes was one of them because it is the Philippines' most remote islands.

A: Really?

B: Yes. And what's even more exciting was that for a week, my friend and I camped out and slept in tents on the beach.

A: I see... So, what else did you do there for a week?

B: We spent most of days swimming and diving in water. Batanes has the sparkling clear blue waters I've ever seen. And our tour guide took us to the vast rolling hills, traditional stone houses, amazing lighthouses, and famous local restaurants.

A: Did you enjoy any nightlife there?

B: Not really. Batanes doesn't have much nightlife. People living there seem to spend a lot of time with families. 28 (And unlike other islands, there were only a few bars and restaurants that were open late,) so we had to start every morning early to buy something to eat and drink.

A: Really? What did you eat?

B: There was a local unique restaurant where it serves dishes with fresh ingredients the locals grow themselves. I loved crispy sweet potato chips, shrimp and coconut simmer in coconut milk and rolls filled with pork.

A: That sounds appetizing, but still I don't find the island charming. 29 (For me, it doesn't sound exciting). Can you tell me what makes Botanes special?

B: Well, I believe it's quiet and untouched. Peaceful and natural landscape makes the island a must-see travel destination. 30 (And do you remember how I've always wanted to sleep under the stars and to wake up on the beach?)

A: Yes, I do.

B: I made my dream come true in Batanes.

A: I envy you.

B: 31 (If it had been another island, sleeping on the beach would have been impossible because there are a lot of tourists and crimes.) But on Batanes, I could lie out there on the white soft sand without anyone bothering and harming us.

A: Well, the island's security must be tight.

B: I didn't see any police officers while staying, but I felt I was safe there. The locals aren't hostile towards strangers and are so kind and courteous.

A: That kind of atmosphere is rare these days.

B: Right. And the locals make an effort to keep their island clean.

A: Does the government force the locals to clean the island?

B: Not at all. 32 (They believe that it's their responsibility to preserve and protect the island as it is.) They deeply value nature.

A: It sounds like a beautiful place. The people there will make you want to go back.

B: I agree. In fact, I booked an airline ticket on sale so that I can visit there again next summer. I'm sure it'll be even more fun then.

A: 33 (Can I go with you?)

B: Of course! You'd better hurry because the ticket sale doesn't last long.)

27 정보 찾기(일치)

What kind of beaches does Donna like to visit?

(a) beaches that are easy to reach
(b) muddy beaches
(c) beaches with lots of tourists
(d) remote beaches

28 정보 찾기(일치)

How are the beaches on Batanes different from other islands?

(a) The water there is cloudy.
(b) There are many bars and restaurants that keep people up all night.
(c) There are not many bars and restaurants that stay open late.
(d) There is no delicious food.

29 정보 찾기(일치)

After speaking with Donna, what is one of Sam's first impressions of Batanes?

(a) that it is exotic
(b) that it is unexciting
(c) that it is exciting
(d) that it is polluted

30 정보 찾기(일치)

What has Donna always wanted to do when she travels?

(a) to visit a secluded beach
(b) to explore underwater caves
(c) to sleep on a beach at night
(d) to relax on the sand

31 추론

Based on the conversation, why most likely would Donna be unable to sleep on a beach in different islands?

(a) because sleeping on a beach can be dangerous
(b) because the weather is unpredictable
(c) because there are many dangerous insects
(d) because tourists are not allowed to sleep on a beach

32 정보 찾기(일치)

Why do the islanders keep the beaches clean?

(a) to attract more tourists
(b) to increase the number of marine animals
(c) to save their environment
(d) to obey the law of the country

33 추론

What will Sam probably be doing after the conversation?

(a) He'll be booking a flight to Batanes.
(b) He'll be thinking about when to quit his job.
(c) He'll be flying to Batanes with Donna.
(d) He'll be planning what to do for next summer vacation.

TEST 1 | part 1 27~33 |

문제풀이

A: Donna, 돌아왔군요! 바타네스 여행은 어땠어요? 저는 그것이 정말 놀랍다고 들었어요.

B: 맞아요. 그 섬은 숨이 멎는 듯한 자연 경치를 가지고 있어요. Sam! 27 「제가 ▣외딴 섬으로 여행하는 걸 얼마나 ▣좋아하는지 알지요?」 음, 바타네스는 필리핀에서 가장 외진 섬이기 때문에 그들 중 하나였어요.

A: 그래요?

B: 네, 더 신나는 것은 일주일 동안 친구와 함께 캠핑을 하면서 해변에서 텐트를 치고 잤던 거에요.

A: 그렇군요... 그래서 일주일 동안 거기서 또 뭘 했나요?

B: 우리는 대부분의 날을 물에서 수영하고 다이빙하면서 보냈어요. 바타네스는 내가 본 것 중 가장 반짝이는 맑고 푸른 물을 가지고 있어요. 그리고 우리의 여행 가이드는 우리를 거대한 구릉지, 전통적인 돌집, 놀라운 등대, 그리고 유명한 지역 식당으로 데려갔어요.

A: 거기서 밤에 즐겁게 보냈어요?

B: 그렇지 않습니다. 바타네스에는 밤에 할게 별로 없어요. 그곳에 사는 사람들은 가족과 함께 많은 시간을 보내는 것 같아요. 28 「그리고 다른 섬들과 달리, ▣늦게 문을 여는 술집과 식당이 몇 개 밖에 없었기 때문에,」 우리는 먹고 마실 것을 사기 위해 매일 아침 일찍 시작해야 했어요.

A: 정말요? 뭘 먹었어요?

B: 현지인들이 직접 재배한 신선한 재료로 요리를 제공하는 현지 고유의 레스토랑이 있었어요. 저는 바삭바삭한 고구마 칩, 코코넛밀크쉬림프와 포크롤을 좋아했어요.

A: 먹음직스럽게 들리지만, 그래도 섬이 매력적이라고는 생각하지 않아요. 29 「저에게는, 그곳은 ▣별로 신나 보이지 않아요.」 무엇이 바타네스를 특별하게 만드는지 말해줄 수 있어요?

B: 음, 그곳은 고요하고 손상되지 않은 것 같다고 생각해요. 평화롭고 자연적인 풍경이 그 섬을 꼭 가봐야 하는 여행지로 만들어요. 30 「그리고 제가 항상 ▣별빛 아래에서 자고 해변에서 일어나고 싶어 했던 것을 기억하나요?」

A: 네, 그래요.

B: 저는 바타네스에서 제 꿈을 이루었어요.

A: 부럽네요.

B: 31 「다른 섬이었다면, ▣관광객들과 범죄가 많기 때문에 해변에서 자는 것은 불가능했을 거에요.」 하지만 바타네스에서는 아무도 우리를 괴롭히고 해치지 않고 하얀 부드러운 모래 위에 누워 있을 수 있었어요.

A: 글쎄, 그 섬의 보안이 철저했을 거에요.

B: 머물면서 경찰관을 보지 못했지만, 그곳에서는 안전하다고 느꼈어요. 지역 주민들은 낯선 사람들에게 적대적이지 않고 매우 친절하고 공손해요.

A: 요즘은 그런 분위기가 드물어요.

B: 맞아요. 그리고 그 지역 주민들은 그들의 섬을 깨끗하게 유지하기 위해 노력해요.

A: 정부가 지역 주민들에게 섬을 청소하도록 강요하나요?

B: 전혀요. 32 「그들은 ▣이 섬을 있는 그대로 ▣보존하고 보호하는 것이 자신들의 책임이라고 믿고 있어요.」 그들은 자연을 매우 소중하게 여겨요.

A: 아름다운 곳 같아요. 그곳에 있는 사람들이 당신이 다시 돌아오고 싶게 만들 거에요.

B: 맞아요. 사실, 저는 내년 여름에 다시 방문할 수 있도록 할인 중인 항공권을 예약했어요. 훨씬 더 재미있을 거라고 확신해요.

A: 33 「▣저도 같이 가도 되나요?」

B: 물론이죠! ▣티켓 할인 판매가 오래 지속되지 않기 때문에 서두르는 것이 좋겠어요.」

27 정보 찾기(일치)

Donna는 어떤 종류의 해변을 방문하기를 좋아하는가?

(a) 닿기 쉬운 해변
(b) 진흙투성이의 해변
(c) 관광객이 많은 해변
(d) 외딴 해변

28 정보 찾기(일치)

바타네스의 해변은 다른 섬들과 어떻게 다른가?

(a) 그곳의 물은 탁하다
(b) 밤새도록 문여는 술집과 식당들이 많이 있다
(c) 늦게까지 문여는 술집과 식당은 많지 않다
(d) 맛있는 음식이 없다

29 정보 찾기(일치)

Donna와 이야기를 나눈 후, Sam이 바타네스에 대해 느낀 첫인상 중 하나는 무엇인가?

(a) 그것이 이국적이라는 것
(b) 흥미롭지 않은 것
(c) 그것이 흥미롭다는 것
(d) 그것이 오염되었다는 것

30 정보 찾기(일치)

Donna는 여행할 때 항상 무엇을 하고 싶어 했는가?

(a) 외딴 해변을 방문하기
(b) 수중 동굴 탐험하기
(c) 밤에 해변에서 잠자기
(d) 모래 위에서 휴식을 취하기

31 추론

대화 내용을 토대로, Donna가 다른 섬의 해변에서 잠을 잘 수 없을 가능성이 가장 높은 이유는 무엇일까?

(a) 왜냐하면 해변에서 자는 것은 위험할 수 있기 때문이다
(b) 왜냐하면 날씨는 예측할 수 없기 때문이다
(c) 왜냐하면 위험한 곤충들이 많기 때문이다
(d) 왜냐하면 관광객들은 해변에서 자는 것이 허용되지 않기 때문이다

32 정보 찾기(일치)

섬 주민들이 해변을 깨끗하게 유지하는 이유는 무엇인가?

(a) 더 많은 관광객을 유치하기 위해
(b) 해양 동물의 수를 늘리기 위해
(c) 그들의 환경을 구하기 위해
(d) 나라의 법을 지키기 위해

33 추론

Sam은 아마도 대화 후에 무엇을 할 것인가?

(a) 그는 바타네스행 비행기를 예약할 것이다
(b) 그는 언제 일을 그만둘지 고민할 것이다
(c) 그는 Donna와 함께 바타네스로 날아갈 것이다
(d) 그는 내년 여름 방학에 무엇을 할지 계획하고 있을 것이다

TEST 2 | part 1 27~33

문제풀이

청취파일 다운로드

- 내용 분류 – 일상 대화
- 주제 요약 – Alice의 더블 베이 여행 후기

Test book 어휘 & 구문독해 p.112

A: Hello, John! It is so great to see you!

B: Hi, Alice! It's been a year since I saw you. How have you been?

A: Well, my husband and I just got back from a holiday in Double Bay.

B: That's where you went for your honeymoon.

A: That's right. **27** We decided to visit because we both wanted to bring back a lot of unforgettable memories we made there.

B: That must have been nice... What was it like?

A: Frankly speaking, I was a little bit disappointed. Double Bay has changed enormously over a decade. For one thing, **28** a high number of tourists from all over the world are visiting there today since it is known as one of the famous tourist attractions. It is no longer the peaceful, quiet, clean, friendly and laid-back beach.

B: Well, I suppose many things can happen in a decade.

A: I agree. There are now many restaurants, shops, hotels, and bars in Double Bay. Streets are dirty and homeless people are begging for money. Every single place we went was always crowded with people.

B: Did that spoil your holiday?

A: Yes, to a certain extent. Although Double Bay was not the same place as we expected, we tried to enjoy our time away from crowds of tourists and focused on the natural surroundings as much as we could.

B: So, how did you spend your holiday?

A: **29** Every early morning, we went to the beach and jumped into the refreshing sea. It was so good to sit by the sea and breathe in the fresh air. Every afternoon or evening, we mostly stayed at a hotel which had its own private swimming pool and beach.

B: That sounds great.

A: That wasn't all. We spent a considerable amount of time on not only swimming, but also surfing.

B: It must have been exciting. I would love to do it.

A: You should do sometimes. **30** Gliding across the water without any tools except the board under the feet makes me feel like I am flying and walking on water. In fact, Double Bay is one of the popular spots for surfers.

B: Really? Why is that?

A: **31** Because the gentle and rolling waves make surfers connect the different sections on the wave, while the water is warm and the scenery from the water is beautiful.

B: It sounds like you had a lot of fun! Was it your first time surfing?

A: No, it wasn't. I have gone surfing many times when I was a teenager. **32** It is just that I'd forgotten how riding on the breaking wave using a surfboard could make me feel energetic.

B: I see. It seems like you had such a great time there.

A: I really did. I can't believe I waited 10 years to go back to Double Bay. **33** Maybe, you should go there with us next time John.

B: That would be wonderful. Alice! I am sure I will love it there too.

27 정보 찾기(일치)

ⓒ Why did Alice and her husband visit Double Bay?

(a) to start a new family business
(b) because they will be moving to Double Bay
(c) to meet their old friends
(d) to experience their memorable moments from the past again

28 정보 찾기(일치)

ⓒ According to Alice, what has changed about Double Bay?

(a) Old buildings are demolished.
(b) Double Bay is now dangerous due to high crime rates.
(c) Tourists do not visit the place anymore.
(d) Double Bay is a popular tourist attraction now.

29 추론

ⓒ How most likely did Alice and her husband spend time away from tourists?

(a) by relaxing on a beach in the very early morning and spending afternoon at the hotel
(b) by staying in the hotel room throughout the morning and going to the beach in the afternoon
(c) by relaxing on a beach only at night
(d) by staying in their hotel room throughout their stay

30 정보 찾기(일치)

ⓒ According to Alice, why should John try surfing?

(a) because surfing is easy to learn
(b) because surfing is one of the most popular water sports
(c) because surfing allows him to experience incredible feelings
(d) because John can be a good surfer

31 정보 찾기(일치)

ⓒ Why is Double Bay popular among surfers?

(a) due to the coral reef
(b) due to the hot weather and the big waves for surfers
(c) due to the huge waves and cold water temperature for surfers
(d) due to the ideal waves and warm water temperature for surfers

32 정보 찾기(일치)

ⓒ What has Alice forgotten about surfing?

(a) how hard surfing was to learn
(b) how surfing made her feel lethargic
(c) how brave she was on her first surfing
(d) how surfing made her feel dynamic

33 정보 찾기(일치)

ⓒ What is Alice suggesting that John do next time?

(a) learn surfing
(b) visit Double Bay with them
(c) tour Double Bay on his own
(d) book a flight ticket

TEST 2 | part 1 27~33 |

문제풀이

A: 안녕, John! 만나서 반가워!
B: 안녕, Alice! 너를 본 지 1년이 지났네. 어떻게 지냈어?
A: 음, 남편과 나는 더블 베이에서 휴가를 마치고 막 돌아왔어.
B: 거기는 네가 신혼여행으로 갔던 곳이잖아.
A: 맞아. 27 〔우리는 그곳에서 우리가 만든 잊을 수 없는 많은 기억들을 되살리고 싶었기 때문에 방문하기로 결정했어.〕
B: 정말 좋았을 거야... 어땠어?
A: 솔직히 말해서. 나는 조금 실망했어. 더블 베이는 10년 동안 엄청나게 변했어. 우선 28 〔그곳은 유명한 관광명소 중 하나로 알려졌기 때문에 오늘날 전 세계에서 수많은 관광객들이 이곳을 방문하고 있어.〕 이곳은 더 이상 평화롭고, 조용하고, 깨끗하고, 친근하고 한가로운 해변이 아니야.
B: 글쎄, 10년 안에 많은 일들이 일어날 수 있을 것 같아.
A: 맞아. 현재 더블 베이에는 많은 식당, 상점, 호텔, 술집이 있지. 거리는 더럽고 노숙자들은 돈을 구걸하고 있어. 우리가 가는 곳마다 항상 사람들로 붐볐어.
B: 그게 네 휴가를 망쳤니?
A: 응, 어느 정도는 그랬어. 더블 베이는 우리가 예상했던 것과 같은 장소는 아니었지만, 우리는 많은 관광객들과 떨어져 있는 시간을 즐기려고 노력했고 최대한 자연환경에 집중했지.
B: 그래서, 휴가는 어떻게 보냈니?

A: 29 〔매일 이른 아침, 우리는 해변으로 가서 상쾌한 바다로 뛰어들었어. 바닷가에 앉아서 신선한 공기를 마실 수 있어서 너무 좋았어. 매일 오후나 저녁, 우리는 개인 수영장과 해변이 있는 호텔에 주로 머물렀지.〕
B: 정말 좋았겠다.
A: 그게 다가 아니었어. 우리는 수영뿐만 아니라 서핑에도 상당한 시간을 보냈어.
B: 분명 재미있었을 거야. 나도 그러고 싶다.
A: 너도 언젠가 그렇게 해야 해. 30 〔발밑 판자 외에는 아무런 도구도 없이 물 위를 미끄러지듯 가로지르면 마치 내가 물 위를 날고 걷고 있는 것 같은 기분이 들어.〕 사실, 더블 베이는 서퍼들에게 인기 있는 장소 중 하나야.
B: 정말? 왜 그런 거야?
A: 31 〔잔잔하게 출렁이는 파도가 서퍼들을 파도 위의 다른 부분들을 연결시켜주는 반면, 물은 따뜻하고 물에서 나오는 풍경이 아름답기 때문이지.〕
B: 넌 정말 재미있게 놀았던 것 같아! 서핑은 처음이었어?
A: 아니, 그렇지 않았어. 내가 10대였을 때 서핑하러 여러 번 갔었어; 32 〔서핑 보드로 부서지는 파도를 타는 것이 어떻게 나를 활기차게 만들 수 있는지를 잊었을 뿐이야.〕
B: 그렇구나. 그곳에서 정말 즐거운 시간을 보낸 것 같아.
A: 정말 그랬어. 내가 10년을 기다려서 더블 베이에 다시 갔다는 게 믿기지 않아. 33 〔John, 다음에 우리와 함께 같이 가는 게 좋을 것 같아.〕
B: 정말 멋질 거야. Alice! 나도 거기서 좋아할 거라고 확신해.

27 정보 찾기(일치)
C Alice와 그녀의 남편은 왜 더블 베이를 방문했는가?

(a) 새로운 가족 사업을 시작하기 위해
(b) 왜냐하면 그들은 더블 베이로 이사할 것이기 때문에
(c) 그들의 오랜 친구를 만나기 위해
(d) 과거의 기억에 남는 순간을 다시 경험하기 위해

28 정보 찾기(일치)
C Alice에 따르면, 더블 베이에 대해 무엇이 바뀌었다고 하는가?

(a) 오래된 건물들이 철거되었다
(b) 더블 베이는 현재 높은 범죄율로 인해 위험하다
(c) 관광객들은 더 이상 그 곳을 방문하지 않는다
(d) 더블 베이는 현재 인기 있는 관광 명소이다

29 추론
C Alice와 그녀의 남편은 관광객들과 떨어져 어떻게 시간을 보냈는가?

(a) 이른 아침에 해변에서 휴식을 취하고 호텔에서 오후를 보내면서
(b) 아침 내내 호텔 방에 머물고 오후에는 해변에 가면서
(c) 밤에만 해변에서 쉬면서
(d) 머무는 동안 호텔 방에 머물면서

30 정보 찾기(일치)
C Alice에 따르면, John은 왜 서핑을 시도해야 하는가?

(a) 왜냐하면 서핑은 배우기 쉽기 때문에
(b) 왜냐하면 서핑은 가장 인기 있는 수상 스포츠 중 하나이기 때문에
(c) 왜냐하면 서핑은 그에게 놀라운 감정을 경험하게 해주기 때문에
(d) 왜냐하면 존은 훌륭한 서퍼가 될 수 있기 때문에

31 정보 찾기(일치)
C 왜 더블 베이가 서퍼들 사이에서 인기가 있는가?

(a) 산호초 때문에
(b) 더운 날씨와 서퍼들에게 큰 파도 때문에
(c) 커다란 파도와 서퍼들에게 차가운 수온 때문에
(d) 이상적인 파도와 서퍼들에게 따뜻한 수온 때문에

32 정보 찾기(일치)
C Alice가 서핑에 대해 잊어버렸던 것은 무엇인가?

(a) 서핑을 배우기 얼마나 어려웠는지
(b) 서핑이 얼마나 그녀를 무기력하게 만들었는지
(c) 그녀가 첫 서핑에서 얼마나 용감했는가
(d) 서핑이 얼마나 그녀를 역동적으로 느끼게 했는지

33 정보 찾기(일치)
C Alice는 John에게 다음번에 무엇을 하라고 제안하고 있는가?

(a) 서핑을 배우다
(b) 그들과 더블 베이를 방문하다
(c) 혼자서 더블 베이를 여행하다
(d) 항공권을 예약하다

TEST 3 | part 1 27~33 |

문제풀이

- 내용 분류 – 일상 대화
- 주제 요약 – Chris의 Paul의 시험을 위한 요청

A: Hi, Chris!

B: Hello, Anna! I dropped by your house the other day to invite you to my birthday party. But your father said you went on a trip with your sister.

A: Oh, really? You see, 27 [my older sister Kate finally passed her diplomat exam after a year of studying, so we had a celebration for her in Singapore.]

B: That is so wonderful! Please congratulate Kate for me. She is the one working at the Foreign Office, right?

A: That's right. She works as an international law assistance at the moment. How did you know?

B: My close friend Paul who is also Kate's friend told me.

A: I see. I know him, too. Anyway, we are really proud of Kate. In fact, 28 [she wasn't able to spend a lot of time with her family and friends for over 6 months because she devoted herself so much to studying for the exam.]

B: I can imagine how much work Kate did.

A: She really did. So, how is Paul doing?

B: Well, he has been studying for the same exam Kate passed. By the way, would you happen to know if Kate attended classes at private institutes in order to prepare for her exam? 29 [Paul is wondering whether he should take exam preparation courses in private institutes.]

A: No, she studied all by herself.

B: Why is that?

A: Well, 30 [she had to work on not only weekdays, but also weekends for several months. She had literally no time to attend classes at private institutes, so she decided to take online exam preparation courses instead.]

B: I see... She must have had a tough time studying.

A: She did, actually. But she had no choice because she did not want to quit her job before she passed the exam. Some of her friends who passed the exam last year helped her, though. 31 [They played roles as tutors.]

B: Wow, it was very nice of them. Anyway, I think Paul already knows the pressures of studying after he failed the exam three times. Over the last weekends, I saw him only studying in the library without meeting his parents and friends.

A: Yeah, that is not a surprising sight. Kate used to sleep less than 3 hours a day and studied hours and hours after work. Fortunately, 32 [she was allowed to take two weeks off work just before the exam.]

B: How lucky she was!

A: I think so, too. Do you want me to call Kate and ask her if she can help Paul? I am sure she won't mind.

B: That'd be wonderful, Anna. Paul would appreciate that. 33 [By the way, are you free for lunch next Friday?]

A: Of course I am, Chris.

B: Fantastic! I'll come and pick you up at 11:30.

A: Ok. It sounds good to me. See you then.

27 ▶ 정보 찾기(일치)

What was Anna doing in Singapore the other day?

(a) She was celebrating Kate's achievement.
(b) ~~She was attending a business meeting.~~
(c) ~~She was meeting her best friend.~~
(d) ~~She was studying with Kate.~~

28 ▶ 정보 찾기(일치)

Why was Anna unable to have a good time with her sister Kate for months?

(a) ~~Kate was living in a different country.~~
(b) Kate was focusing on her ~~work~~.
(c) Kate was preparing for the diplomat exam.
(d) ~~Kate was very sick.~~

29 ▶ 정보 찾기(일치)

According to Chris, what is his friend Paul thinking to do?

(a) ask Kate for help ~~with his studies~~
(b) enroll in exam preparation courses at a private institute
(c) register ~~online~~ exam preparation courses
(d) ~~seek a full-time job~~

30 ▶ 정보 찾기(일치)

Why did Kate attend online courses?

(a) because ~~she didn't want to spend time travelling to private institutes~~
(b) because ~~her boss didn't allow her to attend the courses in private institutes~~
(c) because ~~she wanted to save money~~
(d) because she worked 7 days a week for months

31 ▶ 정보 찾기(일치)

How did Kate's friends help her prepare for the exam?

(a) ~~by giving financial support~~
(b) ~~by buying useful books for her exam~~
(c) ~~by introducing a good tutor~~
(d) by teaching her studies for the exam

32 ▶ 정보 찾기(일치)

What was she permitted to do at work before the exam?

(a) ~~work part-time~~
(b) take time off to study
(c) study for the exam ~~during business hours~~
(d) ~~quit her job~~

33 ▶ 추론

Based on the conversation, what will Anna do on next Friday?

(a) meet ~~Paul~~
(b) have lunch with Chris
(c) have lunch with ~~Paul~~
(d) ~~introduce Paul to Kate~~

TEST 3 | part 1 27~33 |

문제풀이

A: 안녕, Chris!
B: 안녕, Anna! 며칠 전에 내 생일 파티에 초대하려고 네 집에 들렀어. 하지만 네 아버지가 말하길 네가 언니와 여행을 갔다고 했어.
A: 오, 정말? 너도 알다시피, **27** 〖내 언니 Kate는 1년 동안 공부한 후에 마침내 외교관 시험에 합격해서 ▶우리는 싱가포르에서 그녀를 위해 축하해 줬어.〗
B: 정말 멋지다! 나 대신에 Kate를 축하해 줘. 그녀는 외교부에서 일하는 사람 맞지?
A: 맞아. 그녀는 현재 국제법 보조원으로 일하고 있어. 어떻게 알았어?
B: Kate의 친구이기도 한 내 친한 친구 Paul이 내게 말해 줬지.
A: 그렇군. 나도 그를 알아. 어쨌든, 우리는 Kate가 정말 자랑스러워. **28** 〖사실, 그녀는 ▶시험공부에 너무 많은 시간을 할애했기 때문에 6개월 이상 가족과 친구들과 많은 시간을 보낼 수 없었어.〗
B: 나는 Kate가 얼마나 많은 일을 했는지 짐작이 가.
A: 정말로 그랬어. Paul은 어떻게 지내?
B: 글쎄, 그는 Kate가 합격한 것과 동일한 시험을 공부해 오고 있었어. 그런데, 혹시 Kate가 시험을 준비하기 위해 사설학원에서 수업을 들었는지 알아? **29** 〖Paul은 ▶그가 사설학원에서 시험 준비 과정을 수강해야만 하는지 궁금해하고 있어.〗
A: 아니, 그녀는 혼자서 공부했어.
B: 왜 그런 거지?

A: 글쎄, **30** 〖▶그녀는 몇 달 동안 평일뿐만 아니라 주말에도 ▶일을 해야 했어. 말 그대로 학원 수업에 참여할 시간이 없어서, 대신 온라인 시험 준비 과정을 수강하기로 결정했어.〗
B: 그렇군... 그녀는 공부하느라 힘들었음에 틀림없겠어.
A: 실제로 그랬어. 그러나 그녀는 시험에 합격하기 전에 직장을 그만두고 싶지 않았기 때문에 선택의 여지가 없었어. 그렇지만 작년에 시험에 합격한 친구들 중 몇 명이 그녀를 도왔어. **31** 〖▶그들은 가정교사 역할을 했어.〗
B: 와, 정말 친절했네. 어쨌든, 나는 Paul이 세 번이나 시험에 떨어진 후 공부해야 하는 압박감을 이미 알고 있는 것 같다고 생각해. 지난 주말 동안, 나는 그가 부모님과 친구들을 만나지 않고 도서관에서 공부만 하는 것을 봤어.
A: 응, 그건 놀라운 광경이 아니야. Kate는 하루에 3시간도 자지 않고 퇴근 후 몇 시간씩 공부했어. 다행히도, **32** 〖그녀는 ▶시험 직전에 2주간의 휴가를 낼 수 있었어.〗
B: 그녀가 얼마나 운이 좋았는지!
A: 나도 그렇게 생각해. 내가 Kate에게 전화해서 Paul을 도와줄 수 있는지 물어볼까? 내 생각에 그녀는 괜찮다고 할거야.
B: 정말 멋질 거야, Anna. Paul은 그것을 고마워할 거야. 그건 그렇고, **33** 〖▶다음 주 금요일에 점심 한가해?
A: 물론이지, Chris.〗
B: 환상적이야! 11시 30분에 차로 데리러 갈게.
A: 그래. 너무 좋아. 그때 만나.

27 ▶ 정보 찾기(일치)

며칠 전에 Anna는 싱가포르에서 무엇을 하고 있었는가?

(a) 그녀는 Kate의 성취(시험합격)를 축하하고 있었다
(b) 그녀는 업무 회의에 참석하고 있었다
(c) 그녀는 그녀의 가장 친한 친구를 만나고 있었다
(d) 그녀는 Kate와 함께 공부하고 있었다

28 ▶ 정보 찾기(일치)

왜 Anna는 몇 달 동안 언니 Kate와 즐거운 시간을 보낼 수 없었는가?

(a) Kate는 다른 나라에 살고 있었기 때문에
(b) Kate는 그녀의 일에 집중하고 있었기 때문에
(c) Kate는 외교관 시험을 준비하고 있었기 때문에
(d) Kate는 매우 아팠기 때문에

29 ▶ 정보 찾기(일치)

Chris에 따르면, 그의 친구 Paul은 무엇을 하려고 생각하는가?

(a) Kate에게 공부를 도와달라고 부탁하다
(b) 사설 학원에서 시험 준비 강좌를 등록하다
(c) 온라인 시험 준비 과정에 등록하다
(d) 정규직 일자리를 구하다

30 ▶ 정보 찾기(일치)

Kate는 왜 온라인 강좌에 참석했나?

(a) 그녀는 사설 학원을 다니면서 시간을 보내고 싶지 않았기 때문에
(b) 그녀의 상사는 그녀가 사설 학원의 과정에 참석하는 것을 허락하지 않았기 때문에
(c) 그녀는 돈을 저축하고 싶었기 때문에
(d) 그녀는 몇 달 동안 주 7일 일했기 때문에

31 ▶ 정보 찾기(일치)

Kate의 친구들은 어떻게 그녀가 시험 준비를 하는데 도움을 주었을까?

(a) 재정적 지원을 제공함으로써
(b) 그녀의 시험에 유용한 책을 구입함으로써
(c) 좋은 가정교사를 소개함으로써
(d) 그녀에게 시험공부를 가르침으로써

32 ▶ 정보 찾기(일치)

시험 전에 그녀는 직장에서 무엇을 하도록 허락받았는가?

(a) 파트타임으로 일하다
(b) 공부하기 위해서 휴가를 내다
(c) 업무 시간 동안 시험 공부를 하다
(d) 직장을 그만두다

33 ▶ 추론

대화를 토대로 볼 때, Anna는 다음 주 금요일에 무엇을 할 것인가?

(a) Paul을 만나다
(b) Chris와 점심을 먹다
(c) Paul과 점심을 먹다
(d) Paul을 Kate에게 소개하다

TEST 1 | part 2 34~39 |
문제풀이

- 내용 분류 – 공식적 담화
- 주제 요약 – 수제 비누 제작의 이점

Most germs are harmless and some are important for human health, but in the air, soil and on every surface including our bodies, there are several germs that cause problems and these are the ones we prefer not to have on our bodies. To defend against those harmful germs, we use soap everyday. We can easily buy soap anywhere, but have you ever considered making your own soap?

Store-bought soap is cheap and gets you clean. It comes in nice fragrances and has a lot of bubbles, and also the packaging is pretty. However, you can make your soap for own consumption. In fact, thousands of soap lovers have started making their own soaps at home.

We at Handmade Soap School can help you make your first handmade soap. You can make the soap for your own enjoyment and perhaps even start a lucrative business in the future. All you need to do is enroll in our Soap course.

34 (Here are some reasons why you should learn to make your own soap at home): Firstly, making handmade soap is a fun hobby. It can bring out your creativity. **35** (Once you've learned the basic process, you'll start creating your amazing recipes.) There are an abundance of fun patterns, shapes, colors and scents to choose from.

Another reason for making your own soap is to learn how to distinguish good soap from bad soap. Have you wondered how your favourite soap is commercially made in factories? **36** (Once you understand handmade soap, you'll develop a deeper understanding of how high quality soap can be made and feel proud of your soap more.)

The next reason for making handmade soap is to avoid itchy and extremely dry or irritating skin. For cost savings, most commercial soap sold in stores remove glycerin from soap, **37** (but glycerin containing in handmade soap stays on your skin and attracts moisture from the air, which will keep your skin moisturized.)

Making soap according to your taste is easier than you think. All you need to do is get the right ingredients and take your time with the process.

Handmade soap can also save you money. **38** (It is true that initially you'll put out a bit of money to get your supplies,) but your soap won't cost anywhere near a commercial bar of soap costs. You'll be shocked at how much money you'll save on each soap!

At the soap store, a bar of soap costs about $5 on the very low side to over $15. This is for a standard 4.5 ounce bar of soap. When you make your own soap, a handmade bar of soap can be just 0.59 cents to produce! Plus, your soap will be high-quality and fresh.

Finally, making and selling handmade soaps can be extra income that allows you to feed your families and even **39** (your soap can be an incredible gift for occasions and holidays.) Most people love handmade soap made by your own two loving hands. What is a better way to amaze your favorite people than to make a unique and high quality soap?

So, get into making your own soap. Enroll in Handmade Soap School, and discover the fun and fulfillment that homemade soap can bring.

34 정보 찾기(일치)

What is the speaker asking the audience to do?

(a) purchase store-bought soaps more than handmade soaps
(b) purchase the speaker's soaps
(c) learn how to make their own soaps
(d) learn how to get rid of germs

35 정보 찾기(일치)

How can making one's own soap bring out a person's creativity?

(a) It allows a person to spend time with others.
(b) It encourages a person to test diverse recipes.
(c) It helps a person to flush out stress hormones.
(d) It motivates a person to pursue personal goals.

36 정보 찾기(일치)

How does one learn to better feel proud of handmade soap?

(a) by using only high-quality soap
(b) by purchasing store-bought soap occasionally
(c) by avoiding making bad soap
(d) by knowing how good handmade soap is made

37 정보 찾기(일치)

How does glycerin in homemade soap keep one's skin moisturized?

(a) by removing moisture from the air
(b) by absorbing moisture from the atmosphere
(c) by maintaining constant body temperature
(d) by reducing body temperature

38 추론

Based on talk, why most likely does homemade soap initially cost more?

(a) Its ingredients are far more expensive than store-bought soap.
(b) There are extra fees to pay for the supplier.
(c) There are extra fees to buy equipment.
(d) The ingredients cannot be purchased in bulk.

39 정보 찾기(일치)

What is a reason for giving soap as a present once one has learned how to make soap?

(a) to impress friends or families with one's soap making skills
(b) to save money on gifts
(c) to teach friends or families how to make handmade soap
(d) to start a soap business

TEST 1 | part 2 34~39 |
문제풀이

대부분의 세균은 무해하고 일부는 인간의 건강에 중요하지만, 공기, 토양, 그리고 우리 몸을 포함한 모든 표면에는 문제를 일으키는 세균이 몇 가지 있는데 이것들은 우리가 우리 몸에 가지고 있지 않는 것을 선호하는 세균들입니다. 이 해로운 세균들을 방어하기 위해, 우리는 매일 비누를 사용합니다. 우리는 어디서든 비누를 쉽게 살 수 있지만, 여러분은 직접 비누를 만드는 것을 고려해 본 적이 있나요?

가게에서 산 비누는 싸고 여러분을 깨끗하게 해줍니다. 향이 좋고 거품이 많으며 포장도 예쁩니다. 하지만, 여러분은 스스로 비누를 만들 수 있습니다. 사실, 수천 명의 비누 애호가들은 집에서 그들만의 비누를 만들기 시작했습니다.

수제 비누 학교에서 우리는 여러분이 첫 수제 비누를 만들 수 있도록 도울 수 있습니다. 여러분은 자신의 즐거움을 위해 비누를 만들 수 있고 아마도 미래에 수익성이 좋은 사업을 시작할 수도 있습니다. 여러분이 해야 할 일은 우리의 비누 과정에 등록하는 것입니다.

34 【여러분이 집에서 ᴰ자신만의 비누를 만드는 법을 배워야 하는 몇 가지 이유는 다음과 같습니다.】

첫째, 수제 비누를 만드는 것은 재미있는 취미입니다. 여러분은 창의력을 발휘할 수 있습니다. **35** 【일단 기본 과정을 배우면, 여러분은 ᴰ놀라운 제조법을 만들기 시작할 것입니다.】 다양한 재미있는 패턴, 모양, 색상 및 향기를 선택할 수 있습니다.

여러분만의 비누를 만드는 또 다른 이유는 좋은 비누와 나쁜 비누를 구별하는 방법을 배우기 위해서입니다. 여러분이 가장 좋아하는 비누가 공장에서 어떻게 상업적으로 만들어졌는지 궁금한 적이 있습니까? **36** 【일단 여러분이 수제 비누를 이해하게 되면, 여러분은 ᴰ어떻게 고품질의 비누가 만들어질 수 있는지에 대한 ᴰ더 깊은 이해를 하게 될 것이고 여러분의 비누에 대해 더 자부심을 느끼게 될 것입니다.】

수제 비누를 만드는 다음 이유는 가렵거나 극도로 건조하거나 자극적인 피부를 피하기 위해서입니다. 비용 절감을 위해, 매장에서 판매하는 대부분의 상업용 비누는 비누에서 글리세린을 제거하지만, **37** 【ᴰ수제 비누에 함유된 글리세린은 피부에 머물며 공기 중의 수분을 끌어당겨, 피부를 촉촉하게 유지시켜 줍니다.】

여러분의 취향에 따라 비누를 만드는 것은 여러분이 생각하는 것보다 더 쉽습니다. 여러분이 해야 할 일은 올바른 재료를 얻고 그 과정을 천천히 하는 것입니다.

수제 비누는 또한 돈을 절약할 수 있습니다. **38** 【ᴰ처음에는 공급품을 사기 위해 약간의 돈을 들인다는 것은 사실이지만,】 여러분의 비누는 상업용으로 파는 비누 가격 근처 어디에도 가지 않을 것입니다. 여러분은 비누 한 개당 얼마나 많은 돈을 절약할 수 있는지에 대해 충격을 받을 거예요!

비누 가게에서, 비누 한 개의 가격은 최저 5달러에서 15달러 이상입니다. 이것은 일반적인 4.5온스 비누입니다. 여러분이 직접 비누를 만들 때, 수제 비누 한 개를 생산하는 데 단지 0.59센트일 수 있습니다! 게다가, 여러분의 비누는 질 좋고 신선할 거예요.

마지막으로, 수제 비누를 만들고 파는 것은 여러분이 가족을 부양할 수 있게 해주는 부수입이 될 수 있고 심지어 **39** 【여러분의 비누는 ᴰ행사나 휴일에 놀라운 선물이 될 수 있습니다.】 대부분의 사람들은 여러분의 사랑스런 두 손길로 직접 만든 수제 비누를 좋아합니다. 독특하고 질 좋은 비누를 만드는 것보다 여러분이 좋아하는 사람들을 놀라게 하는 더 좋은 방법은 무엇일까요?

그러니, 여러분만의 비누를 만드세요. 수제 비누 학교에 등록하고, 수제 비누가 가져다줄 수 있는 재미와 성취감을 발견해보세요.

34 화자는 청중들에게 무엇을 요청하고 있는가?

(a) 수제 비누보다 시중에서 파는 비누를 더 많이 구입하는 것
(b) 화자의 비누를 구입하는 것
(c) 자신의 비누 만드는 법을 배우는 것
(d) 세균 제거 방법을 배우는 것

35 자신만의 비누를 만드는 것이 어떻게 사람의 창의력을 이끌어 낼 수 있는가?

(a) 그것은 한 사람이 다른 사람들과 시간을 보낼 수 있게 해준다
(b) 그것은 한 사람이 다양한 제조법을 시험하도록 격려한다
(c) 그것은 한 사람이 스트레스 호르몬을 분비하는 것을 돕는다
(d) 그것은 한 사람이 개인적인 목표를 추구하도록 동기를 부여한다

36 수제 비누에 대한 자부심을 더 잘 느끼는 것을 어떻게 배우는가?

(a) 고품질 비누만 사용함으로써
(b) 시중에서 판매하는 비누를 가끔 구매함으로써
(c) 나쁜 비누 만들기를 피함으로써
(d) 수제 비누가 얼마나 잘 만들어졌는지 앎으로써

37 수제 비누의 글리세린은 어떻게 피부를 촉촉하게 유지하게 하는가?

(a) 공기 중의 습기를 제거함으로써
(b) 대기 중의 수분을 흡수함으로써
(c) 일정한 체온을 유지함으로써
(d) 체온을 낮춤으로써

38 이야기에 따르면, 수제 비누가 처음에 비용이 더 많이 들어가는 이유는 무엇인가?

(a) 그 성분이 상점에서 구입한 비누보다 훨씬 비싸다
(b) 공급자에 지불해야 할 추가 비용이 있다
(c) 장비를 구입하는 데 추가 비용이 있다
(d) 재료를 대량으로 구매할 수 없다

39 비누만드는 법을 배웠을 때 비누를 선물로 주는 이유는 무엇인가?

(a) 비누만들기 기술로 친구나 가족에게 깊은 인상을 주기 위해
(b) 선물에 돈을 절약하기 위해
(c) 친구나 가족에게 수제 비누만드는 법을 가르치기 위해
(d) 비누 사업을 시작하기 위해

TEST 2 | part 2 34~39 |
문제풀이

- 내용 분류 – 공식적 담화
- 주제 요약 – 홈스쿨링의 장점

Hello, everyone. I am from Top Education Institute. I am here to introduce a different way of education to all who would like to study at home without going to school everyday, which we call home schooling.

34 ⟨Home schooling, also known as home education is the education that ▶parents teach their children at home instead of sending them to the formal settings of public or private schools.⟩ With home schooling, parents take full responsibility of their children's education.

It is true that families choose home schooling because of dissatisfaction with the educational options available, different religious philosophies, and the belief that children are not progressing within the traditional school structure. Although homeschooled children may not have opportunities to learn social skills and are not taught by qualified instructors with experience in teaching methods, **35** ⟨home schooling is ▶becoming increasingly popular⟩ and sometimes students are even homeschooled at their own request.

Today, I would like to talk to you about the many benefits of home schooling.

First, **36** ⟨home schooling allows parents to ▶customize their children's education to maximize learning, strengthen weaknesses and focus on special areas of interest.⟩ This way highly motivates children to learn at a level they are capable of rather than being stuck at a level because of their grade. As a result, it is shown that homeschooled students on average outperform their peers on standardized tests.

Second, being educated at home causes less stress. There are no cases of bullying, drugs, and all other social pressures. Children have more emotional freedom. In fact, many studies have shown that homeschooled children have no loss of self-esteem and become happier and more emotionally mature adults.

Third, **37** ⟨homeschooled children have ▶flexible schedules that make life easier for the whole family.⟩ Parents can decide the length of lessons and also decide when to take holidays. Many children studying at home can enjoy educational breaks with their parents at off seasons during the year. There are loads of opportunities for field trips, museums visits and parks.

Last, homeschooled children may be more independent. **38** ⟨They are more likely to think independently and unlikely to follow the ideas of a group without first making up their own minds because they know how to think for themselves and ▶aren't influenced by peer pressure.⟩ Also, they are much more independent in seeking out the answers themselves.

With all these rewarding reasons, parents and their children may now become aware of the many advantages of home schooling. We at Top Education Institute are here to help you all. If your children find it difficult to study in the structured environment of a school, you can discuss with us. **39** ⟨We can provide you all the information about home schooling and even we can ▶help you design the curriculum of home schooling for your children,⟩ so you can decide when and how to begin home schooling.

So, join the countless Americans who are being homeschooled successfully. If you have any inquires, contact us or visit our website www.topeducation.com.

34 What is home schooling?

(a) ~~broad education in a field~~
(b) home education provided by ~~either public or private schools~~
(c) educating children at home
(d) ~~domestic training on life-saving skills~~

35 According to the speaker, which is true about home schooling?

(a) ~~that it is chosen by children who do well at school~~
(b) ~~that it is strictly conducted by parents who are teachers~~
(c) ~~that it enhances children's sociability~~
(d) that it is gaining popularity

36 Why are homeschooled students more likely to get higher scores in the exam?

(a) ~~They have a wide range of skills.~~
(b) ~~They are obsessed with academic performance.~~
(c) ~~They study long hours everyday.~~
(d) They study in the personalized learning environment.

37 How can home schooling make the family life easier?

(a) Schedules can be adjusted based on family needs.
(b) ~~Home schooling is economically beneficial.~~
(c) ~~Schedules are only arranged by children.~~
(d) ~~Home schooling helps to develop each family member's potential.~~

38 According to the talk, why are homeschooled students more likely to think independently?

(a) ~~They are only affected by their parents.~~
(b) They aren't affected by their peers.
(c) ~~They do not have many friends.~~
(d) ~~They do not trust their peers.~~

39 How can Top Education Institute assist parents considering home schooling?

(a) ~~by arranging an educational program for them~~
(b) ~~by providing them with financial aid~~
(c) by helping to devise a curriculum of home schooling
(d) ~~by caring their children~~

TEST 2 | part 2 34~39 |
문제풀이

안녕하세요 여러분. 저는 Top Education 연구소에서 왔습니다. 저는 매일 학교에 가지 않고 집에서 공부하고 싶어 하는 모든 사람들에게 다른 교육 방식을 소개하려고 하는데, 우리는 이것을 홈스쿨링이라고 부릅니다.

34 가정 교육이라고도 알려진 홈스쿨링은 ▫부모가 자녀를 공립 또는 사립 학교의 공식적인 환경에 보내는 대신 ▫집에서 가르치는 교육입니다.] 홈스쿨링을 통해, 부모는 자녀 교육에 대한 전적인 책임을 집니다.

이용 가능한 교육적인 선택에 대한 불만족, 다양한 종교적 철학, 그리고 전통적인 학교 구조 내에서 아동이 발전하지 않는다는 믿음 때문에 홈스쿨링을 선택하는 것은 사실입니다. 홈스쿨링을 받은 아동은 사회성 기술을 배울 기회가 없고 교수법 경험이 있는 자격을 갖춘 강사들에 의해 배우지 않을 수도 있지만, 35 홈스쿨링은 ▫점점 인기를 얻고 있으며] 때로는 학생들이 자신의 요청에 따라 홈스쿨링을 받기도 합니다.

오늘 저는 여러분께 홈스쿨링의 많은 장점에 대해 말씀드리고자 합니다.

첫째, 36 홈스쿨링을 통해 부모는 ▫자녀의 교육을 맞춤화하여 학습을 극대화하고 약점을 강화하며 특별한 관심 분야에 집중할 수 있습니다.] 이런 방식은 아이들에게 성적 때문에 어떤 수준에 갇히게 하지 않고 오히려 그들이 할 수 있는 수준에서 배우도록 동기를 부여합니다. 그 결과, 홈스쿨링을 받은 학생들이 표준화된 시험에서 평균적으로 또래보다 더 높은 성적을 거두는 것으로 나타났습니다.

둘째, 가정에서 교육을 받는 것은 스트레스가 적습니다. 괴롭힘, 마약, 그리고 다른 모든 사회적 압력은 없습니다. 아이들은 더 많은 정서적 자유를 가지고 있습니다. 사실, 많은 연구들은 홈스쿨링을 받은 아이들이 자존감을 잃지 않고 더 행복하고 더 감정적으로 성숙한 성인이 된다는 것을 보여주었습니다.

셋째, 37 홈스쿨링을 받은 아동들은 ▫가족 전체의 삶을 더 편하게 해주는 유연한 일정을 가지고 있습니다.] 부모들은 수업의 길이를 결정할 수 있고, 또한 휴일을 언제 보낼지 결정할 수 있습니다. 집에서 공부하는 많은 아이들은 일 년 중 비수기에 부모님과 함께 교육적인 휴식을 즐길 수 있습니다. 현장 학습, 박물관 방문, 공원을 위한 많은 기회가 있습니다.

넷째, 홈스쿨링을 받은 아동은 더 독립적일 수 있습니다. 38 그들은 스스로 생각하는 방법을 알고 있고 ▫또래의 압력에 영향을 받지 않기 때문에 독립적으로 생각할 가능성이 더 높고 먼저 자신의 마음을 정하지 않고 집단의 생각을 따를 가능성이 낮습니다.] 또한 그들은 스스로 답을 찾는 데 훨씬 더 독립적입니다.

이러한 모든 보람 있는 이유 때문에, 부모와 자녀들은 이제 홈스쿨링의 많은 장점을 알게 될 것입니다. 저희 Top Education 연구소는 여러분 모두를 돕기 위해 여기에 모였습니다. 여러분의 자녀가 학교의 구조화된 환경에서 공부하기가 어렵다면, 저희와 상의할 수 있습니다. 39 저희는 홈스쿨링에 대한 모든 정보를 제공할 수 있으며, 자녀를 위한 ▫홈스쿨링 커리큘럼을 설계하는 데 도움을 줄 수 있으므로] 홈스쿨링을 시작하는 시기와 방법을 결정할 수 있습니다.

그러니 성공적으로 홈스쿨링을 받고 있는 수많은 미국인들과 함께하십시오. 문의 사항이 있으시면, 저희에게 연락하시거나 저희 웹 사이트 www.topeducation.com을 방문하십시오.

34. 홈스쿨링은 무엇인가?
(a) 한 분야의 광범위한 교육
(b) 공립 또는 사립학교에서 제공하는 가정교육
(c) 가정에서 아이들을 교육하기
(d) 구명 기술에 대한 가정에서의 훈련

35. 화자에 따르면, 홈스쿨링에 대해 사실인 것은?
(a) 학교에서 성적이 좋은 아이들이 선택한다는 것
(b) 교사인 부모에 의해 엄격하게 실시된다는 것
(c) 그것은 아이들의 사교성을 향상시킨다는 것
(d) 그것은 인기를 얻고 있다는 것

36. 홈스쿨링을 받은 학생들이 시험에서 더 높은 점수를 받는 이유는 무엇인가?
(a) 그들은 다양한 기술을 가지고 있다
(b) 그들은 학업 성과에 사로잡혀 있다
(c) 그들은 매일 긴 시간을 공부한다
(d) 그들은 개인화된 학습 환경에서 공부한다

37. 홈스쿨링이 어떻게 가정생활을 더 편안하게 만들 수 있을까?
(a) 가족의 필요에 따라 일정을 조정할 수 있다
(b) 홈스쿨링은 경제적으로 유익하다
(c) 일정은 아이들에 의해서만 정해진다
(d) 홈스쿨링은 각 가족 구성원의 잠재력을 개발하는 데 도움이 된다

38. 이야기에 따르면, 홈스쿨링을 받은 학생들이 독립적으로 생각하는 이유는 무엇인가?
(a) 그들은 부모에 의해서만 영향을 받는다
(b) 그들은 동년배들로부터 영향을 받지 않는다
(c) 그들은 친구가 많지 않다
(d) 그들은 동년배들을 믿지 않는다

39. Top Education 연구소는 홈스쿨링을 고려하는 학부모를 어떻게 지원할 수 있는가?
(a) 그들을 위한 교육 프로그램을 마련하여
(b) 그들에게 재정적 원조를 제공함으로써
(c) 홈스쿨링의 커리큘럼을 짜는 데 도움을 줌으로써
(d) 그들의 아이들을 돌봄으로써

TEST 3 | part 2 34~39
문제풀이

- 내용 분류 – 공식적 담화
- 주제 요약 – 온라인 영어 강사 모집

Welcome to the Town Hall Annual Job Fair. An increasingly growing number of people are making money through home-based online jobs. Some people take on these jobs on a part-time basis to increase the amount of monthly income, while others have full-time online jobs which are regarded as the main sources of income.

One of the leading sectors in online employment is English as an writing tutorial. This simply means teaching students about how to write academic essays or dissertations. A majority of students are from non-English speaking backgrounds, but highly interested in English academic writing.

34 〔Global English was founded to deliver education on English writing to ᴾnon-native speakers.〕 35 〔ᴾTo ensure academically professional tutorials, we only recruit teachers whose mother tongue is English.〕 This way, students can learn the in-depth language with accuracy.

Who is suited for an English tutor better than you? If you think you are the one, now it is time to move on to the next step.

There are reasons why you should join us:

Firstly, your job will be secure. Since Global English has been known as one of the leading online companies, we have offered jobs for tutors over the past years. And more importantly, you will get paid according to the number of students you teach in a week!

Secondly, your teaching timetables are flexible. At Global English, there are no minimum teaching hours per week, therefore you can design your own teaching schedule. You can even work more than eight hours a day. 36 〔In case you have personal matters or events, ᴾyou can choose to offer tutorials at your convenience as long as your students agree.〕 This will be an ideal way to contribute to your family's income.

Thirdly, 37 〔our tutors are able to ᴾfreely select students of different ages because we are fully aware that this would make you feel more confident and productive without stress.〕 All we want is to connect you with students who fit your teaching level in order to generate high job and student satisfactions.

Lastly, with years of experience providing educational tutorials, 38 〔we have ᴾactively worked on online support for tutors. If you struggle with dealing with difficult students and need more training to upgrade your teaching skills, we are more than happy to help you because you are the potential asset of our company.〕

By now, you will be probably wondering what conditions are required to work with us. Well, 39 〔you ᴾshould be fluent in the English language, which is obviously not an issue for people here with me and also you ᴾshould have a university degree.〕 However, we highly prefer people who majored in English literature or English education with minimum 3 years of English teaching experience.

So, engage in a highly-paid job without leaving home. Start a career in English writing tutorials at Global English. For more information on our company's programs, schedules, and rates, visit us at www.global-english.com.

34 정보 찾기(일치)

Who are the intended students of English writing tutorials?

(a) those who are from families in poverty
(b) those who are not native English speakers
(c) those who want to replace their native language
(d) those who speak English as their first language

35 정보 찾기(일치)

Why does Global English only employ native English speakers?

(a) They will look after their students well.
(b) They have a greater need to earn extra income.
(c) They can easily learn their students' language.
(d) They can teach precise and academic writing skills.

36 정보 찾기(일치)

How can a tutor take advantage of a flexible schedule?

(a) by tutoring many students at the same time
(b) by selecting each student's intelligence
(c) by arranging a convenient teaching timetable
(d) by negotiating tuition fees

37 정보 찾기(일치)

What can a tutor do to make lesson more productive?

(a) freely choose students with higher skill levels
(b) freely choose students of different ages
(c) freely teach subjects the tutor wants
(d) freely attend a teaching training provided by the government

38 정보 찾기(일치)

How does Global English help a tutor who is having difficulty handling students?

(a) by offering online assistance
(b) by replacing the student
(c) by taking time off from work
(d) by reducing teaching hours per week

39 추론

Why most likely are the listeners already qualified to be writing tutors?

(a) Their teaching methods have been widely recognized.
(b) They can easily teach English.
(c) They are currently university students majoring in English.
(d) They are fluent in English and have a university degree.

TEST 3 | part 2 34~39 |
문제풀이

Town Hall 연례 취업박람회에 오신 것을 환영합니다. 가정에 기반을 둔 온라인 직업을 통해 수입을 얻는 사람들이 점점 늘어나고 있습니다. 어떤 사람들은 월 소득을 늘리기 위해 시간제로 이러한 일을 하는 반면, 다른 사람들은 주요 수입원으로 전일제 온라인 직업을 가지고 있습니다.

온라인 취업의 주요 분야 중 하나는 영어작문 지도입니다. 이것은 단순히 학생들에게 학문적 에세이나 논문을 쓰는 방법에 대해 가르치는 것을 의미합니다. 다수의 학생들은 비영어권 출신이지만, 영어로 학문적 글쓰기에 관심이 많습니다.

34 〔Global English는 ▣비영어권 사람들에게 영어 작문 교육을 제공하기 위해 설립되었습니다.〕 35 〔▣학문적으로 전문적인 개인 지도를 책임지기 위해, 우리는 모국어가 영어인 교사만을 모집합니다.〕 이렇게 하면, 학생들은 깊이 있는 언어를 정확하게 배울 수 있습니다.

여러분보다 영어 강사에게 더 적합한 사람은 누구입니까? 여러분이 바로 그 사람이라고 생각한다면, 이제 다음 단계로 넘어갈 시간입니다.

여러분은 우리와 함께해야 하는 이유가 있습니다:

첫 번째로, 여러분의 직업은 안정될 것입니다. Global English가 주요 온라인 회사 중 하나로 알려져 있기 때문에, 우리는 지난 몇 년간 강사들에게 일자리를 제공해왔습니다. 그리고 더 중요한 것은, 일주일에 가르치는 학생 수에 따라 급여를 받게 된다는 것입니다!

두 번째로, 여러분의 수업 시간표는 유연합니다. Global English에서는 주마다 최소 수업시간이 없으므로, 자신만의 수업 일정을 설계할 수 있습니다. 여러분은 심지어 하루에 8시간 이상 일할 수도 있습니다. 36 〔개인적인 문제나 사정이 있는 경우, 학생이 동의하는 한 ▣편리한 시간에 개별지도 시간을 제공할 수 있습니다.〕 이것은 여러분의 가족의 수입에 기여하는 이상적인 방법이 될 것입니다.

세 번째로, 37 〔우리의 선생님들은 ▣다양한 연령대의 학생들을 자유롭게 선발할 수 있습니다. 왜냐하면 우리는 이것이 스트레스 없이 여러분을 더 자신감 있고 생산적으로 느끼게 할 것이라는 것을 충분히 알고 있기 때문입니다.〕 우리가 원하는 것은 양질의 일자리와 학생들의 만족을 발생시키기 위해 당신의 지도 수준에 맞는 학생들과 당신을 연결시키는 것입니다.

마지막으로, 다년간의 교육 개별 지도 시간을 제공한 경험을 바탕으로, 38 〔우리는 ▣강사를 위한 온라인 지원에 적극적으로 임했습니다. 만약 당신이 다루기 어려운 학생들 때문에 고군분투하고 당신의 교육 기술을 향상시키기 위해 더 많은 훈련이 필요하다면, 우리는 당신이 우리 회사의 잠재적인 자산이기 때문에 기꺼이 당신을 도울 것입니다.〕

지금쯤이면, 우리와 함께 일하려면 어떤 조건이 필요한지 궁금하실 겁니다. 음, 39 〔▣영어를 유창하게 구사해야 하는데, 그것은(여러분이 영어를 유창하게 해야 한다는 것은) 나와 함께 여기에 있는 사람들만의 이슈가 아닌 것은 분명합니다. 또한 여러분은 대학 학위도 가져야 합니다.〕 하지만, 우리는 영문학이나 영어 교육을 전공한 3년 이상의 영어 교사 경력을 가진 사람들을 매우 선호합니다.

그러니, 집을 떠나지 않고 고임금 직업에 참여하십시오. Global English에서 영어 작문 개별 지도 경력을 시작하세요. 당사의 프로그램, 일정 및 요금에 대한 자세한 내용은 www.global-English.com을 참조하십시오.

34 정보 찾기(일치)

영어 작문 개인 지도의 대상 학생은 누구인가?

(a) 빈곤 가정 출신인 사람들
(b) 영어가 모국어가 아닌 사람들
(c) 모국어를 대체하고자 하는 사람들
(d) 영어를 모국어로 사용하는 사람들

37 정보 찾기(일치)

교사가 수업을 더 생산적으로 만들기 위해 무엇을 할 수 있는가?

(a) 더 수준 높은 학생을 자유롭게 선발하다
(b) 연령이 다른 학생을 자유롭게 고르다
(c) 교사가 원하는 과목을 자유롭게 가르치다
(d) 정부에서 제공하는 교원 연수에 자유롭게 참석하다

35 정보 찾기(일치)

Global English는 왜 원어민만 고용하는가?

(a) 그들은 학생들을 잘 돌볼 것이다
(b) 그들은 추가 수입을 얻어야 할 필요성이 더 크다
(c) 그들은 학생들의 언어를 쉽게 배울 수 있다
(d) 그들은 정확하고 학문적인 작문 기법을 가르칠 수 있다

38 정보 찾기(일치)

Global English는 학생들을 다루는 데 어려움을 겪고 있는 교사를 어떻게 돕는가?

(a) 온라인 지원을 제공함으로써
(b) 학생을 대신함으로써
(c) 일을 쉼으로써
(d) 주당 수업시간을 줄임으로써

36 정보 찾기(일치)

교사가 어떻게 유연한 일정을 이용할 수 있을까?

(a) 동시에 많은 학생들을 지도함으로써
(b) 각 학생의 지능을 선택함으로써
(c) 편리한 수업 시간표를 마련함으로써
(d) 수업료를 협상함으로써

39 추론

왜 듣고 있는 사람들은 이미 작문 교사 자격을 가지고 있는가?

(a) 그들의 교수법은 널리 인정되어 왔다
(b) 그들은 영어를 쉽게 가르칠 수 있다
(c) 그들은 현재 영어를 전공하는 대학생이다
(d) 그들은 영어에 능통하고 대학 학위를 가지고 있다

TEST 1 | part 3 40~45 |
문제풀이

- 내용 분류 – 일상 대화
- 주제 요약 – Sally의 주거 형태 고민

A: Hi, Sally! I've heard that you got a new job. Congratulation!

B: Thanks Steve! I'm excited more than ever. I really struggled with finding a full-time job because most of big companies have reduced the number of employees they hire every year.

A: That's right. As soon as I got my job, the first thing I did was leaving home to live alone.

B: Really? I have been thinking about living alone too. My office is far from my home. It takes more than 1 hour to commute every morning. My parents ask me to live alone if I want, but I'm not sure 40 ⟦whether I should live alone or stay with parents.⟧

A: I see... Have you tried weighing the advantages and disadvantages of each option? Perhaps doing that can help you make a choice.

B: Yes, I've been doing that. Living alone ensures personal space and privacy. Even if I am a fairly social person, I'll be able to relax in the comfort of my own space.

A: That's true. 41 ⟦And when you live alone, you don't have to take anyone else's needs or requirements into account.⟧ There is no need to ask permissions; You can simply do as you please.

B: Good point. However, there are some downsides to living alone. I've checked several apartments near my office and I found the rent is pricey. I am wondering how I'm going to save up money.

A: Well, apart from paying higher rents, you have to cover the cost of your utility like water and electricity bills.

B: 42 ⟦Another thing about living alone is that I have to spend considerable time on cleaning, ironing, washing and cooking food all by myself. Here will be no one who secretly takes the bins out for me. I'm sure I'll be stressed out.⟧

A: I guess if you live with your parents, you take lots of things for granted. Your parents may do all the housework.

B: Right. Also, 43 ⟦I don't have to pay for rent or worry about a number of other costs like groceries and Internet connection.⟧ So, I can start putting any extra money I earn aside.

A: That's right. Aside from saving money, you have always someone to talk to and rely on while living with your parents. They support you in difficult situations and their life-based wisdom can be very helpful.

B: Exactly. I'm sure that my parents are willing to support me all the time. However, living with parents won't give me as much freedom as I'd like. 44 ⟦I won't be allowed to drink milk from the carton, wake up late and come home late at night.⟧ They'll always treat me as their child.

A: No matter how old you are, you will be a child in the eyes of parents.

B: Yeah, I never knew there were so many things to consider when deciding where to live. However, I think I've reached a decision.

A: Really? What is it?

B: 45 ⟦I prefer the set up where I don't have to worry about payment.⟧ In this way, I can save up money for self-development and investment.

A: That seems like a great choice. Sally! You can live alone anytime later.

B: I agree. Steve!

40 정보 찾기(일치)

C What is Sally trying to decide?

(a) ~~what to do after work~~
(b) ~~whether she should quit her job or not~~
(c) whether she should live alone or with parents
(d) ~~how to spend time with parents~~

41 추론

C According to Steve, how could Sally benefit from living alone?

(a) by being able ~~to visit her parents anytime she wants without asking permissions~~
(b) by being able ~~to have her personal space and privacy without asking permissions~~
(c) by being able to live away from ~~people she doesn't like~~ without considering their needs or requirements
(d) by being able to do something freely without considering somebody's needs or requirements

42 추론

C Why might living alone be stressful to Sally?

(a) ~~She'll have to pay higher taxes~~.
(b) She'll have to do all household chores on her own.
(c) ~~She'll have to take a bus from home to work~~.
(d) ~~She won't be able to save up money~~.

43 추론

C How could living with parents allow Sally to save extra money?

(a) by relying on financial support provided by parents
(b) ~~by paying only~~ the Internet connection and groceries
(c) ~~by asking parents to manage her money~~
(d) ~~by setting up her own business with parents~~

44 추론

C Why most likely would Sally be unable to come home late?

(a) ~~because her parents would want to spend every night with her~~
(b) because her parents wouldn't allow her to come home late
(c) ~~because her parents wouldn't support her financially~~
(d) ~~because her parents would need her care~~

45 추론

C What has Sally probably decided to do after discussing with Steve?

(a) ~~buy an apartment near the company~~
(b) ~~rent an apartment near the company~~
(c) live with parents and commute
(d) ~~live alone~~ and commute

TEST 1 | part 3 40~45 |

문제풀이

A: 안녕, Sally! 네가 새 직장을 구했다고 들었어. 축하해!
B: 스티브 고마워! 나는 그 어느 때보다 흥분돼. 대부분의 대기업이 매년 고용하는 직원 수를 줄였기 때문에 나는 정규직을 구하는 데 정말 어려움을 겪었어.
A: 맞아. 내가 직장을 구하자마자, 내가 가장 먼저 한 일은 혼자 살기 위해 집을 떠나는 것이었어.
B: 정말? 나도 혼자 사는 것에 대해 생각하고 있어. 내 사무실은 집에서 멀리 떨어져 있어. 매일 아침 통근하는 데 1시간 이상 걸려. 부모님은 내가 원하면 혼자 살라고 하는데, **40** 〔▣혼자 살지, 부모님과 함께 있어야 할지〕 모르겠어.
A: 그렇구나... 각 선택의 장점과 단점을 따져보려고 노력해봤어? 아마도 그렇게 하면 선택하는 데 도움이 될 거야.
B: 그럼, 그렇게 해봤지. 혼자 사는 것은 개인적인 공간과 사생활을 보장해. 내가 상당히 사교적인 사람이라 할지라도, 나는 내 공간의 편안함 속에서 쉴 수 있을 거야.
A: 그건 사실이야. **41** 〔그리고 혼자 살 때는, ▣다른 사람의 필요나 요구 사항을 고려하지 않아도 돼.〕 허락을 구할 필요는 없지. 너는 단순히 네가 원하는 대로 할 수 있어.
B: 좋은 지적이야. 하지만, 혼자 사는 것에는 몇 가지 단점이 있어. 내가 사무실 근처에 있는 아파트 몇 채를 확인했는데 집세가 비싸. 내가 어떻게 돈을 모아야 하는지 알고 싶어.
A: 글쎄, 더 높은 임대료를 내는 것 외에도, 너는 수도 요금이나 전기 요금 같은 공공시설의 비용을 부담해야 해.

B: **42** 〔혼자 사는 또 다른 단점은 ▣혼자서 청소하고, 다림질하고, 세탁하고, 음식을 요리하는 데 상당한 시간을 보내야 한다는 거야. ▣나를 위해 몰래 쓰레기통을 비워주는 사람은 없을 거야. 나는 내가 분명히 스트레스를 받을 것이라고 확신해.〕
A: 만약 네가 부모님과 함께 살면 당연하게 여기는 것들이 많을 것 같아. 너희 부모님이 집안일을 다 하시겠지.
B: 맞아. 또한, **43** 〔▣나는 집세를 내거나 식료품과 인터넷 연결과 같은 ▣많은 다른 비용에 대해 걱정할 필요가 없어.〕 그래서, 나는 내가 버는 여분의 돈을 따로 두기 시작할 수 있지.
A: 맞아. 돈을 모으는 것 외에도, 부모님과 함께 사는 동안 너는 대화하고 의지할 누군가가 항상 있어. 그들은 어려운 상황에서도 너를 지지하고 그들의 삶에 기초한 지혜는 매우 도움이 될 거야.
B: 바로 그거야. 내 부모님이 항상 나를 지지해 주실 거라고 확신해. 하지만, 부모님과 함께 사는 것은 내가 원하는 만큼의 자유를 주지 않을 거야. **44** 〔▣나는 우유팩으로 우유를 마시고, 늦게 일어나고, 밤늦게 집에 오는 것이 허락되지 않을 거야.〕 그들은 항상 나를 아이로 대할 거야.
A: 네가 아무리 나이가 많아도, 부모님 눈에는 넌 어린 아이로 보일 거야.
B: 그래, 나는 어디에 살지를 결정할 때 고려해야 할 것들이 그렇게 많은지 몰랐어. 하지만, 나는 결정했어.
A: 정말? 그게 뭐야?
B: **45** 〔나는 ▣지불에 대해 걱정하지 않아도 되는 것을 더 좋아해.〕 이런 식으로 자기계발과 투자를 위해 돈을 모을 수 있어.
A: 그건 좋은 선택인 것 같아. Sally. 넌 언제든 혼자 살 수 있어.
B: 맞아. Steve!

40 정보 찾기(일치)

Sally가 결정하려는 것은 무엇인가?

(a) 퇴근 후 해야 할 일
(b) 그녀가 직장을 그만둬야할지 말지
(c) 그녀가 혼자 살아야 할지 아니면 부모님과 함께 살 아야 할지
(d) 부모님과 함께 시간을 보내는 방법

41 추론

Steve에 따르면, Sally가 어떻게 혼자 사는 것으로부 터 이익을 얻을 수 있는가?

(a) 허락을 구하지 않고 그녀가 원할 때 언제든지 그녀 의 부모님을 방문할 수 있음으로써
(b) 허락을 구하지 않고도 그녀의 개인적인 공간과 사 생활을 가질 수 있게 됨으로써
(c) 그녀가 좋아하지 않는 사람들로부터 그들의 필요나 요구 사항을 고려하지 않고 살 수 있음으로써
(d) 누군가의 필요나 요구 사항을 고려하지 않고 자유 롭게 어떤 일을 할 수 있음으로써

42 추론

왜 혼자 사는 것이 Sally에게 스트레스를 주는가?

(a) 그녀는 더 높은 세금을 지불해야 할 것이다.
(b) 그녀는 모든 집안일을 혼자서 해야 할 것이다.
(c) 그녀는 집에서 회사까지 버스를 타야 할 것이다.
(d) 그녀는 돈을 저축할 수 없을 것이다.

43 추론

부모님과 함께 사는 것이 Sally가 어떻게 여분의 돈 을 저축하도록 하는가?

(a) 부모에 의해 제공되는 재정적 지원에 의지하여
(b) 인터넷 연결과 식료품만 지불하여
(c) 부모님에게 그녀의 돈을 관리하라고 요구함으로써
(d) 부모님과 그녀만의 사업을 차려서

44 추론

Sally가 늦게 집에 돌아오지 못할 가능성이 가장 높 은 이유는 무엇인가?

(a) 왜냐하면 그녀의 부모님은 그녀와 매일 밤을 함께 보내고 싶어 했기 때문이다
(b) 그녀의 부모님은 그녀가 집에 늦게 오는 것을 허락 하지 않았기 때문이다
(c) 왜냐하면 그녀의 부모님이 그녀를 재정적으로 부양 하지 않으려 했기 때문이다
(d) 왜냐하면 그녀의 부모님은 그녀의 보살핌이 필요하 기 때문이다

45 추론

Sally는 Steve와 상의한 후에 무엇을 하기로 결정 했는가?

(a) 회사 근처에 아파트를 사다
(b) 회사 근처에 아파트를 임대하다
(c) 부모와 함께 살면서 통근하다
(d) 혼자 살면서 통근하다

TEST 2 | part 3 40~45 |
문제풀이

- 내용 분류 – 일상 대화
- 주제 요약 – 안면 레이저 치료

A: Good morning, Dr. Smith.
B: Hi! Monica! How can I help you?
A: Well, 40 〔I was wondering if I could undergo face laser treatment instead of a facial massage today.〕
B: How about we discuss the differences between the two procedures?
A: That's a good idea.
B: 41 〔Face laser treatment destroys the outer layers of the skin while simultaneously heating the lower layers in the dermis.〕 This causes new skin to form and promote collagen production that helps fine lines around the mouth and eyes decrease, whereas facial massages move the lymphatic fluid and clear out toxins from our facial skin.
A: I've been doing facial massages for about four years now.
B: That is one advantage of a facial massage. It is a very accessible option. You can go to salons for a professional massage, or do it yourself at home.
A: Right. Another good thing about a facial massage is that it helps blood circulation and sends more oxygen to the skin.
B: If it's been working for you, why are you thinking about undergoing laser skin therapy now?
A: Well, facial massages have disadvantages. 42 〔When a facial massage is done incorrectly, I get bruising and muscle soreness that may last for several days.〕
B: You're lucky you haven't had nerve damage yet.
A: That sounds scary. Another disadvantage of facial massages is that it can cause itching.
B: That's right. Like you said, creams or oils for facial massages contain chemicals causing itchiness.

B: With face laser treatment, however, there are things you don't have to be concerned. Face laser treatment is a non-invasive procedure that improves the skin's appearance or treats minor facial flaws. 43 〔The doctor applies a topical anesthetic to the area being treated to reduce pain.〕
A: You mean the procedure doesn't involve the insertion of instruments and the making of an incision?
B: Face laser treatment is considered to be a short and safe process if done appropriately.
A: I see, but are there any drawbacks to face laser treatment?
B: One disadvantage is the high cost. Since face laser treatment is considered a cosmetic procedure, it is not covered by medical insurance.
A: I see, then how many sessions would I need?
B: It depends on the area being treated, but you will likely need multiple sessions of laser treatment until you achieve your desired results.
A: I see.
B: 44 〔Another disadvantage of face laser treatment is its riskier side effects.〕 Treated skin can become darker or lighter than it was before treatment.
A: Oh no.
B: So, if you decide to push through with face laser treatment, we will thoroughly evaluate the results of each session and proceed accordingly. So, which procedure will you choose?
A: 45 〔I believe laser face treatment is the right one. I'd like to have a consultation for the treatment.〕
B: Sure, Monica.

40 🅟 주제 찾기

ⓒ Why did Monica visit Dr. Smith's office?

(a) ~~to have a job interview~~
(b) ~~to sell a facial laser product~~
(c) to inquire about a medical procedure
(d) ~~to treat her facial pain~~

41 🅟 정보 찾기(일치)

ⓒ According to Dr. Smith, how is collagen production promoted in a laser facial treatment?

(a) ~~by drinking plenty of water~~
(b) ~~by exposing the facial skin to very high temperatures~~
(c) ~~by removing toxins from the skin layers of the face~~
(d) by destroying and heating the different skin layers of the face

42 🅟 정보 찾기(일치)

ⓒ What made Monica suddenly rethink her facial massage?

(a) She finds facial massage ~~too painful~~.
(b) She gets bruising and muscle pain.
(c) ~~She is scared of unknown side effects~~.
(d) ~~Her skin is extremely dry and sensitive~~.

43 🅟 추론

ⓒ Why most likely won't Monica be in pain during the laser procedures?

(a) ~~because her skin is not sensitive and thick~~
(b) ~~because nurses keep talking to her~~
(c) ~~because the doctor is a pain management specialist~~
(d) because the doctor uses a substance that causes loss of pain only to the area to which it is applied

44 🅟 추론

ⓒ Why most likely should each session of laser treatment be assessed?

(a) ~~to ensure that one's skin has been lighter~~
(b) ~~to check if one wants to discontinue laser procedures~~
(c) ~~to calculate how much one needs to pay for each session~~
(d) to prevent any serious side effects

45 🅟 추론

ⓒ What will Monica do after conversation with Dr. Smith?

(a) ~~continue a facial massage~~
(b) ~~see a doctor other than Dr. Smith~~
(c) schedule a consultation for laser treatment
(d) ~~meet friends~~

TEST 2 | part 3 40~45 |

문제풀이

A: 좋은 아침이에요, Smith 박사님.
B: 안녕! Monica! 무엇을 도와드릴까요?
A: 글쎄요. **40** 〔오늘 안면 마사지를 받는 대신 안면 레이저 치료를 받을 수 있을까 해서요.〕
B: 두 시술의 차이점에 대해 논의하는 건 어떨까요?
A: 좋은 생각입니다.
B: **41** 〔안면 레이저 치료는 피부의 외층을 파괴하는 동시에 진피의 하층을 따뜻하게 합니다.〕 이로 인해 새로운 피부가 형성되고 입과 눈 주위의 미세한 주름을 감소하는 데 도움을 주는 콜라겐 생성을 촉진시켜주는 반면, 안면 마사지는 림프액을 이동시키고 얼굴 피부의 독소를 제거해줍니다.
A: 저는 지금까지 약 4년 동안 안면 마사지를 해오고 있습니다.
B: 그게 안면 마사지의 장점 중 하나입니다. 매우 접근하기 쉬운 선택입니다. 전문 마사지를 위해 상점에 가거나 집에서 직접 할 수 있습니다.
A: 맞습니다. 안면 마사지의 또 다른 좋은 점은 혈액 순환을 돕고 피부에 더 많은 산소를 보내는 것입니다.
B: 만약 그것(안면 마사지)이 당신에게 효과가 있다면, 왜 지금 레이저 피부 치료를 받을 생각을 하고 있는 겁니까?
A: 글쎄요, 안면 마사지는 단점이 있어요. **42** 〔안면 마사지가 잘못되면, 며칠 동안 멍과 근육통이 생깁니다.〕
B: 아직 신경 손상을 입지 않았다니 다행이군요.
A: 무서운 것 같네요. 안면 마사지의 또 다른 단점은 가려움증을 유발한다는 것입니다.
B: 맞아요. 말씀하신 대로, 안면 마사지용 크림이나 오일에는 가려움을 유발하는 화학물질이 들어 있습니다.

A: 상상이 가네요.
B: 하지만 안면 레이저 치료는 걱정할 필요가 없습니다. 안면 레이저 치료는 피부의 외관을 개선하거나 사소한 안면 결점을 치료하는 비외과적인 시술입니다. **43** 〔의사는 통증을 줄이기 위해 치료 중인 부위에 국소 마취제를 바릅니다.〕
A: 그 시술은 기구를 삽입하고 절개를 하는 것이 아니라구요?
B: 안면 레이저 치료는 적절하게 수행된다면 짧고 안전한 과정으로 간주됩니다.
A: 그렇군요, 하지만 안면 레이저 치료에 대한 단점이 있나요?
B: 한 가지 단점은 높은 비용입니다. 안면 레이저 치료는 미용 시술로 간주되기 때문에, 의료 보험이 적용되지 않습니다.
A: 그렇군요, 그러면 몇 회가 필요하나요?
B: 시술 부위에 따라 다르지만, 원하는 결과를 얻기 전까지는 여러 번의 레이저 치료가 필요할 수 있습니다.
A: 알겠습니다.
B: **44** 〔안면 레이저 치료의 또 다른 단점은 더 위험한 부작용입니다.〕 치료 전보다 치료된 피부가 더 어둡거나 더 밝아질 수 있습니다.
A: 어머, 안 돼요.
B: 그래서 안면 레이저 치료를 하기로 결정하시면, 각 단계의 결과를 철저히 평가하고 그에 따라 진행하도록 하겠습니다. 그러면, 어떤 시술을 선택할 건가요?
A: **45** 〔저는 안면 레이저 치료가 좋다고 생각합니다. 치료를 위해 상담을 받고 싶습니다.〕
B: 그래요, Monica.

40 주제 찾기

Monica는 왜 Smith 박사의 사무실을 방문했는가?

(a) 취업 면접을 보기 위해
(b) 안면 레이저 제품을 판매하기 위해
(c) 의료 시술에 대해 문의하기 위해
(d) 그녀의 얼굴 통증을 치료하기 위해

41 정보 찾기(일치)

Smith 박사에 따르면, 안면 레이저 치료에서 콜라겐 생성은 어떻게 촉진되고 있는가?

(a) 많은 물을 마심으로써
(b) 얼굴 피부를 매우 높은 온도에 노출시킴으로써
(c) 얼굴의 피부 층에서 독소를 제거함으로써
(d) 얼굴의 다양한 피부층을 파괴하고 가열함으로써

42 정보 찾기(일치)

Monica는 왜 갑자기 안면 마사지를 다시 생각하게 되었나?

(a) 그녀는 안면 마사지가 너무 아프다는 것을 알게 되다
(b) 그녀는 멍이 들고 근육통이 생기다
(c) 그녀는 알려지지 않은 부작용을 두려워하다
(d) 그녀의 피부는 극도로 건조하고 민감하다

43 추론

왜 Monica는 레이저 치료 중에 통증을 느끼지 않을 수 있는가?

(a) 왜냐하면 그녀의 피부는 민감하지 않고 두껍기 때문이다
(b) 왜냐하면 간호사들이 계속 그녀에게 말을 걸기 때문이다
(c) 왜냐하면 의사는 통증관리 전문가이기 때문이다
(d) 왜냐하면 의사는 그것이 발라지는 부위에만 고통을 감소시키는 물질을 사용하기 때문이다

44 추론

레이저 치료의 각 단계가 평가받아야 하는 이유는 무엇인가?

(a) 피부가 더 밝아지는 것을 보증하기 위해
(b) 레이저 시술을 중단하기를 원하는지를 확인하기 위해
(c) 각 회당 얼마를 지불해야 하는 지를 계산하기 위해
(d) 심각한 부작용을 막기 위해

45 추론

Monica는 Smith 박사와 대화한 후에 무엇을 할 것인가?

(a) 안면 마사지를 계속하다
(b) Smith 박사 외와의 의사를 찾아가다
(c) 레이저 치료를 위한 상담 일정을 잡다
(d) 친구를 만나다

Listening 청취 269

TEST 3 | part 3 40~45 |

문제풀이

- 내용 분류 – 일상 대화
- 주제 요약 – Jenny의 집 구매에 대한 고민

A: Hello, Jenny! I heard that you are looking for a new house in the city.

B: That is not quite right, George. **40** ⟨I mean I want to buy a house in the city, but my husband insists on buying a house in the countryside.⟩ Which do you think is better?

A: We can discuss the advantages and disadvantages of both types of living.

B: Thank you. Let's start with living in cities.

A: Okay. One good thing about living in the city is that you will have proper medical care services. **41** ⟨You don't have to travel plenty of miles to visit a doctor and you don't need to spend long hours waiting for the ambulance to arrive in case of emergency.⟩ The number of doctors in cities is higher than in the countryside.

B: That is right. I also think that the city has the comprehensive transportation systems. Since I don't drive, taking subways and buses always helps me get from one place to another. Besides that, I can focus on reading a book with taking my eyes off the road while travelling.

A: I agree. In addition, there are better job opportunities. Over the past few years, employment has grown drastically in metropolitan areas.

B: That means I can pursue my career while living within the city. What about its disadvantages, though?

A: One disadvantage of living in the city is that the cost of living is typically high.

B: I also think pollution is a sad reality for big city life. Smog, high carbon emission rate, and the increased number of vehicles cause air pollution and lead people to suffer from heart diseases and respiratory diseases, like asthma and lung cancer.

A: Not only that: **42** ⟨due to the large concentration of population and an innumerable number of vehicles in the city, it is hard to avoid noise pollution that could damage mental health and increase stress as well as pressure.⟩

B: I see. How about the benefits of living in the countryside?

A: Well, if you live in the countryside, you will be free from pollution. The abundance of green trees and plants, and less amount of toxic pollutants improve the quality of the air.

B: That's nice, but what about its disadvantages?

A: A downside to rural living is that most of the rural areas do not have good educational facilities. For example, **43** ⟨unlike other big cities, there are a small number of schools, colleges and universities due to a low number of students.⟩ This is why people believe the quality of education in rural areas is poor.

B: Oh, that is worrying. Aside from that, lack of health facilities is one of the major issues faced by residents in rural areas. Good hospitals are lacking. You need to move to a city for medical treatment.

A: Yes, that is true. **44** ⟨Weather could be an issue, too. During blizzards in the winter, you have to regularly plow the snow, otherwise, you will be stuck down under the snow for days until help can reach you. During the rainy season or flood, you can be completely isolated in your house because most of the roads will be underwater.⟩

B: That is a good point. Thanks for discussing the pros and cons of both options with me. George.

A: No problem, Jenny. So, where are you going to buy your house?

B: I think, I'd like to live in harmony with nature. Both my husband and I pursue a happy life free from stress, money and competition. **45** ⟨So living in the countryside will not be a bad idea.⟩

40 ⓟ 정보 찾기(일치)

ⓒ What are Jenny and her husband planning to do?

(a) sell a house in the city
(b) rent a house in the city or countryside
(c) buy a house or an apartment
(d) live in the city or countryside

41 ⓟ 추론

ⓒ If they decide to live in the cities, what will they be able to do when they are sick?

(a) They will need to make a doctor's appointment.
(b) They will travel a short distance to see a doctor.
(c) They will get medical care services at a low price.
(d) They will be treated by the best doctors in the world.

42 ⓟ 정보 찾기(일치)

ⓒ Why is it difficult to protect noise pollution in the cities?

(a) because there are less electric cars than gas vehicles
(b) because there are too many factories
(c) because there are too many people
(d) because there are too many people with mental illnesses

43 ⓟ 정보 찾기(일치)

ⓒ According to George, what could negatively affect the quality of education in rural areas?

(a) a small number of students
(b) a small number of teachers
(c) poor government support
(d) the noise the neighbors cause

44 ⓟ 추론

ⓒ Based on the conversation, what most likely causes isolation in rural living?

(a) the location of a house
(b) extreme weather conditions
(c) the number of family members
(d) road conditions

45 ⓟ 추론

ⓒ What will Jenny and her husband most likely do?

(a) They will find a house near their workplace.
(b) They will be by a house in the city.
(c) They will buy a house in the countryside.
(d) They will rent a house in the countryside.

TEST 3 | part 3 40~45 |
문제풀이

A: 안녕, Jenny! 나는 네가 이 도시에서 새 집을 찾고 있다고 들었어.
B: 그건 사실이 아니야, George. **40** 〔나는 시내에 집을 사고 싶지만, 내 남편이 시골에 집을 사겠다고 고집하고 있거든.〕 어느 쪽이 더 낫다고 생각해?
A: 우리는 두 종류의 생활에서 장점과 단점에 대해 토론할 수 있어.
B: 고마워. 도시 생활부터 시작하자.
A: 알았어. 도시 생활의 한 가지 좋은 점은 적절한 의료 서비스를 받을 수 있다는 것이야. **41** 〔의사를 방문하기 위해 수 마일을 이동할 필요도 없고, 응급상황에 대비해 구급차가 도착할 때까지 오랜 시간을 기다릴 필요도 없어.〕 의사 수는 도시가 시골보다 많아.
B: 맞아. 나는 또한 도시가 포괄적인 교통 시스템을 가지고 있다고 생각해. 나는 운전을 하지 않기 때문에, 지하철과 버스를 타는 것은 한 장소에서 다른 장소로 가는 데 항상 도움이 돼. 그 외에도, 나는 이동 중에 길에서 눈을 떼고 책을 읽는 데 집중할 수 있어.
A: 나도 동의해. 게다가, 더 나은 직업의 기회가 있어. 지난 몇 년 동안, 수도권에서 고용이 급격히 증가해왔어.
B: 도시에 살면서 직장생활을 계속해나갈 수 있다는 뜻이야. 하지만 단점은 어떨까?
A: 도시에서 사는 것의 단점 중 하나는 생활비가 일반적으로 높다는 거야.
B: 나는 또한 오염도 대도시 생활에 슬픈 현실이라고 생각해. 스모그와 높은 탄소 배출률과 차량 증가는 대기 오염을 유발하고 심장질환과 천식이나 폐암과 같은 호흡기질환을 앓게 해.
A: 그뿐만 아니라, **42** 〔도시의 인구 밀도가 높고 차량 수가 많기 때문에, 정신 건강을 해치고 압박감뿐만 아니라 스트레스를 증가시킬 수 있는 소음 공해를 피하기는 어려워.〕
B: 그렇군. 시골에서 사는 것의 장점은 어떨까?
A: 글쎄, 시골에 살면 오염으로부터 자유로워질 거야. 녹색 나무와 식물이 풍부하고 독성 오염 물질의 양이 적으면 공기의 질이 향상돼.
B: 그거 좋긴 한데, 단점은 어때?
A: 시골 생활의 단점은 대부분의 시골 지역이 좋은 교육 시설을 가지고 있지 않다는 거야. 예를 들어, **43** 〔다른 대도시들과는 달리, 학생 수가 적기 때문에, 학교, 대학, 대학교 수가 적어.〕 이것이 사람들이 농촌 지역의 교육의 질이 좋지 않다고 믿는 이유야.
B: 아, 걱정되네. 그것과는 별도로, 보건시설 부족은 농촌 지역 주민들이 당면한 주요 문제 중 하나야. 좋은 병원은 부족하지. 넌 의료 시술을 위해 도시로 이사해야만 해.
A: 그래, 맞아. **44** 〔날씨도 문제가 될 수 있어. 겨울에 눈보라가 치는 동안, 너는 규칙적으로 눈을 치워야만 해. 그렇지 않으면, 너는 도움을 받을 때까지 며칠 동안 눈 밑에 갇혀 있을 거야. 장마철이나 홍수 때, 대부분의 도로가 물에 잠기기 때문에 집 안에 완전히 고립될 수 있어.〕
B: 좋은 지적이야. 두 가지 선택의 장단점을 나와 함께 논의해줘서 고마워, George.
A: 문제없어, Jenny. 그래, 어디에 집을 살 거야?
B: 내 생각에, 나는 자연과 조화를 이루며 살고 싶어. 남편과 나는 스트레스, 돈, 경쟁으로부터 자유로운 행복한 삶을 추구해. **45** 〔그래서 시골에서 사는 것은 나쁜 생각이 아닐 거야.〕

40 　　　　　　　　　　ⓟ 정보 찾기(일치)

ⓒ Jenny와 그녀의 남편은 무엇을 할 계획인가?

(a) 시내에서 집을 팔다
(b) 도시나 시골에 집을 빌리다
(c) 집이나 아파트를 사다
(d) 도시나 시골에 살다

41 　　　　　　　　　　　　　ⓟ 추론

ⓒ 만약 그들이 도시에서 살기로 결정한다면, 그들은 아플 때 무엇을 할 수 있는가?

(a) 의사를 만나려면 예약을 해야 한다
(b) 그들은 의사를 만나기 위해 짧은 거리를 이동할 것이다
(c) 그들은 저렴한 가격에 의료 서비스를 받을 것이다
(d) 그들은 세계 최고의 의사들에 의해 치료될 것이다

42 　　　　　　　　　ⓟ 정보 찾기(일치)

ⓒ 왜 도시에서 소음 공해를 보호하는 것이 어려운가?

(a) 왜냐하면 가스차보다 전기차가 적기 때문에
(b) 왜냐하면 공장이 너무 많기 때문에
(c) 왜냐하면 사람이 너무 많기 때문에
(d) 왜냐하면 정신병을 가진 사람들이 너무 많기 때문에

43 　　　　　　　　　ⓟ 정보 찾기(일치)

ⓒ George에 따르면, 농촌 지역에서 교육의 질에 부정적인 영향을 미치는 것은 무엇인가?

(a) 소수의 학생들
(b) 소수의 교사들
(c) 부실한 정부 지원
(d) 이웃들이 일으키는 소음

44 　　　　　　　　　　　　　ⓟ 추론

ⓒ 대화에 따르면, 농촌 생활에서 고립을 야기할 가능성이 가장 높은 것은 무엇인가?

(a) 집의 위치
(b) 심각한 기상 조건
(c) 가족 수
(d) 도로 상황

45 　　　　　　　　　　　　　ⓟ 추론

ⓒ Jenny와 Jenny의 남편은 무엇을 할 것 같은가?

(a) 그들은 직장 근처에 집을 구할 것이다
(b) 그들은 도서에 있는 집 옆에 있을 것이다
(c) 그들은 시골에 집을 살 것이다
(d) 그들은 시골에 있는 집을 빌릴 것이다

TEST 1 | part 4 46~52 |

문제풀이

- 내용 분류 – 일반 설명
- 주제 요약 – 중개 계좌 개설 방법

Good morning, everyone! Having your own brokerage account or stock account is a great way to grow your wealth. It gives you access to the securities exchange where you can buy and sell stocks. However, to many of you, setting up a brokerage account can seem complicated, but it is a simple process once you know. 46 (Today, I'll tell you how to open your first brokerage account.)

First, decide what you need a brokerage account for. Do you want to use it to invest your money for a short-term or long-term goal? or do you just want a convenient way to store and access mutual funds? 47 (The type of account you should open will depend on your financial goals and needs,) so it is significant to identify them as soon as possible.

Second, based on your goals, choose what type of brokerage account to open. People who open an account for the first time usually choose either a traditional brokerage account or a retirement account. Both accounts allow you to save money but they have differences. A traditional brokerage account leads you to pay tax on investment profits but you are free to withdraw your money whenever you'd like. On the other hand, 48 (a retirement account can get you tax deductions, but you won't be able to use your money until you are retired.)

Third, select a brokerage account provider that is right for you. If you want to purchase and manage your own investments by yourself, a brokerage account at an online broker is right for you. 49 (Online brokers do not charge inactivity and maintenance fees.) On the other hand, a managed brokerage account in a full-service brokerage firm is typically commission-based and comes with investment management by a human investment advisor who manages your investments. Since this is a full-service investment option, you have to pay for fees.

Fourth, directly apply to your preferred brokerage firm. You can open a new account by completing an application online. 50 (This is ideal for investors who want a quick and painless process with online brokers.) Alternatively, you can head down to the branch office in person to open your brokerage account. You'll be asked to fill out new account application forms that will ask about your risk tolerance, net worth, investment objectives, employment status and the extent of your financial knowledge in order to build an investor profile.

Finally, fund the account. Once you've opened the investment account, you'll need to initiate a deposit or funds transfer. 51 (After the transfer is complete and your brokerage account is funded, you can begin investing.) When funding your new account, be sure to keep your broker's minimums in mind. Many have different minimums for taxable accounts and retirement accounts.

After you have funded your account, it'll be a good idea to spend some time searching and learning the basics of how to responsibly choose stocks or funds.

Thank you for listening! 52 (If you'd like to open a brokerage account now, please stay! We at E-Trade charge no commission fees for a year and our broker-dealers are ready to offer various investments that are suitable for you and they will answer all your inquiries.)

46 주제 찾기

What is the main subject of the talk?

(a) choosing the right brokerage account provider
(b) ways to invest money
(c) how to overcome financial difficulties
(d) setting up a brokerage account

47 정보 찾기(일치)

What should one consider when choosing the type of account to open?

(a) what his brokerage account provider will be doing with the money
(b) what he will be doing with the money
(c) how much money he has
(d) how many money his brokerage account provider has

48 추론

How most likely can people avoid paying tax through a brokerage account?

(a) by withdrawing money anytime people want
(b) by choosing a brokage account
(c) by withdrawing money before people are retired
(d) by choosing a retirement account

49 정보 찾기(일치)

According to the speaker, which is an advantage of online brokers over human investment advisors?

(a) having no inactivity and maintenance fees
(b) having lower inactivity and maintenance fees
(c) providing a full-service investment option
(d) offering free investment management

50 정보 찾기(일치)

Why is it ideal for one to apply online when opening an account?

(a) so he can build an investor profile
(b) so he can save time on a process with online brokers
(c) so he can avoid sending his application forms
(d) so he can ask the online brokers questions

51 정보 찾기(일치)

When will one be able to start investing?

(a) before the brokerage account is funded
(b) after the brokerage account is funded
(c) after a deposit or funds transfer is initiated
(d) before a deposit or funds transfer is complete

52 추론

What is probably the speaker's purpose in delivering the talk?

(a) to encourage brokerage account owners to increase their financial profits
(b) to persuade people to open a brokerage account at E-Trade
(c) to inform people about what a brokerage account is
(d) to help people in managing their finances

TEST 1 | part 4 46~52 |
문제풀이

좋은 아침입니다. 여러분! 자신의 중개 계좌 또는 주식 계좌를 갖는 것은 부를 늘리는 좋은 방법입니다. 그것은 주식을 사고 팔 수 있는 증권거래소에 접근할 수 있게 해줍니다. 그러나 많은 분들에게 중개 계좌를 설정하는 것은 복잡해 보일 수 있지만, 일단 알고나면 간단한 절차입니다. 46 오늘은 ▣첫 중개 계좌 개설 방법을 알려드리겠습니다.

먼저 중개 계좌를 여러분이 원하는 것으로 결정하십시오. 단기 또는 장기 목표를 위해 돈을 투자하는 데 사용하고 싶습니까? 아니면 뮤추얼 펀드를 저장하고 접근하는 편리한 방법을 원하십니까? 47 개설해야 하는 계좌 유형은 ▣재정 목표와 필요에 달려있기 때문에, 가능한 한 빨리 재정 목표와 필요를 확인하는 것이 중요합니다.

둘째, 목표에 따라 어떤 종류의 중개 계좌를 개설할지를 선택하십시오. 처음으로 계좌를 개설하는 사람들은 일반적으로 전형적인 중개 계좌 또는 퇴직 계좌를 선택합니다. 두 계정 모두 돈을 저축할 수 있지만 차이점이 있습니다. 전형적인 중개 계좌는 투자 수익에 대한 세금을 내도록 하지만 여러분이 원할 때 언제든지 돈을 인출할 수 있습니다. 한편, 48 ▣퇴직 계좌는 세금 공제를 받을 수 있지만, 퇴직할 때까지 돈을 사용할 수 없을 것입니다.

셋째, 귀하에게 적합한 중개 계좌 제공 업체를 선택하십시오. 만약 자신의 투자를 직접 구매하고 관리하고 싶다면, 온라인 브로커의 중개 계좌가 적합합니다. 49 ▣온라인 브로커는 비활성 및 유지 관리 비용을 부과하지 않습니다. 반면에, 전문 증권 중개업 회사의 관리 중개 계정은 일반적으로 수수료 기반이며 투자를 관리하는 인적 투자 고문의 투자 관리와 함께 제공됩니다. 이것은 포괄적 업무를 제공하는 투자 옵션이므로 수수료를 지불해야만 합니다.

넷째, 선호하는 증권사에 직접 신청하십시오. 온라인으로 신청서를 작성하여 새 계좌를 개설할 수 있습니다. 50 이것은 ▣온라인 브로커와 함께 빠르고 힘들지 않은 과정을 원하는 투자자에게 이상적입니다. 또는 직접 지점으로 가서 중개 계좌를 개설할 수 있습니다. 투자자 프로필을 작성하기 위해 위험 허용 범위, 순 자산, 투자 목표, 고용 상태 및 재무 지식의 범위에 대해 묻는 새 계정 신청서를 작성해야 합니다.

마지막으로 계정에 자금을 입금하십시오. 투자 계좌를 개설한 후에는 입금 또는 자금 이체를 시작해야 합니다. 51 ▣이체가 완료되고 중개 계좌에 자금이 입금되면 투자를 시작할 수 있습니다. 새 계정에 자금을 입금할 때, 중개인의 최소 금액을 염두에 두십시오. 많은 사람들이 과세 계정과 퇴직 계정에 대해 서로 다른 최소 금액을 가지고 있습니다.

계정에 자금을 입금한 후에는, 책임감 있게 주식이나 자금을 선택하는 방법에 대한 기본 사항을 검색하고 학습하는 데 시간을 보내는 것이 좋습니다.

들어주셔서 감사합니다! 52 ▣지금 중개 계좌를 개설하고 싶으시면 그대로 계십시오! 저희 E-Trade는 1년간 수수료가 부과되지 않으며, 당사의 중개업자들은 귀하에게 적합한 다양한 투자를 제공할 준비가 되어 있으며, 귀하의 모든 문의에 답변해 드릴 것입니다.

46
그 이야기의 주요 주제는 무엇인가?

(a) 올바른 중개 계좌 제공 업체 선택
(b) 돈을 투자하는 방법
(c) 재정적 어려움을 극복하는 방법
(d) 중개 계좌 개설하기

47
개설할 계좌의 종류를 선택할 때 고려해야 할 사항은?

(a) 크의 중개 계좌 제공자가 그 돈으로 무엇을 할 것인가
(b) 그가 그 돈으로 무엇을 할 것인가
(c) 크가 얼마나 많은 돈을 가지고 있는지
(d) 크의 중개 계좌 제공자가 얼마나 많은 돈을 가지고 있는지

48
사람들이 중개 계좌를 통해 세금 납부를 피할 수 있는 방법은 어떤 것 인가?

(a) 사람들이 원할 때 언제든지 돈을 인출함으로써
(b) 중개 계좌를 선택함으로써
(c) 사람들이 은퇴하기 전에 돈을 인출함으로써
(d) 퇴직 계좌를 선택함으로써

49
화자에 따르면, 인적 투자 고문에 비해 온라인 브로커의 장점은 무엇인가?

(a) 비활성 및 유지 관리 비용이 없음
(b) 낮은 비활성 및 유지 관리 비용
(c) 전체 서비스 투자 옵션 제공
(d) 무료 투자 관리 제공

50
우리가 계정을 개설할 때 온라인으로 신청하는 것이 이상적인 이유는 무엇인가?

(a) 투자자의 프로필을 만들 수 있도록
(b) 온라인 브로커와의 과정에 시간을 절약할 수 있도록
(c) 신청서를 보내지 않도록
(d) 온라인 브로커에게 질문할 수 있도록

51
언제부터 투자를 시작할 수 있는가?

(a) 중개 계좌에 자금이 입금되기 전에
(b) 중개 계좌에 자금이 입금 된 후에
(c) 예금이나 자금 이체가 시작된 후에
(d) 예금이나 자금 이체가 완료되기 전에

52
연설자가 강연을 통해 전달하고자 하는 목적은 무엇인가?

(a) 중개 계좌 소유자가 재정적 이익을 높이도록 장려하기 위해
(b) E-Trade에 중개 계좌를 개설하도록 사람들을 설득하기 위해
(c) 사람들에게 중개 계좌가 무엇인지에 대해 알기 위해
(d) 사람들의 재정 관리를 돕기 위해

TEST 2 | part 4 46~52 |
문제풀이

- 내용 분류 – 일반 설명
- 주제 요약 – 좋은 고객 서비스의 중요성

Good morning, everyone. I'm your speaker for today's sales training program. Many of us are mostly concerned about selling products as many as possible. However, after years of working in the sales department, **46** I have a strong belief that improving customer service skills is just as important as selling many products.

Your customers are most likely to remember the company's customer service regardless of how awesome the product is. As a salesperson, good customer service creates return customers that are loyal to you and your company. **47** Also, good customer service is important because it has a huge impact on company's success.

Here are some tips on how to provide excellent customer service.

Tip number one- Be friendly. Try to greet customers with a smile and always be courteous and respectful. Be proactive by paying attention to the customer's needs and offering help or recommendations before they ask. Even if customers appear disappointed or angry, be kind to them.

Tip number two- Respond promptly. Customers appreciate a speedy response to their inquiries, especially when they have a time-sensitive request. **48-c,d** Experts advise returning all phone calls and emails within 24 hours impresses customers and decreases their complaints. **48-b** In addition, let customers know how long it will take you to assist them.

Tip number three- You should know every aspect of the product or service you are selling. If you are able to discuss its features and uses and show your customers the advantages they get from using your product, customers are more likely to buy more than they plan and less likely to ask for a refund.

Tip number four- Listen to your customers. **49** Customers just need to be heard, so be sure to actively listen to what they say. They might have a valid point that you can use to make your product even better. By only listening, you can understand exactly what your customer needs from you.

Tip number five- Say thank you. Customers often remember sincere gratitude and saying thank you reminds them why they shopped at our store. Sending a handwritten thank you note, providing free samples, and offering a special discount, for example, are effective ways of showing how much you thank customers.

Tip number six- Get to know your customers. When you have a better understanding of your customers and what drives them, you'll find it easier to offer them the customer service they need. **50** By asking your customers a few simple questions and conducting a survey, you can find areas where you can stand out from your competition.

Lastly, always focus on relationships. Showing that you care about them may inspire their loyalty and appreciation. You could offer personalized service, greet them by name and makes notes of previous conversations, so you can reference that information the next time you meet. **51** They always remember you if they have received good customer service.

52 Follow these tips and your prospective customers will think you are trustworthy, capable and aggressive in today's competitive market. When customers are satisfied with your customer service, your success will be highly ensured.

46 主제 찾기

C What is the talk about?

(a) how to have a successful career
(b) how to learn customer service skills
(c) strengthening customer service skills
(d) keeping one's hands clean

47 정보 찾기(일치)

C According to the speaker, why is good customer service important?

(a) It increases job satisfaction.
(b) It leads a company to thrive.
(c) It affects the national economy.
(d) It allows customers to buy products at lower prices.

48 정보 찾기(불일치)

C Which advice about prompt response was not mentioned in the talk?

(a) asking for customer feedback on a purchase
(b) informing customers about time to handle their requests
(c) replying emails within 24 hours
(d) returning all phone calls within one day

49 추론

C Based on talk, why most likely should customers need to be heard?

(a) because they can stop complaining
(b) because they will buy more products
(c) because everything they say needs to be recorded
(d) because products can be improved by their opinions

50 정보 찾기(일치)

C What should a salesperson do if he wants to know his customers?

(a) ask customers a few simple questions
(b) call each customer everyday
(c) meet each customer in person
(d) ask customers for help

51 정보 찾기(일치)

C What kind of salesperson do customers tend to remember?

(a) one who wears trendy outfits
(b) one who provides good customer service
(c) one who sells many products
(d) one who has a funny name

52 추론

C Why most likely is providing good customer service favorable to a salesperson's success?

(a) because it makes him an expert in sales
(b) because it helps him have more clients
(c) because it allows him to earn money
(d) because it makes his boss like him

TEST 2 | part 4 46~52 |

문제풀이

여러분, 좋은 아침입니다. 저는 오늘 영업 교육 프로그램의 발표자입니다. 우리들 중 많은 사람들이 가능한 한 많은 제품을 판매하는 것에 대해 대부분 걱정하고 있습니다. 하지만 판매부에서 수년간 근무한 결과, 46 〔저는 ᵃ고객 서비스 기술을 향상시키는 일이 많은 제품을 판매하는 것만큼 ᵇ중요하다는 강력한 믿음이 있습니다.〕

귀사의 고객은 제품이 얼마나 멋진지에 관계없이 회사의 고객 서비스로 기억할 가능성이 가장 높습니다. 영업 사원으로서, 좋은 고객 서비스는 여러분과 귀사에 충실한 재방문 고객을 창출합니다. 47 〔또한, 좋은 고객 서비스는 ᵃ회사의 성공에 큰 영향을 미치기 때문에 중요합니다.〕

여기에 훌륭한 고객 서비스를 제공하는 방법에 대한 몇 가지 팁이 있습니다.

첫 번째 팁 – 친절하게 행동하십시오. 고객을 웃으며 항상 예의 바르고 공손하게 대하세요. 고객이 요청하기 전에 고객의 요구에 주의를 기울이고 도움이나 권장 사항을 제시함으로써 사전 대응하십시오. 고객들이 실망하거나 화가 난 것처럼 보일지라도, 그들에게 친절하게 대하세요.

두 번째 팁 – 즉시 응답하십시오. 고객은 특히 시간에 민감한 요청이 있을 때 문의에 대한 빠른 응답을 높이 평가합니다. 48-c,d 전문가들은 ᵇ24시간 이내에 모든 전화 및 이메일에 응답하면 고객에게 감동을 주고 불만을 줄일 수 있다고 조언합니다.〕 48-b 〔또한, ᵇ고객에게 지원하는 데 ᵃ시간이 얼마나 걸릴지 알려주십시오.〕

세 번째 팁 – 여러분이 판매하는 제품 또는 서비스의 모든 측면을 알아야 합니다. 그것의 기능과 용도에 대해 논의하고 고객에게 제품 사용으로 얻는 이점을 보여줄 수 있다면, 고객은 계획한 것보다 더 많이 구매하고 환불을 요청할 가능성이 적습니다.

네 번째 팁 – 고객의 말에 귀를 기울이십시오. 49 〔고객은 그저 들어주는 것을 원하기 때문에, 고객의 말에 적극 귀를 기울이시기 바랍니다. ᵇ그들은 여러분이 여러분의 제품을 훨씬 더 좋게 만드는 데 사용할 수 있는 타당한 견해를 가지고 있을 것입니다.〕 귀담아 듣는 것만으로, 고객이 여러분에게 요구하는 것이 무엇인지를 정확히 이해할 수 있습니다.

다섯 번째 팁 – 감사하다고 말하십시오. 고객들은 종종 진심 어린 감사를 기억하며 감사하다고 말하는 것은 그들이 왜 우리 가게에서 구매를 했는지를 상기시킵니다. 예를 들어, 손으로 쓴 감사 편지를 보내고, 무료 견본을 제공하고, 특별 할인을 제공하는 것은 고객에게 얼마나 감사하는지를 보여주는 효과적인 방법입니다.

여섯 번째 팁 – 고객에 대해 알아보십시오. 고객과 고객을 이끄는 요소에 대해 더 잘 이해하면, 고객에게 필요한 고객 서비스를 더 쉽게 제공할 수 있습니다. 50 〔ᵇ고객에게 몇 가지 간단한 질문을 하고 설문 조사를 수행하여, 경쟁사와 차별되는 영역을 찾을 수 있습니다.〕

마지막으로, 항상 관계에 집중하십시오. 여러분이 그들에게 관심을 보인다는 것을 보여주는 것은 그들에게 의리와 감사를 불러일으킬 수 있습니다. 맞춤 서비스를 제공하고, 이름을 부르며 인사하고, 이전 대화 내용을 메모하여 다음에 만날 때 해당 정보를 참조할 수 있습니다. 51 〔그들은 ᵇ좋은 고객 서비스를 받았다면 항상 ᵇ여러분을 기억합니다.〕

52 〔이러한 팁을 따르면 ᵇ잠재 고객은 당신을 오늘날의 경쟁 시장에서 신뢰할 수 있고, 능력이 있으며, 적극적이라고 생각할 것입니다.〕 고객이 고객 서비스에 만족하면, 여러분의 성공이 크게 보장될 것입니다.

46 ⓟ 주제 찾기
ⓒ 무엇에 대한 이야기인가?

(a) 성공적인 경력을 쌓는 방법
(b) 고객 서비스 기술을 배우는 방법
(c) 고객 서비스 기술 강화하기
(d) 손을 깨끗하게 유지하기

47 ⓟ 정보 찾기(일치)
ⓒ 화자에 따르면, 좋은 고객 서비스는 왜 중요한가?

(a) 그것은 직업 만족도를 높인다
(b) 그것은 회사가 번영하도록 이끈다
(c) 그것은 국가 경제에 영향을 미친다
(d) 그것은 고객들이 더 낮은 가격에 제품을 살 수 있게 해준다

48 ⓟ 정보 찾기(불일치)
ⓒ 신속한 대응에 대한 어떤 조언이 강연에서 언급되지 않았는가?

(a) 구매에 대한 고객 피드백 요청하기
(b) 고객에게 요청을 처리할 시간에 대해 알리기
(c) 24시간 이내에 이메일 회신하기
(d) 하루 안에 모든 전화에 응답하기

49 ⓟ 추론
ⓒ 대화에 따르면, 고객의 의견을 들어야 하는 이유는 무엇인가?

(a) 왜냐하면 그들은 불평하는 것을 멈출 수 있기 때문에
(b) 왜냐하면 그들은 더 많은 제품을 살 것이기 때문에
(c) 왜냐하면 그들이 말하는 모든 것을 기록해야 하기 때문에
(d) 왜냐하면 제품은 그들의 의견에 의해 향상될 수 있기 때문에

50 ⓟ 정보 찾기(일치)
ⓒ 영업 사원이 고객을 알고 싶다면 무엇을 해야 하나?

(a) 고객에게 몇 가지 간단한 질문을 한다
(b) 매일 각 고객에게 전화를 건다
(c) 각 고객을 직접 만난다
(d) 고객에게 도움을 청한다

51 ⓟ 정보 찾기(일치)
ⓒ 고객들은 어떤 종류의 영업사원을 기억하는 경향이 있는가?

(a) 유행하는 옷을 입은 사람
(b) 좋은 고객 서비스를 제공하는 사람
(c) 많은 제품을 판매하는 사람
(d) 재미있는 이름을 가진 사람

52 ⓟ 추론
ⓒ 영업사원의 성공에 호의적인 좋은 고객 서비스를 제공하는 것이 가장 좋은 이유는 무엇인가?

(a) 왜냐하면 그것이 그를 영업 전문가로 만들기 때문이다
(b) 왜냐하면 더 많은 고객을 확보하는 데 도움이 되기 때문이다
(c) 왜냐하면 그것은 그가 돈을 벌 수 있게 해주기 때문이다
(d) 왜냐하면 그것이 상사가 그를 좋아하게 만들기 때문이다

Listening 청취 **281**

TEST 3 | part 4 46~52 |
문제풀이

- 내용 분류 – 일반 설명
- 주제 요약 – 전화로 까다로운 고객을 처리하는 방법

Hello, everyone. While a lot of customers you will speak on the phone are polite and considerate, some customers start yelling at you on the phone. Today, I'm going to talk to you about how to effectively deal with tough customers on the phone because this will be part of your job as a call center professional.

It is inevitable to speak to angry or frustrated customers on the phone. These people can be very unreasonable and feel like they have every right to be rude to you. Handling this type of people is not easy at all, but it's your job duty to provide them with quality customer service. **46** 〔So, here are some tips on how to deal with difficult customers on the phone.〕

The first tip is **47** 〔to listen to difficult customers speaking on the phone.〕When you really listen to what they are trying to tell you, you are simultaneously showing concern and gaining insight into the issue they are having, which helps you find a solution.

The second tip is to provide validation to the customer. Instead of telling customers to "calm down", try saying "You're right, this is a problem, and we are going to find a solution."

Third, do not react emotionally. When you're in the middle of a tense conversation, you might say something sarcastic or yell back, however, as a call center professional, you need to keep your voice calm and pleasant. At times, customers can test your patience to the limit, but the trick is to separate yourself from their emotion. **48** 〔If you react in anger, this will only exacerbate the situation.〕

You can actually practice your tone of voice. The more experience you have with handling your customers, the more proficient you will become. Train yourself to maintain a pleasant and calm tone of voice, no matter what the customer says to you.

Fourth, offer solutions. You should express an apology for the trouble the customer is having, but you can't keep apologizing forever. **49** 〔Give your customer a single and definite solution if you have one, but offering a variety of solutions for a difficult issue is helpful because customers can decide for themselves how they would like to proceed.〕

The fifth tip is to avoid placing customers back on hold because that will usually only irritate them further. Whenever possible or appropriate, complete any support tasks while the customer can hear you. If you need to put them on hold, be sure to set clear expectations by describing what you are going to do and approximately how long it will take until you return to the line.

If you don't figure out what's wrong, simply tell them that you don't have a solution. **50** 〔Don't make promises you can't keep, but you can still make a deliberate effort to show empathy. This can be very effective for calming someone down.〕If your customers won't listen to reason and continue to yell at you, then it's probably time to hang up the phone.

Finally, take a few minutes to rest. **51** 〔Dealing with angry customers is stressful and speaking to a new customer while still feeling the tension of previous experience might lead to an unsatisfactory service.〕So, take a break, do whatever will relax you, and don't let the stress affect you.

Follow the tips I've presented, and be a better call center professional. **52** 〔When you succeed in handling a difficult customer on the phone over and over again, your self-confidence will be boosted and you will find answering the next regular customer complaint so much easier.〕

46 🅿 주제 찾기

What is the talk about?

(a) how to identify a problem customer on the phone
(b) how to avoid customer complaints on the phone
(c) how to attract good customers on the phone
(d) how to deal with difficult customers on the phone

47 🅿 정보 찾기(일치)

How should a call center professional respond when speaking to a difficult customer on the phone?

(a) by raising his voice
(b) by listening to the customer
(c) by asking the customer to stay calm
(d) by hanging up and calling the customer back in a few minutes

48 🅿 정보 찾기(일치)

Why should call center professionals need to keep their voice calm and pleasant?

(a) to identify customers' emotions
(b) to end the conversation with customers quickly
(c) to prevent the situation from getting worse
(d) to let customers buy more products

49 🅿 정보 찾기(일치)

What is the benefit of offering various solutions to difficult customers?

(a) customers can choose a solution they want.
(b) customers can feel their complaints are right.
(c) customers will be less angry.
(d) customers will stop complaining quickly.

50 🅿 추론

Why most likely should a call center professional try to show empathy?

(a) because customers would appreciate his attitude
(b) because customers like someone listening to what they say
(c) because the service has been inadequate
(d) because customers can calm down

51 🅿 정보 찾기(일치)

How can speaking to a new customer on the phone while still stressed out affect service?

(a) It may result in satisfactory service.
(b) It may lead to an inappropriate service.
(c) It can contribute to poor mental health.
(d) It can make the customer hang up the phone.

52 🅿 정보 찾기(일치)

According to the speaker, what makes one's self-confidence increase?

(a) dealing with a tough customer on the phone repeatedly
(b) solving a difficult complaint on one's own
(c) meeting tough customers in person
(d) addressing a difficult problem immediately

TEST 3 | part 4 46~52 |

문제풀이

안녕하세요, 여러분. 여러분이 전화로 이야기할 많은 고객들이 정중하고 사려 깊은 반면, 어떤 고객들은 전화로 여러분에게 소리를 지르기 시작합니다. 오늘은 당신의 일 중 하나인 콜센터 전문가로서 전화상으로 다루기 힘든 고객을 효과적으로 상대하는 방법에 대해 말씀드리겠습니다.

화를 내거나 좌절감을 느낀 고객들과 전화로 대화하는 것은 불가피합니다. 이 사람들은 매우 비합리적이고 여러분께 무례할 모든 권리가 있다고 느낄 수 있습니다. 이러한 유형의 사람들을 다루는 일은 결코 쉬운 일이 아니지만, 품격 있는 고객 서비스를 그들에게 제공하는 것이 바로 여러분의 임무입니다. 46 따라서, 여기에 전화로 까다로운 고객을 처리하는 방법에 대한 몇 가지 조언이 있습니다.

첫 번째 조언은 47 까다로운 고객이 전화로 말하는 것을 듣는 것입니다. 그들이 여러분에게 말하려는 것을 정말로 들을 때, 여러분은 동시에 관심을 보이고 그들이 가지고 있는 문제에 대한 통찰력을 얻음으로써 해결책을 찾는 데 도움이 됩니다.

두 번째 조언은 고객에게 타당성을 제공하는 것입니다. 고객에게 "진정하세요"라고 말하는 대신, "당신이 옳습니다. 이것은 문제이며, 우리는 해결책을 찾을 것입니다."라고 말해 보십시오.

세 번째로, 감정적으로 반응하지 마십시오. 긴장된 대화 중에는 비꼬는 말을 하거나 소리를 지르는 경우도 있지만, 콜센터 전문가로서 목소리를 차분하고 유쾌하게 유지해야 합니다. 때때로, 고객은 여러분의 인내심을 극단적으로 시험할 수 있지만, 요령은 자신을 감정에서 분리하는 것입니다. 48 만약 분노에 반응하면, 이것은 상황을 악화시킬 뿐입니다.

여러분은 실제로 목소리 톤을 연습할 수 있습니다. 고객을 다루는 경험이 많을수록 더 능숙해질 것입니다. 고객이 여러분에게 어떤 말을 하든 즐겁고 차분한 목소리 톤을 유지하도록 스스로를 훈련하십시오.

네 번째로, 해결책을 제시하세요. 고객이 겪고 있는 문제에 대해 사과를 해야 하지만, 영원히 사과할 수는 없습니다. 49 만약, 여러분이 확실한 하나의 해결책을 가지고 있다면 고객에게 제공하되, 고객이 원하는 진행 방식을 스스로 결정할 수 있기 때문에, 어려운 문제에 대해 다양한 해결책을 제시하는 것은 도움이 됩니다.

다섯 번째 조언은 고객은 기다리는 것에 짜증을 내기에 그들을 기다리게 하는 상황을 피하는 것입니다. 가능하거나 필요할 때마다, 고객이 여러분의 말을 들을 수 있는 동안 모든 지원 작업을 완료하십시오. 만약 여러분이 고객을 기다리게 만든다면, 반드시 여러분이 무엇을 할 것인지 그리고 여러분이 다시 통화에 돌아올 때까지 대략 얼마나 걸릴 것인지를 설명함으로써 명확한 기대치를 설정하십시오.

만약 여러분이 무엇이 문제인지 알지 못한다면, 간단히 그들에게 해결책이 없다고 말하세요. 50 지킬 수 없는 약속은 하지 말고, 그래도 공감할 수 있도록 의도적인 노력을 할 수 있습니다. 이것은 누군가를 진정시키는 데 매우 효과적일 수 있습니다. 만약 여러분의 고객이 충고에 따르지 않고 계속해서 여러분에게 소리를 지른다면, 아마도 전화를 끊어야 할 때일 것입니다.

마지막으로, 몇 분 정도 휴식을 취하세요. 51 화가 난 고객을 상대하는 것은 스트레스이고 이전 경험의 긴장감을 여전히 느끼면서 새로운 고객에게 말하는 것은 불만족스러운 서비스로 이어질 수 있습니다. 그러니, 휴식을 취하고, 긴장을 풀 수 있는 어떤 것이든 하고, 스트레스가 여러분에게 영향을 미치지 않도록 하세요.

제가 제시한 조언을 따르고 더 나은 콜센터 전문가가 되십시오. 52 전화로 까다로운 고객을 계속 상대하는 데 성공하면, 자신감이 높아지고 다음 일반 고객 불만 사항에 대한 대답이 훨씬 더 쉬워질 겁니다.

46
무엇에 대한 이야기인가?

(a) 전화상으로 문제 고객을 식별하는 방법
(b) 전화상으로 고객의 불만을 피하는 방법
(c) 전화상으로 좋은 고객을 끌어들이는 방법
(d) 전화상으로 까다로운 고객을 상대하는 방법

47
콜센터 전문가는 전화상으로 까다로운 고객과 통화를 할 때 어떻게 대응해야 하는가?

(a) 목소리를 높임으로써
(b) 고객의 말을 들음으로써
(c) 고객에게 침착하라고 요구함으로써
(d) 전화를 끊고 몇 분 후에 다시 고객에게 전화를 걸어 봄으로써

48
왜 콜센터 전문가는 목소리를 차분하고 즐겁게 유지하는 것이 필요한가?

(a) 고객의 감정을 파악하기 위해
(b) 고객과의 대화를 빨리 끝내기 위해
(c) 상황이 악화되는 것을 막기 위해
(d) 고객들이 더 많은 제품을 사도록 하기 위해

49
까다로운 고객에게 다양한 해결책을 제공하면 어떤 이점이 있나?

(a) 고객은 원하는 해결책을 선택할 수 있다
(b) 고객들은 그들의 불만이 옳다고 느낄 수 있다
(c) 고객은 화를 덜 낼 것이다
(d) 고객은 불평하는 것을 빨리 멈출 것이다

50
콜센터 전문가가 공감을 표현해야 하는 이유는 무엇인가?

(a) 왜냐하면 고객들은 그의 태도에 감사할 것이기 때문이다
(b) 왜냐하면 고객들은 그들이 말하는 것을 듣는 누군가를 좋아하기 때문이다
(c) 왜냐하면 서비스가 부적절했기 때문이다
(d) 왜냐하면 고객들은 진정할 수 있기 때문이다

51
스트레스를 받으면서도 새로운 고객과 통화를 하는 것이 서비스에 어떤 영향을 미칠 수 있나?

(a) 그것은 만족스러운 서비스 결과를 낳는다
(b) 그것은 부적절한 서비스로 이어질 수 있다
(c) 그것은 나쁜 정신 건강에 기여할 수 있다
(d) 그것은 고객이 전화를 끊게 만들 수 있다

52
화자의 말에 따르면, 무엇이 자신감을 증가시키는가?

(a) 전화상으로 까다로운 고객을 반복적으로 대하기
(b) 혼자서 힘든 불평을 해결하기
(c) 까다로운 고객을 직접 만나기
(d) 어려운 문제를 즉시 해결하기

문제 풀이는 Skill! 빠르게 푸는 전략으로 지텔프 졸업!

시대에듀
답이 보이는 지텔프 독해 실전편

고득점을 위한 문제 풀이 전략!
혼자서도 학습 가능한 자세한 지문 분석!
지텔프 독해 돌파를 위한 3단계 문제 풀이 스킬!

| 2026 |

스피드
지텔프
레벨2

SPEED G-TELP LEVEL 2

공저 정윤호·이정미

실전 모의고사

G-TELP 핵심이론 + 상세한 문제풀이 + 모의고사 3회분

다양한 학습 콘텐츠 제공
온라인 강의
sdedu.co.kr

시대에듀

TEST 1

GENERAL TESTS OF ENGLISH LANGUAGE PROFICIENCY
G-TELP™

LEVEL 2

GRAMMAR SECTION

DIRECTIONS:

The following items need a word or words to complete the sentence. From the four choices which follow each item, choose the best answer. Then blacken in the correct circle on your answer sheet.

Example:

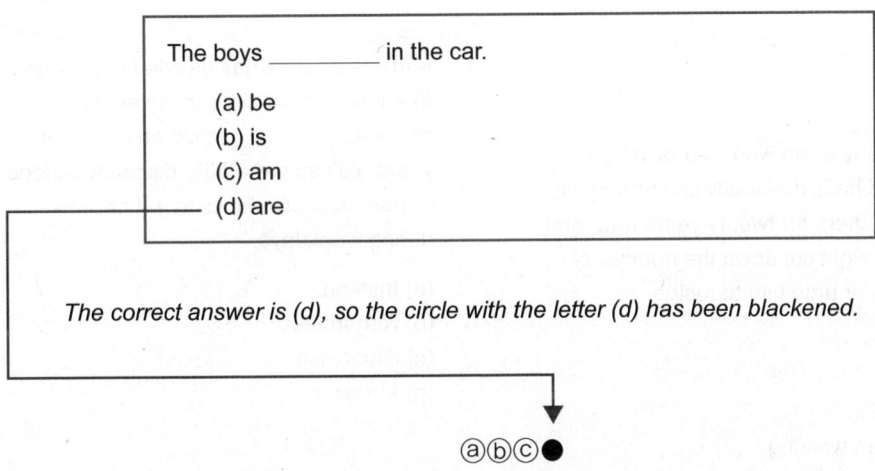

The correct answer is (d), so the circle with the letter (d) has been blackened.

NOW TURN THE PAGE AND BEGIN

1. Even with governmental subsidies, many individual business owners still won't have enough funds to maintain their businesses this year. Particularly, restaurant owners have therefore recommended _____ food prices if they are to continue business operations.

   (a) increasing
   (b) to be increasing
   (c) to increase
   (d) having increased

2. The company Brian works for is in bad shape, and he is extremely concerned. He _____ there for twenty years now, and is afraid it might cut down the number of employees or urge him to resign.

   (a) will work
   (b) works
   (c) is working
   (d) has been working

3. Living in the city is starting to harm Vicki's health because air pollution is severe. She thinks that if she lived in the country, she _____ fresh air everyday.

   (a) breathes
   (b) will breathe
   (c) would have breathed
   (d) would breathe

4. Macarthur High School's choir will be performing next. Right now, the choir members _____ plenty of water to keep their vocal cords from drying out.

   (a) drink
   (b) have drunk
   (c) are drinking
   (d) would drink

5. Kim's restaurant has decided to provide free lunch to the city's impoverished citizens. _____, children under 14 years old can get a 50% discount on food or non-alcoholic drinks to eat or drink during weekdays.

   (a) Instead
   (b) Regardless
   (c) Otherwise
   (d) Moreover

6. Linda was late for work this morning. She had to go back home to get the materials for meeting she'd left on the desk. She _____ the bus when she remembered about the documents.

   (a) would already get off
   (b) already got off
   (c) was already getting off
   (d) had already got off

7. Luke wishes that he had better self-control around computer games. If he had not played games all day yesterday, he _____ his math exam.

(a) could be passing
(b) was passing
(c) passed
(d) could have passed

8. In many countries, the high unemployment rate is causing a stagnant economy, forcing people _____ cities or their countries by emigrating to places where they can find a job.

(a) having left
(b) leaving
(c) to leave
(d) to have left

9. Prince Laboratories has poured massive sums into a new drug for diabetes. However, the FDA is still examining the drug's safety. By October, the company _____ for FDA approval for two years before they can distribute the drug to people all over the world.

(a) will have been waiting
(b) has waited
(c) would have waited
(d) will wait

10. Eric is disappointed that he cannot go to the cinema with his friends on the weekend. He is considering _____ them after the movie, but is worried that he will not be able to finish work.

(a) to be meeting
(b) having met
(c) meeting
(d) to meet

11. Many roads in the countryside are so narrow that accidents commonly happen. While farmers and residents have sent request letters for road construction, the government advises that the public _____ bikes, bicycles and small cars in the meantime.

(a) are using
(b) will use
(c) use
(d) uses

12. Melissa was very nervous when she first started swimming in the sea. She only had experienced _____ in the swimming pool.

(a) to be swimming
(b) swimming
(c) to swim
(d) having swum

13. Sandra has just left home, and is on her way to the office. Given how close her office is to her house, I'm sure she _____ be here before the meeting starts.

    (a) should
    (b) may
    (c) will
    (d) could

14. I was supposed to go shopping with my sister yesterday, but my last client meeting went longer than expected. She was really angry because she _____ for an hour by the time I finally met her.

    (a) waited
    (b) would have waited
    (c) was waiting
    (d) had been waiting

15. We expect a huge crowd at the Korean music concert tomorrow. To get a good seat, it is imperative that you _____ at the venue at least four hours before the concert begins.

    (a) will arrive
    (b) have arrived
    (c) arrive
    (d) to arrive

16. Sales of printed newspapers are decreasing in many countries because newspapers are increasingly replaced by online news sources. If Internet technologies did not develop today, printed newspapers _____ prevalent.

    (a) would have remained
    (b) remain
    (c) have remained
    (d) would remain

17. The police wanted to ensure that their primary suspect was definitively the one who smuggled drugs. Therefore, several witnesses were asked _____ the man in police custody.

    (a) having identified
    (b) identifying
    (c) to identify
    (d) to have identified

18. Jack is regretting buying a new laptop too soon because the laptop is now on sale. If he had waited a little bit longer, he _____ a fair amount of money on the purchase.

    (a) saved
    (b) would have saved
    (c) was saving
    (d) would save

19. Rehabilitating old buildings to their original appearance can help attract investment as well as tourists if the structures are historically significant. _____, a historic but abandoned industrial building can be turned into small business space.

    (a) Moreover
    (b) For instance
    (c) In fact
    (d) Thus

20. Did you know that Maggie has already returned home from her business trip? I saw her this afternoon while she _____ coffee with her mom at the cafe.

    (a) would drink
    (b) drank
    (c) was drinking
    (d) had drunk

21. Lisa can't wait to finish work. Her husband is not preparing dinner for her. She is sure their kitchen _____ of baked lamb, and pizza when she gets home later.

    (a) smells
    (b) is smelling
    (c) has smelled
    (d) will be smelling

22. My grandfather Tony knocked over a glass of orange juice while I was cleaning in the living room. _____ the juice, I would have prepared dinner to serve before 6 pm.

    (a) He had not spilled
    (b) If he did not spilled
    (c) Had he not spilled
    (d) Were he not spilled

23. Cindy is reluctant to eat lunch and dinner because she is afraid of putting on weight. Her doctor insists that she _____ more, so she can burn more calories or speed up her metabolism.

    (a) will exercise
    (b) is exercising
    (c) exercises
    (d) exercise

24. Jimmy's math teacher is very strict about punctuality. In fact, she said that missing the school bus, _____ for tardiness, is the last explanation she wants to hear when one student is late for school.

    (a) what she never allows as an excuse
    (b) that she never allows as an excuse
    (c) whom she never allows as an excuse
    (d) which she never allows as an excuse

25. Stella took a medical leave of absence for two weeks. I wanted to visit her house to check on her. However, I was afraid Stella _____ feel uncomfortable with my visit.

    (a) can
    (b) might
    (c) will
    (d) must

26. Anthony's expenses for ongoing roof repairs have just reached $1000. He is on a tight budget nowadays, and if he could make the repairs himself, he _____ to use that $1000 to donate for families living in poverty.

    (a) would be able
    (b) would have been able
    (c) was able
    (d) has been able

THIS IS THE END OF THE GRAMMAR SECTION

LISTENING SECTION

DIRECTIONS:

The Listening Sections has four parts. In each part you will hear a spoken passage and a number of questions about the passage. First you will hear the questions. Then you will hear the passage. From the four choices for each question, choose the best answer. Then blacken in the correct circle on your answer sheet.

Now you will hear an example question. Then you will hear an example passage.

Now listen to the example question.

Example:

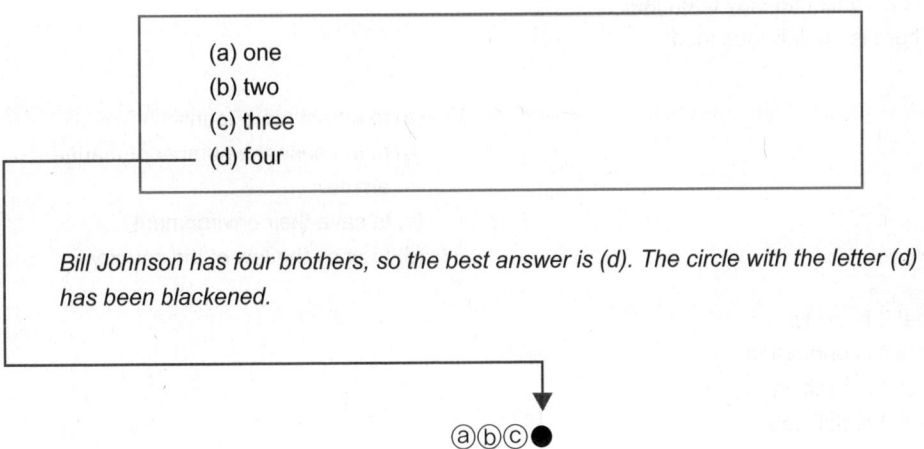

Bill Johnson has four brothers, so the best answer is (d). The circle with the letter (d) has been blackened.

NOW TURN THE PAGE AND BEGIN

PART 1. You will hear a conversation between two people. First you will hear questions 27 through 33. Then you will hear the conversation. Choose the best answer to each question in the time provided.

27. (a) beaches that are easy to reach
    (b) muddy beaches
    (c) beaches with lots of tourists
    (d) remote beaches

28. (a) The water there is cloudy.
    (b) There are many bars and restaurants that keep people up all night.
    (c) There are not many bars and restaurants that stay open late.
    (d) There is no delicious food.

29. (a) that it is exotic
    (b) that it is unexciting
    (c) that it is exciting
    (d) that it is polluted

30. (a) to visit a secluded beach
    (b) to explore underwater caves
    (c) to sleep on a beach at night
    (d) to relax on the sand

31. (a) because sleeping on a beach can be dangerous
    (b) because the weather is unpredictable
    (c) because there are many dangerous insects
    (d) because tourists are not allowed to sleep on a beach

32. (a) to attract more tourists
    (b) to increase the number of marine animals
    (c) to save their environment
    (d) to obey the law of the country

33. (a) He'll be booking a flight to Batanes.
    (b) He'll be thinking about when to quit his job.
    (c) He'll be flying to Batanes with Donna.
    (d) He'll be planning what to do for next summer vacation.

PART 2. You will hear a man talking to a group of people. First, you will hear questions 34 through 39. Then you will hear the talk. Choose the best answer to each question in the time provided.

34. (a) purchase store-bought soaps more than handmade soaps
    (b) purchase the speaker's soaps
    (c) learn how to make their own soaps
    (d) learn how to get rid of germs

35. (a) It allows a person to spend time with others.
    (b) It encourages a person to test diverse recipes.
    (c) It helps a person to flush out stress hormones.
    (d) It motivates a person to pursue personal goals.

36. (a) by using only high-quality soap
    (b) by purchasing store-bought soap occasionally
    (c) by avoiding making bad soap
    (d) by knowing how good handmade soap is made

37. (a) by removing moisture from the air
    (b) by absorbing moisture from the atmosphere
    (c) by maintaining constant body temperature
    (d) by reducing body temperature

38. (a) Its ingredients are far more expensive than store-bought soap.
    (b) There are extra fees to pay the supplier.
    (c) There are extra fees to buy equipment.
    (d) The ingredients cannot be purchased in bulk.

39. (a) to impress friends or families with one's soap making skills
    (b) to save money on gifts
    (c) to teach friends or families how to make handmade soap
    (d) to start a soap business

PART 3. *You will hear a conversation between two people. First you will hear questions 40 through 45. Then you will hear the conversation. Choose the best answer to each question in the time provided.*

40. (a) what to do after work
    (b) whether she should quit her job or not
    (c) whether she should live alone or with parents
    (d) how to spend time with parents

41. (a) by being able to visit her parents anytime she wants without asking permissions
    (b) by being able to have her personal space and privacy without asking permissions
    (c) by being able to live away from people she doesn't like without considering their needs or requirements
    (d) by being able to do something freely without considering somebody's needs or requirements

42. (a) She'll have to pay higher taxes.
    (b) She'll have to do all household chores on her own.
    (c) She'll have to take a bus from home to work.
    (d) She won't be able to save up money.

43. (a) by relying on financial support provided by parents
    (b) by paying only the Internet connection and groceries
    (c) by asking parents to manage her money
    (d) by setting up her own business with parents

44. (a) because her parents would want to spend every night with her
    (b) because her parents wouldn't allow her to come home late
    (c) because her parents wouldn't support her financially
    (d) because her parents would need her care

45. (a) buy an apartment near the company
    (b) rent an apartment near the company
    (c) live with parents and commute
    (d) live alone and commute

PART 4. You will hear an explanation of a process. First you will hear questions 46 through 52. Then you will hear the explanation. Choose the best answer to each question in the time provided.

46. (a) choosing the right brokerage account provider
    (b) ways to invest money
    (c) how to overcome financial difficulties
    (d) setting up a brokerage account

47. (a) what his brokerage account provider will be doing with the money
    (b) what he will be doing with the money
    (c) how much money he has
    (d) how many money his brokerage account provider has

48. (a) by withdrawing money anytime people want
    (b) by choosing a brokage account
    (c) by withdrawing money before people are retired
    (d) by choosing a retirement account

49. (a) having no inactivity and maintenance fees
    (b) having lower inactivity and maintenance fees
    (c) providing a full-service investment option
    (d) offering free investment management

50. (a) so he can build an investor profile
    (b) so he can save time on a process with online brokers
    (c) so he can avoid sending his application forms
    (d) so he can ask the online brokers questions

51. (a) before the brokerage account is funded
    (b) after the brokerage account is funded
    (c) after a deposit or funds transfer is initiated
    (d) before a deposit or funds transfer is complete

52. (a) to encourage brokerage account owners to increase their financial profits
    (b) to persuade people to open a brokerage account at E-Trade
    (c) to inform people about what a brokerage account is
    (d) to help people in managing their finances

THIS IS THE END OF THE LISTENING SECTION

READING AND VOCABULARY SECTION

DIRECTIONS:

You will now read four different passages. Each passage is followed by comprehension and vocabulary questions. From the four choices for each item, choose the best answer. Then blacken in the correct circle on your answer sheet.

Read the following example passage and example question.

Example:

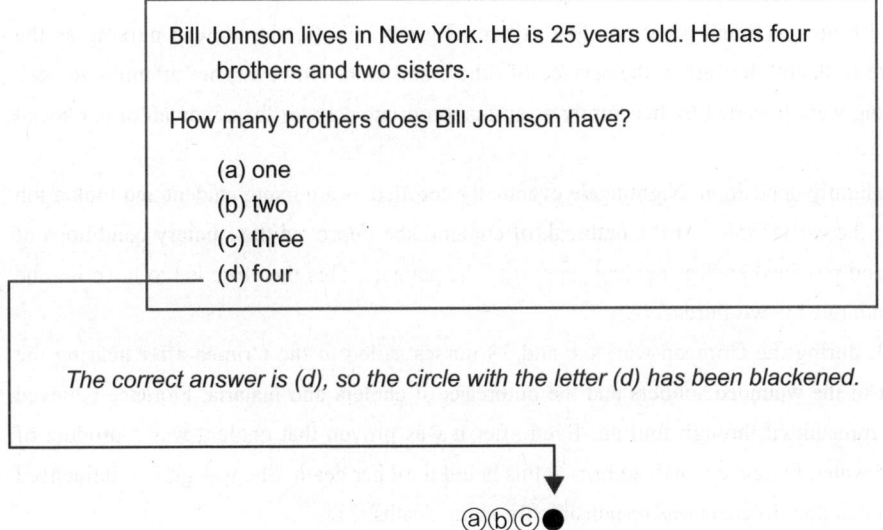

> Bill Johnson lives in New York. He is 25 years old. He has four brothers and two sisters.
>
> How many brothers does Bill Johnson have?
>
> (a) one
> (b) two
> (c) three
> (d) four

The correct answer is (d), so the circle with the letter (d) has been blackened.

NOW TURN THE PAGE AND BEGIN

PART 1. Read the following biography article and answer the questions. The underlined words in the article are for vocabulary questions.

FLORENCE NIGHTINGALE

Florence Nightingale was an English social reformer, statistician, and nurse. She is best known as the founder of modern nursing. Nightingale, who was called the "Angel of the Crimea", tirelessly devoted her life to preventing disease and ensuring safety and compassionate treatment for soldiers.

Florence Nightingale was born on May 12, 1820, in Florence, Italy. As the second of two daughters, Nightingale excelled in mathematics and was able to read and write different languages at an early age. Since she was never satisfied with traditional female skills of home management, she preferred to read the great philosophers and to engage in serious political and social discourse with her father.

Because Florence found great comfort in her religious beliefs, she viewed nursing as the suitable route to devote herself to the service of others and God. However, her attempts to seek nurse's training were thwarted by her family as an inappropriate activity for a woman of her social stature.

Despite family opposition, Nightingale eventually enrolled as a nursing student and took a job in London in the early 1850s. At the outbreak of cholera, she improved the sanitary conditions of the hospital and provided endless nursing support to the patients. This therefore led to lowering the hospital's death rate by two-thirds.

In 1853, during the Crimean war, she and 38 nurses sailed to the Crimea after hearing the mistreatment of the wounded soldiers and the outbreaks of cholera and malaria. Florence believed cholera was transmitted through foul air. Even after it was proven that cholera was a product of contaminated water, Florence remained firm in this belief until her death. She was greatly influenced by the notion that poor hygiene was responsible for many deaths.

In 1860, the Nightingale School of Nurses aimed at making nursing a viable and respectable profession for women. After she passed away in 1910, the Florence Nightingale Medal was awarded to nurses for outstanding service and the Florence Nightingale Museum was established to recognize her pioneering work in nursing and her social reforms that included improving healthcare for all sections of British society.

53. What was the reason for Nightingale's preference in philosophy or political and social discourse?

    (a) her talent in home management
    (b) her religious beliefs
    (c) her satisfaction with the conventional role of women in household
    (d) her dissatisfaction with the traditional role of women in household

54. Why was Nightingale's family against Nightingale becoming a nurse?

    (a) Males did not like women working as a nurse.
    (b) Working as a nurse wasn't suitable for her social position.
    (c) She was far good at mathematics and languages.
    (d) Her family wanted her to be a politician.

55. How did Nightingale reduce the hospital's death rate?

    (a) by distributing medical supplies to war casualties
    (b) by volunteering to work in patient services
    (c) by promoting hygiene practices of the hospital
    (d) by providing education about the prevention of infectious diseases

56. What did Nightingale strongly believe until her death?

    (a) Cholera was responsible for many deaths.
    (b) Cholera could be treated by nurses.
    (c) Cholera was contaminated by polluted water.
    (d) Cholera was contaminated by dirty air.

57. Which serves as a recognition of Nightingale's contributions to nursing and social reforms?

    (a) She was honored by nursing students.
    (b) Her school was designated as a heritage site.
    (c) Her museum was established in England.
    (d) British society named all nursing medals in her honour.

58. In the context of the passage, discourse means _____.

    (a) conflict
    (b) discussion
    (c) lesson
    (d) matter

59. In the context of the passage, viable means _____.

    (a) feasible
    (b) suitable
    (c) sustainable
    (d) versatile

PART 2. Read the following magazine article and answer the questions. The underlined words in the article are for vocabulary questions.

LACK OF SLEEP CAUSES ALZHEIMER'S DISEASE

Several studies have found an association between sleep problems and a higher risk of accumulating beta-amyloid in the brain. The studies showed that people who do not sleep enough are more likely to suffer from Alzheimer's disease, one of the most pervasive and debilitating forms of dementia.

Based on a research conducted by Dr. Nora D. Volkow and Dr. Gene-Jack Wang of NIH's National Institute on Alcohol Abuse and Alcoholism, after a loss of sleep, levels of beta-amyloid were 5% more than after adequate sleep. During a good night's sleep, the brain has time to flush out the beta-amyloid known as a protein being a catalyst in Alzheimer's, whereas beta-amyloid builds up and forms plaque on the brain tissue when sleep gets interrupted at night.

Studies published in Nature Neuroscience discovered that adults over age 65 with beta-amyloid plaques in their brain have reduced the deep sleep, even though these people do not yet show signs of Alzheimer's, like memory loss and cognitive decline.

The recent research by Dr. Kristine Yaffe, professor of psychiatry, neurology and epidemiology at the University of California, also revealed that those who reported spending less time in bed actually sleeping were more likely to develop dementia five to ten years earlier than those who got the deep sleep. However, the good news is that beta-amyloid starts to build up in healthy adults before the onset of symptoms of Alzheimer's. So, it might be possible to delay the onset of more severe symptoms of dementia, if it could be detected early through screening.

According to Dr. Michael Twery, director of the National Heart, Lung, and Blood Institute Center on Sleep Disorders Research, for the brain to fully rest and reset, adults generally require 7-8 hours of quality sleep, infants need 16 hours, young children need 10 hours, and teenagers should aim for 9 hours. Moreover, there is strong evidence that regular aerobic exercise helps to improve sleep quality.

60. What is the result of people experiencing sleep deprivation?

    (a) They become dependent on alcohol.
    (b) They are invulnerable to Alzheimer's disease.
    (c) They have a low deposition of beta-amyloid protein plaque in the brain.
    (d) They are likely afflicted with an illness associated with Alzheimer's disease.

61. What could happen to the brain if people are lacking in night sleep?

    (a) Poor night sleep clears beta-amyloid out of the brain.
    (b) The level of beta-amyloid is elevated on the brain.
    (c) No plaque on the brain tissue is shown in the brain.
    (d) The level of beta-amyloid is lowered on the brain

62. Based on the passage, which of the following statement about beta-amyloid in the brain is true?

    (a) Elderly people with beta-amyloid plaques frequently experience the deep sleep.
    (b) Elderly people with beta-amyloid plaques always indicate the decreased deep sleep along with signs of Alzheimer's.
    (c) Adequate sleep at night prevents the formation of beta-amyloid in the brain.
    (d) Adequate sleep at night promotes the formation of beta-amyloid in the brain.

63. According to Dr. Kristine Yaffe, how can screening be used?

    (a) as a means to promptly relieve symptoms of Alzheimer's
    (b) as the best way to get the deep sleep
    (c) as a means to quickly discover beta-amyloid in adults
    (d) as a means to measure the severity of symptoms in adults

64. Why are recommended hours of sleep different depending on age?

    (a) because the brain needs time to remove plaques on brain tissues
    (b) because the brain needs time to arrange the function of each body organ
    (c) because the brain needs time to relax and return to its original and functioning condition
    (d) because each body organ burns a different amount of calories

65. In the context of the passage, interrupted means _____.

    (a) disturbed
    (b) obstructed
    (c) shortend
    (d) postponed

66. In the context of the passage, onset means _____.

    (a) treatment
    (b) end
    (c) beginning
    (d) peak

PART 3. *Read the following encyclopedia article and answer the questions. The underlined words in the article are for vocabulary questions.*

GREAT DANE

The Great Dane is a breed of German origin. The Great Dane descends from hunting dogs known from the Middle Ages and is recognized as the largest dog breed in terms of height.

Great Danes are huge. Males can reach 87cm tall and weigh anywhere from about 50 to 54kg, while females may be 81cm tall and weigh from about 45 to 50kg. Their massive head is narrow and flat on top. The ears drop forward. The neck is long and strong. The body is long and muscular, and the front legs are straight.

The Great Dane is a giant breed. The breed is thought to have been around for more than 400 years. They were bred by German nobility to protect country estates and hunt wild boar. In the 18th century, Great Danes were prestigious guardians of estates and carriages. In 1880, the Germans banned the name "Great Dane" and called the breed "Deutsche Dogge", which means German mastiff, however, the breed continues to be called Great Dane in English speaking countries.

Great Danes have a fast metabolism. This results in more energy and food consumption than in small breeds. Because of their size, their average lifespan is 6 to 8 years. A health condition known as bloat, which involves gas buildup and possible twisting of the stomach, is the number-one killer of Danes. Since these dogs do grow at a rapid pace, it takes a while for the bones and joints of Great Danes to become stable, so puppies are not allowed to jump and run until they are at least 18 months old.

Great Danes are considered gentle giants. They are moderately playful, affectionate and good with children. However, they must be obedience trained to assure they are manageable when fully grown because some individuals in the breed can be aggressive with dogs they do not know, although Great Danes generally get along with other animals.

These dogs are primarily family pets and have become popular today among city dwellers who keep them to help guard against robbers.

67. Which statement best characterizes the Great Dane?

    (a) It is the first hunting dog in the Middle Ages.
    (b) It lives in Germany.
    (c) It is the world's tallest dog.
    (d) It is the world's heaviest dog.

68. Which of the following descriptions about the Great Dane is false?

    (a) that the top of its head is flat
    (b) that a male dog is about 6 cm taller than a female dog
    (c) that its body is made up of firm muscles
    (d) that it can walk upright on his hind legs

69. Why were Great Danes raised by Germans holding the highest social status in the 18th century?

    (a) because Great Danes were able to keep properties safe from danger
    (b) because raising Great Danes could cost a lot of money
    (c) because Great Danes ate wild boars
    (d) because Germans did not want Great Danes to be called German mastiff

70. What is the major reason for the Great Dane's high intake of food compared to small dogs?

    (a) its ability to store food in the stomach for a long time
    (b) its ability to convert food into energy at a very fast rate
    (c) its body condition called bloat
    (d) its short lifespan

71. How most likely do Great Danes become compliant?

    (a) by playing with other animals
    (b) by a small amount of food
    (c) through obedience instruction
    (d) through animal hunting

72. In the context of the passage, moderately means _____.

    (a) gradually
    (b) hugely
    (c) massively
    (d) reasonably

73. In the context of the passage, aggressive means _____.

    (a) hostile
    (b) friendly
    (c) obsessive
    (d) addictive

> **PART 4.** Read the following business letter and answer the questions. The underlined words in the article are for vocabulary questions.

Robert Kensington
Manager
Alpha Electrical Store

Dear Mr. Kensington:

I bought a Loyald fridge that cost $2500 from your shop on 11th August 2020, bill No. LTN/22/17. Only after 3 days, the fridge has started giving me the trouble.

The freezer compartment was not cooling properly. It took a lot of time to freeze the food items kept inside and the frozen foods kept inside the freezer got spooled. I called your customer service and informed them of the problem. Julia Kylim whom I spoke with, told me that your company would send a replacement for the faulty product. She also assured me that it would arrive within a week.

No replacement arrived, although I waited for two weeks. I have made several phone calls to your shop stating the trouble. This time, I was told that the replacement would be delayed again because the manufacturer needed another week to deliver a new fridge. Had I not called, I would have been kept waiting longer and putting up with inconveniences.

I am urging you to resolve this concern promptly. Since the fridge is under the warranty period, I demand a refund immediately. In case you fail to address this issue within the next 5 days, you can be assured of hearing from my lawyer soon because I will file a formal complaint with the Better Business Bureau.

I have enclosed in this letter a copy of the order receipt and a photograph of the defective product. You can e-mail your response to me at goldstar@email.com or call me at 555-666-0000.

Annabelle Lee

74. Why is Annabelle Lee writing a letter to Robert Kensington?

   (a) to order a new product
   (b) to make changes of the delivery date and address
   (c) to ask for more information concerning a product
   (d) to complain about a defective product

75. What did Julia Kylim tell Lee that the company would do about her concern?

   (a) offer a full refund
   (b) report the concern to the manufacturer
   (c) exchange the item with a new one
   (d) repair the item back to its original condition

76. Why most likely was Alpha Electrical Store unable to deliver the new fridge straight away?

   (a) The manufacturer needed more time to deliver a new fridge.
   (b) There were many customers waiting for their products to arrive.
   (c) The manufacturer could not make fridges in large quantities.
   (d) The deliveryman was off sick for a week.

77. How will Lee respond if she doesn't receive a refund for her purchase quickly?

   (a) by purchasing the same fridge from another store
   (b) by reporting to the police
   (c) by lodging a compensation claim against the store
   (d) by filing a complaint with the Consumer Ombudsman Center

78. Why most likely is Lee sending a photo of the defective product with her letter?

   (a) She wants to compare the new product with the defective product.
   (b) She wants to use it as proof of her complaint.
   (c) She intends to threaten the store.
   (d) She wants to upload the photo to social media.

79. In the context of the passage, urging means.

   (a) begging
   (b) demanding
   (c) convincing
   (d) offering

80. In the context of the passage, address means.

   (a) tackle
   (b) delay
   (c) write
   (d) mail

THIS IS THE END OF THE TEST

TEST 2

GENERAL TESTS OF ENGLISH LANGUAGE PROFICIENCY
G-TELP™

LEVEL 2

GRAMMAR SECTION

DIRECTIONS:

The following items need a word or words to complete the sentence. From the four choices which follow each item, choose the best answer. Then blacken in the correct circle on your answer sheet.

Example:

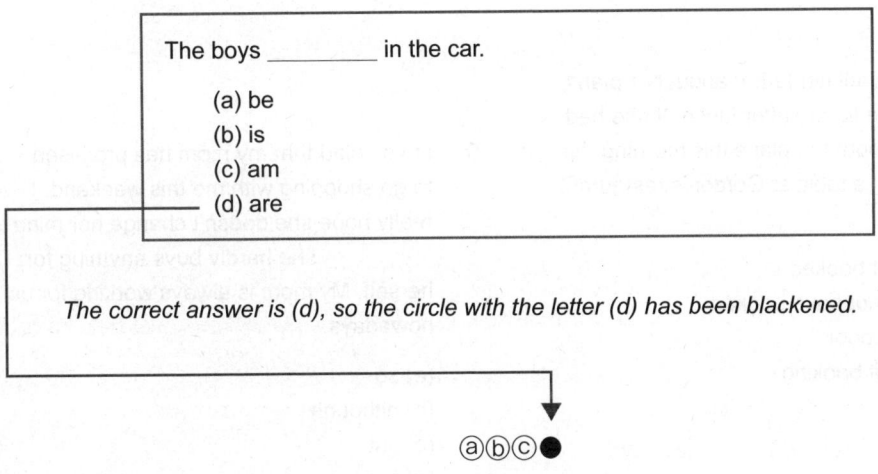

The correct answer is (d), so the circle with the letter (d) has been blackened.

NOW TURN THE PAGE AND BEGIN

1. It's been a year now since Kim lost her job. Nonetheless, she has intentionally avoided _____ a new job because she doesn't want to work.

   (a) to find
   (b) will find
   (c) finding
   (d) having found

2. Tina didn't tell her father about her plans to go to the library after lunch. If she had told him about her plans this morning, he _____ a table at Gordon's restaurant for dinner.

   (a) has not booked
   (b) would not have booked
   (c) did not book
   (d) was not booking

3. Jack was one of the national top marathon runners. He _____ five gold medals at the 1936 Olympic Games in Berlin until he had a car accident.

   (a) would win
   (b) was winning
   (c) won
   (d) had been winning

4. Graham bought a bracelet for his wife to wear for their 5th wedding anniversary. The bracelet, _____ , caused Graham to pay a fair amount of money. The bracelet is designed by a famous designer.

   (a) what is made of platinum with 1000 sparkling diamonds
   (b) how it is made of platinum with 1000 sparkling diamonds
   (c) which is made of platinum with 1000 sparkling diamonds
   (d) that is made of platinum with 1000 sparkling diamonds

5. I'm so glad that my mom has promised to go shopping with me this weekend. I really hope she doesn't change her mind _____ she hardly buys anything for herself. My mom is always working for us nowadays.

   (a) so
   (b) although
   (c) but
   (d) because

6. Our dog Felix is home now. He had been missing for three days before we found him near the park this morning. We are still wondering what he _____ have eaten for three days.

   (a) will
   (b) might
   (c) should
   (d) can

7. Jackson is leaving on a trip to Taiwan this Wednesday. _____ he is taking a long vacation, he is bringing a small suitcase. Perhaps he plans to buy a big suitcase once he arrives there.

    (a) Despite
    (b) Even though
    (c) Unless
    (d) As long as

8. Jack has good memories of his high school music teacher, Ms. Hampton. Aside from giving interesting music theory lessons, she _____ students who were not confident in playing musical instruments.

    (a) always encourages
    (b) had always encouraged
    (c) was always encouraging
    (d) would always have encouraged

9. When I was growing up, I wished that I was speaking fluent French. My dream still holds true today. _____ to France, I would make as many friends as possible.

    (a) I could travel
    (b) Could I travel
    (c) If I had traveled
    (d) If I travels

10. It was so windy this afternoon. I called my mother to close the window in my room as soon as she gets home. I asked that she _____ slowly and safely due to strong wind.

    (a) drove
    (b) drive
    (c) drives
    (d) was driving

11. Julia is often late for work because she has to take her daughter to school every morning. If she could allow her daughter to walk to school by herself, she _____ complaints from her work colleagues.

    (a) isn't getting
    (b) doesn't get
    (c) wouldn't get
    (d) hadn't got

12. It is already nine o'clock in the morning, and I still have a lot of housework to do. I _____ home until noon cleaning rooms and washing dishes.

    (a) am staying
    (b) have stayed
    (c) stay
    (d) will be staying

13. I really respect mothers who completely devote themselves to child-rearing. One of those I admire most is my mother, who _____ for 7 days a week to support my family as well as other poor people.

    (a) is working
    (b) works
    (c) has been working
    (d) will work

14. Christine and Annabelle have been friends since they were in kindergarten. Even after they got married, they have been enjoying _____ time for their favorite hobbies together.

    (a) having spent
    (b) to spend
    (c) will spend
    (d) spending

15. Seoul National University Hospital is the oldest public hospital in South Korea. Since 1946, _____, the hospital has hired professional doctors and nurses to ensure proper treatment.

    (a) when it was established
    (b) how it was established
    (c) where it was establishd
    (d) that it was established

16. Mr. Lee is advising his sister to exercise at least three times a week instead of eating one meal a day. He warns that she may regret _____ her health, since regular exercise is the most effective way to prevent weight gain.

    (a) harming
    (b) to harm
    (c) being harmed
    (d) to be harming

17. Amy vomited more than three times and complained about nausea this early morning, so we took her to the hospital. If we hadn't done so, we _____ that she has severe gastritis which is inflammation of the lining of the stomach.

    (a) were not knowing
    (b) didn't know
    (c) have not known
    (d) wouldn't have known

18. Harris has to conduct his study all over again because he found an error in calculating chemical formulas. The professor recommends that he _____ a new model of calculator.

    (a) will use
    (b) uses
    (c) use
    (d) is using

19. Greenfield, a new fiber optic cable system designed to prevent power outages, has been developed. It _____ eliminate the possibility of electrical outages and even detect an outage before it happens.

    (a) can
    (b) may
    (c) would
    (d) must

20. I had no idea passengers were advised to arrive well ahead of listed departure time at least two hours, so I missed the flight to New York. If I _____ about the announcement, I would have left home earlier.

    (a) would know
    (b) knew
    (c) had known
    (d) was knowing

21. The profits earned by milk companies should have been reviewd when higher taxes were imposed on their products. However, these companies have increased the prices of their milk products _____ for their losses.

    (a) making up
    (b) to make up
    (c) to have made up
    (d) having made up

22. Annabelle is in her last year as a nursing student and is looking forward to graduation. By the time she finishes this semester, she _____ nothing but how to improve patient care for more than four years.

    (a) was studying
    (b) will have been studying
    (c) studied
    (d) would have studied

23. Beth asked me to go with her to the newly opened hair salon on Milson Street. She will be going on a date with Greg on Christmas Eve, and needs _____ a haircut for the date.

    (a) to have got
    (b) to be getting
    (c) getting
    (d) to get

24. My mom will open her second Italian restaurant on George Street this weekend. To attract a crowd, I am requiring that all my friends and relatives _____ the opening party to act as regular customers.

    (a) have attended
    (b) are attending
    (c) will attend
    (d) attend

25. I'm so happy that I joined the dancing team our school formed early this semester. I usually prefer dancing alone or with close friends. However, if it weren't for the dancing team, I _____ trouble developing my dancing skills on my own.

   (a) was having
   (b) would be having
   (c) am having
   (d) will be having

26. James is unable to make it to the post office before it closes. Fortunately, his girlfriend works near the post office. He _____ to her over the phone about letters and parcels she needs to pick up from the post office.

   (a) now talks
   (b) is now talking
   (c) would now talk
   (d) has now talked

THIS IS THE END OF THE GRAMMAR SECTION

LISTENING SECTION

DIRECTIONS:

The Listening Sections has four parts. In each part you will hear a spoken passage and a number of questions about the passage. First you will hear the questions. Then you will hear the passage. From the four choices for each question, choose the best answer. Then blacken in the correct circle on your answer sheet.

Now you will hear an example question. Then you will hear an example passage.

Now listen to the example question.

Example:

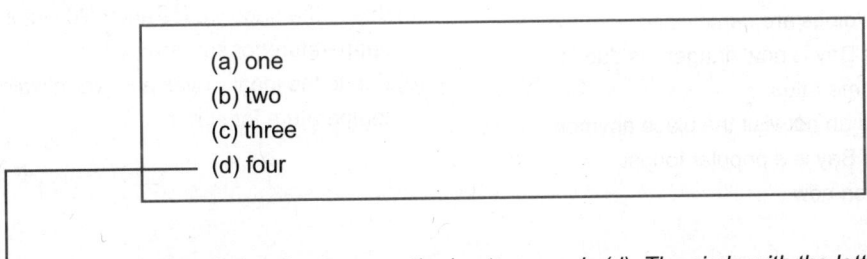

Bill Johnson has four brothers, so the best answer is (d). The circle with the letter (d) has been blackened.

ⓐⓑⓒ●

NOW TURN THE PAGE AND BEGIN

PART 1. You will hear a conversation between two people. First you will hear questions 27 through 33. Then you will hear the conversation. Choose the best answer to each question in the time provided.

27. (a) to start a new family business
    (b) because they will be moving to Double Bay
    (c) to meet their old friends
    (d) to experience their memorable moments from the past again

28. (a) Old buildings are demolished.
    (b) Double Bay is now dangerous due to high crime rates.
    (c) Tourists do not visit the place anymore.
    (d) Double Bay is a popular tourist attraction now.

29. (a) by relaxing on a beach in the very early morning and spending afternoon at the hotel
    (b) by staying in the hotel room throughout the morning and going to the beach in the afternoon
    (c) by relaxing on a beach only at night
    (d) by staying in their hotel room throughout their stay

30. (a) because surfing is easy to learn
    (b) because surfing is one of the most popular water sports
    (c) because surfing allows him to experience incredible feelings
    (d) because John can be a good surfer

31. (a) due to the coral reef
    (b) due to the hot weather and the big waves for surfers
    (c) due to the huge waves and cold water temperature for surfers
    (d) due to the ideal waves and warm water temperature for surfers

32. (a) how hard surfing was to learn
    (b) how surfing made her feel lethargic
    (c) how brave she was on her first surfing
    (d) how surfing made her feel dynamic

33. (a) learn surfing
    (b) visit Double Bay with them
    (c) tour Double Bay on his own
    (d) book a flight ticket

PART 2. You will hear a presentation about a new product. First you will hear questions 34 through 39. Then you will hear the presentation. Choose the best answer to each question in the time provided.

34. (a) broad education in a field
    (b) home education provided by either public or private schools
    (c) educating children at home
    (d) domestic training on life-saving skills

35. (a) that it is chosen by children who do well at school
    (b) that it is strictly conducted by parents who are teachers
    (c) that it enhances children's sociability
    (d) that it is gaining popularity

36. (a) They have a wide range of skills.
    (b) They are obsessed with academic performance.
    (c) They study long hours everyday.
    (d) They study in the personalized learning environment.

37. (a) Schedules can be adjusted based on family needs.
    (b) Home schooling is economically beneficial.
    (c) Schedules are only arranged by children.
    (d) Home schooling helps to develop each family member's potential.

38. (a) They are only affected by their parents.
    (b) They aren't affected by their peers.
    (c) They do not have many friends.
    (d) They do not trust their peers.

39. (a) by arranging an educational program for them
    (b) by providing them with financial aid
    (c) by helping to devise a curriculum of home schooling
    (d) by caring their children

PART 3. *You will hear a conversation between two people. First you will hear questions 40 through 45. Then you will hear the conversation. Choose the best answer to each question in the time provided.*

40. (a) to have a job interview
    (b) to sell a facial laser product
    (c) to inquire about a medical procedure
    (d) to treat her facial pain

41. (a) by drinking plenty of water
    (b) by exposing the facial skin to very high temperatures
    (c) by removing toxins from the skin layers of the face
    (d) by destroying and heating the different skin layers of the face

42. (a) She finds facial massage too painful.
    (b) She gets bruising and muscle pain.
    (c) She is scared of unknown side effects.
    (d) Her skin is extremely dry and sensitive.

43. (a) because her skin is not sensitive and thick
    (b) because nurses keep talking to her
    (c) because the doctor is a pain management specialist
    (d) because the doctor uses a substance that causes loss of pain only to the area to which it is applied

44. (a) to ensure that one's skin has been lighter
    (b) to check if one wants to discontinue laser procedures
    (c) to calculate how much one needs to pay for each session
    (d) to prevent any serious side effects

45. (a) continue a facial massage
    (b) see a doctor other than Dr. Smith
    (c) schedule a consultation for laser treatment
    (d) meet friends

PART 4. You will hear an explanation of a process. First you will hear questions 46 through 52. Then you will hear the explanation. Choose the best answer to each question in the time provided.

46. (a) how to have a successful career
    (b) how to learn customer service skills
    (c) strengthening customer service skills
    (d) keeping one's hands clean

47. (a) It increases job satisfaction.
    (b) It leads a company to thrive.
    (c) It affects the national economy.
    (d) It allows customers to buy products at lower prices.

48. (a) asking for customer feedback on a purchase
    (b) informing customers about time to handle their requests
    (c) replying emails within 24 hours
    (d) returning all phone calls within one day

49. (a) because they can stop complaining
    (b) because they will buy more products
    (c) because everything they say needs to be recorded
    (d) because products can be improved by their opinions

50. (a) ask customers a few simple questions
    (b) call each customer everyday
    (c) meet each customer in person
    (d) ask customers for help

51. (a) one who wears trendy outfits
    (b) one who provides good customer service
    (c) one who sells many products
    (d) one who has a funny name

52. (a) because it makes him an expert in sales
    (b) because it helps him have more clients
    (c) because it allows him to earn money
    (d) because it makes his boss like him

THIS IS THE END OF THE LISTENING SECTION

READING AND VOCABULARY SECTION

DIRECTIONS:

You will now read four different passages. Each passage is followed by comprehension and vocabulary questions. From the four choices for each item, choose the best answer. Then blacken in the correct circle on your answer sheet.

Read the following example passage and example question.

Example:

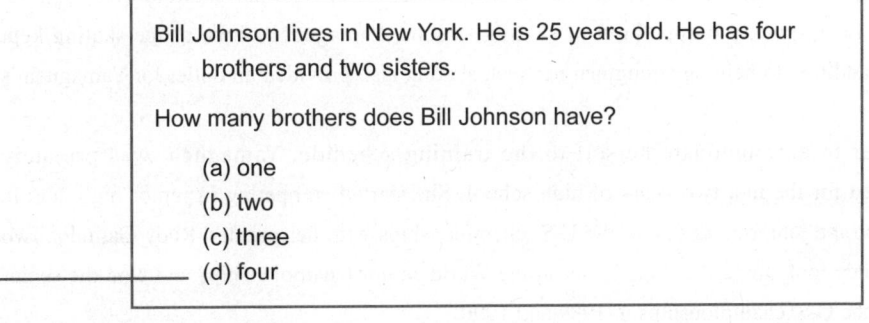

Bill Johnson lives in New York. He is 25 years old. He has four brothers and two sisters.

How many brothers does Bill Johnson have?

    (a) one
    (b) two
    (c) three
    (d) four

The correct answer is (d), so the circle with the letter (d) has been blackened.

NOW TURN THE PAGE AND BEGIN

PART 1. *Read the following biographical narrative and answer the questions. The underlined words in the article are for vocabulary questions.*

KRISTI YAMAGUCHI

Kristi Yamaguchi is an American former figure skater. Yamaguchi, a two-time world champion, the 1992 Olympic champion, and the 1992 U.S. champion, is one of the most decorated figure skaters in U.S. history.

Yamaguchi was born on July 12, 1971, in Hayward, California, to Jim, a dentist, and Carole Yamaguchi, a medical secretary. She has two siblings, Brett and Lori. Because she was born with clubfoot, she put casts on legs for much of the first year of her life and then wore corrective shoes connected by a brace for the next year.

At the age of 6, Yamaguchi started skating as physical therapy for her clubfoot. Although her older sister, Lori, quickly dropped out of skating lessons, Yamaguchi's love of ice skating kept growing. In addition to helping strengthen her feet, skating also provided an outlet for Yamaguchi's shyness.

In order to accommodate herself to the training schedule, Yamaguchi was privately homeschooled for the first two years of high school. She started competing in junior high, and in 1986 she won the junior pairs title at the U.S. championships with her partner, Rudy Galindo. Two years later, they took home the same honor at the World Junior Championships and won the senior pairs title at the U.S. championships in 1989 and 1990.

After graduating from high school, she moved to Alberta, Canada, to train full-time with her coach, Christy Ness and to focus on her singles figure skating. Yamaguchi developed her artistry and triple-triple combinations in hopes of becoming a more well-rounded skater.

Yamaguchi won the 1991 World Championships. In the 1992 Winter Olympics in Albertville, France, she won a gold medal in the ladies' singles figure skating. After her Olympic win, Yamaguchi toured for many years with *Stars on Ice*. Yamaguchi was inducted into the U.S. Figure Skating Hall of Fame in 1998 and the World Figure Skating Hall of Fame in 1999.

In 1996, she established the Always Dream Foundation, a nonprofit organization that provides funding for underprivileged, disabled and at-risk children. Her foundation has been trying to make a positive difference in children's lives through education. Yamaguchi is also an author. In 2011, she published an award-winning children's book and received the Gelett Burgess Children's Book Award. In 2018, she was honored by the U.S. Olympic Committee with the Jesse Owens Olympic Spirit Award.

53. What made Kristi Yamaguchi begin skating as a child?

    (a) her outgoing personality
    (b) watching her brother skate
    (c) her parents' insistence
    (d) her rotated feet

54. Why most likely did Yamaguchi study from home for a couple of years of high school?

    (a) because her parents could no longer pay for her training
    (b) because she needed to adapt to her training schedule
    (c) because she could not find a training coach
    (d) because she did not cope with school stress well

55. What did Yamaguchi do in Canada?

    (a) She was trained for her singles figure skating.
    (b) She competed at the Olympics.
    (c) She was trained with Rudy Galindo.
    (d) She succeeded in triple-triple combinations for the first time.

56. Which did not happen to Yamaguchi from the early 1990s onwards?

    (a) She won the junior pairs title at the U.S. championships.
    (b) She won first place in an Olympic event.
    (c) She became a world champion.
    (d) She joined *Stars on Ice*.

57. What was the reason that the Always Dream Foundation was founded?

    (a) to help poor kids to learn figure skating
    (b) to prevent kids from crimes
    (c) to help kids with financial and physical difficulties
    (d) to help kids find their parents

58. In the context of the passage, well-rounded means _____.

    (a) famous
    (b) inspirational
    (c) healthy
    (d) versatile

59. In the context of the passage, underprivileged means _____.

    (a) needy
    (b) advantaged
    (c) wealthy
    (d) illiterate

PART 2. Read the following magazine article and answer the questions. The underlined words in the article are for vocabulary questions.

STUDIES FIND THAT COW'S MILK MAY PREVENT MUSCLE LOSS

Recent studies have found that cow's milk is good for building muscle. The findings show that milk prevents the loss of muscle mass and is effective in increasing muscle strength.

In a study published in the American Journal of Clinical Nutrition, researchers from McMaster University found that the daily consumption of cow's milk after workout including resistance exercise promotes greater muscle growth than soy or sport drinks.

To conduct the study, for 12 weeks, 56 young male participants were asked to drink either cow's milk, a soy protein drink or a carbohydrate drink after completing weight lifting workouts. The results showed that the group drinking the cow's milk came out on top in terms of muscle gain with an estimated 40 percent more muscle mass than the soy protein drinkers. In addition, milk drinkers gained 63 percent more muscle mass than the carbohydrate drinkers.

An earlier study demonstrated the effects of cow's milk consumption on young athletic women. Researchers from Texas University found that only women in the cow's milk consumption group experienced greater muscle gains. After a workout, regular consumption of cow's milk is likely to support the build-up of muscle mass. This is because cow's milk contains two types of proteins named casein and whey. Most importantly, casein protein provides a high amount of leucine which is responsible for muscle growth by reducing protein breakdown.

The studies shed light on the type of milk people drink in recent years. Stuart Phillips, associate professor of kinesiology from the American College of Sports Medicine believes drinking whole fat milk after lifting weights promotes muscle growth 2.8 times more than drinking skim milk does.

However, the studies in established literature were mainly based on consuming cow's milk-based protein after workouts. Thus, the study was only able to conclude the effectiveness of cow's milk for increasing muscle mass. The researchers hope to do future studies about how other proteins like eggs or lean meats affect muscle growth after workouts.

60. What did researchers find out?
    (a) that cow's milk helps build more muscle
    (b) that people who prefer to drink cow's milk are healthy
    (c) that cow's milk helps weight loss
    (d) that cow's milk is better than soy and sports drinks

61. How could the cow's milk drinking group be described?
    (a) They gain weight easier than the soy and carbohydrate drinking groups.
    (b) They have 63 percent more muscle growth than the soy protein drinkers.
    (c) They drink a large amount of milk after weight lifting workouts.
    (d) They have greater muscle mass than the soy and carbohydrate drinking groups.

62. Why does drinking cow's milk enhance muscle mass?
    (a) because cow's milk has the only one protein that cannot be found in other kinds of drinks
    (b) because cow's milk accelerates protein breakdown
    (c) because cow's milk has casein protein that gives high concentrations of leucine
    (d) because cow's milk hinders the production of proteins in the muscle

63. What do the recent studies tell cow's milk drinkers?
    (a) Whole fat milk is more effective than skim milk if drinkers want to build muscle mass.
    (b) Skim milk is more effective than whole milk if drinkers want to build muscle mass.
    (c) Drinkers need to do lifting weights if they want to build muscle mass.
    (d) Drinking both whole fat milk and skim milk before lifting weights is highly recommended.

64. What does the article suggest that the researchers should do in the future?
    (a) The researchers should measure the period muscle growth after workouts.
    (b) The researchers should investigate the influences of other kinds of proteins on muscle growth after workouts.
    (c) The researchers should compare advantages and disadvantages of each protein drink.
    (d) The researchers should prove that the ingestion of eggs or lean meats is better than drinking cow's milk in terms of health.

65. In the context of the passage, consumption means _____.
    (a) waste   (b) expenditure
    (c) intake   (d) utilization

66. In the context of the passage, demonstrated means _____.
    (a) concealed   (b) determined
    (c) measured   (d) proved

PART 3. Read the following encyclopedia article and answer the questions. The underlined words in the article are for vocabulary questions.

RAFFLESIA ARNOLDII

The Rafflesia Arnoldii is a species of flowering plant, which produces the largest individual flower in the world. It is found in the rainforests of Sumatra and Borneo, Indonesia.

Rafflesia Arnoldii is a parasitic plant which has no visible leaves, roots, or stems. Similar to fungi, it grows as a mass of thread-like strands of tissue completely embedded within and in intimate contact with surrounding host cells from which nutrients and water are obtained. It can only be seen outside the host plant when it is ready to reproduce. The only part of Rafflesia that is identifiable as distinctly plant-like are the flowers. Rafflesia Arnoldii has been found to infect hosts growing in alkaline, neutral and acidic soils.

The flower of Rafflesia Arnoldii grows to a diameter of around one meter and weighs up to 11 kilograms. These flowers emerge from very large cabbage-like or dark brown buds typically about 30 centimeters wide.

The buds take many months to develop and the flower lasts for just a few days. When Rafflesia is ready to reproduce, a tiny bud forms outside the root or stem of its host and develops over a period of a year. The cabbage-like head that develops eventually opens to reveal the flower.

Thriving in rainforests, Rafflesia Arnoldii is in danger of extinction due to habitat loss as well as poaching. Its buds are harvested and sold for medicinal properties. The plant cannot grow in captivity and, as most occurrences of Rafflesia contain only male or female flowers, pollination is rare.

The flower of Rafflesia Arnoldii has a foul smell that attracts flies and beetles. A fly must land first on a male flower, avoid being eaten, and then transport the pollen to a female flower. If pollination occurs, the flower produces a smooth-skinned fruit, which is actually a berry about 13 centimeters in diameter. Fortunately, squirrels and birds enjoy this fruit, and are therefore able to help with seed dispersal.

These days, Rafflesia Arnoldii have been found from 490 to 1024 meters in altitude and ecotourism is known as a main threat to the species since the number of flower buds at locations where many tourists visit, has decreased.

67. Which statement best characterizes the Rafflesia Arnoldii?

    (a) It grows in areas with dry summers and snowy winters.
    (b) It is the world's biggest flowering plant.
    (c) It provides the biggest flower in the world.
    (d) It is the world's tallest flowering plant.

68. Which of the following descriptions about the Rafflesia Arnoldii is true?

    (a) It gets nutrients and water from fungi.
    (b) Its flowers are only distinguishable.
    (c) It is infected by host plants.
    (d) It has roots or stems but no leaves.

69. What is most likely the reason why Rafflesia Arnoldii has the largest flower on earth?

    (a) The flower of Rafflesia Arnoldii has a long diameter and heavy.
    (b) The flower of Rafflesia Arnoldii is from the largest bud.
    (c) The flower of Rafflesia Arnoldii lasts for months to produce fruits.
    (d) The flower of Rafflesia Arnoldii is grown by humans.

70. Why most likely are Rafflesia Arnoldii endangered?

    (a) because Rafflesia Arnoldii can be grown by humans
    (b) because climate change leads to forest degradation
    (c) because people sell flowers of Rafflesia Arnoldii for therapeutic purposes
    (d) because people illegally remove Rafflesia Arnoldii from their natural habitats

71. What roles do flies play before pollination successfully takes place?

    (a) Flies transfer pollen from the male flower to the female flower.
    (b) Flies make a disgusting smell to protect flowers from birds.
    (c) Flies produce more pollen
    (d) Flies land on a female flower prior to a male flower.

72. In the context of the passage, emerge means _____.

    (a) vanish
    (b) appear
    (c) express
    (d) arrive

73. In the context of the passage, foul means _____.

    (a) ordinary
    (b) unusual
    (c) pleasant
    (d) stinking

PART 4. Read the following business letter and answer the questions. The underlined words in the article are for vocabulary questions.

May 5, 2021
Cathy Tick
Manager
Forbitt Corporation

Dear Mr. Tick:

Please let this letter serve as my resignation as shift supervisor due to unsatisfactory work conditions. In accordance with our company policy, my last day of employment will be June 4, 2021.

On repeated occasions, I have been asked to work back-to-back shifts on weekends and holidays. Initially, I understood the need to help out with the increase in production. But I was also promised that more employees would be hired to relieve the stress on current staff members.

To this point, many months later, there has been no added staff to take the pressure off the employees putting in upwards of 90 hours per week. I have been afraid that I can work in unsafe conditions I do not want to be responsible for heavy workload and long working hours.

To the HR department, I have raised concerns on several occasions and have even submitted these concerns in writing. Nonetheless, I was merely told to wait for the resolution of the matter. The extra strain has now started to affect my health and I am forced to conclude that my needs are no longer part of the company's interests. Therefore, I must take immediate action and resign.

It would be a great kindness to ensure that my leaving documents and dues are processed on time. I will train anyone you deem appropriate to replace me. And I wish the company all the best in your future endeavors.

Sincerely,
Keith Jung

74. Why did Keith Jung write Cathy Tick a letter?

    (a) to request a promotion
    (b) to negotiate his salary
    (c) to complain his poor work conditions
    (d) to tell her that he is quitting his job

75. Regarding working on weekends and holidays, which of the following was the company's assurance?

    (a) regular performance incentives
    (b) recruiting extra staff
    (c) a reduction in production
    (d) an all-expense-paid vacation

76. Based on the letter, which of the following statement about Keith Jung is true?

    (a) He has worked less than 90 hours every week.
    (b) His responsibility was to take care of current staff members.
    (c) He has overworked for months.
    (d) He has worked with new and old staff members.

77. How did the HR department respond to his complaints?

    (a) by requesting an appointment to meet with Cathy Tick
    (b) by solving them as soon as possible
    (c) by offering monthly bonuses
    (d) by telling him to wait without a specified time

78. What most likely will Keith Jung do for the company before the termination of his employment?

    (a) He will be interviewing a number of candidates.
    (b) He will train his replacement.
    (c) He will look for a suitable replacement.
    (d) He will claim his insurance benefits.

79. In the context of the passage, resolution means _____.

    (a) continuation
    (b) solution
    (c) agreement
    (d) intention

80. In the context of the passage, deem means _____.

    (a) demand
    (b) identify
    (c) count
    (d) consider

THIS IS THE END OF THE TEST

TEST 3

GENERAL TESTS OF ENGLISH LANGUAGE PROFICIENCY
G-TELP™

LEVEL 2

GRAMMAR SECTION

DIRECTIONS:

The following items need a word or words to complete the sentence. From the four choices which follow each item, choose the best answer. Then blacken in the correct circle on your answer sheet.

Example:

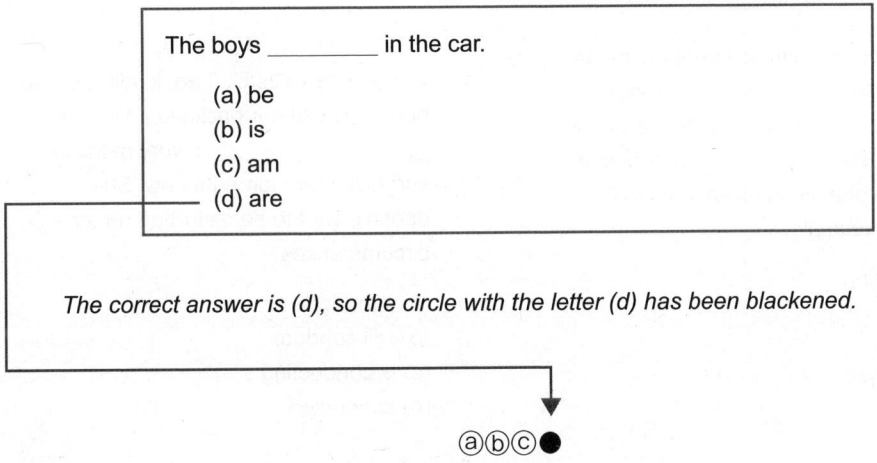

The correct answer is (d), so the circle with the letter (d) has been blackened.

NOW TURN THE PAGE AND BEGIN

1. Parents have warned us not to eat fast food. They say that fast food has high calories, sugar, salt, and cholesterol and is harmful to health. _____ , we still eat fast food because its taste is irresistible.

   (a) Otherwise
   (b) Eventually
   (c) Nevertheless
   (d) In fact

2. The majority of animals in Antarctica are dying due to rising water temperatures. That is why environmentalists are urging that the public _____ urgent action on climate change in order to save the remaining animals.

   (a) are taking
   (b) take
   (c) to take
   (d) will take

3. The Seoul City Council has set up a new public bike-sharing system which makes use of an online application. Called Ddareungi, the app allows bikers _____ for renting a bicycle by using their smartphones.

   (a) to be paid
   (b) having paid
   (c) to be paying
   (d) to pay

4. Karis Kulas is a famous hip-hop composer who has worked with many high-profile celebrities. My friend Jack, who is always a fan of her, _____ it if he were to be given the opportunity to collaborate with her in writing a new piece of music.

   (a) had greatly appreciated
   (b) is greatly appreciating
   (c) will greatly appreciate
   (d) would greatly appreciate

5. If someone rings Dr. Lee, kindly ask the person to call her back later. Dr. Lee _____ a very delicate surgical operation right now. She doesn't want to be disturbed under any circumstances.

   (a) conducts
   (b) will conduct
   (c) is conducting
   (d) conducted

6. Children and teenagers can be physically and psychologically damaged by their smartphones and tablet computers. Thus, doctors strongly claim that parents _____ limit their children's screen time.

   (a) may
   (b) would
   (c) should
   (d) will

7. Not all people who take a nap are lazy and wasting their time. A study shows that people _____ have improvements in their working memory and a 37% less chance of contracting a fatal heart condition.

   (a) which are fond of a short nap in the afternoon
   (b) who are fond of a short nap in the afternoon
   (c) when are fond of a short nap in the afternoon
   (d) whom a short nap in the afternoon are fond of

8. A new hybrid car was lately recalled from the market. _____ the car was banned due to a faulty engine control system. So, affected customers were offered full refunds.

   (a) Selling
   (b) Having sold
   (c) To sell
   (d) To have sold

9. Mina wasn't able to get a ticket for Maroon 5's London concert because the tickets were already sold out. If she had known that a lot of people would go to the concert tonight, she _____ a ticket online instead of lining up for a ticket.

   (a) was buying
   (b) bought
   (c) would buy
   (d) would have bought

10. Olivia is upset with her brother for not washing dad's car with her. He _____ computer games since this early morning without having breakfast and lunch.

    (a) plays
    (b) is playing
    (c) has been playing
    (d) played

11. One week ago, Heather decided to take a short trip. She _____ nonstop for ten years before she was appointed as a full professor of anatomy at Cambridge last month. She's now on her way to Bangkok in Thailand.

    (a) studied
    (b) studies
    (c) had been studying
    (d) was studying

12. Thousands of factory workers are staging a protest over the permanent termination of employment. They have been standing in front of factories since yesterday, insisting that the company _____ workforce planning.

    (a) rethink
    (b) would rethink
    (c) rethinks
    (d) is rethinking

13. Due to sexual discrimination, Stacey quitted her job. Today, she constantly reminds herself that if she had endured that poor working environment, she _____ from various mental disorders.

    (a) was suffering
    (b) would suffer
    (c) would have suffered
    (d) suffered

14. Kids sometimes say something unexpected. Today, my six-year-old daughter said that if she were a bird, she _____ in the sky because she can be a good friend with all kinds of birds.

    (a) will be flying
    (b) would fly
    (c) had flied
    (d) flied

15. The teachers are having a difficult time choosing the best essay of this year's writing competition. Many of the essays are equally outstanding. Nevertheless, they promised _____ the winner at 11 a.m.

    (a) will report
    (b) reporting
    (c) to report
    (d) to have reported

16. *Hypothyroidism* is a disorder of the endocrine system in which the thyroid gland does not produce thyroid hormone. Many people find this serious since untreated cases of hypothyroidism _____ pregnancy can lead to delays in body growth and intellectual development in the baby.

    (a) therefore
    (b) during
    (c) although
    (d) but

17. George has been working as a car salesman for 15 years. Although he loves his job, dealing with complaints from bad customers stresses him out enormously. If given the chance, he _____ get a stress management therapy.

    (a) may
    (b) should
    (c) can
    (d) would

18. On his way home, Jeff, by chance, saw Brandy, an old friend who has been working as an accountant in England. He couldn't resist _____ her to dinner.

    (a) having invited
    (b) to invite
    (c) inviting
    (d) to be inviting

19. The Sea level rises faster. In order to survive, polar bears _____ walk a long way to search for food. Sometimes, they forage in garbage dumps placed in the areas where the locals live.

    (a) must
    (b) can
    (c) might
    (d) should

20. While I _____ for an important exam the other night, I found my lovely dogs sleeping on my bed peacefully.

    (a) studied
    (b) was studying
    (c) would study
    (d) had studied

21. If you really want to be a doctor, you need to put more effort into your study. _____, you won't get into a medical school and will regret what you have done.

    (a) Instead
    (b) Therefore
    (c) Additionally
    (d) Otherwise

22. Every summer, Clare tries one of the water activities she has on her wish list. She has already done snorkeling, sea walking, and jet skiing. Next summer, she will go _____ with her sisters and parents.

    (a) to be windsurfing
    (b) windsurfing
    (c) to windsurf
    (d) having windsurfed

23. Jenny was late for school yesterday. She had to go back home to bring her history assignment. She wanted to ask her old brother for a ride, but he _____ at that time.

    (a) would sleep
    (b) had slept
    (c) slept
    (d) was sleeping

24. Working in a group is not easy because people have different qualifications, knowledge, ideas, and work experience. In order to avoid conflicts or arguments, it is essential that you _____ communication and interpersonal skills.

    (a) are improving
    (b) will improve
    (c) improved
    (d) improve

25. Adam Miller, one of the best neurologists, was actually a pianist during his high school years. In fact, he _____ the piano over a year due to his busy schedule.

(a) weren't playing
(b) isn't playing
(c) didn't play
(d) hasn't been playing

26. Devastated after breaking up with his girlfriend, William wasn't sure whether he should go and see a therapist until his sister convinced him to go. If he _____ for all his pain to go away, his life would have been miserable.

(a) is waiting
(b) had waited
(c) waited
(d) would wait

THIS IS THE END OF THE GRAMMAR SECTION

LISTENING SECTION

DIRECTIONS:

The Listening Sections has four parts. In each part you will hear a spoken passage and a number of questions about the passage. First you will hear the questions. Then you will hear the passage. From the four choices for each question, choose the best answer. Then blacken in the correct circle on your answer sheet.

Now you will hear an example question. Then you will hear an example passage.

Now listen to the example question.

Example:

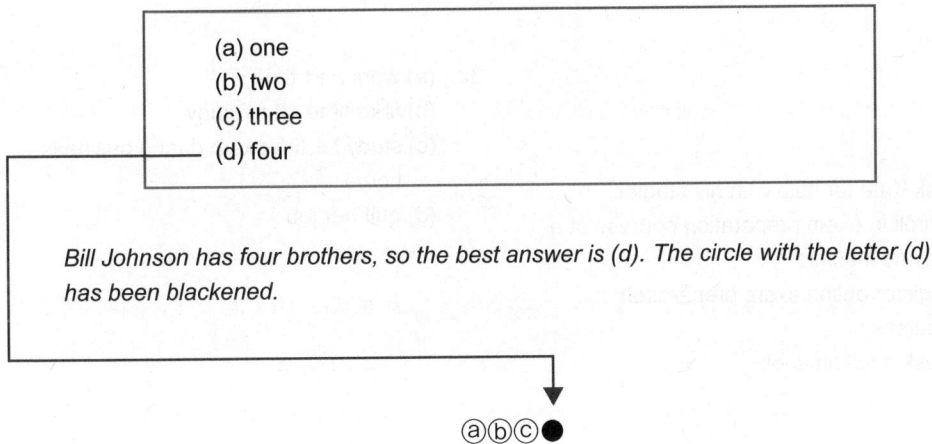

(a) one
(b) two
(c) three
(d) four

Bill Johnson has four brothers, so the best answer is (d). The circle with the letter (d) has been blackened.

ⓐⓑⓒ●

NOW TURN THE PAGE AND BEGIN

PART 1. *You will hear a conversation between two people. First you will hear questions 27 through 33. Then you will hear the conversation. Choose the best answer to each question in the time provided.*

27. (a) She was celebrating Kate's achievement.
    (b) She was attending a business meeting.
    (c) She was meeting her best friend.
    (d) She was studying with Kate

28. (a) Kate was living in a different country.
    (b) Kate was focusing on her work.
    (c) Kate was preparing for the diplomat exam.
    (d) Kate was very sick.

29. (a) ask Kate for help with his studies
    (b) enroll in exam preparation courses at a private institute
    (c) register online exam preparation courses
    (d) seek a full-time job

30. (a) because she didn't want to spend time travelling to private institutes
    (b) because her boss didn't allow her to attend the courses in private institutes
    (c) because she wanted to save money
    (d) because she worked 7 days a week for months

31. (a) by giving financial support
    (b) by buying useful books for her exam
    (c) by introducing a good tutor
    (d) by teaching her studies for the exam

32. (a) work part-time
    (b) take time off to study
    (c) study for the exam during business hours
    (d) quit her job

33. (a) meet Paul
    (b) have lunch with Chris
    (c) have lunch with Paul
    (d) introduce Paul to Kate

PART 2. *You will hear a man talking about a product. First you will hear questions 34 through 39. Then you will hear the talk. Choose the best answer to each question in the time provided.*

34. (a) those who are from families in poverty
    (b) those who are not native English speakers
    (c) those who want to replace their native language
    (d) those who speak English as their first language

35. (a) They will look after their students well.
    (b) They have a greater need to earn extra income.
    (c) They can easily learn their students' language.
    (d) They can teach precise and academic writing skills.

36. (a) by tutoring many students at the same time
    (b) by selecting each student's intelligence
    (c) by arranging a convenient teaching timetable
    (d) by negotiating tuition fees

37. (a) freely choose students with higher skill levels
    (b) freely choose students of different ages
    (c) freely teach subjects the tutor wants
    (d) freely attend a teaching training provided by the government

38. (a) by offering online assistance
    (b) by replacing the student
    (c) by taking time off from work
    (d) by reducing teaching hours per week

39. (a) Their teaching methods have been widely recognized.
    (b) They can easily teach English.
    (c) They are currently university students majoring in English.
    (d) They are fluent in English and have a university degree.

PART 3. *You will hear a conversation between two people. First you will hear questions 40 through 45. Then you will hear the conversation. Choose the best answer to each question in the time provided.*

40. (a) sell a house in the city
    (b) rent a house in the city or countryside
    (c) buy a house or an apartment
    (d) live in the city or countryside

41. (a) They will need to make a doctor's appointment.
    (b) They will travel a short distance to see a doctor.
    (c) They will get medical care services at a low price.
    (d) They will be treated by the best doctors in the world.

42. (a) because there are less electric cars than gas vehicles
    (b) because there are too many factories
    (c) because there are too many people
    (d) because there are too many people with mental illnesses

43. (a) a small number of students
    (b) a small number of teachers
    (c) poor government support
    (d) the noise the neighbors cause

44. (a) the location of a house
    (b) extreme weather conditions
    (c) the number of family members
    (d) road conditions

45. (a) They will find a house near their workplace.
    (b) They will by a house in the city.
    (c) They will buy a house in the countryside.
    (d) They will rent a house in the countryside.

PART 4. You will hear an explanation of a process. First you will hear questions 46 through 52. Then you will hear the explanation. Choose the best answer to each question in the time provided.

46. (a) how to identify a problem customer on the phone
    (b) how to avoid customer complaints on the phone
    (c) how to attract good customers on the phone
    (d) how to deal with difficult customers on the phone

47. (a) by raising his voice
    (b) by listening to the customer
    (c) by asking the customer to stay calm
    (d) by hanging up and calling the customer back in a few minutes

48. (a) to identify customers' emotions
    (b) to end the conversation with customers quickly
    (c) to prevent the situation from getting worse
    (d) to let customers buy more products

49. (a) customers can choose a solution they want
    (b) customers can feel their complaints are right
    (c) customers will be less angry
    (d) customers will stop complaining quickly

50. (a) because customers would appreciate his attitude
    (b) because customers like someone listening to what they say
    (c) because the service has been inadequate
    (d) because customers can calm down

51. (a) It may result in satisfactory service.
    (b) It may lead to an inappropriate service.
    (c) It can contribute to poor mental health.
    (d) It can make the customer hang up the phone.

52. (a) dealing with a tough customer on the phone repeatedly
    (b) solving a difficult complaint on one's own
    (c) meeting tough customers in person
    (d) addressing a difficult problem immediately

THIS IS THE END OF THE LISTENING SECTION

READING AND VOCABULARY SECTION

DIRECTIONS:

You will now read four different passages. Each passage is followed by comprehension and vocabulary questions. From the four choices for each item, choose the best answer. Then blacken in the correct circle on your answer sheet.

Read the following example passage and example question.

Example:

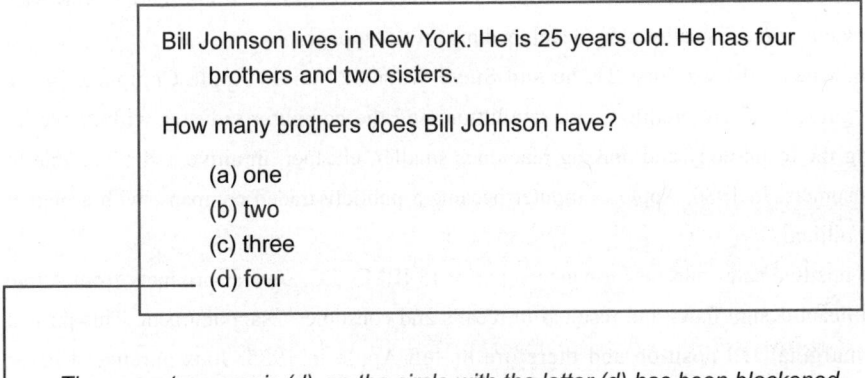

Bill Johnson lives in New York. He is 25 years old. He has four brothers and two sisters.

How many brothers does Bill Johnson have?

(a) one
(b) two
(c) three
(d) four

The correct answer is (d), so the circle with the letter (d) has been blackened.

ⓐ ⓑ ⓒ ●

NOW TURN THE PAGE AND BEGIN

PART 1. Read the following biographical narrative and answer the questions. The underlined words in the article are for vocabulary questions.

STEVE JOBS

Steve Jobs was an American inventor, designer and entrepreneur who was the co-founder, chief executive and chairman of Apple Computer. Jobs is also widely recognized as a pioneer of the personal computer revolution of the 1970s and 1980s.

Steve Jobs was born on February 24, 1955, in San Francisco, California. As an infant, Jobs was adopted by Clara and Paul Jobs. As a boy, Paul showed his son how to take apart and reconstruct electronics, a hobby that instilled confidence, tenacity and mechanical prowess in young Jobs. While Jobs was always smart and innovative thinker, he was directionless and dropped out of college after six months and spent the next 18 months dropping in on creative classes at the school. Jobs later recounted how one course in calligraphy developed his love of typography.

In 1976, when Jobs was just 21, he and Steve Wozniak started Apple Computer in the Jobs' family garage and are credited with revolutionizing the computer industry with Apple by democratizing the technology and making machines smaller, cheaper, intuitive and accessible to everyday consumers. In 1980, Apple Computer became a publicly-traded company, with a market value of $1.2 billion.

Despite positive sales and performance superior to IBM's PC, several products from Apple suffered significant design flaws and resulted in recalls and consumer disappointment. This pushed Jobs into a marginalized position and therefore he left Apple in 1985. Jobs purchased Pixar Animation Studios in 1986. The studio went on to produce wildly popular movies and these films have collectively netted $4 billion. The studio merged with Walt Disney in 2006, making Jobs Disney's largest shareholder.

In 1997, Jobs returned to his post as Apple's CEO. With a new management team, altered stock options and a self-imposed annual salary of $1 a year, Jobs put Apple back on track. Jobs' ingenious products, effective branding campaigns and stylish designs caught the attention of consumers once again. Jobs died in 2011 after battling pancreatic cancer. He was 56 years old.

53. What is Steve Jobs known for?

   (a) being the second chairman of Apple Computer
   (b) being the sole founder of Apple Computer
   (c) being the first popular Apple Computer personality
   (d) being the leader of the personal computer revolution

54. When most likely did Jobs find out about his interest in typography?

   (a) upon establishing Apple Computer
   (b) before he left college
   (c) after dropping out of college
   (d) while he was in high school

55. How did Jobs and Wozniak revolutionize the computer industry?

   (a) They decreased prices of all products they were selling.
   (b) They led the widespread use of computers.
   (c) They competed with IBM.
   (d) They made Apple as the most famous company in the world.

56. Why most likely did Jobs leave Apple?

   (a) Because he was Disney's largest shareholder.
   (b) Because he bought Pixar Animation Studios.
   (c) Because Walt Disney was merged with Pixar Animation Studio.
   (d) Because he was responsible for product recalls and customer dissatisfaction caused by faulty design.

57. How did Jobs catch consumers' eyes again?

   (a) by encouraging them to buy Apple's stock
   (b) by producing creative and stylish products
   (c) by inspiring them to design Apple's computer
   (d) by persuading them to join in a new management team

58. In the context of the passage, tenacity means _____.

   (a) ambition
   (b) persistence
   (c) courage
   (d) patience

59. In the context of the passage, democratizing means _____.

   (a) distributing
   (b) specifying
   (c) developing
   (d) popularizing

PART 2. Read the following Web article and answer the questions. The underlined words in the article are for vocabulary questions.

STUDY SHOWS AUTISTIC CHILDREN TEND TO BE OBESE

Recent studies have found a link between obesity and autism among children. The studies showed that the risk of obesity is highest among the children with autism and childhood obesity further raises the risk of several disorders like diabetes, heart disease, sleep apnoea, menstrual irregularities and orthopaedic problems.

Based on a study conducted by Chanaka N. Kahathuduwa, clinical assistant professor in the department of psychiatry at Texas Tech University Health Sciences Center, children with autism have a 41.1% greater risk for development of obesity than typically developing children. Also, the prevalence of obesity among children and adolescents between ages 2 and 19 years in the United States is 16.3% and the prevalence of those that are overweight is 31.9%.

In the study performed by Carol Curtin, co-director of the Healthy Weight Research Network at the University of Massachusetts, children with autism have unusual eating habits and prefer energy dense foods including high fat foods. It is possible that these eating patterns may contribute to the development of obesity. Particularly, children with severe autism are more than three times as likely to be obese as those with mild autism because they tend to be less active and have more restricted diets than other autistic children.

Meanwhile, a survey by Tanja Kral, associate professor of nursing at the University of Pennsylvania in Philadelphia found that it is still unclear why children with autism are more likely to be obese than their peers. The study carried out by researchers from Duke University Medical Center and Virginia Commonwealth University revealed that women who were overweight before they became pregnant have about a one-third increased risk of having a child with autism, compared with normal-weight women.

However, many studies are unable to prove there is a direct link between autism and women who were overweight or obese before falling pregnant. This is because the findings are based on observational studies that varied widely in their studied populations and it is possible that genetics, health, lifestyle and other family environmental factors could have played a role in the likelihood of having a child with autism.

60. What is the result of children with autism?

    (a) They have a greater risk of suffering from a number of disorders.
    (b) They have a greater risk of being overweight or obese.
    (c) They are highly affected by many disorders.
    (d) They have a lesser risk of being overweight or obese.

61. According to Carol Curtin, which of the following statement about autistic children's eating patterns is true?

    (a) Their eating habits are similar to typically developing children.
    (b) They avoid eating foods that have the high amount of energy or calories per gram of food.
    (c) They enjoy eating foods that have the low amount of energy or calories per gram of food.
    (d) They favor foods that have the high amount of energy or calories per gram of food.

62. What could happen to children born to mothers who were severly obese before pregnancy?

    (a) They could be more likely to be underweight than their friends.
    (b) They might be more vulnerable to autism.
    (c) They could be within the healthy weight range.
    (d) They could be fatter than their friends.

63. Why are children with high level autism more likely to be obese than those with low level of autism?

    (a) because they do not stay active as much as those with low level of autism
    (b) because they spend more time eating than those with low level of autism
    (c) because they do not have a diet that limits or increases specific foods
    (d) because they take medications that increase hunger

64. What do many researchers find it hard to demonstrate?

    (a) how exactly pregnant women in different ages are associated with autism
    (b) how normal-weight women and obese women are different while they are pregnant
    (c) how exactly women who were obese before having a baby are associated with autism
    (d) how exactly women who were obese after pregnancy are having autistic children

65. In the context of the passage, typically means _____.

    (a) mainly   (b) normally
    (c) regularly   (d) frequently

66. In the context of the passage, likelihood means _____.

    (a) consequence   (b) perception
    (c) probability   (d) severity

PART 3. *Read the following encyclopedia article and answer the questions. The underlined words in the article are for vocabulary questions.*

STONEFISH

The stonefish is a marine fish that is found in shallow water of the tropical Indo-Pacific. Stonefish are sluggish bottom-dwelling fish that live among rocks or coral and in mudflats and estuaries. They are known as the most venomous fish in the sea.

Stonefish's dorsal areas is lined with 13 spines which are sharp and stiff and can even pierce boot soles. Through its dorsal fin spines, the stonefish can inject a venom that is capable of killing an adult person in less than an hour. In nature, the stonefish does not use its venom to capture prey, but instead to avoid predation. The venom, which consists of a mixture of toxin proteins, is extremely painful and quite effective at turning away even the strongest potential predators.

The stonefish has evolved many adaptations to help them succeed in the reef bottom. They have large heads and mouths, and small eyes. Their bumpy skins covered with wartlike lumps and fleshy flaps can help them hide and remain camouflaged in between rocks and corals. They reach up to 30~40 centimeters long.

They eat mostly other reef fish and some bottom dwelling invertebrates like shrimp. They capture prey by sitting motionless on the reef floor and waiting for potential prey to swim by. They have been recorded striking their prey in 0.015 seconds. Their powerful jaws and large mouths create so much pressure that they are easily able to suck down their unsuspecting prey and swallow it whole.

There is no evidence to suggest that human activity threatens the stonefish. Although individuals are sometimes caught for the private aquarium trade, stonefish are rarely eaten by people and there is not a targeted fishery for this species. Therefore, they are unlikely to become endangered anytime soon.

67. What are stonefish famous for?

    (a) being the most abundant fish on earth
    (b) being one of the extinct fish on earth
    (c) being the world's ugliest fish
    (d) being the most poisonous fish on earth

68. How are stonefish able to kill humans quickly?

    (a) by sucking the blood of humans in the water
    (b) by infecting the venomous wound
    (c) by releasing a toxin from dorsal fin spines
    (d) by laying toxic eggs from dorsal fin spines

69. What is the benefit of the stonefish having rocky skins?

    (a) getting less exhausted by the activity
    (b) not being exposed to another type of prey and predator
    (c) swimming easily between rocks and corals
    (d) sustaining the high pressure in the deep ocean

70. What is most likely the reason why stonefish have strong jaws and big mouths?

    (a) to produce venoms quickly
    (b) to protect themselves from predators quickly
    (c) to eat prey quickly
    (d) to hide from potential predators quickly

71. Why are stonefish unlikely to become an endangered species?

    (a) They have long average lifespans.
    (b) They are not affected by seawater contamination.
    (c) They still have a large population.
    (d) They are not fished for food.

72. In the context of the passage, camouflaged means _____.

    (a) disguised
    (b) engulfed
    (c) exposed
    (d) protruded

73. In the context of the passage, unsuspecting means _____.

    (a) inedible
    (b) targeted
    (c) unsuspicious
    (d) unrecognizable

PART 4. Read the following business letter and answer the questions. The underlined words in the letter are for vocabulary questions.

October 11, 2020
Mr. John Nile
111 Cloudy Heights
Canterbury, NY 10000

Dear Mr. Nile:

It gives us pleasure to inform you that our bank has decided to open a branch this coming November1, 2020. The new branch is located near the Transport Center in Canterbury.

You will realize that to open a branch at a place where business opportunities are still in the infancy requires great courage and <u>conviction</u> of duties. Fortunately, our bank is never found wanting where such courage is required. It is so because it has faith in its tradition of public goods and in its clients. We are, therefore opening the new branch even against all odds.

You have been our old patron. We invite you to open your account with us at the new branch and make full use of other banking facilities to be provided there. We have decided to give 25% more interest on deposits in the new branch to the first 300 deposits for one year. Also, you will get all the customer facilities along with the foreign exchange facilities. From now, you will be able to receive any kind of foreign remittance within 48 hours and also can maintain accounts in foreign currency. It is our <u>earnest</u> desire that you make use of our offer and give us an opportunity to serve the public in greater good.

Should you have any inquires, don't hesitate to contact us at 300-40001 or at auzbank@uk.com. Thank you for your continued support of our bank.

Respectfully,
Brian Jo
Manager
AUZ Bank

74. Why did Brian Jo write John Nile a letter?

    (a) to notify John Nile that his bank account is closed
    (b) to inform John Nile that AUZ Bank is closing
    (c) to inform that John Nile has been registered for a service
    (d) to inform John Nile that AUZ Bank opens a new branch

75. What is the reason why opening the new branch is very unlikely to succeed?

    (a) Business chances in the region of the new branch are just starting to develop.
    (b) There are more young customers than old customers.
    (c) Running a business in the region of the new branch is very difficult.
    (d) The new branch is not ready to provide excellent customer service.

76. Why was John Nile chosen to benefit from the new branch?

    (a) because he is one of bank's founder members
    (b) because he has been a regular customer of the bank
    (c) because he has been a rich business man
    (d) because he never borrows money from the bank

77. What will most likely happen if Nile opens his account at the new branch?

    (a) He will be able to transfer money to overseas within 48 hours.
    (b) He will have extra interests on foreign accounts.
    (c) He will have an instant account in foreign currency.
    (d) He will have higher interests on his deposits within a given period of time.

78. What should Nile do if he has inquires about the new branch?

    (a) visit other branches
    (b) meet Brian Jo
    (c) ring up the bank
    (d) send email to Brian Jo

79. In the context of the passage, conviction means _____.

    (a) persuasion
    (b) belief
    (c) judgement
    (d) uncertainty

80. In the context of the passage, earnest means _____.

    (a) sincere
    (b) intense
    (c) willing
    (d) keen

THIS IS THE END OF THE TEST

ANSWER KEY

TEST 1

	SCORE
GRAMMAR	/ 26
LISTENING	/ 26
READING & VOCABULARY	/ 28
TOTAL	/ 80

GRAMMAR SECTION

01	02	03	04	05	06	07	08	09	10
(a)	(d)	(d)	(c)	(d)	(c)	(d)	(c)	(a)	(c)
11	12	13	14	15	16	17	18	19	20
(c)	(b)	(c)	(d)	(c)	(d)	(c)	(b)	(b)	(c)
21	22	23	24	25	26				
(d)	(c)	(d)	(d)	(b)	(a)				

LISTENING SECTION

27	28	29	30	31	32	33	34	35	36
(d)	(c)	(b)	(c)	(a)	(c)	(a)	(c)	(b)	(d)
37	38	39	40	41	42	43	44	45	46
(b)	(c)	(a)	(c)	(d)	(b)	(a)	(b)	(c)	(d)
47	48	49	50	51	52				
(b)	(d)	(a)	(b)	(b)	(b)				

READING AND VOCABULARY SECTION

53	54	55	56	57	58	59	60	61	62
(d)	(b)	(c)	(d)	(c)	(b)	(a)	(d)	(b)	(c)
63	64	65	66	67	68	69	70	71	72
(c)	(c)	(a)	(c)	(c)	(d)	(a)	(b)	(c)	(d)
73	74	75	76	77	78	79	80		
(a)	(d)	(c)	(a)	(d)	(b)	(b)	(a)		

TEST 2

	SCORE
GRAMMAR	/ 26
LISTENING	/ 26
READING & VOCABULARY	/ 28
TOTAL	/ 80

GRAMMAR SECTION

01	02	03	04	05	06	07	08	09	10
(c)	(b)	(d)	(c)	(d)	(b)	(b)	(c)	(b)	(b)
11	12	13	14	15	16	17	18	19	20
(c)	(d)	(c)	(d)	(a)	(a)	(d)	(c)	(a)	(c)
21	22	23	24	25	26				
(b)	(b)	(d)	(d)	(b)	(b)				

LISTENING SECTION

27	28	29	30	31	32	33	34	35	36
(d)	(d)	(a)	(c)	(d)	(d)	(b)	(c)	(d)	(d)
37	38	39	40	41	42	43	44	45	46
(a)	(b)	(c)	(c)	(d)	(b)	(d)	(d)	(c)	(c)
47	48	49	50	51	52				
(b)	(a)	(d)	(a)	(b)	(b)				

READING AND VOCABULARY SECTION

53	54	55	56	57	58	59	60	61	62
(d)	(b)	(a)	(a)	(c)	(d)	(a)	(a)	(d)	(c)
63	64	65	66	67	68	69	70	71	72
(a)	(b)	(c)	(d)	(c)	(b)	(a)	(d)	(a)	(b)
73	74	75	76	77	78	79	80		
(d)	(d)	(b)	(c)	(d)	(b)	(b)	(d)		

ANSWER KEY

TEST 3

	SCORE
GRAMMAR	/ 26
LISTENING	/ 26
READING & VOCABULARY	/ 28
TOTAL	/ 80

GRAMMAR SECTION

01	02	03	04	05	06	07	08	09	10
(c)	(b)	(d)	(d)	(c)	(c)	(b)	(a)	(d)	(c)
11	12	13	14	15	16	17	18	19	20
(c)	(a)	(c)	(b)	(c)	(b)	(d)	(c)	(a)	(b)
21	22	23	24	25	26
(d)	(b)	(d)	(d)	(d)	(b)

LISTENING SECTION

27	28	29	30	31	32	33	34	35	36
(a)	(c)	(b)	(d)	(d)	(b)	(b)	(b)	(d)	(c)
37	38	39	40	41	42	43	44	45	46
(b)	(a)	(d)	(d)	(b)	(c)	(a)	(b)	(c)	(d)
47	48	49	50	51	52
(b)	(c)	(a)	(d)	(b)	(a)

READING AND VOCABULARY SECTION

53	54	55	56	57	58	59	60	61	62
(d)	(c)	(b)	(d)	(b)	(b)	(d)	(b)	(d)	(b)
63	64	65	66	67	68	69	70	71	72
(a)	(c)	(b)	(c)	(d)	(c)	(b)	(c)	(d)	(a)
73	74	75	76	77	78	79	80
(c)	(d)	(a)	(b)	(d)	(c)	(b)	(a)

G-TELP

※ TEST DATE

MO.		DAY		YEAR			

감독확인란	

등급	①	②	③	④	⑤

성 명	

성명란																				
초성	ㄱ	ㄴ	ㄷ	ㄹ	ㅁ	ㅂ	ㅅ	ㅇ	ㅈ	ㅊ	ㅋ	ㅌ	ㅍ	ㅎ						
중성	ㅏ	ㅑ	ㅓ	ㅕ	ㅗ	ㅛ	ㅜ	ㅠ	ㅡ	ㅣ	ㅔ	ㅐ	ㅖ	ㅒ	ㅘ	ㅚ	ㅢ	ㅝ	ㅟ	ㅙ
종성	ㄱ	ㄴ	ㄷ	ㄹ	ㅁ	ㅂ	ㅅ	ㅇ	ㅈ	ㅊ	ㅋ	ㅌ	ㅍ	ㅎ	ㄲ	ㄸ	ㅃ	ㅆ	ㅉ	
초성	ㄱ	ㄴ	ㄷ	ㄹ	ㅁ	ㅂ	ㅅ	ㅇ	ㅈ	ㅊ	ㅋ	ㅌ	ㅍ	ㅎ						
중성	ㅏ	ㅑ	ㅓ	ㅕ	ㅗ	ㅛ	ㅜ	ㅠ	ㅡ	ㅣ	ㅔ	ㅐ	ㅖ	ㅒ	ㅘ	ㅚ	ㅢ	ㅝ	ㅟ	ㅙ
종성	ㄱ	ㄴ	ㄷ	ㄹ	ㅁ	ㅂ	ㅅ	ㅇ	ㅈ	ㅊ	ㅋ	ㅌ	ㅍ	ㅎ	ㄲ	ㄸ	ㅃ	ㅆ	ㅉ	
초성	ㄱ	ㄴ	ㄷ	ㄹ	ㅁ	ㅂ	ㅅ	ㅇ	ㅈ	ㅊ	ㅋ	ㅌ	ㅍ	ㅎ						
중성	ㅏ	ㅑ	ㅓ	ㅕ	ㅗ	ㅛ	ㅜ	ㅠ	ㅡ	ㅣ	ㅔ	ㅐ	ㅖ	ㅒ	ㅘ	ㅚ	ㅢ	ㅝ	ㅟ	ㅙ
종성	ㄱ	ㄴ	ㄷ	ㄹ	ㅁ	ㅂ	ㅅ	ㅇ	ㅈ	ㅊ	ㅋ	ㅌ	ㅍ	ㅎ	ㄲ	ㄸ	ㅃ	ㅆ	ㅉ	
초성	ㄱ	ㄴ	ㄷ	ㄹ	ㅁ	ㅂ	ㅅ	ㅇ	ㅈ	ㅊ	ㅋ	ㅌ	ㅍ	ㅎ						
중성	ㅏ	ㅑ	ㅓ	ㅕ	ㅗ	ㅛ	ㅜ	ㅠ	ㅡ	ㅣ	ㅔ	ㅐ	ㅖ	ㅒ	ㅘ	ㅚ	ㅢ	ㅝ	ㅟ	ㅙ
종성	ㄱ	ㄴ	ㄷ	ㄹ	ㅁ	ㅂ	ㅅ	ㅇ	ㅈ	ㅊ	ㅋ	ㅌ	ㅍ	ㅎ	ㄲ	ㄸ	ㅃ	ㅆ	ㅉ	

수험번호

		–					–							
⓪	⓪		⓪	⓪	⓪	⓪		⓪	⓪	⓪	⓪	⓪	⓪	⓪
①	①		①	①	①	①		①	①	①	①	①	①	①
②	②		②	②	②	②		②	②	②	②	②	②	②
③	③		③	③	③	③		③	③	③	③	③	③	③
④	④	–	④	④	④	④	–	④	④	④	④	④	④	④
⑤	⑤		⑤	⑤	⑤	⑤		⑤	⑤	⑤	⑤	⑤	⑤	⑤
⑥	⑥		⑥	⑥	⑥	⑥		⑥	⑥	⑥	⑥	⑥	⑥	⑥
⑦	⑦		⑦	⑦	⑦	⑦		⑦	⑦	⑦	⑦	⑦	⑦	⑦
⑧	⑧		⑧	⑧	⑧	⑧		⑧	⑧	⑧	⑧	⑧	⑧	⑧
⑨	⑨		⑨	⑨	⑨	⑨		⑨	⑨	⑨	⑨	⑨	⑨	⑨

1) Code 1.

	⓪	①	②	③	④	⑤	⑥	⑦	⑧	⑨
	⓪	①	②	③	④	⑤	⑥	⑦	⑧	⑨
	⓪	①	②	③	④	⑤	⑥	⑦	⑧	⑨

2) Code 2.

	⓪	①	②	③	④	⑤	⑥	⑦	⑧	⑨
	⓪	①	②	③	④	⑤	⑥	⑦	⑧	⑨
	⓪	①	②	③	④	⑤	⑥	⑦	⑧	⑨

3) Code 3.

	⓪	①	②	③	④	⑤	⑥	⑦	⑧	⑨
	⓪	①	②	③	④	⑤	⑥	⑦	⑧	⑨
	⓪	①	②	③	④	⑤	⑥	⑦	⑧	⑨

주민등록번호 앞자리						–	고유번호						
						–							
⓪	⓪	⓪	⓪	⓪	⓪		⓪	⓪	⓪	⓪	⓪	⓪	⓪
①	①	①	①	①	①		①	①	①	①	①	①	①
②	②	②	②	②	②		②	②	②	②	②	②	②
③	③	③	③	③	③		③	③	③	③	③	③	③
④	④	④	④	④	④	–	④	④	④	④	④	④	④
⑤	⑤	⑤	⑤	⑤	⑤		⑤	⑤	⑤	⑤	⑤	⑤	⑤
⑥	⑥	⑥	⑥	⑥	⑥		⑥	⑥	⑥	⑥	⑥	⑥	⑥
⑦	⑦	⑦	⑦	⑦	⑦		⑦	⑦	⑦	⑦	⑦	⑦	⑦
⑧	⑧	⑧	⑧	⑧	⑧		⑧	⑧	⑧	⑧	⑧	⑧	⑧
⑨	⑨	⑨	⑨	⑨	⑨		⑨	⑨	⑨	⑨	⑨	⑨	⑨

문항	답 란				문항	답 란				문항	답 란				문항	답 란			
1	ⓐ	ⓑ	ⓒ	ⓓ	23	ⓐ	ⓑ	ⓒ	ⓓ	45	ⓐ	ⓑ	ⓒ	ⓓ	67	ⓐ	ⓑ	ⓒ	ⓓ
2	ⓐ	ⓑ	ⓒ	ⓓ	24	ⓐ	ⓑ	ⓒ	ⓓ	46	ⓐ	ⓑ	ⓒ	ⓓ	68	ⓐ	ⓑ	ⓒ	ⓓ
3	ⓐ	ⓑ	ⓒ	ⓓ	25	ⓐ	ⓑ	ⓒ	ⓓ	47	ⓐ	ⓑ	ⓒ	ⓓ	69	ⓐ	ⓑ	ⓒ	ⓓ
4	ⓐ	ⓑ	ⓒ	ⓓ	26	ⓐ	ⓑ	ⓒ	ⓓ	48	ⓐ	ⓑ	ⓒ	ⓓ	70	ⓐ	ⓑ	ⓒ	ⓓ
5	ⓐ	ⓑ	ⓒ	ⓓ	27	ⓐ	ⓑ	ⓒ	ⓓ	49	ⓐ	ⓑ	ⓒ	ⓓ	71	ⓐ	ⓑ	ⓒ	ⓓ
6	ⓐ	ⓑ	ⓒ	ⓓ	28	ⓐ	ⓑ	ⓒ	ⓓ	50	ⓐ	ⓑ	ⓒ	ⓓ	72	ⓐ	ⓑ	ⓒ	ⓓ
7	ⓐ	ⓑ	ⓒ	ⓓ	29	ⓐ	ⓑ	ⓒ	ⓓ	51	ⓐ	ⓑ	ⓒ	ⓓ	73	ⓐ	ⓑ	ⓒ	ⓓ
8	ⓐ	ⓑ	ⓒ	ⓓ	30	ⓐ	ⓑ	ⓒ	ⓓ	52	ⓐ	ⓑ	ⓒ	ⓓ	74	ⓐ	ⓑ	ⓒ	ⓓ
9	ⓐ	ⓑ	ⓒ	ⓓ	31	ⓐ	ⓑ	ⓒ	ⓓ	53	ⓐ	ⓑ	ⓒ	ⓓ	75	ⓐ	ⓑ	ⓒ	ⓓ
10	ⓐ	ⓑ	ⓒ	ⓓ	32	ⓐ	ⓑ	ⓒ	ⓓ	54	ⓐ	ⓑ	ⓒ	ⓓ	76	ⓐ	ⓑ	ⓒ	ⓓ
11	ⓐ	ⓑ	ⓒ	ⓓ	33	ⓐ	ⓑ	ⓒ	ⓓ	55	ⓐ	ⓑ	ⓒ	ⓓ	77	ⓐ	ⓑ	ⓒ	ⓓ
12	ⓐ	ⓑ	ⓒ	ⓓ	34	ⓐ	ⓑ	ⓒ	ⓓ	56	ⓐ	ⓑ	ⓒ	ⓓ	78	ⓐ	ⓑ	ⓒ	ⓓ
13	ⓐ	ⓑ	ⓒ	ⓓ	35	ⓐ	ⓑ	ⓒ	ⓓ	57	ⓐ	ⓑ	ⓒ	ⓓ	79	ⓐ	ⓑ	ⓒ	ⓓ
14	ⓐ	ⓑ	ⓒ	ⓓ	36	ⓐ	ⓑ	ⓒ	ⓓ	58	ⓐ	ⓑ	ⓒ	ⓓ	80	ⓐ	ⓑ	ⓒ	ⓓ
15	ⓐ	ⓑ	ⓒ	ⓓ	37	ⓐ	ⓑ	ⓒ	ⓓ	59	ⓐ	ⓑ	ⓒ	ⓓ					
16	ⓐ	ⓑ	ⓒ	ⓓ	38	ⓐ	ⓑ	ⓒ	ⓓ	60	ⓐ	ⓑ	ⓒ	ⓓ					
17	ⓐ	ⓑ	ⓒ	ⓓ	39	ⓐ	ⓑ	ⓒ	ⓓ	61	ⓐ	ⓑ	ⓒ	ⓓ					
18	ⓐ	ⓑ	ⓒ	ⓓ	40	ⓐ	ⓑ	ⓒ	ⓓ	62	ⓐ	ⓑ	ⓒ	ⓓ					
19	ⓐ	ⓑ	ⓒ	ⓓ	41	ⓐ	ⓑ	ⓒ	ⓓ	63	ⓐ	ⓑ	ⓒ	ⓓ					
20	ⓐ	ⓑ	ⓒ	ⓓ	42	ⓐ	ⓑ	ⓒ	ⓓ	64	ⓐ	ⓑ	ⓒ	ⓓ					
21	ⓐ	ⓑ	ⓒ	ⓓ	43	ⓐ	ⓑ	ⓒ	ⓓ	65	ⓐ	ⓑ	ⓒ	ⓓ					
22	ⓐ	ⓑ	ⓒ	ⓓ	44	ⓐ	ⓑ	ⓒ	ⓓ	66	ⓐ	ⓑ	ⓒ	ⓓ					

password

⓪	⓪	⓪	⓪
①	①	①	①
②	②	②	②
③	③	③	③
④	④	④	④
⑤	⑤	⑤	⑤
⑥	⑥	⑥	⑥
⑦	⑦	⑦	⑦
⑧	⑧	⑧	⑧
⑨	⑨	⑨	⑨

G-TELP

답안지 (OMR Answer Sheet)

G-TELP
어휘 & 구문독해

READING & VOCABULARY

LISTENING

READING & VOCABULARY
어휘 & 구문독해

G-TELP 독해 & 어휘

PART 1 과거 역사 속의 사건이나 현시대의 이야기
PART 2 잡지나 신문의 기사
PART 3 백과사전
PART 4 비즈니스 편지

TEST 1 part 1 어휘 & 구문독해

Part 1 53~59 FLORENCE NIGHTINGALE

어휘

1st reformer 개혁가 statistician 통계 전문가 be known as ~로 알려져 있다 founder 창립자
Crimea 크림 반도(우크라이나 남단 흑해안의 반도) tirelessly 지칠 줄 모르고
ensure 반드시 ~하게[이게] 하다, 보장하다 compassionate 동정하는

2nd excel in ~에서 뛰어나다 at an early age 젊었을 때 be satisfied with ~에 만족하다
home management 가정 관리 philosopher 철학자 engage in ~에 관여[참여]하다
discourse (진지한) 담론, 토론

3rd find comfort in ~에서 위안을 찾다 suitable 적합한 a route to ~로의 길
be thwarted by ~에 의해 좌절되다 inappropriate 부적절한 stature 지명도, 위상

4th opposition (~에 대한 강한) 반대[항의] enroll as ~로 등록하다 take[accept] a job 일을 맡다
at the outbreak of ~의 발발로 improve 향상시키다 sanitary conditions 위생 상태
endless 무한한 death rate (인구의) 사망률

5th sail to ~로 항해하다 mistreatment 학대 wounded 부상을 입은[다친]
be transmitted through ~을 통해 전해지다 foul air 탁한 공기 even after 이후에도
contaminated water 오염수 firm 확고한 be influenced by ~에 영향을 받다
poor hygiene 불결한 위생 be responsible for ~에 책임이 있다

6th aim at ~을 목적으로 하다 viable 실행 가능한 respectable 존경할 만한 profession 직업
pass away 사망하다 be awarded to ~에게 수여되다 outstanding 뛰어난 museum 박물관
establish [국가·학교·기업 등을] 설립하다 recognize (존재·진실성을) 인정[인식]하다
pioneering 개척[선구]적인 reform 개혁[개선]

구문독해

to가 전치사인 경우
▶ devote A to (동)명사: A를 ~하는 데 몰두(전념)하다
▶ be able to V: ~을 할 수 있다.
▶ prefer to V: ~을 (…보다) 좋아하다
▶ view + 목적어 + as 보어(명사): ~을 ~라고 생각하다(간주하다)
▶ attempt to V: ~하려는 시도
▶ despite + 구: ~에도 불구하고 (양보/대조 전치사)

to가 전치사인 경우
▶ A(원인) + lead to B(결과): A가 B로 이어지다/A라는 원인으로 B라는 결과가 생기다

목적격 종속접속사 that(~것을) 생략
▶ 주어 + 타동사 + (that) + 주어 + 동사

동격을 나타내는 종속접속사 that(~라는)
▶ 추상명사 + that + 주어 + 동사

상태동사 make
▶ make + 목적어 + 목적격보어(형용사/명사): ~을 ~한 상태로 만들다

주격관계대명사 that(~하는)
▶ 선행사(사람/사물/동물) + that + 동사
▶ include + 목적어(동명사): ~을 포함하다

Part 1 53~59 FLORENCE NIGHTINGALE Question

| 어휘 |

53 preference 선호(도) satisfaction with ~에 대한 만족 conventional 관습[관례]적인 household 가정 traditional 전통적인

54 against ~에 반대하여[맞서] work as ~으로 일하다 suitable for[to] ~에 알맞은[어울리는] be good at ~에 능숙하다 far 훨씬, 단연

55 medical supplies 의약 용품 war casualties 전쟁 사상자 work in ~에 종사하다 practices 관례, 실례 infectious diseases 전염병

56 be responsible for ~에 책임이 있다 be contaminated by ~에 의해 오염되다 polluted water 오염된 물

57 serve as ~의 역할을 하다 recognition 인정[승인] a contribution to ~에 대한 공헌[기여] be honored by ~에 의해 영예를 얻다 be designated 지정되다 heritage site 문화 유산 in one's honor(honour) ~에게 경의를 표하여

| 구문독해 |

54 like + 목적어 + 목적격보어(현재분사): ~가 ~하는 것을 좋아하다
want + 목적어 + 목적격보어(to V): ~가 ~하는 것을 원하다

55 by + 동명사: ~함으로써
distribute A to B: B에서 A를 나누어 주다
volunteer + 목적어(to V): ~하는 데 자발적으로 나서다

TEST 2 part 1 어휘 & 구문독해

Part 1 53~59 KRISTI YAMAGUCHI

| 어휘 |

1st former 이전의   decorated 장식된

2nd be born 태어나다   dentist 치과 의사   medical secretary 의학 서기   sibling 형제
be born with 타고 나다   clubfoot 내반족   put a cast on a leg 다리에 깁스를 하다
corrective shoes 교정화   connected 연결된   brace 부목

3rd physical therapy 물리치료   drop out of 중도하차하다   in addition to + (동)명사 ~에 더하여
strengthen 강화하다   provide an outlet for 배출구를 제공하다   shyness 수줍음

4th accommodate oneself to ~에 순응하다   privately 개인으로서   homeschool 홈스쿨링하다
compete 경쟁하다   win the pairs title 2인조 선수권을 획득하다   take A home A를 집으로 가지고 가다
honor 영예

5th graduate from 졸업하다   move[remove] to 이동하다   focus on 집중하다   develop 개발하다
artistry 예술성   combinations 조합   in hopes of ~의 희망을 가지고   well-rounded 다재다능한

6th win a gold medal 금메달을 획득하다   tour 순회공연을 하다   be inducted into 추대되다
Hall of Fame 명예의 전당

7th establish 수립하다   nonprofit organization 비영리 기관   funding 자금 조달
underprivileged 혜택을 못 받는   disabled 장애를 가진   at-risk 위험에 처한
make a difference 변화를 가져오다   positive 긍정적인   education 교육   author 저자
publish 출판하다   award-winning 상을 받은   receive 받다   honor ~에게 명예를 주다

| 구문독해 |

▶ one of + 복수명사: ~중의 하나
▶ keep + 목적어 + Ving: ~가 계속 ~하다(keep + 목적어 + from Ving: ~가 ~하는 것을 못 하게 하다)
▶ help + 목적어(to V): ~하는 것을 돕다
▶ (in order) to V: ~하기 위해서
▶ provide + 목적어(사람) + with 목적어(사물): A를 B에 제공하다[= provide + 목적어(사물) + to/for 목적어(사람)]
▶ try + 목적어(to V: ~하기 위해 노력하다 → 주어의 의지 있음)
▶ try + 목적어(Ving: 시험 삼아 ~하다 → 주어의 의지 없음)

Part 1 53~59 KRISTI YAMAGUCHI Question

| 어휘 |

53 begin 시작하다   outgoing personality 외향적 성격   insistence 고집   rotated 돌아간

54 a couple of years 2년   no longer 더 이상~아닌   pay for 지불하다   adapt to 적응하다
cope with 대처하다

55 compete 경쟁하다   succeed in 성공하다   for the first time 처음으로

56 happen to 일어나다   onwards(onward) 앞으로   win first place 일등하다

57 found 설립하다   find 찾다   financial 경제적   difficulties 어려움

| 구문독해 |

53 make(사역동사) + 목적어 + 목적격보어(V): ~가 ~하게 시키다
watch(지각동사) + 목적어 + 목적격보어(V): ~가 ~하는 것을 보다

54 need + 목적어(to V): ~하는 것이 필요하다

57 help(준사역동사) + 목적어 + 목적격보어(to V): ~가 ~하는 것을 돕다
prevent A from (동)명사: ~하는 것으로부터 A를 막다

TEST 3 part 1 어휘 & 구문독해

Part 1 53~59 STEVE JOBS

어휘

1st inventor 발명가 entrepreneur 사업가 co-founder 공동 창업자 chief executive 최고 경영자 chairman 회장 recognize (recognise) 인정하다 pioneer 선구자 revolution 혁명

2nd be born 태어나다 infant 갓난아기 adopt 입양하다 take apart 분해하다 reconstruct 재건하다 electronics 전자 기기 instill 심어 주다 confidence 자신(감) tenacity 끈기 prowess 능력 innovative 혁신적인 directionless 방향성이 없는 drop out of 중도하차하다 drop in 방문하다 recount 다시 설명하다 calligraphy 서예 typography 활판술, 조판

3rd garage 차고 be credited with 명성을 얻다 revolutionize(revolutionised) 대변혁을 일으키다 democratizing 대중화 intuitive 직감적인 accessible to 접근이 쉬운 publicly-traded company 공개 상장기업 market value 시장 가치 billion 10억

4th performance 성능 superior to ~보다 뛰어난 suffer 경험하다 significant 심각한 flaw 결함 recall 회수하다 push A into B A를 B에 넣다 marginalize 하찮은 존재 같은 기분이 들게 하다 purchase 구입하다 go on to do something 이어서 ~하기 시작하다 collectively 총체적으로 net 순이익을 올리다 merge with 합병되다 shareholder 주주

5th return to 또다시 시작하다 post 지위 CEO 최고 경영자 management team 관리팀 altered 변경된 stock option 주식 매입 선택권 self-imposed 자발적인 annual salary 연봉 put A back on track A을 정상 궤도에 올리다 ingenious 기발한 catch the attention of 주목을 끌다 once again 한 번 더 battle 싸우다 pancreatic cancer 췌[장]암

구문독해

▶ recognize + 목적어 + 목적격보어(as + 보어): ~을 ~이라고 인식하다 [수동태 시, be recognized + 주격보어 (as + 보어)]

▶ spend + 목적어 + (in) 동명사: ~하는 데 ~을 소비하다

간접의문문

▶ 의문문이 문장 내에서 품사적 기능을 가지는데 특히 명사절(주어/목적어/보어)로 주로 사용: 의문사 to V
  = 의문사 + 주어 + should + V

▶ make(상태 동사) + 목적어 + 목적격보어(형용사/명사): ~을 ~한 상태로 만들다

▶ despite(전치사) + 명사: ~에도 불구하고 [although/though/even if/even though(종속접속사) + 주어 + 동사]

▶ A(원인) result in B(결과): A라는 원인이 B라는 결과를 초래하다

▶ A(결과) result from B(원인): A라는 결과는 B라는 원인으로 발생하다

Part 1 53~59 STEVE JOBS Question

| 어휘 |

53 be known for 알려져 있다 sole founder 유일한 설립자 personality 명사

54 find out 알아내다 interest in ~에 대한 관심 establish 설립하다

55 widespread 광범위한 compete with 겨루다 publicly-traded 공개 상장

56 be merged with 병합하다 be responsible for 책임이 있다 dissatisfaction 불만족
be caused by 기인하다 faulty 결함

57 catch one's eye(s) 눈길을 끌다

TEST 1 part 2 어휘 & 구문독해

Part 2 60~66 LACK OF SLEEP CAUSES ALZHEIMER'S DISEASE

| 어휘 |

1st association 연관성 accumulate 축적하다 beta-amyloid 베타-아밀로이드(아밀로이드 단백질)
be likely to V ~할 것 같다 suffer from 고통 받다 Alzheimer's disease 알츠하이머 병
pervasive 만연하는 debilitating 쇠약하게 하는 dementia 치매

2nd based on ~에 근거하여 conducted by ~에 의해 실시된 a loss of sleep 수면 부족 adequate 충분한
good night's sleep 충분한 숙면 flush out 쫓아내다 known as ~으로 알려진 protein 단백질
catalyst 촉매(제) whereas ~반하여 build up 축적하다 form 형성하다 plaque 플라크 tissue 조직
interrupt 가로막다

3rd Nature Neuroscience 자연 신경 과학 cognitive decline 인지력 감퇴

4th psychiatry 정신 의학 neurology 신경학 epidemiology 전염병학 onset 시작 symptom 증상
delay 미루다 detect 발견하다

5th according to ~따르면 infant 유아 aim for 목표로 하다

| 구문독해 |

▶ between A and B: A와 B 사이에
▶ 주격 관계대명사 who: 선행사 + who + 동사
▶ get + p.p.: ~하게 되다
▶ those (who + 복수동사 ~) + 복수동사: ~하는 사람들
▶ report + 목적어(동명사): ~을 보고하다
▶ spend + 목적어 + (in) 동명사: ~하는 데 ~을 소비하다
▶ be likely to V: ~할 것 같다
▶ start + 목적어(to V/Ving): ~를 시작하다
▶ 분리 부정사: to 부사 V
▶ There is + 단수주어/There are + 복수주어: ~이 있다
▶ help + 목적어(to V): ~하는 것을 돕다

LACK OF SLEEP CAUSES ALZHEIMER'S DISEASE Question

| 어휘 |

60 sleep deprivation 수면 부족   invulnerable to 끄떡없는   deposition 퇴적물   be afflicted with 시달리다
illness 병환의   associated with 관련된

61 happen to 일어나다   be lacking in 부족하다   elevate 높이다

62 elderly people 노인   frequently 자주   indicate 나타내다   along with ~와 함께   adequate 충분한
prevent 예방하다   formation 형성   promote 증진하다

63 means 수단   promptly 즉시   relieve 완화하다   discover 발견하다   measure 측정하다   severity 심각성

64 remove 제거하다   arrange 정리하다   return to 돌아가다   body organ 신체 기관   burn 태우다

TEST 2 part 2 어휘 & 구문독해

Part 2 60~66 STUDIES FIND THAT COW'S MILK MAY PREVENT MUSCLE LOSS

어휘

1st recent 최근의 be good for ~에 좋다 build muscle 근육을 키우다 loss 손실 muscle mass 근육량 effective 효과적인 muscle strength 근력

2nd publish 발표하다 clinical 임상 nutrition 영양 researcher 연구원 workout 운동 including 포함하여 resistance exercise 저항 운동 promote 촉진하다 soy 콩

3rd conduct 수행하다 participant 참가자 either A or B A 이거나 B인 protein 단백질 carbohydrate 탄수화물 complete 마치다 weight lifting 역도 come out on top 이기다 in terms of 측면에서 muscle gain 근육 증가 estimated 추정된 in addition 게다가 gain 얻다

4th demonstrate 증명하다 consumption 소비 athletic 운동의 experience 경험하다 regular 규칙적인 be likely to V ~일 것 같다 build-up 증가 contain 포함하다 casein 카세인 whey 유장 amount 양 leucine 류신 be responsible for 책임이 있다 breakdown 분해

5th shed light on 해명하다 associate professor 부교수 kinesiology 운동 생리학 whole milk 전유 promote 촉진하다 skim milk 탈지유

6th established literature 기존 문헌 be based on 기초하다 mainly 주로 milk-based 우유로 만든 be able to V ~할 수 있다 conclude 결론을 내리다 effectiveness 효과 do study 학습을 실행하다 lean meat 살코기 affect 영향을 미치다

구문독해

▶ ask + 목적어 + 목적격보어(to V): ~가 ~하도록 시키다 [수동태 시, be asked + 주격보어(to V)]
▶ This(결과) is because + 주어 + 동사 (원인): 이것이라는 결과는 ~이라는 원인 때문이다.
▶ hope + 목적어(to V): ~하기를 희망하다

Part 2 60~66 STUDIES FIND THAT COW'S MILK MAY PREVENT MUSCLE LOSS Question

어휘

60 find out 발견하다 healthy 건강한 weight loss 체중 감량

61 describe 묘사하다

62 enhance 향상하다 accelerate 가속하다 concentration 농도

63 both A and B A, B 둘 다 recommend 추천하다

64 article 기사 measure 측정하다 period 기간 investigate 조사하다 influence 영향
compare 비교하다 prove 증명하다 ingestion 섭취

구문독해

60 help + 목적어[(to) V]: ~하는 것을 돕다
prefer + 목적어(to V): 오히려 ~을 좋아하다

TEST 3 part 2 어휘 & 구문독해

Part 2 60~66 STUDY SHOWS AUTISTIC CHILDREN TEND TO BE OBESE

| 어휘 |

1st tend to + V (~하는) 경향이 있다 between A and B A와 B 사이에 obesity 비만 autism 자폐증
among 사이의 further 더 나아가 raise 올리다, 들어 올리다 disorder 장애 diabetes 당뇨병
sleep apnoea 수면 무호흡증 menstrual irregularities 월경 불규칙 orthopaedic 정형 외과적

2nd based on ~에 근거하여 conducted by ~에 의해 실시된 clinical assistant professor 임상 조교수
psychiatry 정신 의학, 정신과학 typically 전형적으로 prevalence 만연 adolescent 청소년
overweight 과체중의, 비만의

3rd co-director 공동 이사(책임자) unusual 특이한, 흔치 않은, 드문 dense 밀도가 높은
including ~을 포함하여 eating habits 식습관 contribute to ~에 기여하다 particularly 특히, 특별히
severe 중증의 mild 가벼운[순한/약한] restricted 제한의

4th meanwhile 한편 associate professor 부교수 be likely to V ~일 것 같다 peer 또래
carry out 실행하다, 수행하다 reveal 드러나다 pregnant 임신한 compared with ~과 비교하여

5th be unable to V ~할 수 없다 direct link 직접적인 관련 fall pregnant 임신하다
finding (조사·연구 등의) 결과[결론] be based on ~에 기초하다, 근거하다 observational studies 관찰 연구
varied 차이가 나는 genetics 유전학 play a role ~에서 역할을 하다 likelihood 가능성

| 구문독해 |

▶ There is + 단수주어/There are + 복수주어: ~이 있다
▶ This(결과) is because + 주어 + 동사 (원인): 결과는 ~이라는 원인 때문이다.

Part 2 60~66 STUDY SHOWS AUTISTIC CHILDREN TEND TO BE OBESE Question

| 어휘 |

60 suffer from 고통받다 a number of + 복수명사 많은 be affected by 영향을 받다 lesser 더욱 작은

61 be similar to 비슷하다 avoid + 목적어(Ving) 피하다 enjoy + 목적어(Ving) 즐기다 favor 선호하다

62 happen to 일어나다 born to 태어나다 severly 심하게 underweight 표준 체중 이하의
be vulnerable to 영향을 받기 쉽다, 민감하다

63 specific 특정한 take (a) medication 약을 복용하다

64 be associated with 관련되다 demonstrate 증명하다

| 구문독해 |

61 (전치사) according to ~에 따르면/(종속접속사) according as ~에 따르면

63 as much as: ~만큼, ~정도, ~못지 않게
spend + 목적어 + (in) 동명사: ~하는 데 ~을 소비하다

64 find + it(가목적어) + 형용사/명사(목적격보어) + to V(진목적어): ~가 ~하다는 것을 발견하다

TEST 1 part 3 어휘 & 구문독해

Part 3 67~73 GREAT DANE

어휘

1st breed 품종 origin 태생 descend 유래하다 recognize A as B A를 B로 간주하다 in terms of ~관하여

2nd reach 도달하다 massive 거대한 narrow 폭이 좁은 flat 평평한 forward 앞으로 muscular 근육질의

3rd giant 거대한 nobility 귀족 protect 보호하다 estate 땅 wild boar 멧돼지 prestigious 명망있는 guardians 수호자 carriage 마차 ban 금지하다 mastiff 마스티프

4th metabolism 신진대사 result in 그 결과 ~가 되다 consumption 소비 average lifespan 평균수명 known as ~로 알려진 bloat 부풀다 involve 포함하다 buildup 축적 grow at a rapid pace 빠른 속도로 성장하다 a while 잠시, 잠깐 joint 관절 stable 안정된 at least 적어도

5th moderately 적당히 playful 장난기 많은 affectionate 애정이 많은 obedience 순종 train 훈련시키다 assure 확실하게 하다 manageable 관리할 수 있는 aggressive 공격적인 get along with ~와 잘 지내다

6th primarily 주로 become popular 인기를 얻게 되다 dweller 거주자 guard against ~에 대해 지키다 robber 강도

구문독해

생략
▶ 선행사 + (주격관계대명사 + be동사) + 과거분사{p.p.(~되어진): 형용사}

to 부정사의 완료시제
▶ to have p.p.: 본동사와 to 부정사의 시제가 다를 경우

to 부정사의 수동
▶ to be p.p.

동사의 강조
▶ do/does/did + V(정말로 ~하다)
▶ It takes 시간 + for + 목적격 + to V: 시간이 ~만큼 걸리다

의미상의 주어
▶ consider + 목적어 + 목적격보어[(to be) 보어]: ~을 ~라고 간주하다 〈수동태 시, be considered + 주격보어[(to be) 보어]〉

목적격 관계대명사 that(~하는) 생략
▶ 선행사 + (that) + 주어 + 타동사 + (목적어 없음)

생략
▶ 종속접속사(when) + (주어 + be동사) + 과거분사(given) ~, 주어 + 동사

주격관계대명사 who(~하는)
▶ 선행사(사람) + who + 동사
▶ help + 목적어[(to) V]: ~하는 것을 돕다
▶ want + 목적어 + 목적격보어(to V): ~가 ~하기를 원하다
▶ keep + 목적어 + from Ving: ~하는 것을 못하게 하다(keep + 목적어 + Ving: ~가 계속 ~하다)

Part 3 67~73 GREAT DANE Question

| 어휘 |

67 statement 진술 heavy 무거운(비교급 heavier/최상급 heaviest)

68 description 서술 be made up of 구성되어 있다 firm 단단한
walk upright on his hind legs 뒷발로 서서 걷다

69 be raised by 양육되다 social status 사회적 지위 be able to ~할 수 있다 property 자산 wild boar 멧돼지

70 intake 섭취 compared to ~비교하여 store 저장하다 stomach 위 for a long time 오랫동안
convert A into B A를 B로 전환하다

71 compliant 순응하는 play with ~와 놀다 obedience 복종 through ~을 통해서 instruction 가르침

TEST 2 part 3 어휘 & 구문독해

Part 3 67~73 RAFFLESIA ARNOLDII

어휘

1st Rafflesia Arnoldii 라플레시아아놀디 a species of 일종의 flowering plant 꽃식물 produce 생산하다 rainforests 열대우림 Sumatra 수마트라 주

2nd parasitic plant 기생 식물 visible 눈에 보이는 leaves 잎 root 뿌리 stem 줄기 similar to 비슷한 fungi 곰팡이 thread-like 실과 같은 strand 가닥 tissue 조직 completely 완전히 embedded 박혀 있는 in contact with 접촉하는 intimate 밀접한 surrounding 주변의 host plant 숙주 식물 nutrients 영양분 obtain 얻다 reproduce 번식하다 identifiable 구별되는 distinctly 뚜렷하게 plant-like 식물 같은 infect 감염시키다 alkaline 알칼리성의 neutral 중성의 acidic 산성의 soil 토양

3rd grow to ~이 되다 diameter 지름 weigh 무게가 ~이다 up to 까지 emerge from 벗어나다 cabbage-like 배추 같은 dark brown 짙은 갈색 buds 꽃봉오리 typically 일반적으로

4th take + 시간 ~걸린다 develop 성장하다 last 지속되다 tiny 아주 작은 eventually 결국 open to 공개하다 reveal 드러내다

5th thrive 번성하다 be in danger of 위험이 있다 extinction 멸종 habitat 서식지 poach 밀렵하다 harvest 수확하다 medicinal properties 약효 성분 captivity 포획 occurrence 발생 contain 포함하다 pollination 수분작용 rare 드문

6th foul 역겨운 attract 유인하다 flies 파리들 beetle 딱정벌레 land on 착지하다 avoid 피하다 transport A to B A에서 B로 이동시키다 pollen 꽃가루 occur 발생하다 smooth-skinned 껍질이 매끄러운 berry 열매 fortunately 다행히 squirrel 다람쥐 seed dispersal 종자 분산

7th these days 요즘에는 altitude 고도 ecotourism 생태 관광 be known as 알려져 있다 main threat 주요 위협 species 종족 tourist 관광객 decrease 줄다

구문독해

▶ be ready[willing] to V ~하기를 불사하다
▶ due to(전치사) + 명사: ~ 때문에 (because(종속접속사) + 주어 + 동사)

상관접속사
▶ B as well as A: A뿐만 아니라 B도 (= not only A but also B) (주어로 사용 시, 주어는 B)
▶ avoid + 목적어(Ving): ~를 피하다
▶ 동명사의 수동: being p.p.
▶ the number of + 복수명사: ~수

Part 3 67~73 RAFFLESIA ARNOLDII Question

| 어휘 |

67 statement 진술   characterizes 묘사하다

68 description 설명   get nutrient 양분을 얻다   distinguishable 구별할 수 있는   be infected by 감염되다

69 the reason why + 주어 + 동사 ~의 이유

70 be endangered 위험에 빠지다   therapeutic purpose 치료 목적   illegally 불법적으로   remove 제거하다

71 take place 일어나다   play a role 역할을 하다   disgusting 역겨운   protect A from B B로부터 A를 보호하다   prior to 먼저

| 구문독해 |

70 주어(A: 원인) + lead to + 목적어(B: 결과): A이라는 원인 때문에 B라는 결과가 발생하다.

TEST 3 part 3 어휘&구문독해

Part 3 67~73 STONEFISH

| 어휘 |

1st marine fish 바다 생선 shallow 얕은 tropical 열대의 sluggish 느릿느릿 움직이는 bottom-dwelling 바닥에 거주하는 coral 산호 mudflat 개펄 estuary 어귀 be known as 알려져 있다 venomous 독이 있는

2nd dorsal 등쪽의 be lined with 늘어서 있다 spine 가시 stiff 뻣뻣한 pierce 뚫다 boot sole 구두창 dorsal fin spine 등 지느러미 척추 inject 주사하다 venom (뱀 등의) 독 be capable of ~할 수 있다 less than ~보다 적은 in nature 사실상 capture 잡다 prey 먹이 predation 포식자 consist of 구성되다 toxin 독소 effective 효과적인 turn away 물리치다 potential 잠재적인 predator 포식자의

3rd evolve 진화하다 adaptation 적응 succeed in 성공하다 reef 암초 bumpy 울퉁불퉁한 covered with 덮인 wartlike 사마귀 같은 lump 덩어리 fleshy flaps 살찐 날개 hide 감추다 camouflage 위장하다 up to 까지

4th mostly 주로 invertebrates 무척추동물 shrimp 새우 motionless 가만히 있는 wait for 기다리다 swim by 헤엄쳐 지나가다 strike 공격하다 jaws 턱 suck down 빨아먹다 unsuspecting 의심하지 않는 swallow 삼키다 whole 전적으로, 완전히

5th evidence 증거 threaten 위협하다 catch 잡다 private 개인 소유의 aquarium trade 양어조 매매 rarely 드물게 targeted 목표가 된 fishery 어장 species 종 be unlikely to V 할 것 같지 않다 endangered 멸종 위기에 처한 anytime soon (부정문·의문문에서) 곧

| 구문독해 |

▶ help(준사역동사) + 목적어 + 목적격보어[(to) V]: ~가 ~하는 것을 돕다
▶ so + 형용사/부사 that + 주어 + 동사: 너무 ~해서 그 결과 ~하다
▶ There is + 단수주어/There are + 복수주어: ~이 있다

Part 3 67~73 STONEFISH Question

|어휘|

67 be famous for 유명하다 abundant 풍부한 extinct 멸종된 ugly 못생긴 poisonous 독이 있는

68 by + 동명사 ~함으로써 suck 빨아 먹다 infect 감염시키다 venomous 독이 있는 wound 상처
release A from B A를 B로부터 해방시키다 lay an egg 알을 낳다

69 benefit 이점 get exhausted 탈진하다 be exposed to 노출되다 sustain 계속시키다
high pressure 고기압 a deep ocean 깊은 대양

70 protect A from B B에서 A를 막다 hide from 로부터 숨다

71 endangered 위험에 처한 average lifespan 평균 수명 be affected by 영향을 받다
seawater contamination 바닷물 오염 fish (물고기를)낚다

TEST 1 part 4 어휘 & 구문독해

Part 4 74~80 FAULTY REFRIGERATOR

| 어휘 |

1st   fridge(refrigerator, icebox) 냉장고

2nd   freezer compartment 냉동실   properly 적절하게   freeze 얼다   kept inside 안쪽에 보관된   spool 감대[풀다]   inform A of B A에게 B를 알리다   faulty 흠이 있는   assure 장담하다   arrive 배달되다   within 이내에

3rd   replacement 교체물   wait for 기다리다   make a phone call to 전화를 걸다   state 말하다   manufacturer 제조자   deliver 배달하다   put up with 참다   inconvenience 불편

4th   resolve 해결하다   concern 우려   promptly 즉시   warranty period 보증 기간   demand a refund 환불을 요구하다   immediately 즉시   in case 경우에   address 처리하다   assure A of B A 에게 B를 확신시키다   hear from 연락을 받다   lawyer 변호사   file 제기하다   a formal complaint 정식 고소

5th   enclose in 동봉하다   order receipt 주문영수증   defective 결함 있는   response 응답

| 구문독해 |

▶ start + 목적어(to V/Ving): ~를 시작하다

▶ It takes 시간 + to V: 시간이 ~만큼 걸리다

생략

▶ 선행사 + (주격관계대명사 + be동사) + 과거분사{p.p.(~되어진): 형용사}

▶ 선행사(사람) + whom(목적격관계대명사) + 주어 + 동사 + 전치사 (목적어 없음)

If 생략 가정법 도치

▶ If 주어 had not p.p. (정치) → Had 주어 not p.p. (도치)

▶ keep + 목적어 + Ving: 계속 ~하다(keep + 목적어 + from Ving: ~하는 것을 못하게 하다)

▶ urge + 목적어 + 목적격보어(to V): ~V가 ~하도록 촉구하다

▶ fail + 목적어(to V): ~하지 못하다

Part 4 74~80 FAULTY REFRIGERATOR Question

| 어휘 |

74 write a letter 편지 쓰다   make change of 변경하다   ask for 요청하다   concerning 관련된
   complain about ~에 불평하다

75 a full refund 전액환불   exchange A with B A와 B를 서로 교환하다

76 replace 대체하다   in large[great] quantities 대량으로   deliveryman 상품 배달원   be off sick 병가 중이다

77 purchase 구입하다   report to 신고하다   lodge 제기하다   a compensation claim 손해배상의 요구
   against 맞서   file a complaint with 고소하다   Consumer Ombudsman Center 소비자 고발센터

78 compare A with B A와 B를 비교하다   proof 증거   intend to V 작정이다   threaten 위협하다

| 구문독해 |

▶ There is + 단수주어/There are + 복수주어 : ~이 있다
▶ wait + for + 목적어 + to V: ~가 ~하기를 기다리다

TEST 2 part 4 어휘 & 구문독해

Part 4 74~80 RESIGNATION LETTER

| 어휘 |

1st serve as 역할을 하다 resignation 사직 shift supervisor 교대 감독관직 unsatisfactory 불만족스러운 work conditions 작업여건 in accordance with 부합되게 policy 방침 employment 고용

2nd on repeated occasions 반복적으로 back-to-back 연달아 initially 처음에 help out with 도와주다 employee 직원 hire 고용하다 relieve 덜어주다 current 현행의 staff member 직원

3rd added 추가된 take the pressure off 부담을 덜다 upward[upwards] of ~ 이상 unsafe 불안전한 be responsible for 책임이 있다 heavy workload 과중한 업무량

4th HR department 인력개발부(HR = Human Resources) raise 제기하다 concern 걱정 on several occasions 몇 차례나 submit 제출하다 nonetheless 그럼에도 불구하고 merely 단지 wait for 기다리다 resolution 해결 strain 부담 affect 영향을 미치다 conclude 결론을 내리다 no longer 더 이상~아닌 take immediate action 재빨리 조처하다 resign 사임하다

5th kindness 친절 ensure 보장하다 leaving document 퇴사 서류 due 회비 process 처리하다 on time 정각에 deem 여기다 appropriate to 적합한 replace 대체하다 endeavor(endeavour) 노력

6th sincerely 진심으로

| 구문독해 |

▶ let(사역동사) + 목적어 + 목적격보어(V): ~가 ~하도록 놓아두다/허락하다
▶ due to(전치사) + 명사: ~ 때문에 (because(종속접속사) + 주어 + 동사)
▶ ask + 목적어 + 목적격보어(to V): ~가 ~하도록 시키다 [수동태 시, be asked + 주격보어(to V)]
▶ There is + 단수주어/There are + 복수주어: ~이 있다
▶ start + 목적어(to V/Ving): ~를 시작하다
▶ force + 목적어 + 목적격보어(to V): ~가 ~하도록 강요하다 [수동태 시, be forced + 주격보어(to V)]
▶ train + 목적어 + 목적격보어(to V): ~가 ~하도록 훈련시키다
▶ deem + 목적어 + 목적격보어[(to be) 보어]: ~가 ~이라고 간주하다
▶ wish + 간접목적어 + 직접목적어: ~에게 ~을 바란다

Part 4 74~80 RESIGNATION LETTER Question

|어휘|

74 request a promotion 승진을 요청하다 negotiate one's salary 연봉 협상을 하다 complain 불평하다
quit one's job 직장을 그만두다

75 regarding ~에 관하여 assurance 보증 performance 성과 incentive 장려금 recruit 채용하다
reduction 감소 production 생산량 all-expense-paid 전액의

76 based on 근거하여 responsibility 책임감 take care of 돌보다 overwork 과로하다
work with 함께 일하다

77 respond to 대응하다 complaint 불평 demand 요구하다 appointment 약속 meet with 만나다
as soon as possible 되도록 빨리 monthly bonuses 월간 보너스 specified 지정한

78 termination 종료 candidate 지원자 employment 고용 replacement 후임자 look for 찾다
suitable 적절한 claim 요청하다 insurance benefit 보험급부

TEST 3 part 4 어휘 & 구문독해

Part 4 74~80 ENCOURAGED TO OPEN AN ACCOUNT

어휘

1st open a branch(office) 지점을 개설하다   be located 위치해 있다   pleasure 기쁨

2nd business opportunities 비즈니스 기회   infancy 유아기는   require 요구하다   courage 용기
conviction 신념   duties 직무   fortunately 다행스럽게도, 운 좋게도   wanting 부족한
faith 믿음   public goods 공공재   client 고객   against all odds 모든 역경에도 불구하고

3rd patron 후원자   open account 계좌를 열다   make full use of 충분히 활용하다   banking facilities 금융기관
interest on deposit 예금이자   along with 함께   foreign exchange 외국환   from now 지금으로부터
receive 받다   remittance 송금   maintain 유지하다   foreign currency 외국 통화   earnest 성실한
desire 욕구   make use of 이용하다   serve the public 대중을 위해 봉사하다   good 선

4th inquires 문의   hesitate + to V 망설이다   thank you for 감사하다   continued support 지속적인 지지

구문독해

▶ give + 간접목적어(사람/동물: ~에게) + 직접목적어(사물: ~을/를): ~에게 ~을 주다
▶ inform + 간접목적어 + 직접목적어(that + 주어 + 동사): ~에게 ~을 알리다
▶ decide + 목적어(to V): ~를 결정하다
▶ find + 목적어 + 목적격보어(분사): ~이 ~하다는 것을 알다[수동태 시, be found + 주격보어(분사)]
▶ invite + 목적어 + 목적격보어(to V): ~가 ~할 것을 권하다, 안내하다

to 부정사의 수동
▶ to be p.p.

▶ It be A that B: B한 것은 바로 A이다 (강조구문)

if 생략 가정법 도치
▶ If + 주어 + should V(정치) → Should + 주어 + V(도치)

직접명령문
▶ 동사원형(V) ~: ~해라

Part 4 74~80 ENCOURAGED TO OPEN AN ACCOUNT Question

| 어휘 |

75 be unlikely to V ~일 것 같지 않다 region 지역 start + 목적어(to V/Ving) ~를 시작하다
be ready to V ~할 준비가 되다 excellent 우수한

76 benefit from 이익을 얻다 founder 설립자 regular customer 단골 borrow money 돈을 빌리다

77 transfer A to B A를 B로 옮기다 overseas 해외에 instant 즉각적인 foreign currency 외화
deposit 예금(액) within a given[certain] period of time 일정한 기간 동안에

80 ring up 전화를 걸다

| 구문독해 |

74 notify + 간접목적어 + 직접목적어(that + 주어 + 동사): ~에게 ~을 알리다
register A for B: A를 B에 등록하다 (수동태 시, A be registered for B)

75 There is + 단수주어/There are + 복수주어: ~이 있다

LISTENING
어휘 & 구문독해

G-TELP 청취

PART 1 개인적인 이야기
PART 2 일의 진행이나 과정에 대한 설명
PART 3 비공식적인 협상 등의 대화
PART 4 공식적인 담화

TEST 1 part 1 어휘 & 구문독해

Part 1 (27~33)

어휘

breathtaking 숨이 멎는 듯한 travel to ~로 여행하다[이동하다] isolated 외딴 remote 외진
camp out 야영하다 sleep in a tent 텐트에서 잠을 자다 what else 그 밖의 또 무슨
for a week 1주(7일)간 sparkling 반짝거리는 take A to B A를 B로 데려가다 vast 거대한
rolling hills 구릉지 traditional 전통적인 a stone house 석조집 lighthouse 등대
nightlife 야간에 할 수 있는 오락 only a few 다만 몇 안 되는 unique 독특한 serve dishes 요리를 내다
ingredient 재료[성분] local 주민, 현지인 simmer 끓이다 crispy 아삭아삭하는
be filled with ~로 가득차다 appetizing[appetising] 구미를 동하게 하는 charming 매력적인, 멋진
untouched 훼손되지 않은 landscape 풍경 must-see 꼭 보아야 할 travel destination 여행지
wake up (잠에서) 깨다 out there 그곳에 bother 괴롭히다 security 보안 tight (관리·단속 등이) 엄격한
hostile 적대적인 courteous 예의바른 atmosphere 분위기 make an effort 노력하다
not at all 전혀 ~하지 않다 responsibility 책임(맡은 일) preserve 보존하다 protect 보호하다
as it is 현 상황에서는 value 가치 있게 생각하다 go back 돌아가다 book 예약하다 on sale 할인 중인
so that ~하기 위해서 go with 함께

구문독해

▶ enjoy + 동명사: ~하기를 즐기다
▶ one of + 복수명사: ~중에 하나
▶ even/still/a lot/far/much + 비교급: 훨씬 더 ~(비교급 강조)
▶ spend + 목적어 + (in) 동명사: ~하는 데 ~을 소비하다
▶ seem + to V: ~처럼 보이다
▶ there is/are + 단수/복수 주어: ~이 있다
▶ find + 목적어 + 목적격보어(현재분사): ~이 ~임을 알다
▶ make + 목적어 + 목적격보어(형용사/명사): ~을 ~한 상태로 만들다
▶ make + 목적어 + 목적격보어(동사원형): ~을 ~하게 시키다
▶ make + 목적어 + 목적격보어(형용사): ~을 ~한 상태로 유지시키다
▶ force + + 목적어 + 목적격보어(to V): ~을 ~하도록 강요하다
▶ sound like + (동)명사: ~처럼 들리다
▶ I'm sure (that) + 주어 + 동사: ~을 확신하다
▶ had better + V: ~하는 편이 더 낫다(had 생략 가능)

Part 1 Question
Part 1 27~33

| 어휘 |

27 what kind[sort] of 어떤 (종류의)　reach ~에 닿다　muddy 진흙투성이인　remote 외딴

28 cloudy 탁한　keep up all night 밤을 세우다

29 speak with ~와 이야기를 나누다　the first impressions 첫인상　exotic 이국적인　polluted 오염된

30 secluded 외딴　an underwater cave 해저동굴

31 based on ~에 근거하여　most likely 아마　unpredictable 예측할 수 없는　insect 곤충

32 islander 섬사람　attract 끌어들이다　marine animals 해양 동물　obey 지키다

33 think about ~에 관해 생각하다　quit one's job 사직하다　fly to ~까지 비행기로 가다　what to do 무엇을 할지께 가다

| 구문독해 |

31 be unable to V: ~할 수 없다
allow + 목적어 + 목적격보어(to V): ~가 ~하는 것을 허락하다[수동태 시, be allowed 주격보어(to V)]

32 the number of + 복수명사: ~수

33 의문사 + to V(= 의문사 주어 should V)

TEST 2 part 1 어휘 & 구문독해

Part 1 (27~33)

어휘

get back from ~에서 돌아오다　bring back ~을 기억나게 하다　unforgettable 잊을 수 없는
frankly speaking 솔직히 말해서　a little bit 조금　enormously 엄청나게　decade 10년
from all over the world 전 세계에서　be known as ~로서 알려지다　tourist attraction 관광 명소
no longer 더 이상 ~아닌　laid-back 느긋한　beg for ~을 구하다　be crowded with ~로 혼잡하다
spoil 망치다　to a certain extent 어느 정도　away from ~에서 떠나서　focus on ~에 집중하다
jump into ~로 뛰어들다　sit by 앉아서 구경만 하다　breathe in 숨을 들이쉬다　mostly 주로
stay at[in] a hotel 호텔에 묵다　a considerable time 꽤 많은 시간　glide across ~를 가로질러 가다
except ~을 제외하고는　scenery 풍경

구문독해

▶ 주어 + 현재완료진행(have been Ving) + since + 과거 시점: ~한 이래로 ~해오고 있다
▶ decide + 목적어(to V): ~를 결정하다
▶ must have p.p.: ~했음에 틀림없다(과거 일에 대한 강한 추측)
▶ a number of + 복수명사 + 복수동사: 많은
▶ one of + 복수명사: ~중의 하나
▶ There is + 단수주어/There are + 복수주어: ~이 있다
▶ the same A as B: B와 같은 동일한 A
▶ try + 목적어(to V): ~하기 위해 노력하다 → 주어의 의지 있음
▶ as 형용사/부사 as one can: 가능한 한 ~한/하게, 될 수 있으면 ~한/하게(= as 형용사/부사 as possible)
▶ spend + 목적어 + on (동)명사: ~하는 데 ~을 소비하다
▶ not only A but also B = B as well as A: A뿐만 아니라 B도(주어로 사용 시, 주어는 B)
▶ must have p.p.: ~했음에 틀림없다(과거 일에 대한 강한 추측)
▶ love + 목적어(to V/Ving): ~를 좋아하다
▶ make(사역동사) + 목적어 + 목적격보어(V): ~가 ~하게 시키다
▶ feel like + (that) 주어 + 동사: ~처럼 느끼다(= feel like + (동)명사)
▶ sound like + (that) 주어 + 동사: ~처럼 들리다(= sound like + (동)명사)
▶ go + Ving(동명사): ~하러 가다
▶ seem like + (that) 주어 + 동사: ~처럼 보이다(= seem like + (동)명사)
▶ be sure + (that) 주어 + 동사: ~을 확신하다(= be sure to V/be sure of Ving)

Part 1 Question
Part 1 27~33

| 어휘 |

- **27** move to ~로 이동하다　memorable 기억할 만한
- **28** change about 바뀌다　not ~ anymore 더 이상 ~않다　tourist attraction 관광 명소
- **29** throughout ~동안 쭉, 내내
- **30** incredible 믿을 수 없는
- **31** coral reef 산호초
- **32** lethargic 무기력한
- **33** on one's own 혼자서　book 예약하다　flight ticket 항공권

| 구문독해 |

- **28** due to(전치사) + 명사: ~ 때문에(because(종속접속사) + 주어 + 동사)

TEST 3 part 1 어휘 & 구문독해

Part 1 (27~33)

| 어휘 |

drop by 잠깐 들르다   the other day 며칠 전에   go on a trip 여행을 가다   diplomat exam 외교관 시험
have a celebration 축하연을 열다   congratulate 축하하다   work as ~로 일하다   international 국제적
law assistance 법률 보조   at the moment 바로 지금   anyway 어떻든   be proud of ~을 자랑으로 여기다
by the way 그런데   attend class 수업에 출석하다   private institutes 사설학원   prepare for ~을 준비하다
(all) by oneself 혼자   literally 문자 그대로   instead 대신에   have no choice 선택의 여지가 없다
quit one's job 사직하다   pass the exam 시험에 통과하다   play a role 역할을 하다   sight 광경
hours and hours 몇 시간이나   fortunately 다행히도   take A(시간) off work A만큼의 시간을 휴가 내다
mind 신경 쓰다   appreciate 고마워하다   by the way 그런데   pick A up A를 태우다

| 구문독해 |

▶ devote + 목적어 + to (동)명사: ~을/를 ~하는 데 전념(몰두)하다
▶ happen to V: 우연히 ~하다

간접의문문 if(~인지 아닌지) 용법
▶ 의문사 대용어로 사용된 if는 간접의문문으로 사용될 수 있는데, 이때 if는 whether로 바꿔 사용할 수 있지만, that(~것을)은 사용할 수 없다.
▶ in order to V: ~하기 위해서
▶ not only A but also B = B as well as A: A뿐만 아니라 B도(주어로 사용 시, 주어는 B)
▶ decide + 목적어(to V): ~를 결정하다
▶ must have p.p.: ~했음에 틀림없다(과거 일에 대한 강한 추측)
▶ see(지각동사) + 목적어 + 목적격보어(V): ~가 ~하는 것을 보다
▶ used to V: ~하곤 했다
▶ allow + 목적어 + 목적격보어(to V): ~가 ~하는 것을 허락하다(수동태 시, be allowed to V)
▶ want + 목적어 + 목적격보어(to V): ~가 ~하기를 원하다
▶ ask + 간접목적어 + 직접목적어(if 주어 동사): ~에게 ~인지를 물어보다
▶ be sure + (that) 주어 + 동사: ~을 확신하다(= be sure to V/be sure of Ving)
▶ sound + 형용사: ~처럼 들리다

Part 1 Question
Part 1 27~33

| 어휘 |

27 achievement 성취   attend a meeting 모임(회의)에 참석하다

28 have a good time 즐겁게 보내다   focus on 집중하다   prepare for ~를 준비하다   diplomat exam 외교관 시험

29 according to ~에 따르면   help with ~을 돕다   enroll in ~에 등록하다   register 등록하다
a full-time job 정규직 일자리

31 give financial support 경제적으로 후원하다

| 구문독해 |

30 spend + 목적어 + (in) 동명사: ~하는 데 ~을 소비하다
allow + 목적어 + 목적격보어(to V): ~가 ~하는 것을 허락하다

32 permit + 목적어 + 목적격보어(to V): ~가 ~하는 것을 허락하다(수동태 시, be permitted to V)
take time off to V: ~하기 위해 시간을 내다

33 introduce A to B: A를 B에게 소개하다

TEST 1 part 2 어휘 & 구문독해

Part 2 34~39   Part 2

| 어휘 |

1st important for ~에 있어서 중요한 surface 표면 including ~을 포함하여 germs 세균 cause ~을 야기하다 defend against ~으로부터 지키다 harmless 무해한 soap 비누

2nd store-bought 상점에서 산 come in 들어오다 fragrance 향기 packaging 포장재 consumption 소비

3rd perhaps 아마도 lucrative 수익성이 좋은 enroll in ~에 등록하다

4th bring out ~을 끌어내다 creativity 창조성 abundance 풍부 scent 향기 choose from ~에서 택하다

5th distinguish A from B A와 B를 구별하다 wonder 궁금해하다 favourite 좋아하는 commercially 상업적으로 feel proud of ~을 자만하다

6th itchy 가려운 extremely 극도로, 극히 irritating 자극적인 cost saving 비용 절감 remove A from B B에서 A를 제거하다 contain 함유하다 moisture 수분 moisturize 촉촉하게 하다

7th according to ~에 따르면 ingredient 재료 take your time 여유를 가지다

8th initially 처음에 put out 내놓다 supplies 저장품 a bar of soap 비누 한 개 save on ~를 절약하다

10th extra income 부수입 feed 공급하다 incredible 믿을 수 없는 occasion 특별한 일, 행사 amaze 놀라게 하다

11th get into ~을 (시작)하게 되다 enroll in ~에 등록하다 fulfillment 성취

| 구문독해 |

▶ there is/are + 단수/복수 주어: ~이 있다
▶ prefer + 목적어(to V): ~을 더 선호하다
▶ to 부정사의 부정: not/never to V
▶ consider + 목적어(Ving): ~을 고려하다
▶ get + 목적어 + 목적격보어(형용사): ~이 ~한 상태에 이르게 하다
▶ help + 목적어 + 목적격보어에[(to) V]: ~가 ~하는 것을 돕다
▶ start + 목적어(to V/Ving): ~하기를 시작하다
▶ All [(that) 주어 + need to do] + is + (to) V: ~가 ~하는 데 필요한 모든 것은 ~이다
▶ Here is/are + 단수/복수 주어: 여기에 ~이 있다
▶ learn + 목적어(to V): ~하는 것을 배우다
▶ the reason why + 주어 + 동사: ~하는 이유
▶ keep + 목적어 + 목적격보어(과거분사): ~을 ~한 상태로 유지시키다
▶ allow + 목적어 + 목적격보어(to V): ~가 ~하는 것을 허용하다

Part 2 Question
Part 2 34~39

| 어휘 |

- **34** purchase 구입하다   get rid of 제거하다
- **35** bring out ~을 끌어내다   flush out ~을 쫓아내다   pursue a goal 목표를 추구하다
- **36** occasionally 가끔
- **37** maintain 유지하다
- **38** extra fee 추가 요금   equipment 장비   in bulk 대량으로
- **39** impress 깊은 인상을 주다

| 구문독해 |

- **34** ask + 목적어 + 목적격보어(to V): ~가 ~하는 것을 요청하다
- **35** encourage + 목적어 + 목적격보어(to V): ~가 ~하기를 격려하다
  motivate + 목적어 + 목적격보어(to V): ~가 ~하기를 동기 부여하다
- **36** by + 동명사: ~함으로써
- **37** absorb A from B: B로부터 A를 흡수하다

TEST 2 part 2 어휘 & 구문독해

Part 2 34~39 Part 2

| 어휘 |

1st be from ~에서 오다 institute 연구소 home schooling 홈스쿨링

2nd be known as ~로서 알려지다 send A to B A를 B에 보내다 formal setting 공식적인 자리
take responsibility of ~을 책임지다

3rd dissatisfaction 불만 available 이용할 수 있는 religious 종교적인 philosophy 철학
progress 발전하다 homeschool 자택에서 교육하다 qualified 자격이 있는 instructor 강사
teaching method 교수법 request 요청

4th talk to ~에게 말을 걸다

5th customize 사용자의 사정[희망]에 맞추다 maximize 극대화하다 strengthen 강화하다
weakness 약점 focus on 집중하다 an area of interest 관심 영역 highly 높이 at a level ~의 수준으로
be capable of ~할 수 있다 on average 평균적으로 outperform 더 나은 결과를 내다
peer 또래 standardized 표준화된

6th bullying 약자 괴롭히기 social pressure 사회적 압력 self-esteem 자존감 mature 성숙한

7th a flexible schedule 융통성이 있는 일정 take (a) holiday 휴가를 얻다, 쉬다 break 휴식 시간
at off season 비수기에 loads[tons] of 수많은 field trip 현장 학습

8th independent 독립적인 make up one's own mind 결심하다 for oneself 혼자 힘으로
be influenced by ~에 영향을 받다 peer pressure 또래 압력 seek out ~을 찾아내다

9th rewarding 보람 있는 become aware of ~을 알게 되다 be here 왔다
structured environment 구조화된 환경 discuss with ~와 논의하다

10th countless 셀 수 없이 많은 inquiry 질문의 contact 연락하다

| 구문독해 |

▶ would like to + V: ~하고 싶다
▶ It is true that 주어 + 동사: 사실은 ~이다
▶ because of(전치사) + 명사: ~ 때문에(because(종속접속사) + 주어 + 동사)
▶ although/though/even if/even though(종속접속사) + 주어 + 동사: ~에도 불구하고[despite(전치사) + 명사]
▶ allow + 목적어 + 목적격보어(to V): ~가 ~하는 것을 허락하다
▶ motivate + 목적어 + 목적격보어(to V): ~에게 ~할 동기를 부여하다
▶ A rather than B: B보다 오히려 A
▶ There is + 단수주어/There are + 복수주어: ~이 있다

- make(상태 동사) + 목적어 + 목적격보어(형용사/명사): ~을 ~한 상태로 만들다
- be likely to V: ~할 것 같다
- be unlikely to V: ~할 것 같지 않다
- find + it(가목적어) + 목적격보어(형용사/명사) + to V(진목적어): ~(진목적어)가 ~(목적격보어)하다는 것을 알다
- help(준사역동사) + 목적어 + 목적격보어(to V): ~가 ~하는 것을 돕다

Part 2 Question (34~39)

| 어휘 |

- **34** broad 광범위한   domestic 가정 내의   life-saving 구명 기술
- **35** do well at 성적이 좋다   strictly 엄격히   be conducted by ~에 의해 실시되다   enhances 향상시키다   sociability 사교성   gain popularity 인기를 얻다
- **36** a wide range of 다양한   be obsessed with ~에 사로잡혀 있다   academic performance 학업 성과   personalized 개인이 원하는 대로 할 수 있는
- **37** adjust 조정하다   based on ~에 근거하여   beneficial 유익한   arrange 정하다   develop 개발하다   potential 잠재력
- **38** independently 독립적으로   be affected by ~에 영향을 받다
- **39** assist 돕다   financial aid 재정적인 도움   devise 창안하다

| 구문독해 |

- **34** either A or B: A이거나 B인
- **37** make(상태 동사) + 목적어 + 목적격보어(형용사/명사): ~을 ~한 상태로 만들다
  help + 목적어[(to) V]: ~하는 것을 돕다
- **39** provide + 목적어(사람) + with 목적어(사물): A를 B에 제공하다[=provide + 목적어(사물) + to/for 목적어(사람)]

TEST 3 part 2 어휘 & 구문독해

Part 2 (34~39)

| 어휘 |

1st annual 연례의 job fair 공개 취직 설명회 increasingly 점점 더 make money 수익을 얻다 through ~을 통해 take on a job 일을 떠맡다 monthly income 월 소득

2nd leading sector 주도부문, 선도부문 employment 취업 tutorial 개인 지도 dissertation 논문 a majority of 다수의 be from ~출신이다 be interested in ~에 관심이 있다

3rd deliver 전달하다 non-native 원어민이 아닌 ensure 보장하다 recruit 모집하다 mother tongue 모국어 in-depth 깊이 있는 with accuracy 정확하게

4th be suited for ~에 적합하다 move on to ~로 이동하다

6th secure 안전한 be known as ~로서 알려지다 one of + 복수명사 ~중의 하나 over the past years 여러 해 동안 get paid 봉급을 받다

7th timetable 시간표 flexible 유연한, 융통성 있는 minimum 최소의 therefore 그러므로 design 설계하다 at one's convenience 편한 때에 as long as ~하는 한은

8th confident 자신감 있는 productive 생산적인 connect A with B A와 B를 연계하다 generate 창출하다 satisfaction 만족감

9th work on ~에 노력을 들이다 struggle with ~로 고심하다 deal with ~을 다루다 potential 잠재적인 asset 자산

10th probably 아마 wonder 궁금해 하다 work with ~와 함께 일하다 fluent 유창한 obviously 분명히 degree 학위 highly 매우 prefer ~을 (더) 좋아하다 major in ~을 전공하다

11th engage in ~에 종사하다 highly-paid 고액의 rate 요금

| 구문독해 |

▶ a number of + 복수명사 + 복수동사: 많은
▶ regard + 목적어 + 목적격보어(as + 보어): ~을 ~이라고 여기다[수동태 시, be regarded + 주격보어 (as + 보어)]
▶ mean + 목적어(동명사): ~을 의미하다
▶ found: 설립하다(found – founded – founded – founding)
▶ it is time to V: ~할 시간이다
▶ the number of + 복수명사: ~수
▶ There is + 단수주어/There are + 복수주어: ~이 있다
▶ In case + 주어 + 동사 ~, 주어 + 동사 ~: ~한 경우에는, ~하다
▶ choose + 목적어(to V): ~하는 것을 선택하다

- contribute to (동)명사: ~에 기여하다
- be able to V: ~할 수 있다
- be aware that 주어 + 동사: ~을 알다(= be aware of + (동)명사)
- make(사역동사) + 목적어 + 목적격보어(V): ~가 ~하게 시키다
- All + 주어 + want + is + (to) V: ~가 원하는 모든 것은 ~이다
- in order to V: ~하기 위해서
- require + 목적어 + 목적격보어(to V): ~가 ~하는 것을 요구하다[수동태 시, be required 주격보어(to V)]

Part 2 34~39 Part 2 Question

| 어휘 |

34 intended 계획된 be from ~출신이다 in poverty 가난한 replace 대체하다 first language 모국어

35 employ 고용하다 look after ~돌보다 extra income 추가 수입 precise 정확한

36 take advantage of 이용하다 flexible 유연한 at the same time 동시에 intelligence 지능 arrange 정리하다 convenient 편리한 negotiate 협상하다

37 productive 생산적인

38 take off from work 휴직하다

39 currently 현재 major in ~을 전공하다 be fluent in ~에 유창하다

| 구문독해 |

37 make(상태 동사) + 목적어 + 목적격보어(형용사/명사): ~을 ~한 상태로 만들다

38 have trouble{a hard(difficult) time, difficulty} (in) (동)명사: ~하는 데 어려움이 있다

39 be qualified to V: ~의 자격이 있다

TEST 1 part 3 어휘 & 구문독해

Part 3 (40~45)

어휘

get a job(position) 직장을 얻다　more than ever(before) 어느 때보다도 더　struggle with 고심하다
a full-time job 정규직 일자리　hire 고용하다　as soon as 하자마자　live alone 혼자 살다
think about ~에 관해 생각하다　be far from ~에서 멀다　commute 통근하다　stay with ~의 집에서 머물다
weigh the advantages and disadvantages 득실을 따지다　make a choice 선택하다　ensure 보장하다
fairly 상당히　take A into account A를 고려하다　anyone else 누구든지 다른 사람　requirement 필요(한 것)
permission 허락　as you please 좋을 대로, 원하는 대로　downside 불리한[덜 긍정적인] 면
pricey 값비싼　save up (돈을) 모으다　apart from ~외에는　cover (비용·손실 등을) 보상하다
utility 공공시설　considerable 상당한　ironing 다리미질　by oneself 혼자　take A out A를 제거하다(빼다)
bin 쓰레기통　stress out 스트레스를 받다　take A for granted A를 당연한 일로 여기다
do the housework 가사 일을 돌보다　pay for 대금을 지불하다, 빚을 갚다　worry about ~에 대해 걱정하다
groceries 식료품류　aside 따로 두고, 제쳐 놓고　aside from ~외에는, ~을 제외하고　talk to ~에게 말을 걸다
rely on ~에 의지[의존]하다　wisdom 지혜　all the time 내내　won't ~하지 않을 것이다(will not의 축약형)
carton (우유)곽　wake up late 늦잠 자다　in the eyes of ~이 보는 바로는　reach a decision 결정을 내리다
prefer 좋아하다　set up 설정　in this way 이렇게 하여　save up money for ~에 대비하여 저금하다
self-development 자기 계발[발전]　investment 투자

구문독해

▶ the number of + 복수명사: ~수
▶ It takes 시간 + to V: ~하는 데 시간이 ~만큼 걸리다
▶ ask + 목적어 + 목적격보어[(to) V]: ~가 ~하도록 시키다[수동태 시, be asked + 주격보어(to V)]
▶ be sure + (that) 주어 + 동사: ~을 확신하다(= be sure to V/be sure of Ving)
▶ try + 목적어(Ving): 시험 삼아 ~하다 → 주어의 의지 없음
▶ help(준사역동사) + 목적어 + 목적격보어(to V): ~가 ~하는 것을 돕다
▶ even if/although/though/even though(종속접속사) + 주어 + 동사: ~에도 불구하고 [despite(전치사) + 명사]
▶ be able to V: ~할 수 있다
▶ don't have to V: ~할 필요가 없다
▶ There is + 단수주어/There are + 복수주어: ~이 있다
▶ be going to V: ~할 예정이다
▶ spend + 목적어 + on (동)명사: ~하는 데 ~을 소비하다
▶ start + 목적어(to V/Ving): ~를 시작하다
▶ be sure + (that) 주어 + 동사: ~을 확신하다(= be sure to V/be sure of Ving)
▶ be wiling to V: 기꺼이 ~하다

- as much A as B: B 만큼이나 A하는
- allow + 목적어 + 목적격보어(to V): ~가 ~하는 것을 허락하다[수동태 시, be allowed (to) V]
- treat A as B: A를 B로 취급하다(다루다)
- no matter how + 형용사/부사 + 주어 + 동사: 어떻게 하든, 아무리 ~해도
- seem like + (동)명사: ~처럼 보이다

Part 3 40~45 Part 3 Question

| 어휘 |

- **41** benefit from ~로부터 이익을 얻다   anytime 언제든지   live away from ~로부터 떨어져 살다
- **42** do household chores 가사 노동을 하다   on one's own 혼자서   take a bus 버스를 타다
- **43** financial support 재정적 지원   manage 관리하다   set up 설립[수립]하다
- **44** financially 재정적으로   care 돌봄, 보살핌
- **45** discuss with ~와 논의하다   live with ~와 동거하다   commute 통근하다

| 구문독해 |

- **40** whether A or not: A할지 말아야 할지
  whether A or B: A이든 B이든
- **45** decide + 목적어(to V): ~하기를 결정하다

TEST 2 part 3 어휘 & 구문독해

Part 3 (40~45)

어휘

wonder 궁금해하다   undergo (검열·수술을) 받다   treatment 치료   procedure 시술   destroy 파괴하다
the outer layer 바깥쪽의 막 (외층)   simultaneously 동시에   dermis 진피   form 형성시키다
promote 촉진하다   collagen 콜라겐(피부나 뼈에서 발견되는 단백질 성분)   fine lines 가는(미세한) 주름
decrease 줄다[감소하다]   whereas 반면   lymphatic fluid 림프액   clear out (~을 없애고) 청소하다
toxin 독소   accessible 접근[입장/이용] 가능한   salon 상점   do it oneself 자신이 하다
blood circulation 혈액 순환   oxygen 산소   think about ~에 관해 생각하다   therapy 치료, 요법
incorrectly 부정확하게   bruising 멍이 든   muscle soreness 근육통   last 지속[존속]하다
nerve damage 신경 손상   scary 무서운, 겁나는   itching 가려움증   cosmetics 화장품   used for ~에 사용하는
high concentration 고농도   contain 포함하다   chemical 화학 물질   concerned 걱정하는
non-invasive 비외과적인   flaw 결점   a topical anesthetic 국소 마취제   reduce pain 아픔을 줄이다
involve 포함하다   insertion 삽입   instrument 기계, 기구, 도구   incision (특히 외과 수술 중의) 절개
appropriately 적절하게   drawback 단점   cosmetic procedure 미용 시술   be covered by ~로 처리되다
medical insurance 의료 보험   session 시기, 활동   depend on ~에 의존하다   achieve 얻다
desired 바랐던, 희망했던   side effect 부작용   push through 통과시키다   thoroughly 완전히
evaluate 평가하다   proceed 진행하다[되다]   accordingly 그에 맞춰   have a consultation 상담을 받다

구문독해

간접의문문 if(~인지 아닌지) 용법
▶ 의문사 대용어로 사용된 if는 간접의문문으로 사용될 수 있는데, 이때 if는 whether로 바꿔 사용할 수 있지만, that(~것을)은 사용할 수 없다.
▶ A instead of B: B 대신에 A
▶ cause + 목적어 + 목적격보어(to V): ~가 ~하도록 야기시키다
▶ help(준사역동사) + 목적어 + 목적격보어(to V): ~가 ~하는 것을 돕다
▶ send A to B: A를 B에 보내다
▶ don't have to V: ~할 필요가 없다
▶ apply A to B: A를 B에 사용하다(적용하다, 바르다)
▶ consider + 목적어 + 목적격보어[(to be) 보어]: ~을 ~라고 간주하다〈수동태 시, be considered + 주격보어[(to be) 보어]〉
▶ decide + 목적어 (to V): ~하기를 결정하다

Part 3 Question (40~45)

어휘

40 a job interview 구직면접　inquire about 문의하다

41 promote 촉진하다　plenty of 많은

42 rethink 다시 생각하다　be scared of 두려워하다　extremely 극도로, 극히　sensitive 민감한

43 talk to 말을 걸다　be in pain 아파하다　substance 물질　apply (약 등을) 바르다

44 assess 평가하다　discontinue 중단하다　pay for 대금을 지불하다

45 conversation with ~와의 대화　other than 이외의

구문독해

41 expose A to B: A를 B에 노출시키다
　　remove A from B: B에서 A를 제거하다

42 make(사역동사) + 목적어 + 목적격보어(V): ~가 ~하게 시키다
　　find + 목적어 + 목적격보어{(to be) 형용사}: ~을 ~하다는 것을 알다

43 keep + 목적어 + Ving: ~가 계속 ~하다
　　(keep + 목적어 + from Ving: ~가 ~하는 것을 못 하게 하다)

TEST 3 part 3 어휘 & 구문독해

Part 3 40~45

어휘

look for 찾다, 구하다   insist on ~을 고집하다   countryside 시골   start with 시작하다
proper 적절한   medical care service 의료보호사업   plenty of 많은   mile 마일(약 1.609km)
wait for ~를 기다리다   in case of ~이 발생할 시에는   emergency 비상 (사태)   comprehensive 포괄적인
transportation system 교통 시설(체계)   take a subway 지하철을 타다   take a bus 버스를 타다
from one place to another 한 곳에서 다른 곳으로   besides 그외에도
focus on ~에 주력하다, 초점을 맞추다   take one's eyes off ~에서 눈을 떼다   in addition 게다가
drastically 급격하게   metropolitan areas 대도시권, 수도권   pursue one's career 직장생활을 계속 해나가다
what about? ~하는 게 어때?   cost of living 생활비   typically 일반적으로   pollution 오염
smog 스모그   carbon emission rate 탄소 배출률   vehicle 차량   air pollution 공기[대기] 오염
suffer from ~로 고통받다   heart disease 심장병   respiratory disease 호흡기 질환   asthma 천식
lung cancer 폐암   not only that 비단 그뿐 아니라   concentration of population 인구 집중
innumerable 수없이 많은   noise pollution 소음 공해   be free from 해방되다
toxic pollutant 독성의 오염 물질   improve 향상시키다   quality 품질, 질   rural 시골   facility 시설
aside from that 그것과는 별개로   lack 부족   health facilities 보건시설   resident 주민
move to ~로 이동하다   medical treatment 의학적 치료   blizzard 눈보라   regularly 규칙적으로
plow the snow 눈을 치우다   otherwise 그렇지 않으면   be[get] stuck 갇히다
rainy season 장마철, 우기   flood 홍수   completely 완전히   isolated 고립된   underwater 물속의
hat is a good point 좋은 지적이다   pros and cons 장단점   live in harmony with ~와 좋게 지내다
pursue 추구하다   free from ~으로부터 벗어난, ~이 없는   competition 경쟁

구문독해

▶ don't have to V: ~할 필요가 없다(= don't need to V, need not V)
▶ spend + 목적어 + (in) 동명사: ~하는 데 ~을 소비하다
▶ the number of + 복수명사 + 복수동사: ~수
▶ Since + 주어 + 동사 ~, 주어 + 동사 ~: 이유(~이므로, ~이니까)
▶ help(준사역동사) + 목적어 + 목적격보어[(to) V]: ~가 ~하는 것을 돕다
▶ There is + 단수주어/There are + 복수주어: ~이 있다
▶ due to(전치사) + 명사: ~ 때문에(because(종속접속사) + 주어 + 동사)
▶ B as well as A: A뿐만 아니라 B도(= not only A but also B, 주어로 사용 시, 주어는 B)
▶ This(원인) is why + 주어 + 동사(결과): 그것은(원인) ~ (결과)이다
▶ one of + 복수명사: ~중의 하나
▶ need + 목적어 (to V): ~하는 것이 필요하다

- during(전치사) + 명사: ~동안(while(종속접속사) + 주어 + 동사)
- thank you for + Ving: ~에 대해 감사하다
- go and V = go to V = go V: ~하러 가다
- 예) go see a doctor = go and see a doctor = go to see a doctor: 진찰받으러 병원에 가봐라
- would like to + V: ~하고 싶다
- both A and B: A와 B 둘 다

Part 3 Question (40~45)

| 어휘 |

41 make an appointment ~와 약속을 하다   a short distance 단거리   see a doctor 의사의 진찰을 받다
medical care service 의료보호사업   at a low price 싼 값으로

42 protect 보호하다   mental illness 정신병

43 negatively 부정적으로   a small number of 소수의

44 isolation 고립   extreme 극도의, 극심한

45 workplace 직장

| 구문독해 |

40 plan + 목적어(to V): ~할 작정이다

41 decide + 목적어(to V): ~를 결정하다
be able to V: ~할 수 있다
need + 목적어(to V): ~하는 것이 필요하다

42 It(가주어) ~ to V(진주어): ~한 것은 ~이다
There is + 단수주어/There are + 복수주어: ~이 있다

TEST 1 part 4 어휘 & 구문독해

Part 4 (46~52)

| 어휘 |

1st brokerage account 중개 계좌 stock account 증권 계좌 grow wealth 부를 늘리다
access to ~에의 접근 securities exchange 증권거래소 set up an account 계좌를 개설하다
complicated 복잡한

2nd what ~ for 왜(= why) invest 투자하다 convenient 편리한, 간편한
mutual fund 뮤추얼 펀드(주주에게 배당금의 형태로 나누어 주는 투자 신탁) depend on ~에 의존하다
significant 중요한 identify 확인하다 as soon as possible 가능한 한 빨리

3rd based on ~에 근거하여 open an account 계좌를 개설하다 for the first time 처음으로
traditional 전형의 retirement account 퇴직 예금 계좌 pay tax on ~에 세금을 지불하다
be free to 자유롭게 ~하다, 마음껏 ~하다 withdraw(take out) money 돈을 인출하다
on the other hand 다른 한편으로는, 반면에 tax deduction 세금[소득] 공제(액)

4th purchase 구입[구매/매입]하다 by oneself 혼자 charge 청구하다 inactivity 비활성
maintenance fee 관리비 firm 회사 typically 전형적으로 commission 수수료[커미션]
come with ~이 딸려 있다 pay for 대금을 지불하다

5th apply to 신청하다 preferred 선호하는 complete 완료하다, 끝마치다 ideal for ~에 이상적인
painless 힘들지 않은 alternatively 그렇지 않으면 head down to ~을 향해 나아가다
branch office 지점, 지사 in person 직접[몸소] fill out 작성하다, 기입하다 risk tolerance 투자위험감수도
net worth 순 자산 employment status 고용 상태

6th fund 자금을 제공하다 initiate 시작하다 deposit 예금, 입금 funds transfer 자금 송금
keep A in mind A를 마음에 간직하다 taxable 과세의

8th thank you for + 동명사 ~에 감사하다 would like to V ~하고 싶다 commission fee 수수료
be ready to V ~할 준비가 되다 be suitable for ~에 적합하다 inquiry 문의

| 구문독해 |

▶ either A or B: A이거나 B인
▶ lead + 목적어 + 목적격보어(to V): ~가 ~하도록 이끌다
▶ ask + 목적어 + 목적격보어(to V): ~가 ~하도록 시키다[수동태 시, be asked + 주격보어(to V)]
▶ need + 목적어 (to V): ~하는 것이 필요하다
▶ begin + 목적어(to V/Ving): ~를 시작하다
▶ be sure to V: ~을 확신하다(= be sure + (that) 주어 + 동사/be sure of Ving)
▶ spend + 목적어 + (in) 동명사: ~하는 데 ~을 소비하다

Part 4 Question
Part 4 46~52

|어휘|

- **46** overcome 극복하다
- **48** through ~을 통해
- **50** application form 신청서
- **52** deliver 전하다

|구문독해|

- **48** avoid + 목적어(동명사): ~하는 것을 피하다
- **50** ask + 간접목적어 + 직접목적어: ~에게 ~을 부탁하다
- **52** encourage + 목적어 + 목적격보어(to V): ~가 ~하도록 격려(장려)하다
  persuade + 목적어 + 목적격보어(to V): ~가 ~하도록 설득하다

TEST 2 part 4 어휘 & 구문독해

Part 4 46~52 Part 4

| 어휘 |

1st mostly 일반적으로　be concerned about 걱정하다　sales department 판매부(문), 영업부
improve 향상시키다

2nd regardless of ~에 상관없이　awesome 굉장한, 아주 멋진　salesperson 판매원[외판원]
return customer 재방문 고객　be loyal[faithful, devoted] (to) 충성을 다하다
have a huge impact on ~에 엄청난 영향을 미치다

3rd excellent 훌륭한, 탁월한

4th friendly 친절한　with a smile 빙긋 웃으며　courteous 공손한　respectful 경의를 표하는
proactive 상황을 앞서서 주도하는　pay attention to + (동)명사 ~에 주목하다　recommendation 권고
disappointed 실망한, 낙담한　be kind[gentle, nice, tender] to ~에게 상냥하다

5th respond 대답[응답]하다　promptly 즉시　appreciate 고마워하다　a response to ~에 대한 반응[응답]
inquiry 문의　time-sensitive 분초를 다투는　request 요청[신청]　return a phone call 회답 전화를 하다
impress 감명[감동]을 주다　complaint 불만　in addition 게다가　assist 돕다

6th aspect 측면　feature 특색, 특징, 특성　ask for a refund 환불을 요청하다

7th listen to 귀를 기울이다　valid 타당한

8th sincere gratitude 진지한 감사　handwritten 손으로 쓴　thank you note 감사편지

9th drive 이끌다　conduct a survey 설문조사를 하다　stand out 눈에 띄다　competition 경쟁

10th focus on 초점을 맞추다　care about ~에 관심을 가지다　inspire 고무[격려]하다　loyalty 충성심
appreciation 감사　personalized 개인이 원하는 대로 할 수 있는　greet 인사하다
by name 이름을 부르고　make a note of 필기하다　previous 이전의　reference 참조 하다

11th follow 따르다　prospective 장래의　trustworthy 믿을 만한　aggressive 적극적인　competitive 경쟁적인
be satisfied with 만족하다　highly 크게, 대단히, 매우　ensured 보장된

| 구문독해 |

▶ as 형용사/부사 as possible: 가능한 한 ~한/하게, 될 수 있으면 ~한/하게(= as 형용사/부사 as one can)

▶ as 형용사/부사 as: ~만큼 ~한

▶ be likely to V: ~할 것 같다

▶ Here is + 단수주어/Here are + 복수주어: 여기에 ~이 있다

▶ try + 목적어(to V): ~하기 위해 노력하다 → 주어의 의지 있음

▶ even if/although/though/even though(종속접속사) + 주어 + 동사: ~에도 불구하고[despite(전치사) + 명사]

- let + 목적어 + 목적격보어(V): ~가 ~하도록 허락(허용)하다
- It takes 시간 + to V: ~하는 데 시간이 ~만큼 걸리다
- be able to V: ~할 수 있다
- need + 목적어 (to V): ~하는 것이 필요하다
- be sure to V: ~을 확신하다(= be sure + (that) 주어 + 동사/be sure of Ving)
- make(상태 동사) + 목적어 + 목적격보어(형용사/명사): ~을 ~한 상태로 만들다
- by + Ving: ~함으로써
- remind + 간접목적어 + 직접목적어: ~에게 ~을 상기시키다
- get + to V: ~하게 되다
- find + it(가목적어) + 목적격보어(형용사/명사) + to V(진목적어): ~(진목적어)가 ~(목적격보어)하다는 것을 알다
- allow + 목적어 + 목적격보어(to V): ~가 ~하는 것을 허락하다
- make(사역동사) + 목적어 + 목적격보어(V): ~가 ~하게 시키다

Part 4 Question (46~52)

| 어휘 |

46 strengthen 강하게 하다

47 job satisfaction 직업 만족도   thrive 번창하다

48 prompt response 신속한 대응(반응)   ask for 요청하다   handle 처리하다   within 안에

49 based on 근거하여

50 in person 직접[몸소]

51 trendy outfit 유행하는 옷

52 favorable to 호의적인, 긍정적인   earn money 돈을 벌다

| 구문독해 |

46 keep + 목적어 + 목적격보어(형용사): ~을 ~한 상태로 유지하다

47 lead + 목적어 + 목적격보어(to V): ~가 ~하도록 이끌다
    allow + 목적어 + 목적격보어(to V): ~가 ~하는 것을 허락하다

49 stop + 목적어(Ving): ~하는 것을 멈추다

50 ask A for help: A에게 도움을 요청하다

51 tend to V: ~하는 경향이 있다

52 make(상태 동사) + 목적어 + 목적격보어(형용사/명사): ~을 ~한 상태로 만들다
    help(준사역동사) + 목적어 + 목적격보어(to V): ~가 ~하는 것을 돕다
    allow + 목적어 + 목적격보어(to V): ~가 ~하는 것을 허락하다
    make(사역동사) + 목적어 + 목적격보어(V): ~가 ~하게 시키다

TEST 3 part 4 어휘 & 구문독해

Part 4 (46~52)

| 어휘 |

1st polite 정중한 considerate 사려 깊은 yell at 호통(고함)치다 talk to 말을 걸다 effectively 효과적으로 deal with 상대하다, 다루다 be part of ~의 일부분이다 professional 전문적인

2nd inevitable 불가피한 speak to 이야기를 하다 frustrated 불만스러워하는 unreasonable 불합리한 be rude to ~에게 무례하게 대하다 handle 다루다 quality customer service 품격 있는 고객 서비스

3rd listen to 귀를 기울이다 difficult 까다로운 simultaneously 동시에 concern 관심, 배려, 걱정, 근심 gain (an) insight into 식견을 갖다, 통찰하다 find a solution 해답(법)을 찾다

4th validation 타당성 calm down 진정하다

5th react 반응하다 emotionally 감정적으로 in the middle of 도중에 tense 긴장된 sarcastic 비꼬는 yell back 큰 소리로 반격하다, 대들다 pleasant 유쾌한 at times 때로는 to the limit 극단적으로 trick 비결, 요령 separate A from B B에서 A를 분리시키다 in anger 화가 나서 exacerbate 악화시키다

6th tone of voice 목소리의 톤 proficient 능숙한 maintain 유지하다[지키다] no matter what 비록 무엇이 ~한다 하더라도(= whatever)

7th offer 제공하다 express 나타내다, 표(현)하다 an apology for ~에 대한 사죄 definite 확실한 a variety of 여러 가지의 for oneself 스스로 proceed 진행하다

8th place A back on hold A를 보류 상태로 두다 irritate 짜증나게 하다 further 그 이상으로, 더욱이 whenever 때마다 appropriate 적절한 complete 완료하다, 끝마치다 support task 지원 작업 expectation 기대치 describe 말하다[서술하다], 묘사하다 approximately 대략 return to the line 다시 통화로 돌아오다

9th figure out 생각해 내다, 이해하다 make a promise 약속을 하다 make an effort 노력하다, 애쓰다 deliberate 의도적인 empathy 공감 hang up the phone 전화를 끊다

10th take a few minutes 시간을 내다 deal with 다루다 tension 긴장 previous experience 이전의 경험 unsatisfactory 만족스럽지 못한 take a break 잠시 휴식을 취하다 affect 영향을 미치다

11th present 진술[주장]하다 succeed in 성공하다 over and over again 반복해서 self-confidence 자신감 boost 증가하다, 돋우다 regular customer 단골, 고객, 단골손님 complaint 불평[항의]

구문독해

- start + 목적어(to V/Ving): ~를 시작하다
- be going to V: ~할 예정이다
- feel like + (that) 주어 + 동사: ~처럼 느끼다(= feel like + (동)명사)
- not ~ at all: 전혀 ~하지 않다
- It be A that B: B한 것은 바로 A이다(강조구문)
- provide + 목적어(사람) + with 목적어(사물): A를 B에 제공하다[= provide + 목적어(사물) + to/for 목적어(사람)]
- Here is(are) + 단수(복수)주어: 여기에 ~이 있다
- try + 목적어(to V): ~하기 위해 노력하다 → 주어의 의지 있음
- try + 목적어(Ving): 시험 삼아 ~하다 → 주어의 의지 없음
- help(준사역동사) + 목적어 + 목적격보어[(to) V]: ~가 ~하는 것을 돕다
- Instead of A, B: A 대신에, B하다
- need + 목적어(to V): ~하는 것이 필요하다
- keep + 목적어 + 목적격보어(형용사): ~을 ~한 상태로 유지하다
- the 비교급 A, the 비교급 B: A하면 할수록, 더 B하다
- train + 목적어 + 목적격보어(to V): ~가 ~하도록 훈련시키다
- keep + 목적어 + Ving: ~가 계속 ~하다
- keep + 목적어 + from Ving: ~가 ~하는 것을 못 하게 하다
- would like to + V: ~하고 싶다
- avoid + 목적어(Ving): ~하는 것을 피하다
- be sure to V: ~을 확신하다(= be sure + (that) 주어 + 동사/be sure of Ving)
- It takes 시간 + to V: ~하는 데 시간이 ~만큼 걸리다
- continue + 목적어(to V/Ving): ~을 계속하다
- 주어(A: 원인) + lead to + 목적어(B: 결과): A이라는 원인 때문에 B라는 결과가 발생하다, A는 B로 이어지다
- let + 목적어 + 목적격보어(V): ~가 ~하도록 허락(허용)하다
- find + 목적어 + 목적격보어{(to be) 형용사}: ~을 ~하다는 것을 알다

Part 4 46~52 Part 4 Question

어휘

46 identify 식별하다

47 raise 올리다 stay calm 침착함을 유지하다 hang up 전화를 끊다 call back 다시 전화를 하다 in a few minutes 수분 안으로

48 identify 확인하다 (a) conversation with ~와의 대화 situation 상황 get worse 악화되다

50 appreciate 고마워하다 attitude 태도 inadequate 불충분한, 부적당한 calm down 진정하다

51 be stressed out 스트레스를 받다 inappropriate 부적절한 hang up the phone 전화를 끊다

52 self-confidence 자신감 on one's own 혼자서 in person 직접 address a problem 문제를 해결하다 immediately 즉시, 즉각

| 구문독해 |

47 ask + 목적어 + 목적격보어(to V): ~가 ~하도록 시키다

48 keep + 목적어 + 목적격보어(형용사): ~을 ~한 상태로 유지하다
prevent A from (동)명사: ~하는 것으로부터 A를 막다
let + 목적어 + 목적격보어(V): ~가 ~하도록 허락(허용)하다

49 stop + 목적어(Ving): ~하는 것을 멈추다
stop + 목적어(to V): ~하기 위해 멈추다

51 A(원인) result in B(결과): A라는 원인이 B라는 결과를 초래하다
A(결과) result from B(원인): A라는 결과는 B라는 원인으로 발생하다
주어(A: 원인) + lead to + 목적어(B: 결과): A이라는 원인 때문에 B라는 결과가 발생하다, A는 B로 이어지다
contribute to (동)명사: ~에 기여하다
make(사역동사) + 목적어 + 목적격보어(V): ~가 ~하게 시키다

좋은 책을 만드는 길, 독자님과 함께 하겠습니다.

2026 시대에듀 스피드 지텔프 레벨2

개정3판1쇄 발행	2026년 01월 15일 (인쇄 2025년 09월 17일)
초 판 발 행	2021년 08월 10일 (인쇄 2021년 07월 29일)
발 행 인	박영일
책 임 편 집	이해욱
공 저	정윤호 · 이정미
편 집 진 행	윤승일 · 장민영
표지디자인	김도연
편집디자인	박지은 · 하한우
발 행 처	(주)시대고시기획
출 판 등 록	제 10-1521호
주 소	서울시 마포구 큰우물로 75 [도화동 538 성지 B/D] 9F
전 화	1600-3600
팩 스	02-701-8823
홈 페 이 지	www.sdedu.co.kr
I S B N	979-11-434-0079-6 (13740)
정 가	22,000원

※ 이 책은 저작권법의 보호를 받는 저작물이므로 동영상 제작 및 무단전재와 배포를 금합니다.
※ 잘못된 책은 구입하신 서점에서 바꾸어 드립니다.

스피드 지텔프 레벨2

군무원 | 경찰공무원 | 소방공무원 | 경찰·소방간부후보생 | 5급·7급 공무원
공기업 | 대기업 | 변리사 | 세무사 | 노무사 | 회계사 | 관광통역안내사

시대에듀 지텔프 문법 시리즈
YouTube 강의로 지텔프 시험 한 번에 끝내기!

1주일 만에 끝내는 지텔프 문법

10회 만에 끝내는 지텔프 문법 모의고사

기초부터 확실하게 강의만 들어도 정답이 보이는 마법!
도서의 내용을 바로 설명해주는 동영상 강의로 실력 향상!
단기완성을 위한 왕초보 핵심이론!

▶ YouTube

유튜브 검색창에 **시대에듀 지텔프**를 검색하세요!

시대에듀의 지텔프 최강 라인업

1주일 만에 끝내는 지텔프 문법

10회 만에 끝내는 지텔프 문법 모의고사

답이 보이는 지텔프 독해

스피드 지텔프 레벨2